Institutions under Siege

Much of the research on institutional change shows how systems shift slowly and incrementally. Yet, in the case of former President Donald Trump, change was rapid and radical. In *Institutions Under Siege*, leading political sociologist John L. Campbell offers new insights for understanding the legacy of the Trump presidency. The book examines Trump's attack on the "deep state" through the lens of institutional change theory, and demonstrates how he capitalized on tipping points and distinct leadership tactics to inspire, make deals with, and threaten people to get what he wanted. The book also assesses where the damage caused by the Trump administration is most likely to endure and where long-lasting damage was prevented. Sharp and insightful, *Institutions Under Siege* contrasts existing social science literature to draw attention to the unique significance of tipping points and the characteristics of particular leaders.

JOHN L. CAMPBELL is Class of 1925 Professor and Professor of Sociology Emeritus at Dartmouth College. He is a leading scholar on how institutions and politics affect policymaking and economic performance in advanced capitalist countries. He is the author of several books including *American Discontent: The Rise of Donald Trump and Decline of the Golden Age* (2018) and *What Capitalism Needs: Forgotten Lessons of Great Economists* (2021).

D1548261

Institutions under Siege

Donald Trump's Attack on the Deep State

JOHN L. CAMPBELL
Dartmouth College

CAMBRIDGE
UNIVERSITY PRESS

Shaftesbury Road, Cambridge CB2 8BS, United Kingdom

One Liberty Plaza, 20th Floor, New York, NY 10006, USA

477 Williamstown Road, Port Melbourne, VIC 3207, Australia

314–321, 3rd Floor, Plot 3, Splendor Forum, Jasola District Centre, New Delhi – 110025, India

103 Penang Road, #05–06/07, Visioncrest Commercial, Singapore 238467

Cambridge University Press is part of Cambridge University Press & Assessment, a department of the University of Cambridge.

We share the University's mission to contribute to society through the pursuit of education, learning and research at the highest international levels of excellence.

www.cambridge.org
Information on this title: www.cambridge.org/9781009170185

DOI: 10.1017/9781009170178

First published 2023

A catalogue record for this publication is available from the British Library.

ISBN 978-1-009-17018-5 Hardback
ISBN 978-1-009-17019-2 Paperback

To Kathy, Jessie, John, Ian, Elinore and Alex

Contents

Figures

Tables

Preface

When Donald Trump was elected president in 2016 by the Electoral College despite losing the popular vote to Hillary Clinton by nearly 3 million votes, many Americans were shocked that a political novice – he had never held public office in his life – had won the presidency. And they worried that, combined with his inflammatory rhetoric and sometimes rash behavior, his inexperience would lead to bad judgment and poor policymaking. I worried too as I explained in my book *American Discontent: The Rise of Donald Trump and Decline of the Golden Age*, written shortly after the election. However, nobody, including me, expected Trump to lay siege to America's political institutions as he did. Nor did anybody expect things to go as badly as they did in terms of the damage he caused. That's what this book was originally going to be about.

However, as I began writing, my editor warned me that there would soon be a slew of books appearing that chronicled what had happened on Trump's watch. She urged me to bring a more analytical perspective to the story. She was right. These books have provided a wealth of descriptive information about the unprecedented nature of Trump's presidency. What they don't do, however, is identify either the full extent of the damage he caused to America's political institutions or, more importantly, the factors that enabled him to inflict that damage in the first place. So, this book tackles two questions: How bad was the damage Trump caused? And how did he manage to cause it?

This is a story of good news and bad news. The bad news is that Trump has done a lot of harm to some of our most valuable political institutions – harm with which we will have to live for years if not decades. The good news is that Trump's ability to damage America's institutions is, with one exception, over now that he is no longer president. But even this good news must be tempered with a strong dose of caution. For one thing, Trump is threatening to run for the presidency again in 2024. For another thing, how much of the damage the Biden administration or its successors can repair, and how long it will take, remain open questions. Finally, and this is the exception, although a few Republican politicians like Liz Cheney, Adam Kinzinger, Lisa Murkowski, and Mitt Romney have stood up to Trump and condemned his rhetoric and behavior, particularly his refusal to admit that he lost the 2020 election to Biden, many others – not to mention millions of Republican voters – still take their cues from Trump as some sort of political Messiah.

The darkest days of the Trump administration were during the COVID-19 pandemic. The pandemic has been a disaster. But the lockdown-induced solitude it provided, like it or not, gave me a chance to write this book. And it gave some very generous colleagues time to read an early draft of the manuscript and offer their comments, criticisms, and advice on how to improve it. Among them is John Hall, with whom I have been discussing and writing about politics for years; Francesco Duina, a long-time source of constructive criticism; and Marc Dixon, Eddie Ashbee, and Alex Hicks, three astute observers of American politics. Others either read individual chapters or discussed some of the ideas in the book with me, including Lev Grinberg, Bob Jenkins, Peter Katzenstein, Ove Pedersen, and Sven Steinmo, all of whom helped me think more carefully about conceptual issues. I also owe a debt of gratitude to Richard Samuels, whom I have never met, but who years ago sent me a copy of his marvelous book *Machiavelli's Children*, which inspired me, as I was writing this book, to think about the importance of political leadership as a source of political change. Mike Allen wisely advised me to pare back the book's initially overly ambitious empirical scope. So did Sara Doskow, my first editor at Cambridge University Press, who expressed an early interest in this book and, as noted, convinced me that it needed an analytical frame. Two anonymous reviewers provided invaluable suggestions for improvement. Rachel Blaifeder, my second editor at the press, offered sage advice on how to revise the book once the reviews were in hand. I am grateful to them all.

I discussed some of the ideas in this book with my compatriots at "choir practice" and "prayer group," each held weekly at a local tavern. They continue to remind me that facts matter in debates about politics and many other subjects. More important, they prove week after week that people can use those facts in vigorous yet respectful debate without vilifying one another. I hope that those who read this book will keep that lesson in mind.

Finally, I thank my wife, Kathy Sherrieb, a Harvard-trained social epidemiologist, who has been holed up with me during the pandemic, tracking its morbidity and mortality statistics daily. She has been a source of support, comfort, inspiration, and love for over forty years. As a registered nurse, community health expert, and public health researcher, she devoted her entire professional life to helping others. Since then, she has done all sorts of volunteer and philanthropic work in our town, including starting a food pantry to help those suffering economically from the pandemic and other misfortunes. Donald Trump could learn a lot from her, just as I have.

I

Institutional Guardrails

America's political institutions are the guardrails preventing our democratic system of government from plunging over the cliff into autocracy. But their durability and strength are not guaranteed, particularly when someone like the president of the United States – perhaps the most powerful person in the world – attacks them. Donald Trump laid siege to these institutions. Except for the Civil War, the damage Trump caused to the country's guardrails was unprecedented. This book describes what happened and assesses the damage. But it also does something else that's important.

The bread and butter for many sociologists and political scientists, including myself, is the study of institutions. Most of our work explores how institutions change in slow, incremental, and evolutionary ways. Rarely do we consider how institutions change more radically. Yet Trump's attack on our core political institutions was an attempt at radical change. So, by examining his attack, this book shows how radical institutional change happens. Understanding this is the first step in ensuring that the sort of damage Trump caused doesn't happen again.

The changes that occurred on Trump's watch stemmed in large part from two things often neglected by those who study institutional change: *tipping points* – gradually developing windows of opportunity; and *leadership*, which in Trump's case was frequently neither admirable nor conducive to sound policymaking. Trump's unique leadership style was on full display as he tried to capitalize on various tipping points, often but not always overcoming the resistance he encountered along the way. Much has been written – and will continue to be written – about the political strategies, interest group pressures, and congressional fights involved in what Trump tried to do. All of that is important and I don't mean to diminish its significance. But my intent is to shine a light on tipping points and leadership, which have received short shrift not only in discussions of institutional change but also in the literature on the Trump presidency.

The damage Trump did to America's political institutions is serious. It stemmed from his attack on what his one-time senior policy advisor, Stephen Bannon, and other conspiracy theorists called the "deep state," a system of power allegedly hidden inside the government and its surrounding political apparatus and operating independently of elected political leadership.[1] Part of the damage was done to the country's democratic institutions, notably the electoral and political party systems. But another part of the damage, much less obvious and often neglected by observers but still terribly important, was done to the state apparatus, including the justice system, the federal bureaucracy and civil service, and the government's finances. Both democracy and competent, well-resourced states are integral to the success of any advanced capitalist society. Democracy provides the political stability that capitalism needs by preventing political disagreements from spinning out of control. The state provides the political management capitalism needs either to prevent or correct the harmful effects capitalism may have on society.[2]

Trump's rise to power was the culmination of decades-long changes in America. These included structural changes in the economy; rising racial and ethnic tensions; an ideological shift toward the right; and political polarization. Things had reached a historical tipping point by the time he arrived on the political scene and helped propel him to the White House. Once inaugurated, his leadership style came to light. He inspired, cut deals with and bullied people to get what he wanted, often acting in distrustful, inexperienced, arrogant, and self-centered ways, and often taking advantage of other tipping points.

Trump launched his attack on several fronts. First, he assaulted the nation's electoral institutions about which there had already been growing concerns. Trump turned a blind eye to Russian meddling in the 2016 presidential election, ignoring warnings from his intelligence agencies that it had happened and would likely happen again. Then he solicited foreign interference from Ukraine in the 2020 presidential election and tried to block millions of mail-in ballots in that election. When he lost, he refused to concede and consent to a peaceful transition of power, charged that the election was rigged and stolen from him, and tried to overturn the results. All of this helped set off a violent insurrection at the Capitol on January 6, 2021, as Congress was certifying the Electoral College vote. Looking to future elections, he also tried to manipulate the US Census in ways that would favor Republicans for a decade or more.

Second, even before Trump's arrival, the Republican Party had been drifting in more extreme directions. Trump's inflammatory rhetoric and disregard for political civility pushed the party even farther away from the norms and practices of traditional republicanism. His insistence that he had won the

---

[1] Abramson 2017. See also Green (2017, chap. 7).   [2] Campbell and Hall 2021.

2020 election and that it had been stolen from him – the Big Lie – stoked conspiracy theories galore. As a result, the party was badly split and had trouble functioning as a normal, rational political party – something that America's two-party democratic system must have to work properly.

Third, thanks to an unprecedented backlog of judicial vacancies Trump packed the federal courts with a host of conservative judges he believed would defend his agenda and personal political interests. He appointed three very conservative Justices to the Supreme Court solidifying a conservative super-majority on the high court that he presumed would also do his bidding. In addition, he meddled in the affairs of the Department of Justice, and in doing so tread perilously close to obstructing justice for which he was impeached by Congress.

Fourth, capitalizing on the public's growing dissatisfaction with the size and functioning of government, Trump tried to eviscerate the federal bureaucracy, appointing people to top positions who were often woefully unqualified for their jobs. When those working for him disagreed with his views they often quit if he didn't fire them first. This led to an administration that operated less like a place where people debated and formulated policy rationally and more like an echo chamber filled with sycophants telling Trump what he wanted to hear. Fact-based policymaking was often sidelined, and long-lasting vacuums of expertise and experience were created.

Finally, taking advantage of a rising tide of discontent with what many people believed to be high taxes and exorbitant government spending, Trump engineered a historic tax cut that disproportionately benefited corporations and the wealthy, reduced government revenues, and increased economic inequality. He also tried but failed to slash the federal budget. The result was an amplification of the state's already growing budget deficits, which continued to increase the national debt despite his campaign promise to do just the opposite – a situation that only got worse after the COVID-19 pandemic hit and that may yet have serious implications for both domestic policy and US hegemony abroad.

The conspiratorial nature of the deep state is open to question. But there is no doubt that over the decades, the American state has grown deeper in the sense that its administrative, advisory, and policymaking capacities have expanded and are now marked more than ever by unelected yet professionally trained expert staff.[3] By attacking the deep state, Trump weakened America's electoral, party, justice, civil service, and fiscal institutions – core foundations of American politics and democracy. That said, his attacks weren't always successful and sometimes had serious unintended consequences. That's important not only for America's democracy but also because it has implications for my argument about institutional change.

---

[3] Skowronek et al. 2021, chaps. 1 and 2. See also Skowronek (1982).

To be clear, what I am talking about is not the kind of full-blown revolutionary change seen in the United States or France in the eighteenth century, in Russia in 1917, or in China in 1949. The country was not immersed in armed conflict. The state was not overthrown in a coup d'état. Political leaders were not executed or sent to reeducation camps. In short, what I am talking about did not involve overthrowing and replacing the entire political system but rather making substantial changes *within* it. Nor am I talking about the gradual or routine changes that often stem from the arrival of a new presidential administration or everyday politics, such as finetuning regulations, or modifying legislation and bureaucratic procedures. What I have in mind, then, is neither revolutionary nor evolutionary but something in between – yet still quite radical. The institutional change Trump sought was sudden, dramatic and, to a large extent, unprecedented within the American political system. It was also broad in scope and often likely to be long-lasting. And it was dangerous, which is another reason why understanding how it happened is so important.

Harvard government professors Steven Levitsky and Daniel Ziblatt warned that Trump was a clear and present danger to American democracy having fulfilled all four of their criteria of an ascendant autocratic leader.[4] First, his commitment to democratic rules was weak, as shown by his attempts to undermine the legitimacy of the 2020 presidential election and his refusal to accept its results. Second, he denied the legitimacy of his political opponents charging Hillary Clinton, for example, his Democratic rival in the 2016 election, with having broken various laws and calling for her to be locked up. Third, Trump tolerated and sometimes encouraged political violence. For instance, he egged on protestors to "liberate Michigan" from its pandemic lockdown restrictions, which some of them tried to do by plotting to kidnap Governor Gretchen Whitmer and storming the statehouse. He also helped incite the January 6th Capitol insurrection. Fourth, Trump demonstrated a readiness to restrict the civil liberties of his opponents. Among other things, he accused the network news media of reporting "fake news" about his administration's policies and wondered at what point it would be appropriate to challenge their broadcast licenses – a not-so-veiled threat to a free and independent press.

You might think that the damage Trump caused is much worse than what I am suggesting. As one political scientist suggested to me, rather than radically changing institutions *within* America's political system, Trump has revolutionized the political system itself. By leading the Republican Party in a direction where it is no longer committed to the core tenets of democracy, he told me, we have already had a fundamental regime change very much akin to a Latin American form of presidency with hollowed-out and politicized institutions in which a return to conventional democratic behavior is highly unlikely,

---

[4] Levitsky and Ziblatt 2018.

especially because elections will no longer be accepted due to the politicization of vote counting. I agree that we may be headed in that direction, but I don't think we have arrived there yet or that we necessarily will because, as subsequent chapters explain, there are forces at work both inside and outside of the Republican ranks that are standing up to defend democracy and fighting against this sort of revolutionary institutional transformation. I hope they succeed.

1.1 WHAT OTHERS HAVE SAID

Institutional change has not been the focus of most other books written about the Trump presidency. Some of these either attack or applaud Trump based on the author's personal experience with him. Those that applaud him are often written by close associates.[5] Those that attack him are often written by former members of his team who have resigned, been pushed out or fired, and have an axe to grind.[6] However, several authors have written more even-handed accounts of the Trump presidency. These take several forms.

Some were written early in the Trump administration and looked to the future, such as *One Nation After Trump*, written by syndicated columnist E.J. Dionne and think tank operatives, Norman Ornstein and Thomas Mann, who warned of the dangers that Trump posed to American democracy.[7] David Frum's *Trumpocracy* was another warning cry.[8] Robert Saldin and Steven Teles described in *Never Trump* how some Republicans were also alarmed and tried to stop him from getting elected in the first place before he could damage America's institutions.[9]

Other books reveal the political intrigue inside the Trump administration. For instance, columnist Michael Wolff's *Fire and Fury* exposed the very stormy and confused early days of the Trump White House.[10] The award-winning journalist Bob Woodward gave us *Rage* and with his colleague Robert Costa *Peril*, books based on hours of interviews with hundreds of current and former members of Trump's administration, Congress and in the case of the first book Trump himself.[11] Carol Leonnig and Philip Rucker's two books *A Very Stable Genius* and *I Alone Can Fix It*, also based on interviews with Trump and dozens of insiders, provide another in-depth look at the administration.[12] So does Jonathan Karl's *Betrayal*.[13] These books are rich in description, particularly about Trump's behavior as president, but have little to say about the broad range of institutional problems he caused or what enabled him to do so.

Other authors took a step in that direction, writing about the impact that Trump had on the presidency as an institution. Some describe the damage he

---

[5] Lewandowski and Bossie 2017; Stone 2017.   [6] Cohen 2020; Comey 2018.
[7] Dionne et al. 2017.   [8] Frum 2018.   [9] Saldin and Teles 2020.
[10] Wolff 2018. See also Green (2017).   [11] Woodward 2020; Woodward and Costa 2021.
[12] Leonnig and Rucker 2021; Rucker and Leonnig 2020.   [13] Karl 2021.

caused to that office. For example, Bob Bauer and Jack Goldsmith's *After Trump* explored how Trump violated an array of rules and norms governing various presidential practices and suggested how normative and legal changes might fix the damage and prevent things like this from happening again.[14] Similarly, Susan Hennessey and Benjamin Wittes' *Unmaking the Presidency* catalogued how Trump violated "the deepest normative expectations of the traditional presidency" including telling the truth, behaving presidentially, benefiting financially from holding office, conducting foreign policy, and handling special counsel investigations.[15]

Some academics put the Trump presidency into historical context. Political scientists William Howell and Terry Moe show in *Presidents, Populism, and the Crisis of Democracy* how Trump rose to power in the first place on a wave of populist discontent driven by trends in American society that took decades to develop and that shaped Trump's management of the presidency.[16] Focusing more on the situation in which Trump found himself upon taking office, Stephen Skowronek and colleagues argue in *Phantoms of a Beleaguered Republic* that Trump's power to disrupt the presidency stemmed from the mounting tensions between deep-state professionalism and presidential authority – tensions that were exacerbated by the decades-long centralization of executive branch power that came to a head during the Trump administration.[17] Echoing the theme of rising presidential power, Daniel Drezner turns to psychology to explain how Trump abused that power. He argues in *The Toddler in Chief* that Trump's stunted and infantile cognitive and emotional development led to his rash, unpredictable, and deeply flawed leadership, which caused tremendous harm to the presidency.[18]

All these writers agree that much of what Trump did was a radical break from past institutional precedent. Drezner, for instance, explains that many people believed that Congress, the courts, and the bureaucracy would "tie [Trump] down like Gulliver," but that this didn't happen. More than any previous president, he argues, Trump escaped these constraints and wrought havoc on the presidency.[19] Bauer and Goldsmith write that "Trump operated the presidency in ways that defied widely held assumptions about how a president might use and abuse the powers of the office ... [and] he did so unlike any of his predecessors."[20] Hennessey and Wittes agreed that Trump's behavior was a "radical departure from the traditional presidency."[21]

One notable exception is *The Ordinary Presidency of Donald J. Trump*, written by political scientists Jon Herbert, Trevor McCrisken, and Andrew Wroe, who argued that judging by what Trump managed to do in the first half

[14] Bauer and Goldsmith 2020. See also Jones (2017).   [15] Hennessey and Wittes 2020.
[16] Howell and Moe 2020. See also Campbell (2018).
[17] Skowronek et al. 2021. See also Fukuyama (2014, chaps. 34 and 35).   [18] Drezner 2020.
[19] Drezner 2020, pp. 21–22.   [20] Bauer and Goldsmith 2020, p. ix.
[21] Hennessey and Wittes 2020, p. 11.

of his term, not much unusual happened in the sense that many of his policies were consistent with what other Republican presidents had done for years, including cutting taxes and regulations, beefing up military spending, and appointing conservative judges.[22] Yet critics of their book point out that there was nothing normal about Trump's rhetorical style, his treatment of democratic and diplomatic norms, his ideological inconsistencies, his treatment of America's allies, or his unpredictable and tempermental behavior.[23] In short, Trump's administration did in fact represent a radical break from the past. Similar criticisms apply to *The Myth of the Imperial Presidency*, written by Dino Christenson and Douglas Kriner, who argue that the Trump presidency wasn't all that remarkable insofar as his attempts to change policy were often constrained by public opinion, Congress, and the courts. Yet, like Herbert and his colleagues, their book looks only at the first half of the Trump presidency and so misses some of the most egregious and consequential aspects of his attack on America's political institutions.[24]

What is missing from all this literature is any discussion of the implications of the Trump presidency for our general understanding of institutional change. These books are rich in the detailed description of what Trump did. But they don't connect to the literature on institutional change, which is ironic because much of what Trump did transformed institutions in a remarkable fashion. The same is true for much of the literature in academic journals about the Trump presidency. For example, virtually none of the articles about Trump published in *Presidential Studies Quarterly* during his tenure in office addressed theories of institutional change. Nor did those in a special issue of *Perspectives on Politics* devoted to the Trump presidency.[25] This book aims to correct that omission by drawing out lessons from the Trump presidency for broad theories of institutional change. In doing so, it helps us better understand how Trump caused that change and the damage he inflicted on America's political institutions.

1.2 WHAT'S AN INSTITUTION?

Before going any further, we need to be clear about what we mean by an institution. When people talk about institutions, they are often really talking about organizations.[26] They say, for example, that Congress is an institution or that Harvard University is an institution or that the General Motors Corporation is an institution. That's not quite right. On the one hand, as economic historian Douglass North explained, *institutions* are formal rules and informal norms, the monitoring and enforcement mechanisms that make them work, and the meaning systems associated with them – that is, the often-

---

[22] Herbert et al. 2019.   [23] *Journal of American Studies* 2020.
[24] Christenson and Kriner 2020.   [25] *Perspectives on Politics* 2019.
[26] See, for example, Thelen and Steinmo (1992).

taken-for-granted interpretations of what these rules and norms mean and how they should be implemented. On the other hand, *organizations* are groups of people using their resources to accomplish certain goals, such as passing legislation, educating students, or manufacturing automobiles and trucks.[27]

But there are complexities here. To begin with, institutions structure the behavior of goal-oriented actors like organizations, but organizations also shape institutions. Congress, for instance, must abide by the rules imposed upon it by the US Constitution, but Congress also passes laws that others must follow. Moreover, organizations, such as the courts, interpret the meaning of laws and make sure that we comply with them. So, although organizations create institutions, interpret, and abide by them, and make sure that others abide by them too, they should not be equated with them. Organizations help institutions function but are not institutions in their own right.

Furthermore, institutions involve more than just rules, monitoring and enforcement, and meaning systems. They also involve two other things. The first is people, often in organizations, with the technical know-how, operational experience, professional expertise, managerial skill, and institutional memory necessary to make institutions work and come to life. People are, in sociologist Arthur Stinchcombe's view, "the guts of institutions."[28] The second is resources with which these people carry out their duties.[29] Both people and resources are necessary to create and sustain institutions. How?

First, people use their resources to affect how institutions are *structured*. They do so by writing rules, formulating norms, devising monitoring and enforcement procedures, and interpreting what institutions mean. Second, people use their resources to affect how institutions *function*. This includes influencing institutional *efficacy* – how effective institutions are in fulfilling their intended purposes; how well they work. But it also includes institutional *orientation* – defining the institution's purpose in the first place; what it is supposed to do. The bottom line is that without people and resources, institutions are inert and meaningless. How long would drivers obey speed limits if they knew that there were no police with fast patrol cars to enforce those rules? So, I am arguing that for us to understand how institutions operate we need to pay attention to how people and resources support them or not. I'll have more to say later about how important this is for understanding institutional change but for now, the crucial point is that to understand institutional change, you must pay attention to rules and norms, monitoring and enforcement mechanisms, and meaning systems, but also the people responsible for them and the resources available to them. This book is about how Trump tried to change all of these things in his assault on the so-called deep state.

---

[27] North 1990, chap. 1. See also Campbell (2004, p. 1) and North (2005).
[28] Stinchcombe 1997.   [29] Skowronek et al. 2021, p. 6.

There is a vast literature on institutions and institutional change written by sociologists, political scientists, and economists.[30] Much of it focuses on the formal aspects of institutions like constitutions, laws, regulations, and official standards. But the informal aspects of institutions – that is, norms – are just as important.[31] Why? As Peter Katzenstein and Lucia Seybert show, norms are sites of great uncertainty because their meanings are inherently indeterminate, which means that they present all sorts of possibilities for norm-defying innovation and improvisation.[32] Furthermore, as Robert Lieberman and his colleagues recognize, "institutional restraints are only as strong as the norms that undergird them, binding political leaders to routinized patterns of behavior and instilling in citizens expectations about how democratic governance is to be carried out."[33] In other words, norms help anchor institutions. Several writers that I discussed earlier have noted that much of the damage Trump did to America's political institutions involved shattering long-established norms, not written or enforceable in any formal sense but nonetheless powerfully important.[34] I agree. In fact, it may be harder to fix the damage that Trump did to norms than it will be to fix the damage he did to the more formal aspects of America's political institutions. Some speculate that Trump's norm bashing has made it impossible to return completely to conventional political behavior.[35]

1.3 INSTITUTIONAL CHANGE

Social scientists know that institutions are "sticky." It's hard to change them once they are in place, especially if they've been there for a long time. There are several reasons for this. For example, change may be expensive; constituents may emerge to defend the status quo; and alternatives, even if they can be envisioned, may be deemed impractical and out of reach. In other words, once in place when someone tries to get rid of institutions or dramatically alter them, they are rarely successful. Moreover, institutions don't exist in isolation from each other but rather come in sets. As political scientists have shown, institutions in these sets tend to depend on and complement each other.[36]

---

[30] For reviews, see Campbell (2004, chap. 1), Campbell and Pedersen (2001a) and Jupille and Caporaso (2021).

[31] By one count, there are as many as eighty definitions of "institution" in the social science literature (Jupille and Caporaso 2021). Although there is plenty of overlap, sociological theories of institutions have tended to emphasize the importance of informal rules, norms, and the taken-for-granted cognitive aspects of institutions (e.g. DiMaggio and Powell 1983; Dobbin 1994; Meyer et al. 1987; Scott 2001, chaps. 1 and 2) whereas political scientists and economists have tended to emphasize formal rules, laws, regulations and property rights (e.g. Barzel 1989; Knight 1992, pp. 66–73; Ostrom 1990; Streeck and Thelen 2005b, pp. 10–12).

[32] Katzenstein and Seybert 2018a, p. 40.

[33] Lieberman 2019, p. 475. See also Christenson and Kriner (2020, p. 213).

[34] Kaufman and Haggard 2019, p. 428; Mayer 2021, p. 83.   [35] Howell and Moe 2020, p. 168.

[36] Campbell and Pedersen 2007; Crouch 2005; Hall and Soskice 2001.

For example, German labor market institutions depend on educational institutions to produce highly skilled workers without which German companies would have trouble maintaining the flexible production methods that enable them to compete successfully in international markets for high-quality products like automobiles and machine tools. Conversely, German educational institutions depend on input and resources from manufacturers and labor unions operating in the labor market institutions to help shape the apprenticeship and worker training programs that produce and sustain those highly skilled workers in the first place. Given the institutional complementarities involved in a political system, it is hard to change one institution without changing the others, which is another reason why institutions tend to be sticky.[37] The point is that for all these reasons change usually occurs at the margins.

Those who have made arguments like these assume that institutions typically evolve incrementally.[38] For example, once welfare programs like Social Security, Medicare, Medicaid, and food stamps were established in the United States, there were periodic attempts to cut them back. We saw this when Ronald Reagan was president. But the so-called Reagan revolution failed to get rid of these programs. In fact, the changes Reagan caused turned out to be rather marginal. And, although budgets and staff were trimmed, the programs themselves survived and were later beefed up by different congresses and administrations. Something similar happened when Margaret Thatcher was Britain's prime minister and she tried to roll back various welfare programs there.[39] Even the much more dramatic changes in post-communist Russia and Eastern Europe during the 1990s were not wholesale departures from past institutions. Instead, they contained echoes of each country's unique institutional history.[40]

As such, institutional change is typically a process of baby steps. And sometimes it involves taking two steps forward and one step back, repeatedly in an incremental fashion. Rare is the case when a giant leap forward happens. Yet when it came to the Trump administration, many institutional changes were not incremental; several key institutions experienced much more radical change. And although some of these changes may be reversed in the short term, others are likely to persist much longer as are their consequences, both intended and unintended. In other words, some of Trump's institutional changes are likely to be stickier than others.

Years ago, I wrote a book titled *Institutional Change and Globalization* in which I suggested that two factors went a long way in determining whether attempts at institutional change succeeded and, if they did, whether these

---

[37] Deeg and Jackson 2007, p. 167; Hall and Thelen 2009. See also Campbell (2010, pp. 102–106).
[38] Campbell 2004; Douglas 1986; Greif 2006; Kenworthy 2014; Mahoney and Thelen 2010; Steinmo 2010; Streeck and Thelen 2005a; Thelen 2004.
[39] Kenworthy 2014; Pierson 1994.   [40] Campbell and Pedersen 1996.

changes were likely to be more incremental than radical.[41] One of these factors was "fit." The other was the "institutional entrepreneur." Let's consider each in turn.

1.4 TIPPING POINTS

By "fit" I referred to how easily an idea for institutional change would meld with and complement existing institutions. This was another way of saying that changes at the margins were more likely to be accepted and stick for a prolonged period than changes that struck deeper at the fundamental core of an institution.[42] For instance, tinkering with the laws regulating how guns are purchased, what sorts of guns are legal, and the acceptable capacity of ammunition magazines has been common in the United States. However, changing the core institution governing gun ownership – the second amendment of the US Constitution, the right to bear arms – has not. In fact, nobody has even tried to do that.

Considering Trump's efforts to change America's political institutions, I now see that the notion of fit is an idea of much broader consequence. Institutional change, especially if it is more radical than incremental, is most likely when it fits the times – that is, when conditions are ripe for change. These times are what Malcolm Gladwell would call "tipping points." Like the slow buildup of pressure between tectonic plates that is suddenly released causing a devastating earthquake, tipping points involve the prolonged and gradual accumulation over time of small, incremental changes that eventually culminate in a sudden burst of dramatic change to the status quo. As he puts it, "The tipping point is the moment of critical mass, the threshold, the boiling point."[43] For example, the overwhelming popularity of Air Jordan basketball shoes didn't happen overnight. It occurred as a few boys bought them, and then a few more, and so on until these incremental changes accumulated enough to reach a tipping point where suddenly everybody wanted a pair and sales soared exponentially. Such is the way with most fads.

In a similar vein, social scientists think about threshold effects, a concept that is often used synonymously with tipping points.[44] Some economists, for instance, have used the idea to explain the effect that rising government debt has on economic performance. Not until debt gradually reaches a certain threshold does it undermine economic growth.[45] Timur Kuran, another

---

[41] Campbell 2004. See also Campbell (2010).

[42] "Fit" is also central to other theories of institutional stability (Jupille and Caporaso 2021, chap. 6).

[43] Gladwell 2000, pp. 12–14.

[44] The threshold concept is also found in analyses of things like pandemics, bandwagon effects, and asset bubbles.

[45] US Federal Reserve Bank 2012.

economist, identifies threshold effects to explain a variety of social revolutions.[46] Sociologists and political scientists have used the concept too.[47] A case in point is Frank Baumgartner and Bryan Jones' argument that dramatic policy change occurs when new ideas and ways of defining policy agendas slowly accumulate until suddenly a new way of thinking grips most politicians' imaginations.[48] Likewise, John Kingdon's classic *Agendas, Alternatives and Public Policies* shows that windows of political opportunity develop gradually and afford politicians a chance to suddenly push policymaking in bold new directions.[49]

Tipping points are not the same thing as the "critical junctures" that political scientists are fond of discussing.[50] As Giovanni Capoccia and Daniel Kelemen explain, critical junctures are "brief phases of institutional flux."[51] They are sharp moments of punctuation in the institutional status quo – break points separating two different periods of relative institutional stability or equilibrium. They often stem from a sudden exogenous shock like a war, pandemic, or political-economic crisis. However, they may also stem from slowly developing antecedent conditions.[52] These antecedents may involve institutional conflicts, such as mounting challenges to law or regulation, but they may also involve structural changes in the economy, the evolution of public opinion, the emergence of social movements, or a host of other things. The point is that a critical juncture is the time during which rapid and dramatic change occurs – a time made possible by either the gradual development of a tipping point or a sudden exogenous shock.[53] Insofar as my argument is concerned, tipping points did not suddenly materialize out of thin air. They did not appear from the hand of God. Rather they emerged gradually from a confluence of historical developments and eventually led to critical junctures – moments during which Trump tried to radically transform several of America's political institutions. Capoccia and Kelemen maintain that researchers often invoke the notion of critical junctures to explain change without paying much attention to what causes them in the first place. This book avoids that mistake through the analysis of the development of tipping points.

What surprises me is that the concept of tipping points (or threshold effects) has not received more attention in the literature on institutional change. It is

---

[46] Kuran 1995.
[47] See, for instance, Granovetter (1978), Marwell and Oliver (1993) and Scharpf (1997, pp. 53–54).
[48] Baumgartner and Jones 1993.   [49] Kingdon 1995.
[50] Solingen and Wan (2016) distinguish between critical junctures and tipping points in their empirical analysis of international security institutions.
[51] Capoccia and Kelemen 2007, p. 341.   [52] Mahoney et al. 2016, p. 80.
[53] Capoccia and Kelemen 2007, pp. 341–342, 346, 348, 351. In fact, it's hard to pin down exactly what a "critical juncture" is in the literature because it is defined in a variety of ways often lacking conceptual clarity (Capoccia and Kellemen 2007, p. 347). Mahoney et al. (2016, pp. 77–79) review of some of these definitions.

mentioned only once or twice and not even listed in the index of Joseph Jupille and James Caporaso's exhaustive review of the literature on institutional theory.[54] And when social scientists do discuss it, they typically do so to explain the sudden emergence of collective action, such as social movements, riots, and full-blown political revolutions, rather than the sort of institutional change I am concerned with here – that is, radical pieces of legislation and sudden departures from long-standing political norms and practices within an existing political system.[55]

As useful and enticing as the idea of tipping points or threshold effects may be, these things are notoriously difficult to predict. For example, economists who have tried to identify the tipping point beyond which debt begins to hurt economic performance have admitted that their "threshold estimate is subject to considerable uncertainty."[56] Paul Pierson's review of how political scientists and sociologists have used the concept of threshold effects reveals a similar fuzziness. In his view, the literature simply says that "small movements can push above some critical level" in ways that trigger change.[57] This is true, but not particularly satisfying from a methodological perspective. Similarly, in a famous article on the racial segregation of neighborhoods, Nobel Prize-winning economist Thomas Schelling found that it was difficult to identify the tipping point where an influx of African Americans suddenly triggered an exodus of white residents and the racial composition of neighborhoods shifted sharply. Nevertheless, such thresholds did exist, although he found that several were possible in his models.[58] Gladwell's treatment of the concept is silent on this methodological issue too. He simply knows tipping points when he sees them – a methodological position anathema to social scientists interested in developing positive theories that predict change but not to those who are content with explaining change once it's happened, such as those who failed to predict the collapse of communism in the Soviet Union and Eastern Europe but who recognized in hindsight that it was premised on slowly developing political and economic tipping points.[59]

But what's the reason for all this methodological uncertainty? According to sociologist Mark Granovetter, thresholds are difficult to predict because they are situationally specific and subject to change depending on how people assess the costs and benefits of engaging in collective action. In his words, "Because thresholds are behavioral dispositions, they are difficult to measure with confidence before the behavior actually occurs."[60] Timur Kuran agrees, adding that measurement problems like these often stem from people concealing their true preferences from public view as so often happened in the Soviet-bloc countries

---

[54] Jupille and Caporaso 2021.
[55] See, for example, Granovetter (1978), Schelling (1971), and Pierson's (2004, pp. 83–85,) review.
[56] US Federal Reserve Bank 2012, p. 1.   [57] Pierson 2004, p. 85.   [58] Schelling 1971.
[59] Blanchard et al. 1992; Campbell and Pedersen 1996; Kornai 1992; Kuran 1995.
[60] Granovetter 1978, p. 1440.

that suddenly upended their communist regimes. That's also why, for example, even the CIA and KGB failed to see the 1979 Iranian revolution coming. As Kuran explains, "A society can therefore come to the brink of a revolution without anyone realizing this, not even those with the power to unleash it."[61] What this boils down to is a fundamental problem of epistemology: the political world is a complex, open system with many moving parts and, as such, is riddled with uncertainty.[62] As a result, it is most unlikely that tipping points can be predicted in advance rather than identified after the fact. However, even if we cannot identify them ahead of time and, therefore, can only use the concept to explain things like an institutional change in a post hoc fashion, that doesn't mean that they aren't important. They can still precipitate dramatic institutional change just like earthquakes triggered by unanticipated tectonic tipping points can devastate a community. For these reasons, my use of the concept in this book is descriptive and not predictive.

As noted earlier, Donald Trump's rise to power in 2016 was enabled by a tipping point. Political, economic, and other conditions in the country had deteriorated to a point where a substantial portion of the electorate was fed up with the status quo. Trump presented himself to these people as a leader who would take dramatic steps to change institutions in ways that would fundamentally address their concerns and alleviate their grievances.[63] Once in power, he took advantage of this and other tipping points with a vengeance to pursue his agenda for radical institutional change. In other words, conditions had evolved to a point ripe for someone like Trump to suddenly shake up America's political institutions in a dramatic fashion. Both Trump and his ideas "fit" the times. But it took a special kind of person to do that, which brings us to the issue of institutional entrepreneurs – that is, leaders.

1.5 LEADERSHIP

Early theories of institutions suffered from what scholars call structural determinism – the idea that what people do is caused by surrounding circumstances beyond their control. There are several examples. First, some sociological theories assume that institutions contain taken-for-granted cognitive scripts that people follow automatically.[64] Consider Christmas – a holiday with many institutionalized scripts that people follow routinely like buying a Christmas tree, decorating the house, and giving presents to family members. Sociologist Paul Hirsch, a critic of this view, called these people "institutional dopes" because according to this theory, they were enslaved by these scripts like pre-programmed automatons with no free will.[65] Second, as I mentioned earlier,

---

[61] Kuran 1995, p. 251, chaps. 15 and 16.   [62] Seybert and Katzenstein 2018, pp. 16–25.
[63] Campbell 2018; Howell and Moe 2020.
[64] See Scott (2001, chap. 2) for a review of this argument.
[65] Hirsch 1997; Hirsch and Lounsbury 1997.

those who have written about institutional complementarities recognize that institutions are functionally intertwined and, as a result, resistant to change.[66] Colin Crouch points out that one shortcoming of this theory is that it ignores actors who inhabit these institutions and make them work – and by extension make them change.[67] According to political scientist Daniel Drezner, the tendency toward structural determinism is particularly pronounced among scholars who study the presidency.[68] Drezner says that they "have long privileged structural and institutional factors over the importance of individual leaders," and adds, "The discipline forgot that individual leaders can make a huge difference in governance outcomes."[69] The point is that structural theories like these have a very difficult time explaining institutional change.

Somewhat more forgiving theories acknowledge that people have choices, but those choices are quite limited by preexisting institutional constraints. From this perspective, change is possible but unfolds incrementally in "path-dependent" ways where the direction of change is largely – although not completely – determined by the institutional pathway established earlier.[70] Parents, for instance, may try to change some of the things taught to their kids in high school history, English, math, or science classes, but they don't even think about getting rid of those subjects, which have been institutionalized in their schools for a very long time and are basic requirements for admission to most colleges and universities. This sort of path-dependent argument is a softer version of structural determinism. But it still suffers from the same problem: insufficient attention to human agency, particularly the important role of leaders in the process of change.[71] As Paul Pierson observes, even in the presence of a tipping point, change won't happen unless someone is there to instigate it.[72] Gladwell recognized this too. We have all heard of the straw that broke the camel's back. This metaphor represents the tipping point argument. But the last straw doesn't put itself on the camel's back – that requires a person! Radical institutional change requires not only conditions conducive to change but also someone to tip the balance triggering change.

---

[66] Hall and Soskice 2001.   [67] Crouch 2005.

[68] Drezner's claim is substantiated by Nigel Bowles' (1999) review of the literature on presidential leadership, which identifies five schools of thought on the subject only one of which focuses on leadership characteristics rather than the structural and other factors that facilitate successful presidential leadership. According to Bowles, the one that addresses leadership characteristics – the school of psychological analysis – is the most marginal and the weakest theoretically and methodologically as exemplified, he suggests, by the pioneering work of James Barber (1972) on presidential character. See also Simonton (1987). The more general literature on political (and organizational) leadership is vast and is also tilted heavily toward structural explanations (e.g. Ahlquist and Levi 2011). Only recently have studies of political leadership started to take leadership characteristics seriously (Krcmaric et al. 2020).

[69] Drezner 2020, p. 205. See also Mayer (2021, p. 84) and Shafer and Wagner (2019).

[70] For a discussion of path dependence, see Mahoney (2000, p. 511).   [71] Steinmo 2010, p. 15.

[72] Pierson 2004, p. 85. See also Crouch (2005, p. 3).

Institutional theory has come a long way since the days of structural determinism by trying to bring human agency back into the explanation of political outcomes. The focus has been largely on the issue of preference formation – the reasons why people want what they want. Much of this work focused on how institutions shape people's preferences and then how people act on their preferences within various institutional constraints to change rules, laws, and procedures.[73] However, something is missing. Theorists of this kind neglect how leaders – not just institutions – also shape people's preferences and, in turn, alter those institutions.[74] They simply allude albeit vaguely to the importance of "agency and choice as an important factor in selecting among the options available."[75]

But all is not lost. Sociologists have recognized the importance of institutional entrepreneurs – that is, leaders who have an idea for changing things and possess the capacities and resources – the last straw – to pull it off. Leaders are successful if they can convince other people to follow their lead.[76] Similarly, political scientists James Mahoney and Kathleen Thelen call for a sustained analysis of different types of "change agents," distinguishing among them according to their goals and strategies. Sociologist Colin Crouch urges us to take leaders seriously too because they are the ones who take advantage of opportune moments to trigger change.

However, researchers like these have little to say about the characteristics required for a leader to cause change – that is, the skills, talents, and behavioral predispositions that enable leaders to lead.[77] When they do, they tend to focus on two things. First is the ability to form coalitions and broker settlements among different political factions, all rooted in the constellation of power at the moment.[78] Yet this still begs the question – what sort of qualities or skills are required to forge coalitions and settlements? The second approach, which does a bit better, emphasizes the ability of leaders to shape the perceptions and

---

[73] Rational choice institutionalists were the first to address these issues, but historical and sociological institutionalists eventually followed suit. For a discussion of these three perspectives, see Campbell (2004, chap. 1) and Katznelson and Weingast (2005).

[74] This omission is particularly apparent in Conran and Thelen's (2016, pp. 64–66) review of institutional theories of institutional change.

[75] Capoccia 2016a, p. 90.

[76] Campbell 2004; DiMaggio 1988. There is a hefty literature in political science about the importance of "ideas" (e.g. frames, cognitive paradigms, public sentiments) versus "interests" (e.g. the desire for power, wealth) as the determinants of policymaking outcomes (e.g. Béland and Cox 2011; Campbell 2002, 1998). Bringing leaders and entrepreneurs into structural discussions of institutional change opens the door for considering how ideas affect institutional change.

[77] Mahoney and Thelen 2010, pp. 22–27; Crouch 2005, p. 3. See also Pierson (2004, pp. 136–137) and Steinmo (2010, pp. 218–222). Research on social movements does a much better job showing how leadership is important for causing change (e.g. Ganz 2000; Warren 2001).

[78] These arguments take different forms including rational choice (e.g. Knight 1992, 2001; Ostrom 1990) and historical institutionalist (e.g. Steinmo et al. 1992; Thelen 2004).

identities of people so that they believe in the changes proposed by the leader and are thus willing to form a coalition or agree to a settlement in the first place. In other words, leaders who trigger institutional change do so by articulating and framing innovative ideas in ways that resonate with the people whose support they need – by appealing, for instance, to shared meanings or collective identities that justify or legitimize an institutional change.[79] Much has been written about how important framing is for institutional change.[80] Certainly, when it comes to politics frames, symbolism, pithy metaphors, and memorable slogans matter.[81] Trump's "Make America Great Again" (MAGA) catchphrase comes to mind. But there is more to be said about leadership, particularly insofar as leadership characteristics are concerned.[82]

What leadership characteristics are important for affecting political outcomes is far from settled in the academic literature. But political scientist Richard Samuels' excellent book *Machiavelli's Children* is helpful here.[83] He explains that the ability of a political leader to stretch institutional constraints in truly transformative ways depends on three characteristics, not always used for admirable purposes but often effective, nonetheless. First, as many others have recognized, is the leader's ability to *inspire* people to accept their ideas. This is the notion just discussed of framing ideas, mobilizing symbols, creating myths, and writing new scripts with the cultural tools at the leader's disposal.[84] Martin Luther King Jr. is a good example. His "I Have a Dream" speech on the steps of the Lincoln Memorial in 1963 during the March on Washington is one of the most inspirational leadership moments in American history and helped galvanize the Civil Rights Movement.

But successful leaders may also have the political skills to *buy* support for their ideas in a quid pro quo fashion. In politics, this includes political horse-trading, logrolling, deal-making, co-opting opponents and otherwise trading something for their support. These people are sometimes called transactional leaders. President Lyndon Johnson was reputedly a master of deal-making like this. Notably, his shrewd behind-the-scenes maneuvering won passage of the historic 1965 Voting Rights Act.[85]

[79] Fligstein and McAdam 2012, pp. 16–18, 46–51; Thornton et al. 2012, chap. 5.
[80] Davis et al. 2005.
[81] Edelman 1967; Katzenstein 1996; Schmidt 2002. See Adams (2017) for a discussion of Trump's use of symbols, metaphors, and frames.
[82] As John Hart (1998) explains, this was recognized long ago by Hugh Heclo (1977). Only recently have political scientists started to pay more attention to leadership characteristics through the development of the "personal biography approach" to studying political leadership (Krcmaric et al. 2020). Presidential historians have taken the issue more seriously (e.g. Goodwin 2018).
[83] Samuels 2003.
[84] See also Greenstein (2005) and Goodwin (2018). Swidler (1986) is the crucial statement on the importance of "cultural tool kits" for orchestrating change.
[85] Greenstein 2005, p. 221.

Third, leaders may *bully* people to gain their support for change. Here the leader cajoles, intimidates, strong-arms, and threatens people to submit to their will.[86] And if they refuse, then leaders purge and expel them. Joseph Stalin was an extreme example. If you didn't support him, you ended up in the gulag, or worse. If inspirational leaders motivate and transactional leaders accommodate, then leaders who bully dominate.

While inspiring people requires the utilization of cultural resources, buying and bullying depend more on political and material resources, which is another reason why resources as well as people should be incorporated into our understanding of institutions and institutional change. The more a political leader can inspire, buy, and bully people, the further they can stretch constraints and accomplish radical institutional change. Indeed, many of Samuels' examples are drawn from radical institutional transformations, including the rise of fascism in early twentieth-century Japan and Italy. In short, leaders matter. Why? Because they can provide the straw that breaks the camel's back. As Samuels explains, by deploying these skills, "social, political, and economic forces can be tipped into the balance to abet the leader's scheme" and institutional constraints can be stretched in dramatically transformational ways.[87] Note the connection in his argument between leadership (human agency), tipping point (structure), and fundamental institutional change.

Gladwell also emphasizes the importance of leaders in his tipping point theory. He writes about *mavens*, leaders who can spot windows of opportunity for instigating change – opportunities not always taken but that can lead to those transformative critical junctures noted earlier.[88] In other words, the leader needs to be able to read the contextual tea leaves and know when the time is ripe for change – that a tipping point has arrived.[89] This too is an important leadership characteristic.

Of course, most leaders do not have all these characteristics. Their style of leadership depends on whatever set is available to them. We will see later in this book that Donald Trump possessed all four of these characteristics in spades and did not hesitate to use them. He could spot tipping points and capitalize on them. He also had an uncanny ability to inspire his followers. As one observer noted, "Donald Trump is a brilliant emotional manager...who connects to the public by leveraging political identity to his advantage."[90] His attorney general, William Barr, recognized this too when he told Trump in a conversation with him about the 2020 election that one of his greatest skills was his ability to woo people to his way of thinking.[91] This is a skill that Republican pollster Tony Fabrizio says is rooted in Trump's intuitive sense of what his audience wants to

---

[86] There is a vast literature in political science on the importance of coercion for effective leadership (e.g. Ahlquist and Levi 2011).

[87] Samuels 2003, p. 2.   [88] Capoccia and Kelemen 2007; Katznelson 2003.

[89] See also Crouch (2005, p. 3), Kingdon (1995) and Pierson (2004, p. 85).

[90] Mayer 2021, p. 82.   [91] Woodward and Costa 2021, p. 73.

hear in the first place, repeating it endlessly if they do, and dropping it forever if they don't – something that Trump acknowledges he often does in his speeches.[92] Trump was also a big fan of transactional leadership. For instance, he mended fences with Senator Ted Cruz (R-TX) after the 2016 presidential primary, during which they had leveled scathing personal attacks at each other, and formed a transactional alliance with him to try to win the White House in 2020.[93] But if people didn't bow to his wishes, Trump didn't hesitate to try bullying them into submission.[94] He admitted this in one interview where he surmised that the source of real power was fear – and that he had a talent for instilling fear in people.[95]

As a result, Trump resembled what the brilliant sociologist Max Weber called a charismatic leader. Such a leader, according to Weber, is especially important as a force for radical change and commands the absolute trust and personal devotion – even hero-worship – of his or her followers. The exercise of their authority is sharply opposed to either rational-bureaucratic or traditional authority. In other words, they do not necessarily feel obliged to follow rules, laws, norms, or long-standing precedents to get what they want. Demagogues fit the profile.[96] So did Trump.[97] According to two senior-level officials in previous presidential administrations, Trump is a charismatic personality who traffics in emotional manipulation, who exploits social divisions and blames social elites for the nation's problems, and who tries to decimate institutions that block him from achieving what he wants.[98] And in doing so, he demonstrated incredible political agility in defying control and disrupting previously taken-for-granted rules of the game, particularly during tipping-point times of uncertainty and flux, and often without knowing exactly what the effects would be.[99]

However, even the most gifted leaders have their flaws and weaknesses – characteristics that cloud their judgment and undermine sound decision making. American politics is full of examples of corruption and sex scandals that were the downfall of prominent leaders. Beyond that, however, historians, political scientists, and others have identified several characteristics that can lead to trouble and that concern us in this book. One is a leader's need to surround themselves with people who pledge *personal loyalty* to them no matter what and regardless of whether they have the necessary background, skills, and expertise for the job.[100] The result is to create a personal echo chamber within which the leader only hears one point of view – their own.

---

[92] Peters 2022, pp. 65, 180–181.   [93] Woodward and Costa 2021, p. 179.
[94] Herbert 2019, p. 144; Martin and Burns 2022, chap. 1. Leonnig and Rucker (2021) is full of examples.
[95] Woodward and Costa 2021, p. 418.   [96] Weber 1978, pp. 241–245.
[97] Ghazal Aswad 2019.   [98] Bauer and Goldsmith 2020, p. 4.
[99] Katzenstein and Seybert (2018b, pp. 298–299) refer to this as "protean power."
[100] Drezner 2020; Greenstein 2005.

The world is a complex place and, as research on organizations shows, sound leadership requires listening to various points of view.[101] Shutting out alternative voices can lead to disaster. Senator Joseph McCarthy (R-WI) led an ill-fated crusade to root out communists from the government in the early 1950s – a crusade that proved to be his political downfall and a national embarrassment. He surrounded himself with sycophants like Roy Cohn, McCarthy's chief counsel, who refused to question McCarthy's judgment or dissuade him from his quest. It's worth noting that Cohen later mentored real-estate developer Donald Trump.

Another weakness can be *inexperience*.[102] Leaders themselves may lack the experience and expertise required to do a good job. Of course, inexperienced leaders may rise to the occasion and perform admirably but this requires them to be quick learners, able and willing through long hours of study and briefings to grasp the details and nuances of the issues before them. It also requires appointing experienced staff who have the knowledge and expertise necessary for their jobs. Inexperience can be a serious problem there too. For example, early in his first term as president, Bill Clinton, who had no previous Washington experience, appointed his wife Hillary, a lawyer, and Ira Magaziner, a business consultant, to run his Task Force to Reform Health Care even though neither of them had any experience in Washington politics either. As a result, devising health care reform evolved into a technocratic process largely devoid of congressional input or efforts at bipartisan compromise until the last minute when the president's plan was presented to Congress as a fait accompli. Many believe that this was a politically fatal mistake that contributed to the demise of the Clinton plan, which was never passed into law.[103] Of course, appointing inexperienced staff may stem from the leader's demands for personal loyalty and trustworthiness.

Being smart is often identified as another important leadership characteristic.[104] But *intellectual arrogance* –overconfidence in one's abilities and knowledge – can be a problem for leaders. After all, if one thinks that they are always right, it becomes all too easy to disregard facts and evidence that contradict their views. People who are intellectually arrogant usually aren't honest enough to realize or admit that they are wrong or have made mistakes.[105] Intellectual arrogance also increases the chances that you may fall prey to conspiracy theories and other erroneous explanations that reinforce your initial beliefs. Hitler famously ignored the strategic advice of his generals believing that he knew best how to conduct the Second World War. When they didn't tell him what he wanted to hear, or he suspected that they were undermining his

---

[101] Lester and Piore 2004; Madsbjerg and Rasmussen 2014. See also Goodwin (2018).
[102] Bowles 1999; Greenstein 2005; Krcmaric et al. 2020; Simonton 1987.
[103] Greenstein 2005, p. 225; Skocpol 1996, pp. 180–181.
[104] Bowles 1999; Greenstein 2005, p. 221; Krcmaric et al. 2020; Simonton 1987.
[105] Aichholzer and Willmann 2020.

authority, he was quick to demote them or move them into less important roles. As a result, he made tremendous military blunders that cost him victory in the war.[106]

Finally, although high-ranking political leaders invariably have healthy egos, a modicum of empathy can serve them well. Political scientist Fred Greenstein calls this emotional intelligence and argues that it may be the most indispensable quality in a president.[107] Conversely, an overly inflated sense of self-importance – *narcissism* – can be a devastating leadership characteristic. Narcissistic leaders seek power to realize their own self-interests rather than those of their country or constituents.[108] This is a problem for business leaders too insofar as they put their own interests above those of the companies that they run, losing sight of their company's purpose and why they were hired to run it.[109] Narcissism was Richard Nixon's fatal flaw insofar as he felt no obligation to abide by the law when it came to his reelection campaign in 1972 and approved a break-in at Democratic National Committee headquarters and then the coverup that followed, which led to the Watergate scandal that eventually destroyed his presidency. Nixon's sense of self-importance overrode whatever dedication he may have had once for doing what was best for the country.[110]

The point is that excessive demands for personal loyalty; inexperience, including in one's staff; overconfidence in one's political and policymaking abilities; and a narcissistic sense of self-importance are among the leadership characteristics that may lead to terrible decision making with serious consequences. Trump suffered from all these. According to Republican Senate Minority Leader Mitch McConnell, among others, Trump was unqualified for the job and never grew into it.[111] He had no political or policymaking experience. Nor did several of his top advisors, most notably his daughter Ivanka and son-in-law Jared Kushner, but who were nevertheless unquestionably loyal and trustworthy. Others have noted that Trump's demands for personal loyalty were sometimes so extreme as to resemble a Cosa Nostra-like protection racket.[112] Moreover, Trump often believed that he was the smartest person in the room and, as has been widely reported, had little interest in policy details, suffered from a short attention span in policy discussions, and often ignored briefing reports and the advice of people far more experienced

---

[106] Hitler's intellectual arrogance was extreme, causing him to make terrible mistakes on the eastern front, notably in the battle of Stalingrad, and on the western front during and after D-Day (Beevor 1998, 2009). As historian Anthony Beevor (1998, p. 68) put it, "Hitler, intoxicated with the notion of his own infallibility…would try, godlike, to control every maneuver from afar."

[107] Greenstein 2005, p. 222. See also Goodwin (2018) and Bowles (1999, p. 18).

[108] This is like James Barber's (1972) "active-negative" type of presidential character.

[109] Gulati 2022; Madsbjerg and Rasmussen 2014.   [110] Greenstein 2005, p. 222.

[111] Martin and Burns 2022, p. 218. See also Borowitz (2022, chap. 3).

[112] Cohen 2020; Martin and Burns 2022, pp. 29, 35.

and knowledgeable about the issues at hand than himself.[113] And his sense of self-importance often drove him to put his personal political interests ahead of what was good for the country and America's political institutions, as became especially clear after he lost the 2020 election. As Trump's National Security Advisor, John Bolton, put it, Trump "is a complete aberration in the American system. We've had good and bad presidents, competent and incompetent presidents. But none of them was as centered on their own interest, as opposed to the national interest, [as] Trump."[114] *The New York Times* confirmed Trump's narcissism. Their analysis of over 260,000 words spoken by Trump over more than a month of press briefings found that his most frequently occurring utterances (over 600) were self-congratulations.[115] Trump's sense of self-importance was also obvious in an interview with Jeremy Peters who found that Trump "made it clear that he sees himself as the sole figure responsible for the political and popular success the GOP had during his time as the party's leader."[116]

To be clear, and following others including Timur Kuran, I am not proposing a "great man" theory of history.[117] Exceptional leaders may come and go with little impact. It's only when one emerges at a moment when conditions are ripe for change – a tipping point – and they spot it and take advantage of it that dramatic change occurs. Conversely, I am not advocating some sort of structural theory of historical inevitability. Tipping points do not automatically trigger change either. Leaders must emerge to recognize and exploit them. Remember, for example, that Karl Marx believed that the inherent structural contradictions of capitalism would inevitably lead to its downfall, but Lenin recognized that this wouldn't happen without a vanguard party to lead the revolution. In other words, tipping points create the possibility for moments of radical institutional change – critical junctures – if leaders are skilled enough to spot these opportunities and take advantage of them.

1.6 RESISTANCE AND POWER

Much of what I have suggested implies that the pliability of institutions also depends on power.[118] Whether institutions remain the same, change a little, or change a lot, and shift in a progressive or regressive direction depends on the power struggles that occur over them. To a considerable degree, those with the power get to call the shots. If the forces for change are well-heeled and persuasive, then change is likely. But if the forces defending the status quo hold that advantage, then change is unlikely. Put differently, how institutions change

---

[113] Drezner 2020, chaps. 2, 4, 5; Leonnig and Rucker 2021; Rucker and Leonnig 2020.
[114] Draper 2022.   [115] Peters 2022.   [116] Peters 2022, p. xxiv.
[117] Kuran 1995, pp. 284–288.
[118] See also Ganz (2000), Jupille and Caporaso (2021, chap. 5), Knight (1992), Mahoney and Thelen (2010), and Samuels (2003).

often boils down to the balance of power among the people contesting them, which is why any study of institutional change should pay attention not only to the reformers but also to those resisting reform.[119] An enormous literature explores how power struggles among interest groups, labor unions, business associations, political parties, social movements, and other groups determine how and when political institutions change. But individual leaders also have the power to affect change. That power stems partly from their leadership characteristics.[120]

Trump, like other charismatic leaders, was especially powerful in his ability to disrupt the status quo and initiate major institutional change because he had the leadership characteristics to do so. But his power also stemmed from the resources at his disposal by virtue of being president – an office that enabled him to appoint and fire people, issue executive orders, command media attention, propose or veto legislation, and much more. Nevertheless, we will see that Trump's attacks on the deep state were often met with resistance, sometimes strong enough to weaken if not repel his assault.[121] This was obvious, for example, after the Democratic Party won back the House of Representatives in the 2018 midterm elections and in several successful lawsuits filed against his executive orders. But resistance also came from within the executive branch and his own administration – sometimes from cabinet officials; sometimes from high-ranking political appointees; and sometimes from people within the career civil service.

The fact that power matters also means that there is nothing automatic or inevitable about the outcome of institutional struggles. As a result, we can immediately dispense with any functionalist explanations of institutional change that rest on teleological assumptions that change is always an improvement on the status quo and headed in a more progressive direction.[122] There is nothing inevitably good or bad about institutional change. It depends on the circumstances – the historically given situation and the leaders in charge. This also means that change is not necessarily permanent. For instance, the collapse of the Soviet Union and authoritarian institutions in several East European countries led to more progressive institution building in the 1990s. Democracy began to flourish, people enjoyed more freedom, and their standards of living improved. But later, more reactionary forces seized control in some of these countries reversing some of these trends, proving again that institutional change can go either way and for better or worse. Russia's devastating invasion of Ukraine in 2022 underscores the point.

---

[119] Capoccia 2016b, p. 1118.   [120] Gaventa 1980; Lukes 1974.   [121] Skowronek et al. 2021.
[122] Much has been written about the degree to which institutional change tends toward functionally more efficient outcomes or not. For discussions see Campbell (2004, chap. 3) and Jupille and Caporaso (2021, chap. 4).

1.7 INCREMENTAL VS. RADICAL CHANGE

As noted earlier, institutional theorists tend to focus on incremental and not radical change. Notably, Wolfgang Streeck and Kathleen Thelen developed a now well-known typology of five processes, all of which they say exemplify incremental institutional change.[123] To summarize, displacement occurs when an already existing institution previously of little use becomes more important than another one. Layering occurs when an institutional innovation is grafted onto another institution but becomes increasingly important. Drift happens when an institution gradually erodes or atrophies, becoming less important. Conversion is when an institution is repurposed toward new goals or functions. Finally, exhaustion occurs when an institution slowly breaks down and collapses.[124] Streeck and Thelen ignored how more radical institutional change occurs. Of course, they did so for a perfectly sensible reason: it is much less common in advanced political economies than incremental change.[125] But as they recognized, that doesn't mean that more radical change doesn't occur, that it is any less important, or that we shouldn't try to understand it. As Katzenstein and Seybert note, history doesn't just crawl; it also jumps.[126] In fact, it is precisely because it is so extraordinary and consequential that it deserves our attention in this book. Even scholars like Sven Steinmo who subscribe to an evolutionary theory of institutional change recognize that "history is not a linear process" and that outcomes are sometimes the result of emergent trends.[127] This comes close to the tipping point argument. But all of this raises a very basic question that I have dodged so far. What's the difference between incremental and radical institutional change?

Remember that I am not interested in full-blown revolutions that topple and replace entire political systems but rather radical changes within a political system. That said, Mahoney and Thelen begin to point us in the right direction by explaining that radical change is sudden and unfolds over a short period of time. Incremental change is gradual and develops over a long period of time.[128] Samuels goes a bit further arguing that radical change represents a sharp break from what precedes it. Unlike incremental change, radical change is something relatively new, less path-dependent, and created out of whole cloth. As he puts it, radical change is built *on* the ruins of the old regime while incremental change is built *with* the ruins of the old regime.[129] But there is more to be said.

Institutional change can span a continuum ranging from little or no change to moderate degrees of change to more extreme radical change. Specifying the

---

[123] Streeck and Thelen 2005b.   [124] See also Mahoney and Thelen (2010).
[125] See also Fligstein and McAdam (2012, p. 12) and Thornton et al. (2012).
[126] Katzenstein and Seybert 2018a, pp. 39–40.   [127] Steinmo 2010, pp. 14, 18.
[128] Mahoney and Thelen 2010, pp. 2–3.
[129] Samuels 2003, p. 7. See also Campbell (2004, chap. 2) and Steinmo (2010, p. 17).

difference is important. But how can we differentiate among types of change along this continuum? Three factors are involved: severity, time, and scope.

First, and most important, radical change is a matter of severity. The more severe, dramatic, or extreme the break from past institutional precedent is, the more radical the change is. A tax cut, for instance, that slashes rates by fifty percent is far more radical than one that trims them by only two percent.

Second, time matters in assessing radical change. It does so in two ways – pacing and longevity.[130] As Mahoney and Thelen remind us, radical change happens much faster and more abruptly than incremental change. All of Trump's attempts to change the institutions discussed in this book happened quickly, many by executive fiat. When it comes to longevity, change may be either long-lived or short-lived, depending on the countervailing forces mustered to push back, modify, or reverse it. All else being equal, the more long-lasting an institutional change is, the greater – that is the more radical – its impact will be.[131] Conversely, a sharp break from past institutional precedent that is quickly reversed will have less impact and, in that sense, will be less radical than one that is long-lasting. Insofar as Trump is concerned, some of the changes he wrought were likely to be more long-lasting than others – some survived his presidency while others were reversed soon after he left office.

Third, radical change is also a matter of scope. Institutions have several parts. The greater the number of parts that change, the more sweeping and, therefore, the more radical the change is. There are two ways to think about this. One is substantive. Remember that the American state, indeed any political system, consists of an ensemble of institutions.[132] Trump attacked a wide array of institutions, including those governing elections, his political party, the justice system, the federal bureaucracy, and the tax system and budget. In this sense, his was an unprecedented attempt to radically alter the sweeping, multifaceted institutional terrain of the American political system. However, we can also think about this from a conceptual angle. Remember that institutions involve rules and norms, monitoring and sanctioning mechanisms, and meaning systems as well as the people and resources to run them. In various ways, Trump sought to change all of these. This was another way in which the scope of his attack on America's political system was quite radical.

Keep in mind that institutional change is not limited to structures like rules and norms, monitoring and enforcement, and meaning systems. Institutional functions can also change with significant effect. Streeck and Thelen's types of incremental change describe how institutional functions are displaced,

---

[130] For an extended discussion of how to conceptualize time in historical analysis, see Pierson (2004).

[131] Pierson 1994. My point here resembles Streeck and Thelen's (2005b, p. 9) distinction between abrupt change that results in either a complete "breakdown and replacement" of an institution or the "survival and return" of an institution more or less to its previous condition.

[132] Crouch 2005; Pierson and Skocpol 2002.

converted, exhausted, and drift. So, tracking changes in institutional functions – how well an institution works (its efficacy) and the purposes toward which it is directed (its orientation) – is just as important as tracking changes in institutional structures. There are, of course, complexities here too. For example, even though formal rules and regulations may remain the same, deep cuts in the personnel or budget of a government agency can undermine its ability to monitor and enforce those rules and regulations. As a result, institutional efficacy suffers. But people and resources also matter when it comes to institutional orientation. Replacing liberal judges with conservative ones or vice versa can lead to a dramatic functional reorientation of the law. Trump tried to alter both institutional structures and functions. Remember, however, that the best-laid plans may go awry. Unintended consequences were occasionally a fact of Trump's political life.

Overall, then, the more severe, the more rapid and long-lasting, and the more sweeping institutional change is, the more radical it is. Trump brought radical change to the deep state in less than four years in office. He did this by capitalizing on tipping points and then using his leadership to inspire, buy, and bully people into doing his bidding. But his behavior was also influenced by other leadership characteristics – political inexperience, excessive demands for personal loyalty, his frequent refusal to listen to those whose opinions and beliefs differed from his own, and an overblown sense of self-importance. As a result, his presidency is important both for the radical alterations and damage it did to America's political institutions and for the more general lessons it offers about institutional change. The former cannot be fully explained without the latter.

One caveat is in order. As I mentioned earlier, institutional theorists who have written about abrupt and dramatic institutional change often subscribe to the theory of "punctuated equilibrium." The argument is that radical change is caused suddenly by dramatic exogenous shocks, such as a major technological breakthrough, the outbreak of war, a natural disaster, or the rapid onset of an economic crisis.[133] This is not what I am arguing. First, the punctuated equilibrium approach assumes that prior to the exogenous shock not much is happening – the situation is in balance. This ignores the importance of tipping points, which are central to the story of Trump's assault on American political institutions. His rise to power and subsequent actions benefited from the decades-long accumulation of small, incremental changes that preceded him. If anything, it's a story of what sociologist Colin Hay calls "punctuated evolution."[134] Second, although Trump was a political outsider, his election was not an exogenous shock; he was elected through normal institutional rules and procedures, which he then tried to shred. This was not a coup d'état or foreign invasion. It was endogenous to the American political system's historical development.

---

[133] Baumgartner and Jones 1993; Krasner 1988; Pempel 1998. For a critique, see Thelen (2004, chap. 1) and Conran and Thelen (2016, pp. 54–56).

[134] Hay 2001.

1.8 A LOOK AHEAD

The rest of the book unfolds like this. Chapter 2 examines the long-term changes to America that culminated in Trump's election as president. This is a tale of several trends coalescing in a tipping point that helped bring him to power. It provides historical background and context for the rest of the book. The next five chapters examine some of the most important institutional attacks that Trump launched and the tipping points and leadership characteristics that facilitated them. Each chapter focuses on one of the five things involved in how institutions operate and change. Each one also focuses on a different part of the American political system. So, Chapter 3 looks at his attack on electoral institutions – the most basic *rules and norms* governing American democracy. Chapter 4 investigates how Trump transformed the Republican Party and the *meaning system* that defines republicanism, particularly its norms of civility, tolerance, and cooperation. These two chapters focus on Trump's attack on the heart of American democracy.

The next three chapters deal with Trump's attack on the state apparatus. Chapter 5 looks at his assault on the justice system, including the federal courts, the Supreme Court, and the Department of Justice, which constitute the institutional core of America's political *monitoring and enforcement* apparatus. This was an effort to functionally reorient the justice system not only in a more conservative direction, but often to serve Trump's personal interests. Chapter 6 looks at Trump's crusade against the federal bureaucracy and civil service – an attack on the *people* with professional knowledge, expertise, and experience in administering crucial institutional areas of public policymaking and political management. This attack undermined the functional efficacy of many important parts of the state. Chapter 7 explores how Trump tried to change America's core fiscal institutions – the federal tax system and budget – the source of key *resources* necessary for most other political institutions to operate. Chapter 8 wraps things up by discussing what all this means for institutional analysis, our understanding of radical institutional change, and America's future.

Figure 1.1 provides a simple typology that summarizes much of what lies ahead in forthcoming chapters by locating the institutional changes discussed in them along the first two dimensions of change I described earlier – severity and time. The most important is the horizontal dimension, which locates changes in terms of how sharply they broke with past institutional precedent. Many were more extreme departures from the past than others. The vertical dimension positions them in terms of their presumed longevity and impact. This is a more speculative dimension because longevity depends heavily on future politics and other circumstances, which are hard to predict. The darker each quadrant's shading is, the more radical are the institutional changes located there. The most radical changes in terms of the severity of their break from past precedents and their probable longevity are in the first quadrant. The next most radical changes are in the second quadrant where the breaks were also severe, but their longevity will likely be of shorter duration. The more incremental changes are

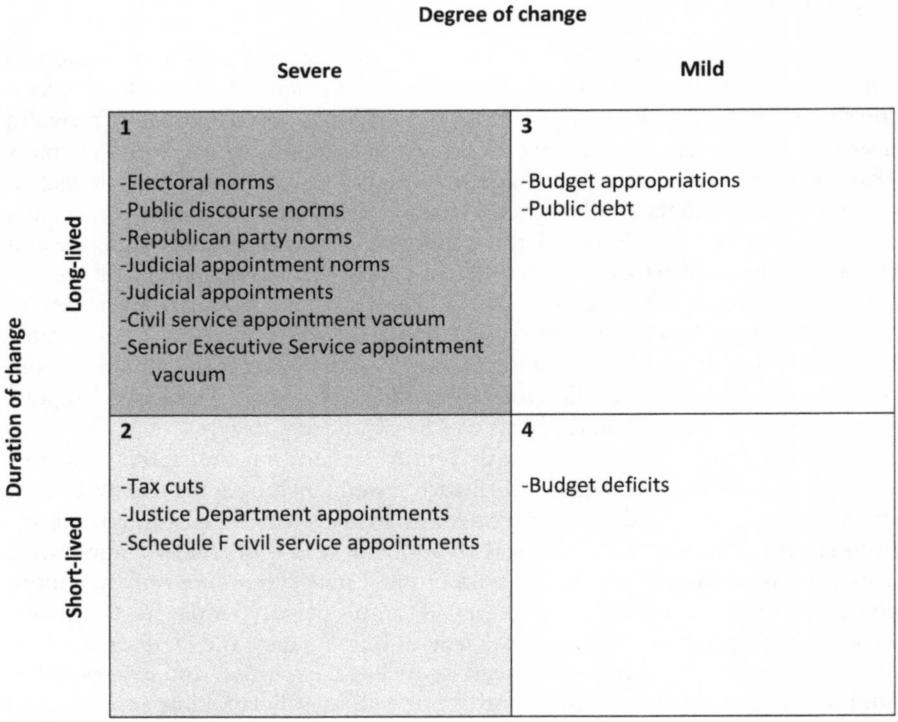

Degree of change

Severe   Mild

	Severe	Mild
Long-lived	**1** -Electoral norms -Public discourse norms -Republican party norms -Judicial appointment norms -Judicial appointments -Civil service appointment vacuum -Senior Executive Service appointment vacuum	**3** -Budget appropriations -Public debt
Short-lived	**2** -Tax cuts -Justice Department appointments -Schedule F civil service appointments	**4** -Budget deficits

Duration of change

FIGURE 1.1. Institutional changes during the Trump regime

in the third and fourth quadrants. The fact that most of the changes are in the first two quadrants – and especially the first one – underscores just how radical Trump's impact on America's political institutions was.

Let me make two final points about this typology. First, regarding scope, the third dimension of change I mentioned earlier, note that Trump pursued a sweeping number of institutional changes, thirteen in all located in Figure 1.1. This is another indication of how radical his attack on America's political system was. Second, keep in mind that many of the most radical changes in the typology (quadrant 1) involved informal norms rather than formal rules, laws, and regulations. This reinforces what others have said about the important but often neglected role of norms for institutions and especially the presidency.[135] We'll get into this more later but before we do, we need to understand how Trump came to power in the first place.

---

[135] Bauer and Goldsmith 2020; Christenson and Kriner 2020, p. 213; Hennessey and Wittes 2020; Skowronek et al. 2021.

2

The Tipping Point

Donald J. Trump was sworn in as the forty-fifth president of the United States on January 20, 2017. How he won the presidency is the subject of this chapter. It is an important story for us because it foreshadows some of the leadership characteristics that he brought to the White House to launch his attack on the "deep state." It's also an important story because Trump's election reflected a tipping point in American politics – a set of structural conditions and national anxieties that had developed gradually over several decades. Trump benefited from other tipping points once he became president, but this was the one that launched his startling rise to the presidency in the first place. Trump recognized and exploited this unique political opportunity to seize power.[1] He was a maven whose inspirational promises and appeal to voters fit the times like a glove, enabling him to pursue his agenda for radical institutional change.

Most explanations of Trump's rise to power have focused on the short-term idiosyncrasies of the election; Russian interference in the campaign; FBI director James Comey's letter to Congress days before the election announcing a renewed investigation into Hillary Clinton's emails; the Clinton campaign's strategic missteps in key swing states like Michigan and Wisconsin; Clinton's lack of charisma on the stump. Other explanations attribute Trump's victory to his use of inflammatory language on the campaign trail, which rallied his base, and how this was made possible because the Freedom Caucus in the House of Representatives, representing the right-wing Tea Party movement, undermined political civility in the years leading up to the election.[2] Of course, Trump's celebrity and deft media skills, honed to perfection in his decades-long

---

[1] For an elaboration of the arguments in this chapter, see Campbell (2018).
[2] Dionne et al. 2017; Gervais and Morris 2018.

relationship with the tabloids and on *The Apprentice*, his reality TV show, helped him too as did his ability to read a crowd and give it what it wanted.

There is some truth in all of this – contingencies like these always affect elections. But there were much deeper long-term trends at work. Trump rode to victory on a wave of public discontent that had been building since the 1970s – a wave consisting of trends in the economy, race and ethnic relations, ideology, politics, and institutions that culminated in a tipping point during Barack Obama's presidency. Trump spotted it and capitalized on it.

2.1 THE ECONOMY

The first trend was economic. Nearly a half-century of wage stagnation, rising inequality, diminishing upward mobility, mounting private debt, and declining private sector employment, particularly in traditional manufacturing industries, are part of the story. During the late 1960s and early 1970s, average wages grew about 2.5 percent annually. Since then, however, they barely budged. Between 1973 and 2000, median family income in the United States stagnated, inched up a bit for the next few years, but then stalled again.[3] This was a particularly tough problem during the latter half of the 1970s and early 1980s, a period marked by stagflation, where, thanks in part to two sudden spikes in oil prices, the economy went into recession, unemployment soared, and inflation hit double digits – only to be brought under control by tight monetary policy that threw the economy into an even worse recession.

To make ends meet, the average American family pursued at least one of three options. One was to work more hours, which many did.[4] The second was to save less money, or spend money already saved. Beginning in 1975 the savings rate for average American families declined. By 2005, it had slipped below zero – people were spending down whatever savings they had.[5] The third option was borrowing money. From 1973 to 2011, the average household debt rose from 67 to 119 percent of disposable personal income.[6] All of this was necessary for the Baby Boom generation to maintain the same standard of living that their parents had enjoyed. The same was true for the Boomer's kids. In short, people had to run faster and faster just to stay in the same place. Many people were unable to do so, which is why American middle-class prosperity became more of an illusion than a reality.[7]

Much of this was due to structural changes in the economy stemming in large part from economic globalization and technological change.[8] Beginning in the early 1970s, many traditional US manufacturing jobs were exported from the Northeast and upper Midwest to the Sunbelt in the South and Southwest where unions were weaker or nonexistent and wages and benefits were lower.

---

[3] Mishel et al. 2012, p. 179.   [4] Leicht and Fitzgerald 2014, p. 47.   [5] Rhee 2013.
[6] Mishel et al. 2012, p. 405.   [7] Leicht and Fitzgerald 2006; Temin 2017.
[8] Howell and Moe 2020, pp. 54–58.

Jobs were also either outsourced to foreign countries or eliminated entirely by technological improvements like computerization and robotics. Downsizing became the watchword for many US firms. Not everyone suffered equally. As the shift from manufacturing to a more service-oriented economy proceeded, those who managed to get good education or upgrade their skills, particularly in ways that made them technologically savvy, did alright. But those who did not, notably people from the working class or the poor, fared worse.[9]

As a result, inequality increased. Wages grew significantly for those in the top 20 percent of the income distribution – and especially for the richest 1 percent – but not for most others. This was reflected in the Gini coefficient, a standard measure of income inequality ranging from 0 to 1. A coefficient of 0 means that the national income is distributed perfectly evenly throughout society – everyone gets an equal share. A coefficient of 1 indicates perfect inequality where one person gets it all and everybody else gets nothing. Between 1975 and 2010, it rose steadily from about 0.301 to 0.365.[10] In short, the rich got richer, but many others were left behind. These trends were exacerbated by the 2008 financial crisis and the Great Recession that followed.

All of this translated into two things of political consequence. First, people's anxiety about their economic fortunes grew over the years, but especially following the financial crisis.[11] Even during the run-up to the 2016 election – years after the crisis had subsided – the economy remained the leading issue in many Americans' minds. When asked what they thought the biggest problem facing the country was, about 40 percent of Americans said it was the economy, with Republicans being more concerned than Democrats by a two-to-one margin.[12] Second, and perhaps most significant, the possibility of upward economic mobility deteriorated. This was an especially important reason why people supported Trump.[13]

Trump identified and tapped the economic angst of millions of Americans and promised to bring traditional manufacturing jobs back to America in industries like steel, automobiles, and coal mining. He threatened to renegotiate the North American Free Trade Agreement (NAFTA) arguing that it had destroyed millions of jobs. He pledged to get tough with China and Mexico to trade fairly with America. And he assured workers that by imposing import tariffs and limiting immigration the economy would flourish, jobs would be restored, their wages would go up, and the possibility of upward mobility would be improved. Above all, he promised that he would accomplish this by cutting taxes and slashing the size of government – the "deep state." This was pure populism. People believed him and were inspired by it.

---

[9] Bluestone and Harrison 1988; Danziger and Gottschalk 1995.
[10] Organization for Economic Cooperation and Development 2011.
[11] Hochschild 2016; Vance 2016.   [12] Gallup Polling 2016b.
[13] Mishel et al. 2012, pp. 142–143; Williams 2016.

2.2 RACE AND ETHNICITY

The second trend underpinning Trump's victory involved race and ethnicity. For several reasons, anti-African American, anti-Hispanic, and anti-Muslim attitudes were rising.[14] To begin with, Republicans like Richard Nixon pioneered the so-called Southern Strategy in the late 1960s and 1970s – an effort to convert white working-class voters to the Republican Party by hinting that their troubles, notably a rising tax burden, were due to the Democratic Party's efforts to provide and pay for welfare and other benefits for African Americans.[15] This fueled a white backlash against minorities and the policies allegedly designed to help them that eventually spread from the south to the north.[16]

Second, the Hispanic population grew significantly during the 1990s and 2000s. The US Census Bureau predicted that by 2044 non-Hispanic whites would be a minority in the country.[17] This was partly due to immigration and partly due to comparatively high Hispanic fertility rates. This upset those who considered this a threat to American culture. It also scared Republicans who began worrying that the country's electoral base was tilting more and more in favor of the Democrats. On average, Hispanics were poorer and less educated than whites – precisely the sort of people who tended historically to vote for Democrats.[18]

Third, anti-Muslim sentiment had been rising since the September 11, 2001, attack on the World Trade Center in New York City and the Pentagon in Washington, DC. Nearly as many Trump supporters believed that radical Islamic terrorism was as serious a problem as immigration was perceived to be.[19] Furthermore, many of those who worried about Muslim immigration believed that Muslims wanted to destroy American values and replace them with an extreme version of Islamic Shari'a law.[20]

Trump capitalized on these trends and sentiments throughout his campaign, pandering to people's worst fears about racial and ethnic minorities.[21] Here he was at odds with the Republican establishment, namely the Republican National Committee, which in 2013 had conducted what was known as "the autopsy" following Mitt Romney's failed presidential campaign. The autopsy concluded that to win the White House, Republican candidates needed to distance themselves from the party's radical wing, which was alienating swing voters, notably fast-growing minority populations. Trump did the opposite.[22] For instance, he blamed African Americans and Hispanics for crime, drugs, and other problems in the inner cities, even though problems like these are often more a matter of economic class than race. The average American believed that

[14] Agiesta and Ross 2012.   [15] Aistrup 1996; US Federal Bureau of Investigation 2017.
[16] McAdam and Kloos 2014, p. 119, chap. 3.   [17] Alba 2015.   [18] Waldman 2016, chap. 12.
[19] Doherty 2016.   [20] Potok 2017.
[21] Edwards III 2020, pp. 311–312; Pfiffner 2021, pp. 98–99; Stuckey 2021, pp. 132–134, 137–139.
[22] Peters 2022, chap. 6.

minorities were much more likely to engage in criminal activity than was true.[23] So, Trump harped incessantly on this theme during his campaign rallies. He was especially hard on Mexicans whom he claimed were streaming across the border creating criminal mayhem. But he also accused them of taking jobs from Americans even though job loss had more to do with automation and corporate downsizing than immigration. In fact, most jobs taken by Mexicans were those that Americans didn't want, and since the Great Recession, more Mexicans had left the country than tried to enter it.[24] Erroneous claims like these illustrated Trump's intellectual arrogance and disregard of facts that didn't suit his fancy. Nevertheless, Trump's pitch about Hispanic immigrants was well placed politically. His supporters believed him.[25]

Finally, Trump blamed Muslims for threatening people's safety and security even though, according to FBI crime statistics, the threat of Muslim terrorism was miniscule, especially compared to the number of homegrown terrorist attacks in school shootings and hate crimes. Since the 9/11 attacks, the Muslim threat had been virtually nonexistent. In the fifteen years prior to the 2016 election, Muslim extremists had been responsible for 0.0005 percent of all murders in the United States. If we include those killed on 9/11, it was still only about 1 percent.[26] Still, he railed about the dangers of radical Islamist terrorists coming to kill innocent Americans. Again, Trump's false sense of intellectual assuredness was evident.

It's not surprising that Trump's accusations resonated with his supporters. Scapegoating minorities for all sorts of things, but particularly for people's economic problems, is a long-standing tradition in America. It had grown recently. And Trump capitalized on it by scapegoating all these groups – mixing racism, nationalism, and promises of rejuvenating the American Dream into a politically toxic yet inspirational populist brew. As William Howell and Terry Moe have noted with reference to Trump and his political base, he "has gone out of his way to excite their race-based resentments, fears and biases."[27] The point is that there were persistent, and in some cases growing, undercurrents of racial and ethnic animosity in America that Trump used to inspire voters and exploit for political advantage. Others have found that Trump's own inflammatory rhetoric exacerbated these growing racial and ethnic animosities.[28]

Racial grievances were tightly intertwined with economic concerns with the most obvious effect among working-class and poor whites living in rural America, particularly in the South and Midwest. Several detailed studies have shown that for years these people had felt left behind by the American Dream.[29] Many believed that they had been ignored by policymakers in Washington,

[23] Ghandnoosh 2014; Ghandnoosh and Rovner 2017; Harrell et al. 2014, tables 6 and 8.
[24] Massey 2015; Massey and Gentsch 2014.   [25] Abrajano and Hajnal 2015; Doherty 2016.
[26] Campbell 2018, pp. 69–70; Kurzman 2017.
[27] Howell and Moe 2020, p. 97. See also Gervais and Morris (2018, p. 29).
[28] Lieberman et al. 2019, p. 474.   [29] Duina 2018; Hochschild 2016; Vance 2016.

who kowtowed to the interests of urban elites. They were also angered by the fact that Washington was broken. The government seemed incapable of doing much to help solve their problems. Many suffered from unemployment and wage stagnation due to changes in the economy noted earlier. Many felt disadvantaged by affirmative action laws designed to aid minorities and especially African Americans in obtaining jobs, education, and government benefits. And many suspected that the same privileged elites who held the upper hand in American politics frowned upon them with disdain. These people often lived in small communities where storefronts had been boarded up, the tax base was eroding, the population was being lost, and many felt that their traditional way of life was under threat, attacked by outside forces beyond their control. Sociologist Robert Wuthnow, who studied these rural communities closely, summarized these people's attitude as one of "moral outrage," not always apparent in conversation but occasionally bubbling to the surface with vehemence, especially when talk turned to politics.[30] They were the sort of people who saw Trump as someone who understood their concerns and was ready to do something about them if elected. And he promised during the campaign that he would take care of people like these who had been left behind by government.

2.3 IDEOLOGY

The third trend that helped Trump win the White House in 2016 was the rise of conservative ideology – a blend of social conservatism, neoliberalism, and concern about big government. Social conservatism emphasized cultural issues. Social conservatives tend to be deeply religious, be pro-life, and favor the repeal of *Roe* v. *Wade*, the Supreme Court decision that legalized abortion. They tend to oppose gay marriage and civil rights protections for the LGBTQ community. They often favor school choice, including public funding for religious and parochial schools. Social conservatives worried that American values were under siege by Democrats, liberals, and others who sought to turn the nation in a direction much different from the nostalgic past they remembered of the 1950s and 1960s that was signified, for example, by television shows like *Father Knows Best* and *Leave It to Beaver*, which portrayed the typical American family as one that was middle class, home-owning, white, and run by a working father and a stay-at-home mother. The social conservative movement came into its own politically, thanks to the rise of the religious right led initially by the Reverend Jerry Falwell, a Southern Baptist mega-church pastor and televangelist who enjoyed considerable influence during the Reagan administration. As I will discuss in Chapter 4, social conservatives helped launch the so-called culture wars in the 1980s that became a mainstay of republicanism

[30] Wuthnow 2018, pp. 110–115.

and upon which Trump capitalized not only during the 2016 presidential campaign but also throughout his presidency.[31]

Neoliberalism – sometimes called market fundamentalism – is a conservative view of economics that also gained a foothold during Ronald Reagan's presidency. Since then, more and more Americans and many of their leaders have fallen under the spell of the neoliberal Sirens believing that the only route to a strong economy was by way of tax cuts, less government spending, and fewer regulations on business. This, it was said, would stimulate economic growth, create jobs, help raise wages, and reduce government deficits and debt.[32]

There is precious little empirical evidence that neoliberalism works as advertised or that it's the golden key to economic prosperity.[33] Nevertheless, several things contributed to neoliberalism's ascendance. First, beginning in the mid-1970s, a very conservative group of think tanks, notably the Heritage Foundation, were established in Washington and pushed neoliberal policies.[34] Second, conservatives gave millions of dollars to infuse higher education with neoliberal teachings.[35] Third, corporations began lobbying for neoliberal policies.[36] Fourth, more and more private money flowed into politics, thanks to changes in campaign finance laws. Most of the increase was from conservative sources outspending liberals two-to-one and pushing neoliberalism.[37] Republicans outspent Democrats in thirteen of the sixteen presidential elections prior to 2016.[38] Finally, key segments of the media began pushing the neoliberal agenda. By 2016 the ten most popular radio talk shows in America featured conservatives touting this view.[39] And, of course, Fox News, America's iconic conservative cable television news channel, did too.

The flip side of neoliberalism was a more general disdain for big government. Since the 1960s, Americans had grown increasingly wary of big government, relative to big business or big labor, as a threat to the United States. In the mid-1960s, about 48 percent of the public held this view, but by 2014, it had reached 72 percent, often because people felt that the federal government threatened individual rights and freedoms. And among the Republicans, the numbers who believed this skyrocketed from 41 to 92 percent.[40] Moreover, since 1970, more Americans felt that their taxes were too high rather than either too low or just about right.[41] The story was similar for government spending. Since the mid-1970s, most Americans have almost always favored small government with fewer services. The difference between Republicans and Democrats was pronounced and grew. By 2015, 80 percent of Republicans

[31] Gervais and Morris 2018, pp. 20–39.   [32] Heilbroner and Milberg 1995.   [33] Blyth 2013.
[34] Campbell and Pedersen 2014, chap. 2.   [35] Cohen 2008; MacLean 2017; Teles 2008.
[36] Domhoff 2014, pp. 15–20; Temin 2017, p. 18.
[37] Cillizza 2014; Clawson 1998; Mayer 2016; Temin 2017, pp. 79–80.   [38] Bartels 2016, p. 76.
[39] Talkers 2017.   [40] Gallup Polling 2015.   [41] Gallup Polling 2017a.

favored smaller government as opposed to 31 percent of Democrats.[42] The public also worried that big government was wasteful, corrupt, and inefficient. Again, the difference between Republicans and Democrats holding this view was substantial – 75 vs. 40 percent, respectively.[43]

Trump built on all these ideological trends. For example, he appealed to social conservatives by staking out a pro-life position on abortion and promising to appoint conservative judges and justices whenever he could. He also addressed people's concerns about big government by pledging to cut taxes, government spending, and regulations. Indeed, much of Trump's economic plan was vintage neoliberalism. For several reasons, millions of people believed his neoliberal pitch. One was that it was already a familiar story that an increasing number of politicians, pundits, and economists had been preaching for decades as they came to accept the neoliberal paradigm.[44] Another reason was that people were simply ignorant of the facts. According to a study from the University of Maryland, when it came to political issues like these, Fox News viewers, the clear majority of whom were conservative and likely Trump supporters, were the most misinformed audience of any major news network.[45] This wasn't surprising insofar as Fox paraded a constant stream of neoliberal advocates across the screen like Larry Kudlow, who became Trump's National Economic Council Director. A third reason was that Trump's plan was simple and easily understood, especially compared to Hillary Clinton's complicated economic plan. Trump lived by the KISS principle – Keep It Simple, Stupid. This was one key to Trump's inspirational skill. He was a pro at packaging his message in a few simple thoughts and sound bites that resonated with crowds. Clinton was not.[46] Finally, he framed it all in ways that resonated with many people's suspicions of big government.

One clarification is necessary. Trump was not a full-blown neoliberal. Neoliberalism is not a monolithic paradigm; it is a menu of policy options from which policymakers pick and choose.[47] And he chose only those parts that fit his agenda. One way in which he deviated from the neoliberal menu was his pledge to revisit America's commitment to free trade agreements like NAFTA, the Trans-Pacific Partnership, and the World Trade Organization. Neoliberalism, after all, strongly favored free trade and opposed protectionism.[48] How did he reconcile this contradiction? When it came to free trade, Trump was particularly hard on China and Mexico. One of his complaints about NAFTA was that Mexico was taking American jobs. Rarely did he mention Canada, the third NAFTA partner. Apparently, it was the Mexicans who were the problem, not the Canadians! In other words, he justified his anti-NAFTA, anti–free trade plan by blending issues of race and jobs. The same

---

[42] Pew Research Center 2015a.   [43] Pew Research Center 2015a.   [44] Mudge 2011.
[45] Brock et al. 2012, pp. 13–14.
[46] Allen and Parnes 2017, p. 323; Stone 2017, pp. 28–29, 265.
[47] Campbell and Pedersen 2001b, pp. 269–273.   [48] Judis 2016, chap. 3.

could be inferred from his remarks about trade with China and, by extension, the rest of the South American and Asian participants in the Trans-Pacific Partnership. Similarly, Trump's anti-immigration policy was at odds with neoliberalism's belief in the benefits of free movement of labor unfettered by government intervention. So, to reconcile the inconsistency, he framed his anti-immigration position, much as he did his position on trade, in terms of race, nationalism, populism, and protecting working and middle-class jobs, but also cracking down on crime, protecting American values, and ensuring national security. Overall, then, he espoused neoliberalism when he thought it would appeal to his base, but tacked in different ideological directions when he thought it wouldn't. His ideological compass pointed in whichever way he thought would best advance his own political interests. Ideological consistency wasn't his concern; getting elected was. Here was a hint of the narcissistic leadership style that would appear more clearly later in his presidency. This was also evidence of his impressive inspirational talents and ability to spot and take advantage of the trends at hand.

2.4 POLITICAL POLARIZATION

The economic, racial, and ideological trends I have been discussing flowed together with a fourth trend – rising political polarization. The ideological gap between Republicans and Democrats had been widening gradually for decades.[49] By some accounts, polarization nowadays is greater than it has ever been since Reconstruction over a century ago.[50] But why? First, since the 1970s, both political parties shifted to the right on most economic issues, thanks in part to the rise of neoliberalism. But the Republicans embraced this ideology much more fervently than the Democrats and, as a result, moved farther to the right.[51] Republicans also embraced more extreme forms of social conservatism, another force pushing them to the right, while on social issues Democrats were trending in a more liberal direction. The Republican shift to the right may seem surprising since it had lost the popular vote in five out of the last six presidential elections. Conventional political science would suggest that a party suffering such a prolonged losing record would tack back to the center. That didn't happen in part due to the growing influence of right-wing billionaires like the Koch brothers and their wealthy political networks who had been exerting more influence within the Republican Party.[52] The religious right's influence was important too. At the same time, both parties became more homogeneous ideologically with fewer moderates holding political office.[53] Furthermore, the numbers of Democrats and Republicans in the House and

[49] Abramowitz 2013; Campbell 2016; Dionne 2016; Edsall 1984; Pew Research Center 2014.
[50] Campbell 2016, p. 140, chaps. 1 and 5; Drezner 2020, p. 25; Edsall 2012, pp. 140–141.
[51] Pew Research Center 2015a.   [52] Mayer 2016.
[53] Howell and Moe 2020, pp. 50–51, 148–149; Shafer and Wagner 2019.

Senate had become more evenly balanced, which exacerbated the other polarization effects.[54]

Second, economic trends were driving polarization too. Organized labor had been a steadfast Democratic Party supporter since the 1930s. But beginning in the late 1950s, the labor movement started growing weaker thanks to the decline of manufacturing, the rise of outsourcing, and other economic trends. Hence, the unions' ability to support Democratic candidates favoring liberal working-class interests and to provide a counterweight to conservative business interests was waning.[55] At the same time, business interests grew more conservative politically because they faced increasing global competition and were less willing to accept expensive Democratic social programs paid for with high taxes.[56] The moderating political voice of America's business elite began to fade.[57]

Racial trends also mattered. Thanks to the Southern Strategy and subsequent white backlash, by the early 2000s, conservative, white, married people viewing themselves as paying taxes to finance programs for undeserving minorities constituted much of the Republican Party's base. Meanwhile, racial and ethnic minorities as well as women, poor people dependent on government services, and comparatively liberal whites comprised the Democratic Party's base.[58] Public opinion polls reflected this in questions about racial discrimination and affirmative action. By 2014, there was a sharp partisan divide between Republicans and Democrats on these issues. Sixty-one percent of Republicans believed that discrimination against whites was at least as big a problem as was discrimination against blacks. Just as many Democrats disagreed. Tea Party Republicans felt particularly strong about this with 76 percent believing that whites suffered from discrimination at least as much as blacks. Moreover, white Republicans outnumbered white Democrats three-to-one in believing that too much attention was being paid to issues of race.[59] To some observers, "One of the central sources of continuity linking the Republican Party that emerged under Nixon in the late '60s and early '70s with the [Republican Party] of today is a sustained politics of racial reaction."[60] In other words, the white backlash assumed a politically partisan flavor that further polarized the two parties.

Trends in immigration made things even worse. By the late 1970s, there was a growing population of new immigrants, which intensified the competition for college admissions, jobs, and promotions. Compounding the problem was the fact that this was happening just as the economy was beginning to suffer from the effects of stagflation, globalization, and rising international competition. As

---

[54] Lieberman et al. 2019.   [55] Frank 2016, p. 51.

[56] Edsall 2012, pp. 69–72; 1985; Ferguson and Rogers 1986; Judis 2016, p. 43.

[57] Mizruchi 2013.

[58] Edsall 2012, p. 41; Edsall and Edsall 1992; Campbell 2016, p. 158; Judis 2016, pp. 36–37.

[59] Johnson 2017, p. 173; Pew Research Center 2016.

[60] McAdam and Kloos 2014, pp. 104, 254–255.

a result, the supply of opportunities did not keep pace with increased demand. Conservative white men – often Republican – increasingly saw themselves as competing against minorities for these opportunities and losing, they believed, because of liberal Democratic affirmative action policies.[61] All of this further amplified racial and ethnic polarization between the Republican and Democratic Parties as the Democrats attracted a growing minority population and the Republicans became increasingly white.[62]

2.5 INSTITUTIONS

Several institutional trends were also in play whose effects accrued gradually over long periods of time and increased political polarization. To begin with, in the 1970s, the Democratic and Republican Parties introduced the primary system for selecting their presidential candidates – a change that shifted control of the nomination process from more moderate party elites to more radical local activists. This often forced otherwise moderate candidates to take relatively more radical positions if they hoped to win their party's nomination. In addition, the whipping systems in Congress – the carrots and sticks that party leaders use to keep their members in line when it's time to vote on legislation and other matters – were beefed up. Furthermore, Congress passed new campaign finance laws that allowed more and more money to flow into political campaigns, often from so-called dark money sources that made it exceedingly difficult to know where the money came from and, therefore, who was supporting a candidate's campaign. As noted earlier, much of this money came from ultra-wealthy right-wing sources to support ever more conservative politicians.[63]

Gerrymandering was also on the rise – the practice of redrawing the geographical boundaries demarcating congressional districts. Every decade the federal government conducts a new census. This often triggers gerrymandering depending on how the population is redistributed between and within states. In most states, redistricting is the responsibility of the party in control of the statehouse, which creates the possibility for the process to be politically biased.[64] And in many states, that's what happened. To an increasing extent, redistricting became politicized so that new lines were drawn to advantage the electoral fortunes of the dominant political party in the state legislature.[65] For example, if Republicans control the state house and a district is dominated by Democrats, then Republicans can draw new lines to cut that district in half and incorporate each half into larger more Republican districts, thereby diluting the electoral influence of the Democrats. Because the favored party in a

[61] Edsall 2012, pp. 68–72.   [62] Abrajano and Hajnal 2015; Abramowitz 2013, chap 2.
[63] Mayer 2016.
[64] A few states have nonpartisan commissions to draw the new lines and districts.
[65] Magleby et al. 2019.

gerrymandered district was unlikely to lose the general election, the real competition was in the primary for that party's nomination. Again, this tended to push the dominant party's candidates toward more extreme policy positions to curry favor with the hard-core party activists who were the people most likely to turn out to vote in the primary.

Overall, then, all these institutional developments tended to push politicians and voters farther apart into their own polarized political tribes reducing the willingness to compromise on policy issues. However, there was another institutional trend at work – not one that amplified political polarization but one that contributed to the public's growing dissatisfaction with the federal government. The core institutional fabric of the American government, based on a constitution written for a time when America was a small agrarian country, had become increasingly ineffective. Members of Congress are elected to serve the interests of their local constituents, not the nation. So, as the country got bigger and policy problems became increasingly national in scope, they became harder for Congress to resolve. Making matters worse, the capacity of Congress to solve national problems also eroded thanks to power gradually shifting toward the executive branch, particularly to the Executive Office of the President. The bureaucracy became deeper and more expansive, and the judiciary expressed increasing deference to the executive branch. Consequently, as several political scientists have argued, public distrust and frustration with the government grew, helping to pave the way for the ascendence of someone like Trump who promised to cut the Gordian knot of political polarization and gridlock and finally get things done in Washington – a particularly bold promise because he had no political experience or familiarity with how politics worked in Washington.[66]

2.6 THE STRAW THAT BROKE THE CAMEL'S BACK

By 2008, all the trends I've been discussing were reaching a political tipping point. And then Barack Obama was elected as America's first African American president. Republican congressional leaders immediately plotted to make him a one-term president by blocking anything he might propose.[67] Then in the wake of the 2008 financial crisis, he launched the most aggressive economic stimulus since the Great Depression, pumping nearly a trillion dollars into the economy – mostly to help corporate America and Wall Street rather than Main Street. He also signed the Dodd-Frank Act, a major increase in government regulation of the financial services industry. And on top of that, he pushed health care reform – the Affordable Care Act, sometimes called Obamacare – through Congress. All of these were massive government interventions that ran against

---

[66] Drezner 2020, pp. 22–29; Howell and Moe 2020, chap. 2; Skowronek et al. 2021. See also Fukuyama (2014, pp. 503–505).
[67] Franken 2017, pp. 235–236, 246; Campbell 2016, pp. 236–237.

the neoliberal grain, consequently infuriating lots of Americans and giving rise to the conservative Tea Party movement.[68] Once the Tea Party's Freedom Caucus emerged in the House of Representatives, much policymaking ground to a halt. Things were not much better in the Senate thanks to the filibuster.

The filibuster is a legislative tactic used to block legislation and other measures in the Senate. Simply put, to filibuster a bill, one or more senators refuse to end debate on the measure, which means that it cannot be brought to a vote. To end a filibuster and force a vote on the measure in question requires a vote on "cloture." Since 1975, a three-fifths supermajority – sixty senators – must vote for cloture to stop a filibuster. So, unless the majority party holds at least sixty seats or can otherwise cobble together a sixty-vote coalition, the minority party can kill a bill by filibustering. The filibuster used to be rare but has become more common in recent decades. As a result, all major legislation except budget appropriations now requires a 60 percent supermajority to pass.[69] The use of the filibuster skyrocketed during Obama's first year in office when the Democrats were in the majority but didn't hold enough seats to stop a filibuster. Historically, the filibuster was used to kill legislative proposals that didn't have strong bipartisan support, but on Obama's watch, Senate Republican Leader Mitch McConnell used it to slow down or torpedo even things that *did* have bipartisan support.[70] It became a bludgeon used often by Republicans to prevent the Obama administration from getting what it wanted from Congress, including matters that were once routine. This was unprecedented in the Senate's history.[71] By the middle of the Obama presidency between 60 and 70 percent of important legislative proposals stalled in Congress.[72] Gridlock set in.

Making matters worse, many administrative and judicial appointments were blocked because the confirmation process had become extremely contentious thanks to polarization. As a result, the number of vacancies in the administration and judiciary soared, especially during Obama's second term. Members on both sides of the aisle agreed that they had never seen things this bad.[73] For example, in his final year in office, the Senate confirmed far fewer nominees to the federal bench than it had for the three previous presidents, all of whom, like Obama, had to contend with Senate confirmation hearings controlled by the opposition party.[74] McConnell's refusal to meet with, let alone convene

---

[68] Abramowitz 2013, pp. 9–12; Tesler and Sears 2010, pp. 155–158. See also López (2014, pp. 205–207).

[69] In 2013 the Senate decided to require only a simple majority vote to end a filibuster for all executive and judicial nominees, excluding Supreme Court nominees, which still required the three-fifths supermajority. In 2017 it voted to require only a simple majority vote to end a filibuster for Supreme Court nominees too.

[70] Franken 2017, pp. 229–230.   [71] Mann and Ornstein 2012, pp. 88–90.   [72] Binder 2014.
[73] Shear 2013.   [74] Wheeler 2016.

confirmation hearings for, Merrick Garland, Obama's nominee to the Supreme Court, epitomized the gridlock.

It's no surprise, then, that people became fed up with Washington politics. Public trust and satisfaction with the government had already been declining but dropped significantly on Obama's watch. And by 2016 the public's approval rating of Congress, also already in decline, had plummeted. Just 17 percent of Americans surveyed believed that it was doing a good job.[75] Obama's approval rating languished too averaging 48 percent during his presidency, worse than any president in over 30 years.[76]

Racism was partly responsible. Obama's election itself was marked with racist overtones as people, including Trump and others in the so-called Birther Movement, charged incorrectly that Obama was born in Africa and, therefore, ineligible for the presidency. According to political scientists Michael Tesler and David Sears, "Barack Obama's candidacy polarized the electorate by racial attitudes more strongly than had any previous presidential candidate in recent times."[77] Their analysis showed that, all else being equal, any issue upon which Obama took a public stand during the 2008 campaign would probably be polarized according to people's racial predispositions. If he supported it during the campaign, people with disparaging racial views would oppose it, and vice versa. Post-election surveys and panel data showed that the impact of racial resentment did not diminish once he took office.[78] One indication was that the highly racialized voting patterns in the 2008 presidential election were repeated four years later.[79] Obama won most of the Hispanic and African American votes. Another indication was that thirty-eight states eventually introduced legislation that many people believed was intended to inhibit voting by minority groups, notably African Americans.[80] It makes sense, then, that over the course of Obama's presidency the percentage of Americans who believed that racism was a big problem in the country doubled from 26 to 50 percent. Nearly three-quarters of African Americans and more than half of Hispanics believed that racism was a serious issue.[81]

The broader point, however, is that the time had become ripe for Trump to launch his bid for the presidency. His campaign involved a two-part strategy. One part was to attack Obama's legacy. He told one reporter soon after announcing his candidacy in 2015 that "I'm going to unify. This country is totally divided. Barack Obama has divided this country unbelievably. And it's all, it's all hatred, what can I tell you. I've never seen anything like it...I will be a great unifier for our country."[82] His narcissistic sense of self-importance in statements like this was hard to miss. He also condemned Obama's handling of the financial crisis. He lambasted the Dodd-Frank legislation for making it "impossible for bankers to function," adding that this made it difficult for

[75] Gallup Polling 2016a.   [76] Gallup Polling 2017b.   [77] Tesler and Sears 2010, p. 9.
[78] Tesler and Sears 2010, pp. 92–93.   [79] Johnson 2017.   [80] López 2014, p. 160.
[81] Pew Research Center 2015b.   [82] Diamond 2015.

Main Street to get the loans it needed to create jobs.[83] He promised to get rid of it. He also promised to "repeal and replace" Obamacare. This too was a bold promise given his lack of political experience.

The second part of Trump's campaign strategy capitalized on the economic, racial, ideological, political, and institutional trends discussed earlier. In doing so he utilized several additional leadership qualities that I identified in Chapter 1. First, with maven-like clarity he spotted opportunities to sway voters that had been developing for decades. Second, he inspired them with all sorts of promises often couched in inflammatory and hyperbolic rhetoric. He promised to be the best job creator God ever gave America by slashing individual and corporate income taxes and easing the regulatory burden on business. To reinforce his conservative credentials, particularly among evangelicals, he promised to appoint a slew of conservative judges and Supreme Court justices whenever possible. He promised to build a wall along the southern border to keep out the Mexicans and other Hispanic immigrants. He promised to crack down on Muslim immigration to prevent terrorism. Third, he pledged to cut through Washington's political gridlock by deploying his transactional skills – that is, making deals that no one else could make. He had, after all, written *The Art of the Deal*, a best-selling book on what a great deal maker he was.[84] And finally, if that didn't work, he vowed to strong-arm his way to success by launching a fusillade of executive orders to bully his way through the congressional logjam. Indeed, his willingness to resort to bullying was already evident given the verbal abuse he delivered to his opponents on the campaign trail, often laced with schoolyard name-calling like "Lyin' Ted" Cruz, "Low Energy Jeb" Bush, "Little Marco" Rubio, and, of course, "Crooked Hillary" Clinton. All of this, he said, would enable him to "Make America Great Again," the core campaign slogan he framed in all sorts of nationalist, racist, xenophobic, and occasionally sexist language.

It worked. Trump was elected. Obama's presidency marked a tipping point long in the making. Trump's victory capitalized on that tipping point and pushed politics beyond it. It was the straw that broke the camel's back enabling him to win the presidency and then, as we shall see, launch an unprecedented assault on America's political institutions.

2.7 THE RISE OF DONALD TRUMP

Exit polling by CNN right after the 2016 election showed that Trump's campaign promises resonated with the fears and anxieties of the American public, which stemmed from all the things I have described.[85] Consider the economic trends first. Roughly two-thirds of people who worried that the economy was in poor shape, and two-thirds who believed that international

---

[83] *Fortune Magazine* 2016.   [84] Trump and Schwartz 2005.   [85] CNN 2016.

trade takes away American jobs voted for Trump. So did about two-thirds of those who felt that life for the next generation would be worse than today. Rural whites were significantly more concerned about economic issues, notably finding jobs in their communities and their children's financial future, than either urban or suburban whites. It shouldn't be surprising, then, that Trump won 62 percent of the small-town and rural vote – twice as much as Clinton.[86] This was crucial to his victories in Pennsylvania, Wisconsin, and Michigan, three states that Clinton was heavily favored to win.

As I explained earlier, Trump pandered effectively to white people's racial concerns. He won 58 percent of the white vote while Clinton won a whopping 74 percent of the non-white vote. People who frowned on racial diversity in America were much more likely to vote for Trump than people who looked kindly upon it. Trump's disparaging comments about African Americans certainly contributed to his loss of the African American and Hispanic vote – he won only 8 percent and 29 percent of their votes, respectively. Finally, 84 percent of those who felt that undocumented immigrants working in the United States should be deported voted for Trump. That said, there is complexity here. Support for Trump varied within as well as across racial and ethnic groups. The within-group variation was due in part to the relationship between race and ethnicity and economic distress. For instance, support for Trump among white voters was greatest for those with racist attitudes as well as those suffering from economic problems. In contrast, blacks suffering similar problems were less likely to vote at all than to vote for Clinton. And people of color who denied the existence of systemic racism, white privilege, and similar racial narratives were also less likely to vote whereas whites denying these narratives were more likely to vote for Trump.[87]

Ideas and ideology were important too. Trump won 81 percent of the conservative vote – people who believed in limited government and the free market, and who yearned for a more conservative judiciary. His promise to overcome political polarization and gridlock resonated with voters too as did his assurances that he would "drain the swamp" by reducing the size of government and attacking the deep state. Fifty-eight percent of those who felt dissatisfied or angry with the federal government went for Trump while 76 percent of those who felt enthusiastic or satisfied with it supported Clinton.

Voters' dissatisfaction with Obama's presidency was evident too. An overwhelming 90 percent of those disapproving of Obama's presidency voted for Trump. And 83 percent of those who believed that Obamacare had gone too far supported him. Lingering concerns about the financial crisis also came into play. 78 percent of those worried that the financial situation of the country was worse than it was four years ago voted for Trump.

---

[86] Morin 2016.
[87] Green and McElwee 2019. See also Gervais and Morris (2018, pp. 214–219).

In short, Trump demonstrated an uncanny ability to take advantage of economic, racial and ethnic, ideological and political trends that had been growing for decades as well as disdain for Obama and his presidency – a perfect storm that increased the possibility that someone like him could capture the White House.[88] Some Americans who voted for him believed what he said. Others saw him as an alternative to what they believed to be a failed political establishment. And the rest hoped that his election would provide them with entrée and influence in Washington.

2.8 CONCLUSION

Trump's rise to power was not entirely of his own making. But he skillfully spotted and took advantage of several trends in the American landscape that had culminated in a tipping point during Obama's tenure in the White House. Then he moved in, inspiring voters with racist, populist, and nationalist rhetoric and promises to either make deals or bully his way through gridlock to achieve his agenda of radical institutional change in American politics. His promises on the campaign trail exposed his sense of self-importance and intellectual arrogance. It is doubtful that more experienced politicians would have dared to make so many sweeping claims about what they could accomplish if elected. The degree to which all these leadership qualities helped him capitalize on other tipping points, affected his ability to fulfill his promises, and damaged the nation's political institutions is the subject of the rest of this book.

---

[88] See also Kaufman and Haggard (2019, p. 424) and Lieberman et al. (2019).

3

The Big Lie

Upon leaving the Constitutional Convention in 1787, Benjamin Franklin is supposed to have been asked whether the framers had given us a monarchy or a republic. As legend has it, Franklin's reply was short and sweet: "A republic, if you can keep it." The principal difference between the two is the presence in a republic of free and fair elections – the institutional core of any democracy.

Reminiscent of Franklin's comment, institutional theorists know that institutions will not last unless people abide by them and, when necessary, defend them. Otherwise, institutions can atrophy and risk collapsing. This is why, in the United States, politicians respect the formal rules under which elections operate as well as the informal norms governing how a candidate behaves. Campaigns can be extremely close and sometimes nasty, peppered with scathing attacks by one candidate on the other. But candidates almost never question the formal rules of the election – how the voting is conducted and how the votes are counted, certified, and reported. And when its finished norms dictate that the loser congratulates the winner and wishes them well just as the winner commends the loser for having run a good race. Although many institutionalists dwell on the formal rules, the informal norms are just as important. Respecting the rules of the election as well as the post-election protocols reinforces the legitimacy of the election.

As this chapter explains, Donald Trump launched an unprecedented attack on America's electoral institutions. He defied informal norms of electoral protocol, impugning the character and integrity of his opponents, and refusing to concede defeat to Joe Biden in 2020 because, as Trump put it, the election had been stolen from him – a baseless charge, now known as the "Big Lie." This was a level of narcissism unprecedented in American politics – Trump's belief in his own electoral infallibility, which led him to extremes revealing how far he was willing to go in the pursuit of his own self-interest at the expense of the country and American democracy. Using that lie to inspire supporters and bully those who stood in his way, he challenged formal election laws to overturn the results of that election. He failed but continued to exacerbate people's already growing doubts about election integrity – doubts that reached a tipping point after his loss to Biden where, with Trump's inspiration, a violent mob stormed the Capitol trying to reverse the election results. He also tried to tamper with the US Census, bullying officials in ways that he hoped would improve his party's electoral fortunes for years to come. This too was unprecedented. Overall, thanks to resistance from several quarters, Trump's attack on these formal institutions was less successful than his attack on informal norms. But it still represented the democratic backsliding that concerned Franklin.[1]

3.1 A TIPPING POINT DEVELOPS

The tipping point that caused the Capitol insurrection was twenty years in the making. It began to develop when George W. Bush defeated Al Gore for the presidency in 2000 but only after the US Supreme Court intervened in a highly controversial decision stopping a recount in Florida and allowing the Republican Secretary of State's vote certification to stand. As a result, Bush beat Gore in the Sunshine State by only about 1,700 votes, less than 0.05 percent of those cast but enough to give him an Electoral College victory and the presidency. One reason why the Florida case is important is that it began to spawn national concerns about election integrity. For example, voters in some Florida precincts had to punch a hole in their paper ballot next to the name of their preferred candidate but didn't punch far enough through the ballot leaving part of the punch hole dangling off the back. Much controversy ensued over whether these "hanging chads" invalidated the ballots. Yet the fight over the Florida results did not question America's electoral institutions. Nobody charged that the election was rigged or that election laws had been broken. And both candidates treated each other respectfully. Gore graciously conceded defeat and as vice president presided in Congress over the certification of the Electoral College votes as the constitution requires. Nevertheless, according to Harvard political scientist Pippa Norris and her colleagues, the litigious war over the Florida ballots established the seismic fault lines that set up the possibility for a collapse of the public's trust in American elections.[2]

That possibility began to morph into reality when Trump began to raise questions in 2011 about Barack Obama's birthright. Trump speculated publicly that Obama wasn't an American citizen, that he was born in Kenya and not Hawaii, and demanded that he produce his birth certificate to prove that he

[1] Bernhard and O'Neill 2019, p. 320; Kaufman and Haggard 2019, p. 424.
[2] Norris et al. 2019, p. 3. See also Gumbel (2016) and; Waldman (2016, chap. 11).

was legally entitled to hold office as president of the United States. This led to the so-called Birther Movement, which found a happy home within the ranks of the Tea Party movement and right-wing media. Even after Obama produced his birth certificate, Trump and various hard-core conspiracy theorists still questioned his American citizenship and, therefore, the legitimacy of his election.[3] In questioning Obama's eligibility, however, their concern was less about challenging electoral institutions than impugning the character of the candidate. That would soon change.

Trump's behavior in the 2016 presidential election constituted a more direct challenge to electoral institutions. It began in the primaries. Trump lost the Republican Iowa caucus to Senator Ted Cruz (R-TX) by about 6,200 votes. He didn't take it lying down. Trump quickly lashed out with a series of nasty tweets like this one: "Based on the fraud committed by Senator Ted Cruz during the Iowa Caucus, either a new election should take place or [the] Cruz results nullified."[4] A tipping point was developing slowly where the legitimacy of presidential elections would eventually crumble in the eyes of millions of voters.[5]

This would not be the last time Trump railed about rigged elections and his self-assured belief that it was impossible for him to lose in a fair one. In fact, it got much worse once he won the nomination. He claimed that if he lost the general election to Hillary Clinton, it would be because the election was rigged against him – a preemptive allegation perhaps preparing the groundwork for a challenge to the results in case she won.[6] In an interview with Fox News before the election, Trump claimed that "You have 1.8 million people who are dead, who are registered to vote, and some of them absolutely vote. Now, tell me how do they do that." He also charged that there were two and a half million people registered to vote in two different places and, therefore, might vote twice. His campaign website – featuring a banner that read "Help Me Stop Crooked Hillary From Rigging This Election!" – urged supporters to go to churches, schools, and other polling places around the country to watch for evidence of voter fraud and wrongdoing. Furthermore, he accused Democrats of manipulating the public opinion polls to make it look like he was trailing Clinton – an effort, he suggested, that was designed to suppress turnout for him on election day. Adding insult to injury, he then blamed the media for reporting those polling numbers. Here was a major party presidential candidate weaponizing the rhetoric of voter fraud and election rigging.[7] It revealed not only his narcissism but also his intellectual arrogance because the facts didn't support his claims. Nevertheless, he did this to inspire and cultivate his political base. And in doing so, he crossed a normative line into unchartered political territory.

[3] Skocpol and Williamson 2012, pp. 78, 126, 194.   [4] Barry 2020.
[5] Norris et al. 2019, pp. 4–9.   [6] Vickery and Szilagyi 2019, p. 194.
[7] Hasen 2019, pp. 30–35.

Trump's accusations spread like wildfire through social media and other right-wing news outlets energizing his followers and stoking their enthusiasm at his rallies. It didn't stop there. In another tweet, he ranted: "Of course there is large scale voter fraud happening on and before election day. Why do Republican leaders deny what is going on? So naïve."[8] Trump even went so far as to blame several establishment Republicans, including Speaker of the House Paul Ryan (R-WI), for being part of a plot to defeat him.[9] None of this was true, except the part about a small group of elite Republicans – the so-called Never Trumpers – who opposed his bid for the presidency arguing publicly that his policies flew in the face of traditional Republican conservatism, smelled of self-important demagoguery, and posed a danger to their party and the country.[10]

Trump eventually beat Hillary Clinton for the presidency, garnering seventy-four more Electoral College votes than she did. But he lost the popular vote by roughly three million votes, which triggered another round of falsehoods by Trump of voter fraud and election rigging: "In addition to winning the Electoral College in a landslide, I won the popular vote if you deduct the millions of people who voted illegally."[11] According to Trump, this sort of cheating was an especially egregious problem in states like New Hampshire, Virginia, and California that went for Clinton, charging as well that the media had refused to report these alleged shenanigans.[12] I live in New Hampshire and was shocked a few days after the election to read in the morning newspaper that Trump had told reporters that Democrats had bussed people into the state from Massachusetts to vote illegally for Clinton.[13] He also asserted that many of these voters were not even US citizens – a claim his Senior Advisor Stephen Miller said they could prove with "enormous evidence."[14] The evidence was never produced. Doubling down on these charges, Trump maintained in an ABC News interview that of the millions of illegal votes cast in the election, none were cast for him – they all went to Clinton.[15] Even the most adamant conspiracy theorist would have been hard-pressed to explain how every one of these millions of allegedly illegal votes went for Clinton while not one went for Trump, and how millions of conspirators had kept so quiet about it. If true, this would have been the best-kept secret in human history!

Trump had shattered the norms of acceptable candidate behavior and, as a result, compromised many people's faith in America's electoral institutions. A Gallup poll found that while about half of Americans surveyed in 2006 expressed confidence that their elections were honest, that percentage dropped to less than a third in 2016.[16] Other polls found that people's belief in

---

[8] Samuelsohn 2016.   [9] Samuelsohn 2016.   [10] Saldin and Teles 2020.
[11] British Broadcasting Company 2016.   [12] British Broadcasting Company 2016.
[13] Leonnig and Rucker 2021, p. 280.   [14] Norris et al. 2019, p. 5; Weiser and Keith 2017.
[15] Blake 2017.
[16] Vickery and Szilagyi 2019, p. 176. According to other polls, these numbers remained fairly stable. *The Washington Post* Fact Checker found that 25 percent of those surveyed in late

the fairness of the 2016 election had dipped even lower than it was in 2000 when Bush beat Gore.[17] With deft inspirational skill, Trump's narcissistic and conspiratorial rhetoric fired up an already energized base to new levels of incandescence.

Despite his victory, Trump continued to argue that the election had been rife with voting fraud and set out to prove it. Soon after taking office, he formed the Presidential Advisory Committee on Electoral Integrity. Headed by Vice President Mike Pence and Kansas Secretary of State Kris Kobach, both Republicans, the commission was tasked with investigating Trump's claims that millions of ballots had been cast illegally. The commission met only twice, found no evidence of voting fraud, and was quietly disbanded without filing a report.[18] Later, however, thanks to a court order, the Trump administration released commission documents. Although Kobach continued to insist publicly that fraud had been rampant, the documents presented virtually no evidence to support that claim. Since 1948 there had been only about 1,000 convictions for voter misconduct in national elections![19] Kobach should have known better. A few years earlier he had led an investigation looking for people registered simultaneously to vote in two places. That search turned up only 14 cases referred for prosecution out of 84 million votes cast in 22 states.[20] This is consistent with a vast number of studies done over the years showing that the number of votes cast fraudulently in US elections due to double voting, deceased registrants, and other means is negligible.[21]

Nevertheless, Trump ignored all the evidence. His complaints about election fraud escalated again in the run-up to the 2020 election, particularly as his standing in the polls started looking grim, but with a twist.[22] This time, thanks to the COVID-19 pandemic, which raised concerns about the safety of voting in person, several states changed their voting rules, such as by permitting mail-in and curbside voting, extending early voting, and lengthening the time allotted for receiving and counting mail-in ballots. Trump and his allies went to court to block these changes while Democrats defended them to make voting safer and easier. Here Trump's strategy turned from inspiring his base to bullying election officials. By election day over 200 lawsuits and countersuits had been filed in courts across the country. Trump objected most notably to mail-in ballots because, as he put it, "Universal mail-in voting is going to be catastrophic; it's going to make our country the laughingstock of the world."[23] But why was he so concerned? He offered two reasons.

First, according to Trump, it would take weeks, months, or even years to know who finally won the election because the US Postal Service wasn't

---

2018 believed that millions of fraudulent votes were cast in the 2016 election; 44 percent didn't believe that; and 31 percent had no opinion (Edwards 2020, p. 308).
[17] Laughlin and Shelburne 2020.   [18] Norris et al. 2019, p. 6.   [19] Villeneuve 2018.
[20] Berman 2015.   [21] Brennan Center for Justice 2020a.   [22] Karl 2021, p. 113.
[23] British Broadcasting Company 2020a.

TABLE 3.1. *Mail-In voter fraud*

	Number of Fraudulent Votes Attempted by Mail	Number of General Election Votes Cast	Percentage of Votes Cast that Involved Mail-in Fraud	Time Period for Collection of Fraud Cases
Colorado	8	15,955,704	0.0000005	2005–2018
Hawaii	0	6,908,429	0.0000000	1982–2016
Oregon	14	15,476,519	0.0000009	2000–2019
Utah	0	971,185	0.0000000	2008
Washington	7	10,605,749	0.0000006	2004–2010

Source: Kamarck and Stenglein (2020).

equipped to handle millions of mail-in ballots, a ridiculous claim for which there was no evidence. Yet he blocked $25 billion in emergency funding for the postal service that would have helped expedite the delivery and return of mail-in ballots. Making matters worse, the administration also consolidated its control over the US Postal Service's board of governors, which led to the appointment of Louis DeJoy, a wealthy Trump loyalist, who ordered 671 massive mail-sorting machines, 10 percent of those in operation, to be decommissioned – a move that could only exacerbate delaying the delivery of mail-in ballots and that appeared to be coordinated with Trump's public attacks on their integrity. Voting rights activists like the League of Women Voters charged that this was a deliberate act of voter suppression.

Second, Trump claimed, again without evidence, that mail-in voting would lead to widespread voting fraud.[24] It would be easy, he said, to duplicate new ballots, forge signatures, and vote on behalf of people who were either dead or had moved. Here again the evidence did not support Trump's claim. Table 3.1 shows that according to the Brookings Institution, using data collected by the conservative Heritage Foundation, the percentage of votes cast fraudulently in previous elections that involved mail-in ballots was virtually nonexistent in the states studied. The odds of such fraud occurring were less than the odds of being struck by lightning, which are about five in a million.

The truth of the matter, however, was that Trump's real concern lay elsewhere. It was expected and widely reported that Democrats were more likely to vote by mail-in ballot than Republicans because Democrats took the risks of being exposed to COVID-19 more seriously than Republicans who would be more willing to vote in person. This was the crux of Trump's vehement opposition to mail-in ballots. Their widespread use would likely increase

---

[24] British Broadcasting Company 2020b; Leonnig and Rucker 2021, pp. 215–216, 240–242.

turnout among Democrats and, therefore, votes for Biden. This turned out to be correct, but mail-in ballots caused another problem too.

Because election officials in many states were only allowed by law to begin processing or counting mail-in ballots on election day, the early returns on election night, were based largely on the ballots cast in person – that is, ballots more likely cast by Republicans voting for Trump. However, once the mail-in vote was counted a so-called "blue wave" of votes for Biden cast by Democrats materialized flipping the results in some states in Biden's favor. This was anticipated and widely reported in the press before the election. But Trump disregarded all of this and in the wee hours of the morning on election night declared victory even though millions of ballots remained to be counted. His premature declaration immediately drew scorn from the mainstream media as he spoke from the East Wing of the White House.[25] Democrats and even a few Republicans were outraged. Maryland's Republican governor Larry Hogan tweeted that "There is no defense for the President's comments tonight undermining our Democratic process. . .No election or person is more important than our Democracy."[26] Here was an acknowledgement – from a fellow Republican – that Trump had crossed another normative line and was damaging the country's democratic institutions.

Once all the votes had finally been counted the results showed that Biden had beaten Trump by more than 7 million votes and earned a 306–232 victory in the Electoral College. Even though Biden's margin of victory in the Electoral College was exactly the same as Trump's victory had been over Clinton four years earlier, which Trump declared a landslide victory, he refused to concede the election to Biden. Instead, he charged that millions of votes had been cast illegally, incorrectly counted or were otherwise fraudulent and that he had won the election. The Big Lie was born.

Democrats and a handful of Republicans continued to push back warning of the dangers that his baseless charges of a rigged election and refusal to concede defeat posed to the nation. For example, Representative Will Hurd (R-TX) put it bluntly: "A sitting president undermining our political process and questioning the legality of the voices of countless Americans without evidence is not only dangerous and wrong, it undermines the very foundation this nation was built upon."[27] That said, most Republicans remained silent for weeks, including their House and Senate leaders, even though Trump's behavior was an unprecedented violation of institutionalized norms in a presidential election.

Why was it so hard for Trump to accept the results of the election? The answer reflects some of the most important characteristics of his leadership style – intellectual arrogance and narcissism. No matter what the issue, Trump had a very difficult time accepting facts that contradicted his views. This was the quality that led him to coin the now-famous phrase "fake news," which he

[25] Darcy 2020.   [26] Gregorian 2020.   [27] Gregorian 2020.

hurled with abandon at any media report that he didn't like. This, combined with his massive ego, was a recipe for his astonishing behavior in the aftermath of the election. He found it impossible to believe that he could lose to Joe Biden, describing him in one interview before the election as "the worst candidate in the history of presidential politics," and adding, "Could you imagine if I lose? My whole life – what am I going to do? I'm going to say I lost to the worst candidate in the history of politics."[28] So, when he was confronted with facts about the election's outcome, he rejected them out of hand and pressed on. Moreover, as we are about to see, he fell prey to various conspiracy theories about how the election had been rigged and victory stolen from him. Now his attack on electoral integrity turned from informal norms to formal institutions. Momentum toward the tipping point accelerated.

3.2 LAWSUITS GALORE

After the election, Trump and his supporters sent legal teams to several battleground states that he had just barely lost, including Pennsylvania, Arizona, Georgia, Wisconsin, and Michigan, demanding recounts and investigations of voter fraud, vote-counting errors, and other alleged procedural improprieties. They filed dozens of lawsuits. These amounted to nuisance suits – legal maneuvers intended to bully state and local officials into changing the vote in Trump's favor. But the courts rejected them due to frivolous legal arguments and a lack of evidence. In fact, some of these lawsuits were so weak that they were eventually withdrawn by those who had brought them in the first place.[29] By late December, the Republicans had lost all of the sixty lawsuits they had filed since the election.[30] In a couple of cases, these suits were so ridiculous that the lawyers representing the Trump campaign quit the case recognizing that their continued representation could damage their own or their firm's reputation.

That didn't stop Trump. He eventually hired former New York City mayor Rudy Giuliani to lead his legal team. This was evidence of another of Trump's leadership characteristics – demands for personal loyalty reinforced by a pattern of surrounding himself with people who told him what he wanted to hear. Giuliani and his team fit the bill to a tee. With Trump's blessing, the Giuliani team persisted in peddling conspiracy theories claiming that voting machines had been hacked, that ballots had been lost in some cases and mysteriously discovered in others, and that millions of them should be thrown out – false claims for which Giuliani was eventually disbarred in New York state. Members of Giuliani's team also pandered in conspiracy theories. His sidekick, Sidney Powell, charged that a cabal including communists, Democratic supporter George Soros, former Venezuelan president Hugo Chavez, the Clinton Foundation, and the CIA among many others manipulated voting machines to

---

[28] Collins 2020.   [29] Deliso et al. 2020.   [30] Rutenberg et al. 2020.

shift votes away from Trump to Biden. Later she was sued by the Dominion Corporation for claiming that their voting machines were rigged to change the results of the election. She was also reprimanded by a Michigan federal judge for filing preposterous lawsuits to undermine public confidence in the election. Eventually, one election law expert blogged that "Rudy Giuliani can say what he wants, and the president can keep declaring that he's won, but there's no plausible legal way this election gets overturned."[31] Nevertheless, Trump continued to tweet messages like this one to inspire his base – a tweet that was retweeted nearly 92,000 times and that received over 385,000 "Likes":

Biden can only enter the White House as president if he can prove that his ridiculous "80,000,000 votes" were not fraudulently or illegally obtained. When you see what happened in Detroit, Atlanta, Philadelphia & Milwaukee, massive voter fraud, he's got a big unsolvable problem![32]

Meanwhile, Trump tried to bully election officials in Michigan and Georgia, among other states, to refrain from certifying the election results. These efforts failed too as election officials – both Republican and Democrat – refused to bow to his wishes. And when the Texas attorney general, with support from Republican attorneys general in seventeen other states, filed suit with the US Supreme Court arguing that key swing states had changed election laws without the necessary approval of state legislatures, Trump asked Representative Mike Johnson (R-LA) to contact all Republicans in Congress and push them to sign an amicus brief supporting the case. Johnson's request to his fellow legislators noted that the president "said he will be anxiously awaiting the final list to review," a not-so-veiled threat that if a member didn't sign, they would pay a price later, perhaps in a barrage of nasty tweets from Trump.[33] His bullying worked. Over 100 Republican members of the House – more than 60 percent of the party's members in that chamber including all its leadership except Liz Cheney (R-WY) – signed. Senator Ted Cruz agreed to argue the case before the high court if it got that far. It didn't. Three days after the suit was filed the Court threw it out. In a short unsigned order, the Court ruled that Texas lacked standing to bring such a case because it had no business interfering in another state's elections.[34]

As these and other efforts by Trump and his allies to alter the election results were going up in smoke, the president turned to his attorney general William Barr, a staunch supporter of the president and someone who had also warned of widespread mail-in voter fraud just weeks before the election. Trump tried to strong-arm Barr into proclaiming that the election had been riddled with fraud. But instead, Barr announced in early December that US attorneys and FBI agents had been investigating complaints and information that they had received about voter fraud. He explained that they had found nothing:

[31] Durkee 2020.   [32] Troyer 2020.   [33] Rutenberg et al. 2021.
[34] Karl 2021, pp. 214–216; Liptak 2020a.

"To date, we have not seen fraud on a scale that could have effected a different outcome in the election." Giuliani, Trump's lawyer, shot back that there hadn't been a serious investigation and so the issue was far from settled. Speculation mounted that Barr might be fired for turning against the president, much like Christopher Krebs, director of the Department of Homeland Security's Cybersecurity and Infrastructure Security Agency, had been sacked just weeks earlier when he pushed back against the president's repeated claims of election fraud by tweeting that his agency had found that the 2020 election was the most secure ever.[35] Both Barr and Krebs were Trump appointees and life-long Republicans, and so had violated whatever transactional quid pro quo Trump may have imagined, which was probably why Trump bullied them so ruthlessly.

3.3 DISREGARDING THE LAW

Trump's efforts to work within the law to challenge formal electoral institutions failed. But he also ratcheted up his attack in ways that came perilously close to breaking the law and crossing the line into criminal territory. At the urging of Michael Flynn, his former National Security Council Advisor, and a few other avid conspiracy theorists, he considered ordering the Defense Department, the Department of Justice, and the Department of Homeland Security to seize voting machines in states that he suspected of voter fraud, presumably to see whether they had been tampered with and flipped votes to Biden. After a heated debate in the Oval Office, a few of his advisors dissuaded him from doing so because he didn't have the authority. But he still tried to persuade local officials in Michigan and Pennsylvania to do so. They refused.[36]

Trump also began putting pressure on politicians and election officials in Michigan, Arizona, and Pennsylvania among other states to overturn their election results. Georgia was the most egregious example. Nearly a month after election day, Trump tweeted that Republican Governor Brian Kemp should overrule his Secretary of State, Brad Raffensperger, who had certified the state's election results giving Biden a razor-thin margin of victory and sixteen electoral votes. For weeks Trump and his Republican allies in Georgia, including its two US Senators, had pressured Raffensperger to change the results claiming mass voter fraud. But Raffensperger had stuck to his guns and refused, insisting that the election had been run fairly.[37] By state law, the governor had no authority to interfere in the election, so Kemp refused to overrule Raffensperger. Trump also urged Kemp to call the legislature back into session to appoint a new slate of Electoral College electors who would defy the will of the voters and cast their ballots for Trump. In short, Trump pressured the governor to break the law not once but twice. Again, Kemp refused.[38] Finally, and perhaps most notoriously,

---

[35] Balsamo 2020.   [36] Feur et al. 2022.   [37] Qiu 2020.   [38] Martin and Herndon 2020.

in a last-minute act of desperation just days before Congress confirmed the Electoral College votes, Trump telephoned Raffensperger. In an hour-long phone conversation recorded by Raffensperger and subsequently published by *The Washington Post* Trump claimed wrongfully that he had won the Georgia vote and asked Raffensperger to "find 11,780 votes" that would flip the Georgia results. At one point Trump told him that if he didn't heed the president's wishes, "it's going to be very costly," a statement that many took to be a personal threat.[39] Again Raffensperger refused. The Fulton County district attorney eventually launched a criminal investigation into Trump's behavior.[40]

When pressuring state officials failed, Trump tried to bully his vice president, Mike Pence, whose responsibility it was to chair the joint session of Congress where the Electoral College votes are confirmed. This was a pro forma process that had never been questioned and that most Americans didn't even know about. Trump told Pence that he wanted him to overturn the Electoral College vote and tried to convince him that he had the constitutional authority to do so. This was another example of Trump's propensity for surrounding himself with people who told him what he wanted to hear. In this case, John Eastman, a conservative lawyer and former member of the Chapman University faculty, had convinced Trump that Pence could flip the election in the Electoral College. Virtually all constitutional scholars thought his reasoning was ridiculous. As specified in the constitution, the vice president's role was administrative only and Pence told him so, as did others. Pence refused Trump's demand and so Trump bullied him relentlessly. Just before Pence headed to the Capitol to chair the joint session Trump called him for one last push and told him "You can either go down in history as a patriot or you can go down in history as a pussy." In the end, Pence did his job, Trump excoriated him publicly, and their personal relationship was destroyed.[41] This was an especially vivid example of Trump's disregard for the law and his unique leadership style of intellectual arrogance and unrelenting bullying.[42] But it was much more than that. More than a year after the election, Trump insisted that Pence could have personally "overturned the election."[43] This was tantamount to a confession that he didn't really care about election fraud at all but rather just preserving his own personal power.

To review briefly, public concerns about election integrity began to develop in 2000 when Bush defeated Gore thanks to Supreme Court intervention. The Birther Movement also raised concerns a few years later. Then in a series of escalating steps, Trump stoked those doubts. First were his persistent charges of

---

[39] Karl 2021, pp. 246–248; Leonnig and Rucker 2021, pp. 442–444; Gardner and Firozi 2021.
[40] For a detailed timeline of the unrelenting pressure Trump put on Georgie state officials to change the election outcome, see Cohen et al. (2021).
[41] Baker et al. 2021.   [42] Swan 2021b.   [43] Feur et al. 2022.

election fraud in 2016 and more so in 2020, especially after he lost the election. Unlike other presidential candidates who had lost very close elections, including Nixon in 1960, Gore in 2000, and Clinton in 2016, Trump refused to accept defeat. He played up concerns about election integrity to rally his base. In this regard, his inspirational leadership skills were on full display. But his intellectual arrogance and propensity for listening only to those who reinforced his own beliefs, not to mention his narcissistic sense of self-importance, were on display too. As a result, long-institutionalized norms governing presidential elections were under siege. Second, Trump's disregard for norms was soon complemented by his numerous legal challenges to the 2020 election. Inspiration now turned toward legal bullying, but the courts refused to accept his arguments. Third, when that failed, he changed tactics again by strong-arming local election officials, politicians, and eventually his own vice president to change the results. That failed too but this time because many of those he tried to squeeze refused to disregard the law.

Nevertheless, all this generated further momentum toward a tipping point where the legitimacy of presidential elections was at stake. According to public policy scholar James Pfiffner, all of this "did serious damage to the American polity."[44] Claims of election fraud undermined public confidence in the 2020 election to the point where public protests became violent. We'll get to this momentarily. But first, it's important to understand that something else also raised questions about the legitimacy of America's presidential elections – foreign interference.

3.4 THE RUSSIANS ARE COMING

Allegations were made that Trump and his allies had solicited foreign interference in the 2016 presidential election. During the 2016 campaign Trump called publicly for the Russians to investigate potentially embarrassing emails from Hillary Clinton that had apparently gone missing and that had been a bone of contention between the two candidates. At a news conference Trump said, "Russia, if you're listening – I hope you are able to find the 30,000 emails that are missing. I think you will probably be rewarded mightily by our press. Let's see if that happens." We learned later from Special Counsel Robert Mueller's report to the attorney general that within hours of Trump's statement Russian hackers infiltrated an Internet domain used by Clinton's personal office as well as seventy-six email addresses at the Clinton campaign.

Suspicions of Russian interference and collusion with the Trump campaign led Assistant Attorney General Rod Rosenstein to appoint Mueller to investigate. Mueller was a highly respected Washington lawyer and former FBI

---

[44] Pfiffner 2021, pp. 103–105, 118.

director with impeccable credentials. Nearly two years later, Mueller issued his heavily redacted report with the following conclusions.[45] Russia's Internet Research Agency (IRA) carried out a social media campaign to sow political and social discord in the United States – an "information warfare" operation specifically targeting the political system. In doing so the IRA contacted Trump supporters and Trump campaign officials, although there was no evidence that the Americans conspired or coordinated with the IRA or the Russian government. The IRA as well as a second Russian organization supported Trump's bid for the presidency. This involved hacking the computer systems of the Clinton campaign and the Democratic National Committee, stealing thousands of documents and emails, and disseminating them online through WikiLeaks and other outlets. The Trump campaign welcomed this activity.

Moreover, according to the Mueller report, Trump's son Donald Jr., his son-in-law Jared Kushner, and his campaign chair Paul Manafort met with a few Russians believing that they would give the campaign incriminating information on Hillary Clinton that would benefit Trump. The meeting occurred but the Russians didn't deliver the goods. Manafort continued his interactions with the Russians, such as providing polling information to them about the presidential race. Despite all this and the fact that the Russians had broken several US laws, the Mueller investigation did not recommend bringing charges associated with these activities against anyone involved with the Trump campaign because there was not enough evidence. However, charges were brought against several individuals, including Manafort, for lying to the Mueller team and Congress about their dealings with the Russians and obstructing the investigation.

Russian meddling does not seem to have affected voting.[46] But it did affect people's perceptions of the election's security and fairness. According to the Pew Research Center, nearly two years after the election 43 percent of Americans said they believed that Russian interference benefited the Trump campaign. As Figure 3.1 shows, the gap between Republicans holding this opinion (14 percent) and Democrats (74 percent) was cavernous. Moreover, as Figure 3.2 illustrates, more than half of all those surveyed doubted that the Trump administration would take serious steps to prevent the Russians from interfering again in future elections. Again, the gap between Republicans and Democrats was large. The point is that there were serious concerns that the electoral system had been and might yet be tainted by foreign influences, perhaps with the approval, acquiescence, and even assistance of Trump, his

---

[45] Mueller 2019.

[46] Abramowitz 2019. See also Brazile (2017), Hasen (2019, pp. 36–39) and Nance (2016) for discussions of possible additional effects of Russian meddling in the election, such as disinformation campaigns.

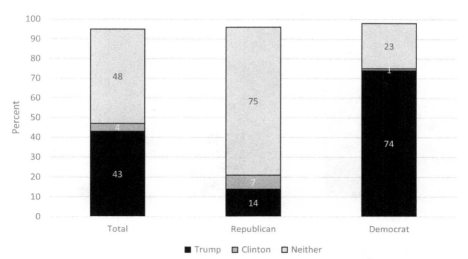

FIGURE 3.1. Percent saying Russian efforts to influence the 2016 election benefited Trump/Clinton campaign.
Note: Poll conducted March 7–14, 2018.
Source: Pew Research Center (2018).

cronies, and his administration. If Republicans worried about election fraud, now Democrats worried about foreign subterfuge.

The Democrats' concerns turned out to be justified. Trump eventually solicited foreign interference in the 2020 presidential election by threatening to withhold military aid for Ukraine unless their new president promised to launch an investigation into Biden's activity in Ukraine while he was Obama's vice president, and to promote a previously debunked conspiracy theory that shifted blame for foreign interference in the 2016 election from Russia to Ukraine. Trump was impeached for this offense. Although the Senate exonerated him on the impeachment charge, the episode cast a long shadow over the 2020 election and added more fuel to the fires of political polarization.[47] It also revealed another example of Trump's willingness to sidestep the law and bully people into submission to further his own personal interests. As such, it pushed the country another step closer to a tipping point in the erosion of public confidence in electoral institutions.

[47] Public opinion polls showed that as early as seven months before the House impeachment inquiry was announced, nearly 77 percent of Democrats already supported impeachment while less than 12 percent of Republicans did. By the time the impeachment inquiry and trial were finished, that number had risen to nearly 85 percent among Democrats but had barely budged for Republicans (Bycoffe et al. 2020).

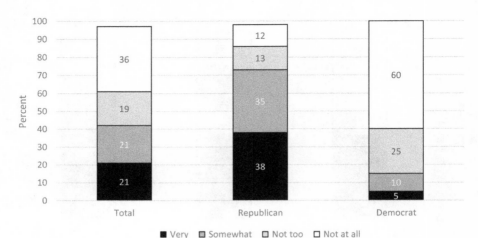

FIGURE 3.2. Percent who are very/somewhat/not too/not at all confident the Trump administration will make a serious effort to prevent Russia from influencing future US elections.
Note: Poll conducted March 7–14, 2018.
Source: Pew Research Center (2018).

3.5 THE EROSION OF PUBLIC CONFIDENCE

In the month leading up to the 2020 election, as Figure 3.3 indicates, only about half of Republicans and Democrats believed that the presidential election would likely be free and fair. But after the election less than a third of Republicans believed that the election had been on the level while over 90 percent of Democrats felt the same. Independents remained about evenly split. Other polls reported similar results well into May 2021 indicating that three-quarters of Republicans still believed that Biden had not legitimately won the election.[48] Of those who doubted the fairness of the election, over three-quarters believed that mail-in voting had led to widespread fraud, that ballots had been tampered with, and that poll watchers and others from one or both campaigns had not been allowed to monitor voting and vote counting. Over half believed that computer systems storing voting information had been hacked, rigged, or otherwise corrupted.[49] Trump had repeated these charges incessantly on his Twitter feed and in public to inspire and expand his base.[50] None of it was true but it worked.

---

[48] Skelley 2021.   [49] Laughlin and Shelburne 2020.
[50] Kim 2020. Faith in the electoral system in general – not just the presidential election – followed similar trajectories (Laughlin and Shelburne 2020).

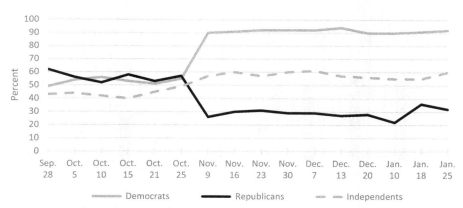

FIGURE 3.3. Share of registered voters saying the November 3, 2020 presidential election "probably" or "definitely" would be/was free and fair.
Source: Laughlin and Peyton (2021).

Two months after the election, over half of Republicans who believed that there was widespread voter fraud reported that they did so because Trump had said so. In fact, Trump was the most frequently cited source of information on the matter for those polled.[51] Of course, people whose candidate wins an election are typically more likely to believe that the election was fair than those whose candidate loses. Yet Figure 3.4 shows that even in states that Trump *won* in 2020 (Texas, Florida, and North Carolina) Republicans trusted their state's results *less* than Democrats did – a gap that grew in most states in the weeks after the election as Trump's charges of fraud grew more frequent and incendiary and his legal challenges mounted. Experimental evidence also supports the conclusion that Trump's rhetoric damaged the election's legitimacy. For instance, in one experiment a team of political scientists found that Trump supporters who were shown Twitter postings of the president disparaging democratic norms were more likely to have lost confidence in the election than those supporters who had not seen these postings.[52]

Let's put this into a broader historical perspective. Figure 3.5 compares how much registered voters trusted the results of the last six presidential elections. People were significantly more dubious about the fairness of the 2016 and 2020 elections, where Trump persistently raised questions about the elections being rigged, than they were of the previous elections, including the controversial

---

[51] Laughlin and Shelburne 2021.
[52] Clayton et al. ND. That said, beliefs in the legitimacy of democratic elections are tricky to measure and may shift over time (Badger 2020).

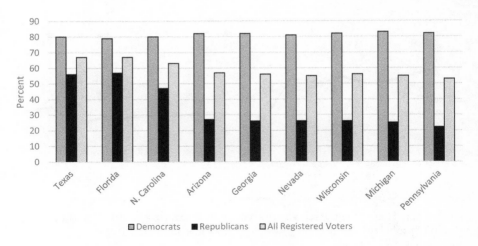

FIGURE 3.4. Share of voters believing the results of the 2020 election in each state are reliable based on what they've seen, read, or heard.
Note: Poll conducted November 13–16, 2020.
Source: Laughlin and Shelburne (2020).

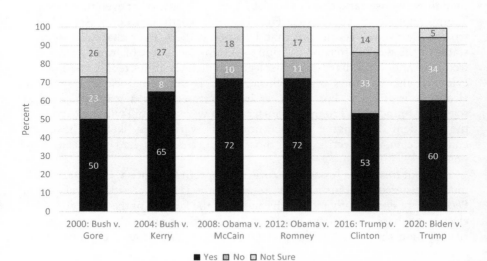

FIGURE 3.5. Percent of registered voters saying they believe each of the following was a free and fair election, or not.
Note: Poll conducted November 6–9, 2020.
Source: N. McCarthy (2020).

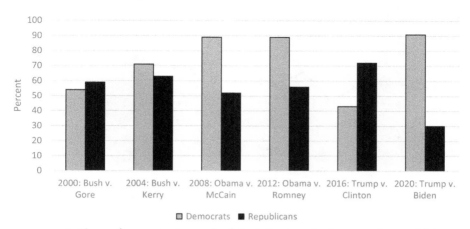

FIGURE 3.6. Share of voters saying each of the following elections was free and fair.
Note: Poll conducted November 13–16, 2020.
Source: Laughlin and Shelburne (2020).

Bush vs. Gore election. Figure 3.6 looks at the same presidential elections. It shows that, except for the 2004 election, Democrats were more trustful than Republicans of the results when the Democrat won, and Republicans were more trustful than Democrats when the Republican won. As noted earlier, this isn't surprising. But what is surprising is that this gap widened over time. In the twenty-first century it grew gradually from single digits to about 30 percent by 2016 and then exploded to 61 percent in 2020 – the election in which rhetoric of voter fraud and legal action was more rampant than ever. Election outcomes are not the only determinant of people's opinion about electoral fairness. Given the experimental and state-by-state data I've already presented, it stands to reason that Trump's continued post-election bluster about fraud, his insistence of having been robbed of victory, his denial of the results, and his refusal to concede all helped undermine Republicans' faith in the fairness of the election. It all mattered.

Confidence in the honesty of US elections overall – national, state, and local, not just presidential – has declined since the Bush vs. Gore election. Figure 3.7 reports Gallup poll data showing that the percentage of respondents expressing such confidence declined while at the same time the percentage expressing doubt increased. The dotted lines represent the linear trends while the solid lines show the annual fluctuations in people's responses. Note that the largest gap occurred in 2016 when Trump ran against Hillary Clinton and warned throughout the campaign that the election was being rigged and people's concerns about Russian interference were beginning to blossom. Unfortunately, I do not have comparable data for the 2020 election. However, it's safe to assume that the gap widened again. A University of Southern California (USC) poll found that the 2020 election further shook voters' confidence in the electoral

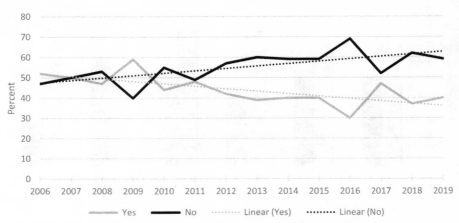

FIGURE 3.7. Do you have confidence in the honesty of US elections?.
Source: Reinhart (2020).

system.[53] And different Gallup data showed that the percentage of Americans who were "very or somewhat confident" that votes for president would be accurately cast and counted dropped from 76 percent in 2004 to a low of 59 percent in September 2020, just two months before the election. According to Gallup, "Confidence is particularly low among Republicans, likely reflecting the repeated warning of their party's standard-bearer [Trump] to be on the lookout for fraud."[54]

Overall, then, confidence in the legitimacy of America's electoral institutions had been eroding slowly but suddenly grew worse due to Donald Trump's foray into politics. His inspirational rhetoric convinced people that the presidential election was rigged. The USC study found that doubts among Trump supporters about the fairness of the 2020 election had increased because they had absorbed Trump's message that mail-in ballots had led to voter fraud. The study also found that Biden supporters feared that voter suppression had been involved. Bob Shrum, director of USC's Center for the Political Future, which co-sponsored the research, warned that "If people lose faith in the fundamentals in the political process – in the fairness of their vote, the way the democracy works – then you have to think the country will end up in very big trouble."[55] His point was that serious institutional damage had been done to the electoral system.

An international perspective underscores the severity of the problem. Figure 3.8 reports survey results from 32 OECD countries where citizens were asked in 2019 whether they were confident in the honesty of their country's elections. Only 40 percent of Americans expressed confidence – one of the

[53] Mason 2020.   [54] J. McCarthy 2020.   [55] Mason 2020.

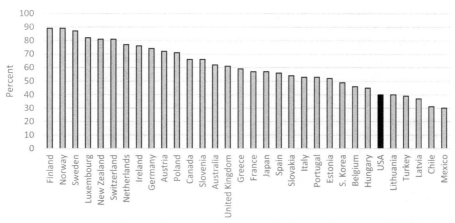

FIGURE 3.8. Percent of respondents in OECD countries saying they are confident in the honesty of their elections, 2019.
Source: Reinhart (2020).

lowest levels of confidence among the world's advanced nations.[56] It's worth noting that Americans' confidence in their elections was even lower than it was in Poland and Hungary, both under authoritarian leadership, as well as countries like Italy and France where right-wing nationalist parties had either been running the government recently or had been an important force otherwise in national politics.

3.6 LEGITIMATION MELTDOWN

It's clear that Trump's radical attack on America's electoral institutions had profound effects. As a result, the presidential electoral system suffered a crisis of legitimacy. Two things are involved in a political legitimation crisis. One is that people inside the political system – that is politicians and other public officials – worry that the system has been corrupted or is otherwise failing. The other is that the public shares these concerns, often because of things that those inside the system say publicly.[57] That's exactly what happened here.

Fears about the legitimacy of the election were raised by officials inside the state, beginning with Trump's own baseless claims of fraud that were then either reiterated – sometimes in court – or echoed by Republican politicians and

[56] Other studies have also ranked the United States low compared to other nations. Moreover, after the 2016 election, international watchdog agencies downgraded America's democratic institutions due to partisan manipulation of the electoral process, another indication of a looming tipping point (e.g. Norris et al. 2019, pp. 17–20).
[57] Campbell 1987.

others in the media. Of course, many election officials insisted otherwise. Meanwhile, several Republican senators, led by Josh Hawley (R-MO) and Ted Cruz, along with over one hundred Republicans in the House – all apparently worried about election fraud, or at least pandering to the Republican base – prepared to object to the Electoral College votes from key swing states when they were to be certified by Congress on January 6, 2021. As the certification began, the first objection raised was to Arizona's vote count. It was soundly defeated, and the certification proceeded again, but not for long.

Concerns about a rigged election had already spilled over into the public realm. There had been demonstrations across the country by Trump supporters convinced that he had been elected for a second term. "Stop the Steal" was their mantra. These were people who had been inspired by and firmly believed Trump's accusations of voter fraud and electoral shenanigans. And their activities had been getting more aggressive for weeks. For instance, election officials and politicians in Georgia, Pennsylvania, Michigan, and other states had been threatened for either having had a hand in an allegedly rigged election or for having refused to overturn it. On Twitter, the Arizona Republican Party called for supporters to be willing to "give [their] life for this fight" or "die for something." Armed protestors had shown up at the Michigan Secretary of State's house after she had certified the election results. One Michigan state representative had received racist death threats after she criticized those who claimed that the election had been rigged. Georgia election officials, mostly Republican, had received death threats too. This was unprecedented and a sharp break from previous presidential elections.[58] It was also indicative of a fast-approaching tipping point. That tipping point arrived on January 6. Trump took full advantage of it.

As Congress was certifying the Electoral College votes, thousands of Trump supporters rallied near the White House where the president addressed them claiming yet again that the election had been rigged and stolen from him. He urged the crowd to march to the Capitol. His remarks were inflammatory at best, seditious at worst, but wholly inspirational either way.[59] The crowd descended on the Capitol. Dozens of protestors, some affiliated with extreme right-wing militias and conspiracy groups like QAnon and the Proud Boys, stormed the building, ransacked congressional offices, seized control of the Senate chamber, and searched for members of Congress who just moments earlier had been evacuated by security to safe spaces elsewhere. Court documents, unsealed later, showed that rioters inside the Capitol said they would have killed Vice President Mike Pence and Speaker of the House Nancy Pelosi if they had found them.[60] The only other time the Capitol had been under siege

---

[58] Corasaniti et al. 2020.
[59] The complete text of Trump's speech can be found at https://abcnews.go.com/Politics/trump-told-supporters-stormed-capitol-hill/story?id=75110558.
[60] Limon 2021.

was during the War of 1812 – and that was when the British, not Americans, attacked it.

Hours later after order was restored in the building, Congress and the vice president returned to finish their business. Some Republicans changed their minds and refused to support further objections to the vote count. But objections to the Pennsylvania votes were raised anyway although quickly defeated. Nevertheless, when it was all over eight senators and 139 representatives had voted to sustain various objections.[61] Five people died because of the melee at the Capitol. By fall 2021, 650 people had been arrested and later charged for participating in the insurrection, including several who said they were simply following Trump's orders – further evidence of Trump's inspirational power.[62] A year later in a startling denial of the facts of what happened on January 6, Trump denied that the insurrectionists had been violent, charged that they were being prosecuted unfairly, and promised that if elected again, he might grant them presidential pardons. In the words of Richard Nixon's White House counsel John Dean, this was the "stuff of dictators."[63]

Both conservative and liberal congressional leaders recognized the damage done to America's democratic institutions. That day, before the Capitol was overrun, Senate Majority Leader Mitch McConnell warned Congress that the voters had spoken and that "If we overrule them, it would damage our republic forever." Then, after the Congress returned to finish its business, Senate Minority Leader Charles Schumer rose to speak. He referred to Franklin Roosevelt's famous address to Congress in 1941 where he called the Japanese attack on Pearl Harbor a day that would live in infamy. And then he said this: "We can now add January 6, 2021 to that very short list of dates in American history that will live forever in infamy." Foreign leaders from around the world also expressed shock and concern about the damage done to America's democratic institutions and standing in the world.[64] A YouGov Direct poll on the evening of the insurrection found that almost two-thirds of registered voters saw the storming of the Capitol building as a threat to democracy. However, 56 percent of those surveyed still believed that enough fraud had taken place to have changed the outcome of the presidential election and 45 percent of Republicans supported the storming of the Capitol.[65] The Big Lie was still alive and as dangerous as ever.

An institutional tipping point had finally been reached and then suddenly and violently breached thanks to Trump and his allies' persistent claims of voter fraud, corruption, and electoral malfeasance, not to mention suspicions

[61] Yourish et al. 2021.
[62] Allam et al. 2021; Blumenthal 2021. The FBI received numerous tips and warnings even before January 6 that right-wing extremists were planning on violence that day and believed that they were acting on the president's orders (Allam et al. 2021).
[63] Pengelly 2022.   [64] Daly 2021.   [65] Smith et al. 2021.

of foreign interference. Never had an incumbent president refused to accept his electoral defeat; never had an incumbent president tried to obstruct the peaceful transition of power.[66] Millions of people believed that the 2020 election had been rigged and that Joe Biden was not the legitimately elected president. An institutional cornerstone of American democracy, in place since the founding of the republic and Washington's willingness to turn over the reins of power to his successor, John Adams, had been broken. This was the culmination of Trump's radical assault on America's electoral institutions. It was motivated by his intellectual arrogance and refusal to face facts and his narcissistic belief that he couldn't possibly have lost the election, all bolstered by those loyalists with whom he had surrounded himself who reinforced that belief. Then, relying heavily on his inspirational skills, but also resorting to bullying when he felt it necessary, Trump undermined people's faith in the institutions as never before.

It's worth noting that questions about the legitimacy of the Bush vs. Gore election stemmed from concerns over voting technology, which could be fixed with improvements in things like voting machines. The legitimation crisis engulfing the Trump vs. Biden election was different and far more serious. As one political scientist explained, "This is a much more complicated problem that has to do with the incentives of elites to stoke anger in the American population. That's not something we can solve by coming up with a different ballot casting process."[67]

The damage is likely to be long-lasting. For instance, several well-heeled conservative organizations, wealthy philanthropists, and right-wing think tanks continued to push the Big Lie long after the 2020 election was decided, such as by financing an Arizona election ballot audit that election experts and even Arizona election officials viewed as deeply flawed and politically biased.[68] Mike Lindell, the MyPillow chief executive, financed several efforts to overturn the 2020 election. Stephen Bannon refused to acknowledge on his podcasts that Biden had won the election fair and square. And in February 2022, nearly a year and a half after the election, vocal Republicans marched on the state house in Wisconsin demanding that the legislature decertify the results and rescind the state's ten electoral votes – a move fueled by bogus legal theories and a Republican state representative and candidate for governor, Timothy Ramthun, who enjoyed Lindell's support. A similar decertification movement was afoot in Arizona.[69] According to J. Michael Luttig, a leading conservative lawyer and former appeals court judge that George W. Bush once considered nominating to the US Supreme Court, "This is the clearest and most present danger to our democracy...Trump and his supporters in Congress and in the states are preparing now to lay the groundwork to overturn the election in

[66] Leonnig and Rucker 2021, p. 279.   [67] Badger 2020.   [68] Mayer 2021.
[69] Epstein 2022.

2024 were Trump, or his designee, to lose the vote for the presidency."[70] It didn't stop there. A host of Republicans competing for national and state office in the 2022 primary elections in Ohio, Nevada, West Virginia, and several other states touted the Big Lie and mimicked Trump's claims of election fraud. By summertime more than one hundred Republicans had won primaries after repeating Trump's claims about the Big Lie. Many also promised to improve electoral security without offering any evidence that current practices had been compromised. A few, such as Doug Mastriano, who won Pennsylvania's Republican gubernatorial primary, and J.R. Majewski, the Republican primary winner for an Ohio congressional district, attended the January 6 riot at the Capitol. All of this demonstrated that Trump's legacy continued to live well beyond his presidency.[71]

Furthermore, Republicans used the Big Lie as an excuse to launch an attack on voting rights that posed further threats to democracy. And they did so even though nobody had turned up any evidence of significant voter fraud or vote tampering after the election. Some of Trump's own lawyers admitted that no reasonable person could conclude that there was any truth to the claims that the election had been rigged.[72] Yet by late 2021, Republican lawmakers had proposed more than 400 bills in states around the country to restrict voting – more than seven times the number introduced the year before. If successful, they would limit things like mail-in, absentee, and early in-person election day voting as well as impose stricter requirements for voter identification and reduce the number of neighborhood ballot drop boxes. Many of these restrictions would disproportionately affect African Americans, other minority groups, and people living in cities – all likely Democratic voters. Summarizing the views of many scholars and historians, *The Washington Post* called it "the most sweeping contraction of ballot access in the United States since the end of Reconstruction." Congressional Democrats countered with a bill that would expand rather than restrict voting rights nationwide – a bill Senate Republicans refused to consider.[73] But Republicans didn't stop there. By May 2021 Republicans in twenty states had introduced at least forty bills that would expand the powers of poll watchers, which critics charged would lead to voter intimidation and more disruption during voting and vote counting. By some accounts, "The Republican drive to empower poll watchers adds to the mounting evidence that much of the party continues to view the 2020 election through the same lens as Mr. Trump, who has repeatedly argued that his losses in key states must have been because of fraud."[74] As of October 2021, 33 Trump-inspired voting laws had been passed in 19 states, including bills granting new powers to partisan actors to challenge ballot counting and make it easier to replace local nonpartisan election officials.[75] Dozens of local election

---

[70] Haberman et al. 2022.   [71] Oladipo 2022.   [72] Rupar 2021.   [73] Gardner et al. 2021.
[74] Corasaniti 2021.   [75] Barrett et al. 2021.

officials across the country have now been replaced by Trump acolytes who believe that the system they are now supposed to oversee was rigged.[76] It will be hard to put the genie of electoral suspicion back in the bottle now that the legitimacy of America's electoral institutions has been so radically compromised.

3.7 ATTACKING THE CENSUS

Donald Trump is an avid golfer. To succeed at golf, one needs to be good at both the short game, chipping and putting, and the long game, driving the ball hundreds of yards down the fairway. Trump's accusations of voter fraud were an assault on America's formal and informal electoral institutions. Here he was playing the short game – trying to win an election right now. But he was also playing the long game, which involved trying to change the rules by which the decennial US Census was conducted. It was an effort to alter the composition of election districts at the state level, the distribution of seats in the House of Representatives, and votes in the Electoral College – all to benefit the electoral fortunes of the Republican Party for a decade or more to come.[77] This too was an attempt at radical institutional change.

A little historical background is in order. Ever since America's founding, there have been efforts to restrict people from voting. The Electoral College itself was established to ensure that in presidential elections if the unruly masses voted for a dangerous demagogue or anyone else who was anathema to the political establishment, the Electoral College could overrule the popular vote in favor of someone else, thereby disenfranchising a majority of the electorate. Women didn't win the right to vote until 1920. Many institutional obstacles preventing African Americans from voting remained until the 1965 Voting Rights Act. As recently as 2010, nearly six million Americans were forbidden from voting due to a past criminal conviction.[78]

Most recently, several states have passed voter identification laws making it more difficult for registered voters to vote who lack proper identification.[79] Behind many of these voter ID laws were Republican concerns about demographic changes that were eating into their base of political support. As I explained in Chapter 2, non-Hispanic whites, the core of the Republican base, were slowly shrinking as a percentage of the population while the percentage of African American, Hispanic, and other minority groups who typically vote for Democrats was rising. Some argue that strict voter ID laws tend to benefit Republicans more than Democrats. This is true at both the state and county levels.[80] According to Michael Waldman, president of the Brennan Center for Justice, this was by design:

---

[76] Alberta 2022.   [77] Chinni 2020.   [78] Waldman 2016, pp. 174–179.
[79] Waldman 2016, pp. 201–202.   [80] Bergman et al. 2019.

A Republican Party strategy was evident. Of the eleven states with the highest African American turnout in 2008, seven made it harder to vote. Nine of the twelve states with the largest Hispanic population growth imposed new restrictions. These groups favored Democrats.[81]

This brings us to Donald Trump. His concerns about voter fraud, on the one hand, and the Republican Party's shrinking demographic base, on the other hand, led to another assault on America's electoral institutions – less direct than those discussed so far, but insidious, nonetheless. In 2018 his administration ordered the US Census Bureau to add a question to the 2020 census about whether an individual was a US citizen. Census Bureau experts pushed back arguing that this would lower response rates among undocumented immigrants and their families, particularly Hispanics, who feared being identified and then deported. Questions have been added to and subtracted from the census over the years, but this was different because it would radically distort the count.

Why would Trump want an undercount like this? To begin with, it was suspected that the undercount would be worse for states tending to vote for Democrats – states like California and New York with large numbers of undocumented immigrants.[82] In turn, these states might lose some seats in the House of Representatives, which are awarded according to the size of a state's population. It was possible, then, that an undercount would cause seats to shift from blue states to red ones through reapportionment. In turn, this would cause some blue states to lose some Electoral College votes, which are distributed partly according to how many seats a state holds in the House. As a result, a census undercount might improve Trump's or any other Republican's chances of winning another presidential election someday. The Trump administration had been quite open about its desire to change the formula by which House seats were divvied up among the states by excluding noncitizens from the population count. This would leave an older, whiter official population in states with large immigrant populations and presumably benefit Republicans at election time.[83] Furthermore, as discussed in Chapter 2, the census often triggers congressional redistricting in states opening the door for gerrymandering.[84] In recent years Republicans controlled many state legislatures and governorships, so the odds were that a significant change in a state's population due to an undercount would trigger reapportionment, redistricting, and gerrymandering that would give the Republicans an electoral advantage going forward in several states.[85] This, too, would benefit Trump or another Republican running for election.

---

[81] Waldman 2016, p. 201.   [82] Wines and Fausset 2020.   [83] Wines 2022.
[84] A few states have established nonpartisan commissions to draw the new lines and districts.
[85] Magleby et al. 2019; Waldman 2016, pp. 225–229.

With all this in mind, Democrats and activists challenged the census citizenship question in court. Plaintiffs argued that the question violated the US Constitution, which called for a decennial count of all *persons* – not just *citizens* – living in the United States.[86] In short, they argued that Trump was violating constitutional law. The administration's defense was that they were simply trying to uphold the Voting Rights Act, better protect minority voter rights, and ensure against voter fraud – an argument that didn't make much sense. The US Supreme Court ruled against the administration in a 5-to-4 decision in part because it did not believe the administration's rationale for adding the question to the census. Chief Justice John Roberts provided the deciding vote, writing that his problem was not with the question itself but with the explanation for its inclusion, which he found to be flimsy and unconvincing. Indeed, documentary evidence revealed later that Republicans wanted to add the question to the census to undermine the political influence of minority groups who tended to vote for Democrats.[87] One might think that this level of resistance would have stopped Trump in his tracks. But he didn't give up the fight.

Having lost in court, Trump turned to procedural strategies. First, according to documents obtained by the Brennan Center for Justice under the Freedom of Information Act, Trump issued a presidential memorandum instructing the Census Bureau to illegally strip undocumented immigrants from the apportionment count after the census had been completed. But how could this be done without the citizenship question? He directed the Census Bureau to produce citizenship statistics based on information in state driver's license and welfare records. The idea was that these data could be used to identify and exclude undocumented people from the reapportionment and redistricting data reported to Congress. Bureau statisticians and methodologists were very skeptical that these data would be useful in accurately calculating citizenship statistics. Nor did they have a methodology for analyzing them in which they were confident.[88]

Second, the Census Bureau was required by law to provide the state-by-state census count to the president by December 31, 2020 for him to report the reapportionment data to Congress. But census data collection in the field nearly ground to a halt that spring thanks to the COVID-19 pandemic, so the administration asked Congress to extend the deadline for delivering reapportionment numbers to April 2021. However, in July, perhaps suspecting that he would lose the November election, Trump changed his mind, ordering the Bureau to stick to the December deadline. This meant that it had to cut short counting people in the field and squeeze five months of data processing into half that time. This too would have run the risk of undercounting the number of

---

[86] See Article 1, Section 2, Clause 3 of *The Constitution of the United States of America*.
[87] Prokop 2019.   [88] Brennan Center for Justice 2022; Wines 2022.

undocumented people in the country – a group notoriously difficult to locate and count by door-to-door census takers.

In short, the Brennan Center concluded that the Trump administration, "attempted to exert extreme partisan influence over the Census Bureau as it was conducting the 2020 Census."[89] Doing these things was unprecedented in American history. However, for technical reasons the data analysis could not be finished by the end of the year unless analysts took methodological shortcuts that would have jeopardized the accuracy of the census.[90] About a month before the December deadline, Rob Santos, president-elect of the American Statistical Association told reporters that:

They [Census Bureau] could be in a situation where they don't know what they don't know, and by the time they find out, it's too late. I don't have high confidence that this can be done in two weeks, or three weeks, or a month. I think the Census Bureau needs time to do its due diligence, sort out the problems and fix them.[91]

But Trump didn't care about accuracy. Nor did he worry about the professional integrity of the Bureau's staff. So, he resorted to bullying. His political appointees at the Census Bureau ratcheted up pressure on their analysts to get the job done so that Trump could report the numbers he favored to Congress before he left office.[92] It didn't work. The Bureau's leadership, methodologists and statisticians refused to abide by the speed-up or kowtow to the administration's demand for tallies of undocumented immigrants.[93] This was spelled out in no uncertain terms in an internal Bureau memo, which said that "the Census Bureau views the development of the methodology and processes as its responsibility as an independent statistical agency."[94] Another memo that Bureau officials wanted to send to Commerce Secretary Wilber Ross explained that the Commerce Department, which houses the Census Bureau, was "demonstrating an unusually high degree of engagement in technical matters...unprecedented relative to the previous censuses."[95]

In the end, Trump's long game failed. Just as the Court had blocked his attempt to circumvent constitutional law, professional staff at the Census Bureau stopped his effort to sidestep their expertise and standard operating procedures. The census numbers including the undocumented count went to Biden instead.

It's worth noting that Trump's effort to change the census was radical in another sense too. After reapportionment in 1981 California Congressman Phil Burton, a Democrat, made a hand-drawn map repositioning the electoral

[89] Brennan Center for Justice 2022.   [90] Clark 2020; Wang 2020; Wines and Bazelon 2020.
[91] Wines and Bazelon 2020.   [92] Clark 2020; Wang 2020; Wines and Bazelon 2020.
[93] Brennan Center for Justice 2022.   [94] Wines 2022.
[95] Brennan Center for Justice 2022; Wines 2022.

districts in his state that benefited his party. This was a crude but effective means of gerrymandering California. A decade later, Republicans used computer programs for the same purpose to increase their hold on politics throughout the southern states. In 2000 and 2010 these analytic techniques grew more sophisticated. In some states, both parties cooperated in gerrymandering to ensure that their incumbents remained in office. But in other states one party or the other moved aggressively to dominate the process. Republicans were particularly successful in Texas, Virginia, North Carolina, and Pennsylvania. For example, in the 2012 midterm elections in Pennsylvania, Democrats won the total state-wide vote for people running for seats in the House of Representatives, but Republicans won most of the seats in the House – thirteen of eighteen – thanks to gerrymandered districts.[96] Trump's effort, however, took this to a new level. Whereas this sort of political monkey business had always been restricted to the state level, he tried to elevate it to the national level by inserting the citizenship question into the 2020 census and otherwise meddling in its administration.

3.8 CONCLUSION

Trump's frontal assault on electoral institutions was paired with a flanking attack on the US Census. His maneuvering was successful in normative terms insofar as his persistent claims about rigged elections, voter fraud, mishandled ballots, and all the rest helped convince more and more people that the electoral system was not free and fair. Concerns mounted reaching a tipping point where a mob descended on the Capitol, questioning the legitimacy of the election as never before. No presidential election in modern history had suffered such a severe legitimation crisis. But institutionalized norms were not the only casualty. Formal institutions were too, at least judging by the post-election moves to pass laws restricting voting in various ways at the state level, all in the name of countering unfounded allegations of election fraud. To the extent that these laws pass, they illustrate how the institutional impact of the Big Lie has trickled down to the states and why the damage caused by Trump's assault on America's electoral institutions will last for years to come. In contrast, damage to the US Census and by extension the country's representative institutions was avoided.

It's hard to argue that Trump's attack on America's electoral system fits the standard incremental model of institutional change. In this case change wasn't a matter of drift, displacement, conversion, or other subtle processes unfolding slowly and largely unnoticed. On the contrary, it fit the criteria for radical change that I detailed in Chapter 1. It was all quite dramatic and

---

[96] Waldman 2016, p. 228.

visible, representing a sharp break with past institutional practices. Trump's efforts were also broad in scope, focusing on several formal rules, procedures, and laws as well as all sorts of informal norms. Furthermore, it all happened quickly, driven by Trump, his minions and his enablers capitalizing on a tipping point that had been developing for years but that he had exacerbated in relatively short order with his inflammatory rhetoric and aggressive behavior.

It is important to recognize the leadership characteristics with which Trump went about all of this. To begin with, his attack on election integrity was driven by his refusal to accept the fact that he could possibly have lost to Joe Biden. Many of the loyalists surrounding him, including members of his own legal team, told him that he was right and that he should fight to overturn the results. In short, three of Trump's leadership qualities were to blame: his own intellectual arrogance and inflated sense of self-importance coupled with his demands for personal loyalty and trustworthiness from those advising him.

Furthermore, inspiration was his primary means for drawing the legitimacy of the electoral system into question. He railed about rigged elections and voter fraud in the media, at large campaign rallies across the country and, of course, on Twitter. As one supporter remarked at a Trump rally after the 2020 election, "Donald Trump's not going away. And that whole movement that he created was a movement that inspired a certain population of people. I just don't think that feeling is going anywhere soon."[97] Inspiration is the operative concept in that quotation.

Once the election was over, Trump also resorted to bullying. He went to extraordinary lengths to pressure state officials and Republicans in Congress to overturn the election and demanded that his vice president ignore the constitution and block congressional confirmation of the Electoral College results. When it came to the census and reapportionment scheme, Trump resorted to bullying again. He tried to strong-arm the Census Bureau into placing the citizenship question on the 2020 census. When he lost that fight in court, his political appointees leaned on analysts to speed up the data analysis to get the numbers to him by the December 31 deadline. He lost that fight too, which raises two final points about radical institutional change.

First, there was plenty of conflict and struggle over Trump's attempts to transform these institutions. To the extent that he failed, several people got in his way, including state election officials, governors, his vice president, and Census Bureau civil service professionals who resisted his efforts to bully them into submission in the service of his personal political interests. But the courts were perhaps his chief stumbling block. I'll have more to say about that in

---

[97] Martin and Herndon 2020.

Chapter 5. The point is that Trump ran into formidable resistance that stymied his attempt to overturn the election and revise Census Bureau protocol. Second, Trump's attack was directed at formal rules, procedures, and laws as well as informal norms. He was most successful in changing norms, which underscores how fragile and easily damaged norms are, and how devastating normative damage can be. As we are about to see, that damage spilled over into his own Republican Party.

4

Reinterpreting Republicanism

According to the old proverb, "An elephant never forgets." Indeed, during severe drought in Africa, old elephants have been known to lead the herd to distant watering holes that they remember visiting only as calves sixty years earlier during previous dry spells. It's ironic, then, that the Republican Party's mascot is the elephant. The party used to be dedicated to traditional political norms and values, particularly those of civility and compromise.[1] It also used to focus on economic and national security issues. Yet thanks to Donald Trump many in the party seem to have forgotten this. As a result, the party has embraced identity politics driven by anger, incivility, intolerance, and divisiveness. Trump alone was not responsible for this shift. For instance, figures like Patrick Buchanan, who twice sought the party's presidential nomination, former Speaker of the House Newt Gingrich, and one-time vice presidential candidate Sarah Palin had been nudging the party in this direction for years, aided by the right-wing media. But Trump took this to unprecedented extremes that now dominate the party.[2] The consequences have been dire.

Recall that institutions involve meaning systems as well as rules and norms. People must interpret what rules and norms mean to enact them. These interpretations are generally taken for granted until someone challenges them. When it comes to political institutions, politicians and political parties provide these interpretations through political discourse.[3] This chapter shows that with Trump's political ascendance the Republican Party reached and surpassed a tipping point and changed dramatically, falling into political extremism based on a cult of personality. What it meant to be a Republican was radically transformed.[4] The tipping point involved two trends. One was a rising level

---

[1] Lieberman et al. 2019, p. 475.   [2] Peters 2022.   [3] Kjaer and Pedersen 2001; Schmidt 2008.
[4] Howell and Moe 2020, pp. 79–80.

of incivility in Republican discourse. The other was the escalating ferocity of the culture wars. Trump capitalized on both trends pushing the party past the tipping point with extraordinarily inflammatory rhetoric, ad hominem attacks, lies, and wild conspiracy theories. As a result, in addition to the deterioration of political civility, Republicans became deeply divided within their own ranks, engulfed in a civil war over norms and values that continued after Trump left office. This was a fight over the meaning of republicanism, which severely damaged the party. But it also damaged national politics by undermining the norms of negotiation and compromise that had long governed America's two-party system – one of the pillars of American democracy. Much of this was fueled by Trump's inspirational, transactional, and bullying leadership style as well as his narcissism and demands for personal loyalty.

Trump was never a conventional Republican. Although he advocated neo-liberal tax and spending cuts, which were consistent with long-held Republican beliefs, when it came to issues of civility and cultural matters, he operated far outside mainstream republicanism. It's worth noting that he also failed in other ways to fit the Republican mold. Cozying up to the Russian president Vladimir Putin didn't fit the party's long-standing distrust of Russia or the former Soviet Union. His personal conduct was often at odds with conservative Republican morality. Breaking up immigrant families crossing the southern border didn't sit well with the party's traditional family values. Banning travel from predominantly Muslim countries to the United States and building a wall to keep out immigrants from Mexico and Latin America didn't jibe with many Republicans' belief in the neoliberal virtues of unrestricted movement in free labor markets. Moreover, as is clear from the discussion in Chapter 3, Trump was obsessed with his own reelection, willing to throw democratic institutions under the bus to achieve it. After he lost the election, Trump continued to obsess over the Big Lie, railed about having been cheated out of a second term, and proceeded to tighten his grip over the Republican Party, preparing to reward those who still supported him and the Big Lie, punishing those that didn't, and setting up another possible run for president. In short, Trump's version of republicanism, which was always tailored to his own rather than the party's interests, was often at odds with the traditional version. And it ripped the party apart.

4.1 CIVILITY ABANDONED

Rising incivility was one part of the tipping point that helped Trump transform the meaning of republicanism. Unlike other modern presidents, Trump decimated the norms of political civility, but he didn't do it single-handedly.[5]

---

[5] The literature on this subject is vast. See, for instance, Edwards (2020), Hart (2020), Howell and Moe (2020), Drezner (2020), and Reuning and Dietrich (2019).

Incivility within the Republican ranks had been growing before Trump arrived on the scene but reached new heights with him.[6] It began in earnest with the Tea Party's emergence during the Obama administration. The Tea Party was a movement that opposed what it perceived to be a socialist turn in American politics energized during the 2008 financial crisis by the government's massive financial bailouts and then the passage of the Affordable Care Act, commonly known as Obamacare. Its members were farther to the right than traditional Republicans. They held strong anti-government – often libertarian – views and were socially conservative on moral and cultural issues ranging from abortion to immigration.[7] The Tea Party was emboldened by the media, particularly Fox News, which encouraged and empowered it to redefine the limits of acceptable political discourse, lowering the bar farther and farther.[8]

The Tea Party became a powerful force, particularly in the House of Representatives where the Tea Party caucus, which had little appetite for compromise, began to undermine mainstream republicanism and replace it with what Bryan Gervais and Irwin Morris call "reactionary republicanism." The primary discursive feature of reactionary republicanism was an emotionally negative, disrespectful mode of communication. It was facilitated by the rise of social media platforms like Twitter that enabled politicians to speak directly and whenever they wanted to voters rather than going through the traditional media filters like newspapers and network television, which might not report everything they said.[9] Trump took this discourse to a new, more extreme level. According to political scientist James Pfiffner, "From the beginning of his campaign for the presidency and continuing through four years, Donald Trump undermined the norms of civility in modern American politics. Of course, American politics have always been filled with invective, but Trump exceeded the normal give-and-take."[10]

Even before he was elected, concern was mounting in some quarters of the Republican Party about Trump's unusually incendiary rhetoric. During the 2016 presidential campaign a vocal group of elite Republican operatives, including officials in previous administrations, donors, lawyers, and political strategists, mobilized to oppose Trump's nomination for the presidency and then, after he secured it, fought to defeat him in the general election. These so-called Never Trumpers feared that Trump's rhetoric reflected his disdain for the conventional norms not only of civility but of democracy too. They feared that this was the rhetoric of a dangerous demagogue.[11] Similar sentiments were held by much of the Republican establishment, including both former president Bush and former Republican presidential candidates Bob Dole, John McCain, and Mitt Romney as well as several party luminaries who denounced Trump in

---

[6] Dionne et al. 2017, pp. 9–10. [7] Skocpol and Williamson 2012. [8] Peters 2022, p. 85.
[9] Gervais and Morris 2018. [10] Pfiffner 2021, p. 97. [11] Saldin and Teles 2020.

a special symposium in the *National Review*, a legendary mouthpiece for mainstream republicanism.[12]

Their concerns were not without merit. For example, although presidential candidates talk about America's problems, they typically lace their campaign speeches with references to how wonderful and exceptional America is. But in Trump's interpretation, America was no longer exceptional or a world leader. He harped on how swaths of the country were trapped in poverty, littered with rusted-out factories, saddled with failing schools, and terrorized by gangs and drug dealers so badly that America's wealth, strength, and confidence had disappeared. This sharp pessimistic turn in rhetoric was particularly clear in his inaugural address, which was dubbed "American Carnage." Furthermore, indicative of his intellectual arrogance, Trump ridiculed his opponents for not being smart enough to restore American greatness and, in a glaring example of his narcissistic sense of self-importance, praised himself as the only person clever enough to do so.[13]

Of course, many presidents have engaged from time to time in hyperbole, insulted their opponents, and lapsed into crass language. Lincoln's successor Andrew Johnson was impeached in part for using inflammatory rhetoric that violated the discursive norms of the day. Those norms eroded gradually over the twentieth century and presidential rhetoric assumed an increasingly anti-intellectual character. It became less about logical argument and debate over complex ideas and more about simplistic applause-rendering platitudes, partisan punchlines, and appeals to emotion.[14] But Susan Hennessey and Benjamin Wittes showed that "Trump represents a radical acceleration of [these] trends already long underway in presidential rhetoric."[15] In their view, far more than any other president, Trump engaged in a near-endless stream of ad hominem attacks, insults, and offensive accusations – often taking to Twitter or Fox News to do so – all designed to inspire and rally his base of supporters rather than unite the country or build coalitions as past presidents have done. In short, as others have concluded, this was a sharp break from past presidential precedent.

For instance, one study compared how often presidents from Franklin Roosevelt to Trump engaged in name-calling in their speeches, press conferences, interviews, and other formal communications. Trump smashed the record for name-calling. And when his tweets were added to the analysis, his performance was even more extraordinary. He called people names more than three times as often on Twitter as he did in all of his other forms of communication combined.[16] Another study found that Trump's rhetorical style was more paranoid and drawn to conspiracies, ethnocentrism, racism, and nativism than any major-party presidential candidate since the Second World War.[17]

---

[12] Howell and Moe 2020, p. 72.   [13] Gilmore et al. 2020. See also Ghazal Aswad (2019, p. 66).
[14] Lim 2008.   [15] Hennessey and Wittes 2020, p. 93. See also Drezner (2020).
[16] Coe and Park-Ozee 2020.   [17] Hart 2020, pp. 348–350.

It also reflected policies that were sometimes radically different from traditional Republican policies, such as his proposals for restricting immigration and weaponizing tariff protection against America's trading partners – another indication that Trump was reinterpreting the meaning and norms of republicanism.[18]

Trump's ramping up of incivility was not lost on the public. The Pew Research Center found that 85 percent of Americans surveyed in 2019 said that political debate in the country had become significantly more negative, disrespectful, and uncivil. Three-quarters also said it had become less fact-based and 60 percent felt that it had become less focused on substantive policy issues. Most important, over half believed that Trump was responsible because he had poisoned the tone of political debate.[19] Indeed, Trump's shattering of the norms of civil discourse was extraordinary.[20] And as Gervais and Morris predicted, this was dangerous because it carried with it the possibility of normalizing violence.[21] We know now that they were right as the January 6 assault on the Capitol proved. Several people who broke into the Capitol that day and were subsequently arrested and indicted, including Jacob Chansley, who wore a horned headdress and face paint during the attack, and Dominic Pezzola, a leading member of the Proud Boys, a right-wing extremist group, said that they did so because they were following Trump's exhortations just hours before the riot to "stop the steal" and "fight like hell" to preserve their country.[22]

Trump's discursive impact was facilitated by two related developments. One that I've already mentioned was the emerging popularity and use of social media, notably Twitter. In 2010 there were about 10 million Twitter users in the United States – a number that grew steadily to a peak of about 65 million in 2015 just as Trump was entering the presidential race.[23] He was the first president to use Twitter on a regular and frequent basis. The average number of tweets from Trump's account skyrocketed almost tenfold from about 5 per day to 47 per day during his presidency.[24] The second development was rising market pressure faced by mainstream media companies and journalists to provide stories that interested consumers. As the competition among news outlets increased thanks to the proliferation of cable news channels, talk radio, online news publications, and social media platforms, it became more difficult for traditional media organizations to maintain viewers and readers and, therefore, revenues. As a result, Trump's unusually brash and inflammatory rhetoric received widespread media attention because it was sales-worthy.[25] As

---

[18] Reuning and Dietrich 2019, pp. 335.
[19] Drake and Kiley 2019. See also Edwards (2020, p. 290).
[20] Drezner 2020; Hennessey and Wittes 2020, chap. 4.   [21] Gerais and Morris 2018, p. 250.
[22] Wolfe 2021.   [23] Statista 2021a.   [24] Statista 2021b.
[25] Angelucci et al. 2020; Godes et al. 2009.

a result, he garnered far more media coverage than would have been expected otherwise. During the 2016 campaign, for instance, he received an estimated $2 billion in free media coverage – more than twice as much as any other candidate. This too helped undermine the civility of political discourse and boost his popularity among voters.[26]

In sum, Trump jumped on the bandwagon of political incivility, driven in part by supreme overconfidence in his own intellect and abilities as well as an inflated sense of self-importance, often bullying his opponents with name-calling and other insults. All of this helped generate a tipping point that transformed the norms of traditional Republican civility. But the development of that tipping point also involved the rise of the culture wars.

4.2 CULTURE WARS

Trump's incivility often meant disparaging racial, ethnic, and religious minorities as well as women. In this regard, he capitalized on the culture wars that had been growing since the 1980s.[27] The culture wars were deeply polarizing conflicts between conservatives and liberals over cultural norms and values regarding religion, identity politics, multiculturalism, and gender rights. Trump himself alluded to this during his first Republican primary debate in 2015 when, in response to a question about his derogatory remarks about women, he said that "I think the big problem this country has is being politically correct. I've been challenged by so many people, and I don't frankly have time for total political correctness."[28]

Trump exploited and exacerbated the culture wars unlike any president before him. As one Never Trumper put it, "He is a culture warrior" with a talent for finding incendiary ways of raising hot-button identity issues.[29] Nowhere was this clearer than when it came to issues of race. Trump announced his candidacy in 2015 accusing Mexican immigrants of being criminals and rapists. In contrast to politicians' use of dog-whistle politics that disparaged racial minorities through innuendo and inference, Trump tossed that aside and took a more direct and explicit approach. For instance, as president, he criticized African American athletes like Colin Kaepernick, the San Francisco Forty Niners' star quarterback, for kneeling during the national anthem to protest police brutality and racial inequality. He refused to remove the names of Confederate generals from military bases. He balked at criticizing violent white supremacists and neo-Nazis at a Charlottesville, Virginia rally that turned violent. And as Black Lives Matter protests emerged across the country in the wake of the murder of George Floyd, an African American, at the

---

[26] Fontaine and Gomez 2020; Reuning and Dietrich 2019.   [27] Hall and Lindholm 1999.
[28] Bump 2021.   [29] Saldin and Teles 2020, p. 36.

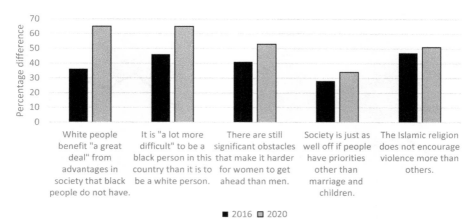

FIGURE 4.1. Gap between Clinton/Biden and Trump voters on key cultural issues.
Source: Pew Research Center (2020b).

hands of a white Minneapolis police officer, rather than supporting the mostly peaceful law-abiding demonstrators, Trump portrayed them as violent insurrectionists led by professional anarchists and Antifa radicals.[30] Trump's shift to an explicitly racist discourse was hard to miss.

Other scholars agree that Trump was "unique among modern presidents in his overt willingness to articulate these noxious beliefs against the higher ideals of the nation" and that his rhetoric often divided the polity by undermining civil public discourse.[31] For example, Pew Research found that the divisions between Republicans and Democrats on a series of fundamental political and social values had grown since the mid-1990s but climbed to unprecedented heights on Trump's watch.[32] Trump divided Republicans and Democrats on these issues more than any president in three decades.[33] Figure 4.1 shows the difference in reactions between Republican and Democratic voters to a series of statements about race, gender, and religion – issues central to the culture wars. Those who voted for Trump rather than Hillary Clinton in 2016 and those who voted for Trump rather than Joe Biden in 2020 tended to disagree with each statement while those voting for the Democrats tended to agree with these statements. What matters for us is that the gap between Democrat and Republican reactions to each statement, already significant in 2016, grew during Trump's term in office, especially for racial issues, which were at the core of Trump's cultural rhetoric. For example, when asked if whites benefit from advantages in society that blacks don't have, roughly 35 percent more Democrats agreed with that statement in

[30] Liasson 2020.   [31] Stuckey 2021, p. 137. See also Drezner (2020).
[32] Pew Research Center 2017.   [33] Dimock and Gramlich 2020.

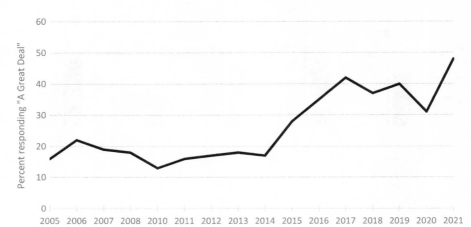

FIGURE 4.2. How much do you personally worry about race relations?.
Note: Gallup did not ask this question for 2009.
Source: Gallup Polling (2021b).

2016 than Republicans, but by 2020 the gap between Democrats and Republicans had widened to 65 percent. Political scientists agree that presidential language matters in shaping this sort of public opinion.[34] According to Roderick Hart, Trump's rhetoric "found a happy home among his supporters" who now often emulate his style.[35] The danger, as political psychologists have found, is that when people withdraw into their tribes – that is, identity groups based on things like race, ethnicity, gender, religion, and political affiliation – the level of incivility between tribes tends to rise.[36] The point is that Trump's culture war rhetoric was inspiring his Republican base but driving a wedge into the American body politic.

Putting this into a cross-national perspective underscores how serious the situation had become. According to surveys conducted by Pew Research, in the United States, Britain, Germany, and France, people on the left were more likely to embrace political correctness in various forms than people on the right. However, by the time Trump left office Americans on the left and right were roughly four times more divided on these cultural issues than their European counterparts.[37] Cultural disagreements in Europe were more like mild skirmishes while in America they were more like fierce battles.

There is further evidence suggesting that Trump's inflammatory rhetoric was associated with an escalation of the culture wars. For instance, Figure 4.2

---

[34] For discussions of the important effects presidential language has, see, for example, Stuckey (2021), Coe and Park-Ozee (2020), Lim (2008), Hennessey and Wittes (2020, chap. 4), and Drezner (2020).
[35] Hart 2020, p. 349.   [36] American Psychological Association 2016.   [37] Bump 2021.

shows that the percentage of Americans reporting that they were very worried about race relations began to rise sharply beginning in 2015, the year Trump announced his bid for the presidency and began publicly denigrating African Americans, Mexicans, and immigrants. This supports the research of political scientist George Edwards and others, who have found that although racial and ethnic differences drove political polarization before Trump, their impact strengthened after he arrived on the political scene. As Edwards explains, "There is evidence that the president's rhetoric ushered in a climate that favored expression of prejudices...A majority of the public thought Trump made race relations worse and that it had become more common for people to express racist or racially insensitive views."[38] Another example concerns the use of gender-neutral language in Congress. According to data collected from the Facebook and Twitter accounts of members of Congress, between the time Trump was elected until he left office use of the politically correct term Latinx – the binary, gender-neutral term for people who are of or relate to Latin American origin or descent – increased significantly among Democrats but, following Trump's aversion to political correctness, was almost never used by Republicans.[39] Of course, these data aren't definitive. But they are consistent with the argument that Trump's toxic rhetoric exacerbated the culture wars in America.

As this last example illustrates, not only the Republican base but the Republican Party itself had become increasingly obsessed with the culture wars during Trump's tenure in office. Indeed, the Republican National Committee (RNC) resolved not to formulate a new platform for the 2020 presidential campaign other than to reaffirm its support for the 2016 platform.[40] Instead, it chose to deflect attention from substantive policy issues at its nominating convention, preferring to emphasize hot-button cultural issues and push back against what Republicans called the "cancel culture" – efforts by politically correct Democrats to muzzle conservative points of view on cultural issues. Trump and other speakers at the convention used their platform to inflame the culture wars. For example, speakers warned that if the Democrats won, the country would descend into anarchy, violence, and oppression because in their view the Biden-Harris ticket was hell-bent on pushing a politically correct agenda that would destroy America's traditional norms and values.[41] The Republican Party was learning from Trump's success and was now emulating his rhetorical tactics. It didn't stop here.

Keep in mind that radical change involves not only a sharp but also a long-lasting break from the past. The impact of Trump's break with norms of political civility seems poised to last long beyond his presidency. Republicans continued to echo his cultural attacks even after he lost the 2020 election. For

[38] Edwards 2020, p. 312.   [39] Shah 2020.   [40] Republican National Committee 2020.
[41] Leonnig and Rucker 2021, p. 250.

instance, the theme for the 2021 Conservative Political Action Committee (CPAC) conference was "America Uncancelled," a direct repudiation of the Democrats' cancel culture and concern with political correctness.[42] Similarly, that same year at a meeting of the RNC in Palm Beach, Florida, Senator Tom Cotton (R-AR) urged Republicans to oppose Democrats' positions on transgender youth, abortion, election reforms that enabled more minorities to vote, and several other explosive cultural issues.[43]

One of the most glaring demonstrations of the longevity of Trump's culture war rhetoric occurred after the 2020 election, where several Republican-controlled state legislatures moved to pass laws restricting how issues of racism and sexism were taught in schools. The idea was to ban schools from teaching "divisive concepts" like the notion that American institutions are inherently racist and sexist and, as a result, that white males enjoy systemic privileges. Trump had already supercharged the issue in two ways. One was his announcement during the 2020 campaign that he would form a 1776 Commission to investigate what he claimed to be the left-wing indoctrination of students in public schools and universities to things like "critical race theory," which stressed that blacks were still institutionally disadvantaged in America compared to whites. The other was his September 2020 Executive Order 13950 prohibiting the teaching of divisive concepts like "systemic racism and sexism" and "white privilege" in workplace training programs. Biden quickly rescinded the executive order when he became president but Republicans in several states adopted Trump's executive order language to write their own legislation – another example of how Trump's influence trickled down to the state level. In New Hampshire, for instance, Republicans drafted HB544 – a bill that was remarkably similar in language to Trump's executive order although targeted at forbidding the teaching of divisive concepts in public schools and universities. It was appended to the budget and signed into law by the governor.[44] Taking a page from Trump's playbook, all of this was in sync with the party's strategy of running on culture war issues in the 2022 midterm elections rather than criticizing Biden's substantive policies, which a majority of the public favored.[45] The irony in all this was breathtaking; having accused Democrats of engaging in a cancel culture that shut down discussions of hot-button cultural issues, now Republicans were doing exactly the same thing.

Overall, then, Trump's fiery rhetoric took advantage of the culture wars, which had been gathering momentum for years, and pushed them beyond the tipping point inspiring the Republican Party and driving it farther to the right on cultural issues in ways that increasingly divided the country. This was an unprecedented change in the meaning of what passed as an acceptable political

---

[42] Bump 2021.   [43] Peoples and Colvin 2021.

[44] Critical details in New Hampshire HB544 (New Hampshire 2021) are virtually identical with those in Executive Order 13950 (US Federal Register 2020).

[45] Gabriel and Goldstein 2021.

discourse among many Republicans. The effects of that change promised to persist long after Trump left the political stage. But the combination of Trump's departure from civil political discourse combined with his passion for inflaming the culture wars led to another radical institutional change. His discourse became so inflammatory, his condemnation of political correctness so obsessive, and his passion for conspiracy theories so intense that it finally ripped the Republican Party apart. At issue was a fight over what it meant to be a Republican in the first place.

4.3 THE REPUBLICAN CIVIL WAR

Even before Trump's arrival, the deterioration of political civility in Republican discourse and the escalation of culture wars had created problems within the Republican Party. Conflicts began to emerge between old-school Republicans like John Boehner (R-OH) and John Kasich (R-OH) and more rambunctious upstarts like the Tea Party's Michelle Bachman (R-MN) and Tom Price (R-GA). By 2015 the situation had become untenable for Boehner, Speaker of the House, who quit politics in frustration over the unwillingness of the Tea Party wing to engage in civil negotiations and compromise either with the party's more moderate wing or with Democrats.

The rise of the Tea Party movement, Boehner's resignation, and the emergence of the Never Trumpers signified that a fissure was forming within the Republican Party between the mainstream and reactionary Republicans. But Trump's divisive rhetoric split that crack wide open during the 2016 campaign, his presidency, and his 2020 campaign. A civil war had erupted within the Republican Party. An initial sign of that split appeared when Paul Ryan (R-WI), Boehner's replacement as Speaker of the House, quit politics in 2019 after finding it impossible to continue working with Trump whose rhetoric and personality he found "sickening" and whose leadership he found erratic and unpredictable.[46] Things got even worse after Trump lost the 2020 election, refused to concede defeat, insisted that the election had been stolen from him, and eventually taunted a crowd of supporters on January 6 to march on the Capitol and "fight like hell" to make things right. Of course, the party had experienced internal rifts before, as all parties do. Barry Goldwater's radical conservatism and Nelson Rockefeller's moderate liberalism divided the Republican Party in the early 1960s. So did Ronald Reagan in the 1980s and then the Tea Party in the 2000s. But nobody had seen anything like this. The party's leadership tied itself in knots trying to bridge the divide. Two examples personify the problem.

The first concerns Republican Senate Minority Leader Mitch McConnell's behavior regarding Trump's second impeachment trial where Trump stood

---

[46] Woodward and Costa 2021, chap. 2.

accused of having incited the mob that stormed the Capitol building on January 6. After telling allies privately that "If this isn't impeachable, I don't know what is" and that conviction was warranted, McConnell flipped and voted to acquit him.[47] But minutes later he flipped again, saying this on the Senate floor condemning Trump's actions: "This was an intensifying crescendo of conspiracy theories orchestrated by an outgoing president who seemed determined to either overturn the voters' decision or else torch our institutions on the way out...There is no question, none, that president Trump is practically and morally responsible for the events of the day."[48] McConnell's depiction of an "intensifying crescendo" of inflammatory rhetoric to "torch our institutions" pointed to the tipping point, discussed in Chapter 3, where conspiracy theories and other falsehoods had reached a zenith. More important, McConnell was trying to have it both ways – pandering to Trump's critics as well as his supporters.

The second personification of the Republican Party's civil war was Kevin McCarthy, the Republican leader in the House. Soon after the insurrection, he told other Republican leaders on a conference call that "I've had it with this guy" and that he was going to urge Trump to resign from the presidency.[49] He also publicly condemned Trump's language for triggering the Capitol insurrection saying this: "The president bears responsibility for Wednesday's attack on Congress by mob rioters. He should have immediately denounced the mob when he saw what was unfolding." He added that Trump needed to "quell the brewing unrest and ensure [that] president-elect Joe Biden is able to successfully begin his term."[50] But despite these words McCarthy never encouraged Trump to resign. He turned around and then supported Trump by voting against his second impeachment. And two weeks later he went to Mar-a-Lago, Trump's exclusive golf resort and post-White House home, to pay homage to Trump and seek his political blessing.

McCarthy as well as McConnell embodied the fissure within the Republican Party. Both men simultaneously defended and condemned Trump's rhetoric and behavior in a whipsaw fashion. But the fact that neither man voted against Trump during the second impeachment saga spoke volumes about how they had been cowed by Trump's popularity, pressure tactics, and demands for personal loyalty. Referring to the groundswell of Republican support for Trump during his second impeachment trial, one Trump aide said, "We got to everyone. We got to McConnell, we got to McCarthy," if you vote for impeachment, "you're screwed."[51]

In fact, Trump had gotten to lots of Republican legislators. When Congress gathers in joint session to certify the Electoral College votes, only one member of the House and one member of the Senate need to sign the challenge to a

[47] Burns and Martin 2022; Martin and Burns 2022, p. 231.   [48] Segers and McDonald 2021.
[49] Burns and Martin 2022; Martin and Burns 2022, pp. 222–223.   [50] Niedzwiadek 2021.
[51] Barrett et al. 2021.

state's Electoral vote count to force the two chambers to separate and debate whether to accept it. Yet on January 6, many Republicans wanted to prove that they were in Trump's corner, so several dozen signed their names to the challenges being brought forward. Indicating how this was driven by their desire to curry Trump's favor, one member lamented about, "The things we do for the Orange Jesus," as he signed the challenge documents. Later that day while the Capitol was under siege and as members and their staff hid fearing for their lives, several Republican legislators tried to telephone the president to get him to call off the insurrectionists. But in the same breath many asked his aides to remind him that they still supported him and promised not to certify the Electoral College count once order was restored.[52] They understood Trump's transactional style of leadership and feared his bullying even in this unprecedented moment of great danger to themselves and the republic.

McCarthy wasn't the only Republican to trek to Florida to curry Trump's favor. Three months later CPAC brought hundreds of donors, congressional leaders, and several presidential hopefuls to Orlando, just four miles from Mar-a-Lago. Trump was the keynote speaker at the invitation-only weekend retreat where connections were made, money was raised, and political strategy was discussed. Trump's allies also held fundraising events at his estate that weekend. Illustrating the deep divisions within the party as defined by one's allegiance to Trump, the weekend retreat excluded leading Republicans who had disparaged Trump, including McConnell, Wyoming Representative Liz Cheney, Utah Senator Mitt Romney, and Maryland Governor Larry Hogan, among others. It was clear now that Trump remained in control of the Republican Party and had convinced many of its members to accept his rhetoric and interpretation of what republicanism was all about. One Republican donor, Dan Eberhart, told reporters that "The venue for the quarterly meeting along with Trump's keynote speech at CPAC shows that the party is still very much in Trump's grip."[53]

A particularly cutthroat illustration of how Trump's inflammatory and conspiratorial rhetoric split the party involved Liz Cheney. In January 2021 Representative Matt Gaetz (R-FL) went to Wyoming and at a rally lambasted his Republican colleague for having voted to impeach Trump after the Capitol insurrection. Cheney was the third highest-ranking Republican in the House and the daughter of former Republican vice president Dick Cheney. Her conservative credentials were impeccable. Yet Gaetz vowed to campaign against her for, in his view, conspiring with McConnell, Biden, and Speaker of the House Nancy Pelosi (D-CA) to sustain the status quo in Washington rather than working for the American people. As Gaetz put it, "The truth is that the

---

[52] Alemany et al. 2021. Even after order was restored in the Capitol, six Republican senators objected to counting Arizona's votes and seven objected to Pennsylvania's. In the House 121 Republicans objected to the Arizona votes and 138 objected to the Pennsylvania votes.

[53] Peoples and Colvin 2021.

establishment in both political parties have teamed up to screw our fellow Americans for generations." Much of Gaetz's speech was remarkably like those speeches that Trump gave at his mega-rallies in which he accused Cheney of being a "weak" member of Congress, or worse.[54] Gaetz was not alone in paying homage to their fallen leader in both word and deed.

At the time, Kevin McCarthy had urged Gaetz not to attack Cheney but later went on the attack himself, maneuvering to push her out of her leadership position in the Republican caucus. McCarthy backed Representative Elise Stefanik (R-NY), a more moderate Republican than Cheney on policy issues, but a strong supporter of Trump now that he had won her district in upstate New York in the 2020 election.[55] Now that McCarthy had turned against Cheney, the game was over. In May 2021 she was stripped of her leadership position and Stefanik was installed as her replacement. The next day Cheney reiterated her concerns about Trump's discursive influence on the party telling reporters that "We have seen the danger that he continues to provoke with his language."[56] Put differently, she warned that Trump's uncivil, deceitful, and divisive rhetoric was a radical threat to America's democratic institutions, including the peaceful transfer of power. Trump's response was typically vindictive and personal, illustrating precisely the sort of divisive language to which Cheney had referred, not to mention his bullying style of leadership:

Liz Cheney is a bitter, horrible human being. I watched her yesterday and realized how bad she is for the Republican Party. She has no personality or anything good having to do with politics or our country. She is a warmonger whose family stupidly pushed us into the never-ending Middle East disaster, draining our wealth and depleting our great military, the worst decision in our country's history. I look forward to soon watching her as a paid contributor on CNN or MSDNC![57]

Thanks to Trump's willingness to bully his enemies, and his talent for inspiring his supporters with bombastic rhetoric, conspiracy theories and lies, the party had turned into a dangerous cult of personality. This was about much more than the Big Lie. This was about what it meant to be a Republican, which had shifted radically from being beholden to certain conservative principles to being beholden to Trump. There could be no doubt that a crucial tipping point had been passed and that Trump's narcissism had prevailed.

Other Republicans also took heat for speaking out against Trump, including Congressman Adam Kinzinger (R-IL) and Mitt Romney, who was booed at a party convention in his home state of Utah just before its members tried to censure him. Senator Susan Collins (R-ME) told a CNN reporter that she was appalled by the crowd's reaction to Romney. More to the point, she warned

---

[54] Choi 2021.   [55] Zanona et al. 2021.   [56] Hudak et al. 2021.

[57] Smith 2021. Note that "MSDNC" is not a misprint. Trump was mocking MSNBC, the liberal cable news channel, and implying that it was a mouthpiece for the Democratic National Committee (DNC).

that her party needed to remember that it was united by fundamental principles and was "not a party that is led by just one person."[58] In other words, she warned that the Republican Party had forgotten the once taken-for-granted norms and principles it was supposed to stand for. It had forgotten what it meant to be a Republican and succumbed to Trump's demands for personal loyalty.

Illustrating Collins' point, Kevin McCarthy's treatment of Marjorie Taylor Greene (R-GA), a newly elected member of Congress in 2021, stood in sharp contrast to his treatment of Liz Cheney. Greene was a far-right conspiracy theorist, whose public and social media statements took Trump's incivility and culture war rhetoric to a new level. For instance, she alleged that Democratic billionaire George Soros – a Jewish Holocaust survivor – was a Nazi. She embraced QAnon and white supremacist conspiracy theories. She believed that the mass shooting at a Parkland, Florida high school was a hoax. She accused members of the Democratic Party of being involved in child sex, satanism, and the occult. And unlike Cheney, she insisted that the 2020 election was stolen from Trump. As all this came to light, McCarthy refused to take away her committee assignments, so House Democrats did it instead. But Greene continued to propagate all sorts of wild theories and hit the road with Matt Gaetz holding a series of rallies where they railed against political correctness and continued to insist that Trump's election had been stolen from him. Ironically, given Greene's claim that Democrats were involved with pedophilia, Gaetz was under investigation for having trafficked in sex with underage girls. Then, in May 2021, Greene equated employers' COVID-19 mask mandates to the Nazi's requirement that Jews wear a Star of David during the Holocaust – a remark that sparked widespread outrage, even from some members of her own party. But it was nearly a week before McCarthy and other party leaders finally condemned her statements – and then only after being hounded by the media and lobbied hard by some Republican Party members and others including the Republican Jewish Coalition.[59] Why such hesitancy?

Throughout all this Trump continued to support Greene in his transactional style because she paid deference and loyalty to him and represented his views on cultural issues, which is one reason why McCarthy and other Republican leaders were so slow to reprimand her; they didn't want to upset Trump by appearing to be disloyal and risking his retaliation. Another reason was that they worried that doing so would elevate her platform, alienate voters – notably, Trump's base – and jeopardize the party's chances of regaining control of the House in the 2022 midterm elections as well as McCarthy's chances of becoming Speaker of the House. Finally, Greene's outrageous comments had enabled her to raise millions of dollars for the Republican Party.[60] The fact that

[58] Firozi 2021.   [59] Edmondson 2021a; Jacobs 2021; Sprunt 2021.   [60] Edmondson 2021a.

McCarthy had turned on Cheney but balked at punishing Greene spoke volumes about how the party had lost its traditional moorings.

The party had indeed begun to morph into the Party of Trump. As noted earlier, Trump had never perfectly fit the mainstream Republican Party profile but now the party was beginning to accept that Trump's version was the one they should emulate. By April 2021, over 40 percent of registered Republican voters said that they were more supportive of Trump than the Republican Party itself.[61] According to long-time political journalist Jeff Greenfield, "The party is talking with one voice; the voice is Trump's, and it's one that plenty of Americans are still perfectly receptive to."[62] Political scientist William Mishler was more pointed: "What worries me is not that there's a minority of crazies in the party. It's that there's a majority of crazies."[63] Others weren't so sure that all was lost – at least not yet. Conservative radio host Erick Erickson warned that "[Republicans] are going to have to make room for each other or let the Democrats run over them in the midterms." Moderates like Congressman Adam Kinzinger, who had long decried Trump's rhetoric and behavior, insisted that "we [Republicans] are in a battle. And it may be a battle that really needs to happen for our party to say, what does it stand for? Are we aspirational or are we a party that feeds on fear and division?"[64]

The point is that Trump's extraordinary incivility, driven to a considerable degree by his engagement with the culture wars, his refusal to accept facts, and his embrace of self-serving conspiracy theories had, as Mitch McConnell noted, reached and transcended a tipping point where what it meant to be a Republican was under siege. This was a radical and historic institutional break. In fact, some went so far as to argue that the party faced the sort of existential crisis that had destroyed American political parties in the past and might do so now.[65] Soon after Cheney was stripped of her leadership position over 100 Republicans released a letter threatening to form a third party unless the Republican Party extricated itself from Trump's stranglehold and returned to its core principles. Echoing Cheney's remarks, their statement warned that the Republican Party had fallen under the spell of a despotic and self-absorbed leader who fostered conspiracy theories and divisiveness that threatened American democracy. The group involved former Republican leaders, including governors, members of Congress, ambassadors, cabinet secretaries, state legislators, and Republican Party chairmen.[66] Former New Jersey Governor Christie Todd Whitman, one of the signatories, said that the party had become "centered around one person" and referring to Republicans like herself added that "There's literally millions of people who feel homeless."[67] Why? Because they couldn't embrace the new and unprecedented meaning of what it meant to

---

[61] Jacobs et al. 2019, p. 463; NBC News Survey 2021, p. 19.   [62] Greenfield 2021.
[63] Wines 2021.   [64] Warren 2021b.   [65] Cobb 2021.   [66] Milligan 2021; Montague 2021.
[67] Heyboer 2021.

be a Republican – ideological rigidity, extreme cultural intolerance, and a propensity for fearmongering, nativism, and demagoguery.[68]

So, despite his defeat in 2020, Trump's hold on the Republican Party seemed secure. His reinterpretation of the norms and values defining what it meant to be a Republican was now deeply rooted in the party. According to freshman Congressman Peter Meijer (R-MI), the party used to stand for things like local control of political institutions, small and more efficient government, and policies that improved people's lives and made the future a more promising place. Instead, the party now relies on grievance, fear, and misinformation to scare voters into its ranks.[69] As one Republican donor explained, "The party doesn't seem to have the ability to hit escape velocity from its former standard bearer."[70] Senator Lindsay Graham (R-SC), a leading figure in the party, went even further acknowledging that Trump had become a necessity for the Republican Party without whom it would be terribly difficult to come back from the party's defeat in 2020.[71]

4.4 A VERY TIGHT GRIP

How Trump's grip on the party became so tight had much to do with his extraordinary leadership traits. To begin with, Trump continued to inspire his base and they continued to support him in return. For instance, election officials received hundreds of threats to their personal safety or lives after the January 6 uprising. Most were concentrated in the six states upon which Trump focused his attacks on election integrity.[72] Moreover, Trump's job approval ratings among Republicans vacillated between 84 percent and 74 percent throughout most of his presidency until slipping after the 2020 election but still hovering around 60 percent. Moreover, as noted earlier, many Republicans expressed greater allegiance to Trump than to the party. In keeping with that sentiment, just before Biden was inaugurated, 57 percent of Republicans polled said that Trump should remain a major political figure for many years to come.[73] Some members of the party's extreme right wing went even further. Less than six months into Biden's presidency, some called for a coup d'état and Trump's "reinstatement" as president by the end of summer 2021.[74] Finally, nearly ten months after the 2020 election, 78 percent of Republicans polled said that Biden didn't legitimately win enough votes to be president.[75] What was particularly disturbing was that this was an *increase* from only a few months earlier when roughly two-thirds of Republicans surveyed said they believed this – and half said they believed incorrectly that the Capitol insurrection was led by violent left-wing protestors trying to make Trump look bad.[76]

---

[68] Howell and Moe 2020, pp. 152–153.   [69] Alberta 2022.   [70] Peoples and Colvin 2021.
[71] Woodward and Costa 2021, p. 343.   [72] Barrett et al. 2021.
[73] Pew Research Center 2021a.   [74] Shephard 2021.   [75] CNN 2021.
[76] Ipsos/Reuters 2021.

Trump's inspirational touch extended into fundraising. He activated a new set of conservative mega-donors who, according to their social media postings, often shared his divisive views and the views of some of his most extreme supporters. Using Federal Election Commission records, ProPublica identified twenty-nine super-rich individuals and couples who increased their political donations to Trump and the party at least tenfold since 2015, each recently giving at least $1 million and often far more, primarily to super PACs supporting Trump or his fundraising operation, Trump Victory, which channeled money to various Republican Party campaign committees. The list of donors included Julia Fancelli, who helped finance the January 6 pre-insurrection rally in Washington and supported the Big Lie, and Palmer Luckey, who had donated to an anti-Hillary Clinton group trafficking in misogynistic and white supremacist messaging.[77]

The Republican Party recognized Trump's inspirational power and continued to use his brand for fundraising on an unprecedented scale, especially to appeal to small donors. According to Brad Parscale, Trump's first 2020 campaign manager, "The Republican Party has never had small-dollar fundraising at this scale before Donald Trump and they probably never will at this scale after Donald Trump." It seemed unlikely that the Republican Party wanted to, or even could, break from Trump in the foreseeable future because his grip on the party's grassroots base was so strong.[78]

This is not to say, however, that Trump and the party saw eye-to-eye on all fundraising matters. And so, Trump often resorted to bullying to get his way. After leaving office Trump's lawyers sent cease-and-desist letters to the RNC, the National Republican Senatorial Committee (NRSC), and the National Republican Congressional Committee (NRCC) demanding that they stop using his name, image, or likeness in their fundraising efforts. These are the three largest Republican fundraising organizations. Instead, Trump urged Republicans to contribute to his own Save America political action committee. The idea, he said, was to stop giving money to the so-called Republicans in Name Only (RINOS) – that is, party members who stuck to traditional conservative Republican principles rather than abandoning them for Trump's views. It was a label that signified the civil war within the Republican Party. Of course, money donated to Trump's organization was money that he, not the party, controlled.[79] Trump's Save America PAC had over $31 million in hand by the end of 2020. A little more than half of this was from those small donors – contributing $200 or less – that I mentioned before, indicating strong support from his electoral base. By comparison, at the end of 2020 the RNC had about $81 million left, the NRSC had about $14 million, and the NRCC had about $13 million.[80] The squabble between Trump and these other fundraising

---

[77] Arnsdorf 2021.   [78] Goldmacher 2021.   [79] Coleman 2021; Peoples and Colvin 2021.
[80] Center for Responsive Politics 2021.

organizations was settled eventually. But Trump had plenty of money with more coming in to use at his discretion to further his political interests, back his congressional supporters, attack his enemies, and promote his interpretation of what it meant to be a true Republican. All this was indicative of his willingness, if not need, to put his own interests above the party's interests in narcissistic fashion.

Since then, Trump and his allies continued scheduling events and raising millions of dollars to back Trump supporters in the 2022 midterm elections. For instance, a planned Mar-a-Lago event in February 2022 included a private dinner with Trump for donors who had each raised at least $375,000. The forum was for federal candidates endorsed by Trump, including Harriet Hageman who was challenging Liz Cheney of Wyoming. In December 2021, there was another candidate forum at Mar-a-Lago including a $125,000-a-plate dinner with Trump. Trump and his team also planned rallies around the country especially in places where those he endorsed were running for office. "The efforts seem intended to reinforce the former president's grip on the Republican Party and its donors amid questions about whether Mr. Trump will seek the party's nomination again or settle into a role as a kingmaker." Trump's own PACs amassed over $100 million by summer 2021. If that wasn't enough to solidify his grip on the party, a new think tank called the America First Policy Institute was formed in 2021 for Trump and his supporters. It's raised over $20 million and had 110 employees including several former Trump cabinet members, such as former Interior Secretary David Bernhardt, former Energy Secretary Rick Perry, and former EPA Director Andrew Wheeler. It held two events at Trump properties – one at Mar-a-Lago as a fundraiser; another at Trump's Bedminster, New Jersey golf club – to promote a lawsuit Trump filed against the Big Tech companies that barred him from their platforms.[81]

Trump's efforts to dominate the Republican Party didn't stop with inspirational rhetoric and fundraising. For instance, Trump also granted audiences to a stream of Republicans seeking his political blessing. By early 2022 he had issued nearly 100 endorsements for Trump supporters running for political office.[82] He also threatened to help "primary" Republicans who didn't support him. In other words, he would back people who supported him if they wanted to run for office against sitting Republican politicians who had either criticized or otherwise opposed him. Here was Trump's inclination for transactional deal-making with those who genuflected toward him – I'll support your candidacy, if you support me – and bullying those who stood up to him. And it seemed to work at least some of the time. For instance, Trump's endorsement of author and venture capitalist J.D. Vance for the US Senate propelled Vance to a stunning come from behind victory in the Ohio Republican primary in 2022.[83]

[81] Vogel and Goldmacher 2022.   [82] Vogel and Goldmacher 2022.
[83] Goldmacher and Haberman 2022.

Of course, driving this behavior was Trump's insistence on personal loyalty and trustworthiness. Those who didn't show it soon found themselves in his crosshairs. For instance, he vowed to go to Alaska and campaign against Republican Senator Lisa Murkowski who had voted against him in the second impeachment trial. Underscoring the desire to have Trump's endorsement, several Washington state Republicans considering running for a congressional seat in 2022 agreed that those not endorsed by Trump would drop out of the race.[84] He also began quizzing candidates seeking his endorsement, suggesting that if they didn't believe that the election was stolen, he wouldn't support them. And by late summer 2021 Trump had called Republican leaders in a half-dozen states pressuring them not to stop re-litigating the 2020 election results.[85] Finally, by not announcing whether he would seek reelection in 2024, Trump limited what other possible Republican contenders could do for fear of alienating him and his supporters and losing his possible endorsement.[86] Again, his personal interests took precedence over the party's.

Another way in which Trump's hold on the Republican Party had tightened involved congressional house cleaning – an indirect extension of his bullying modus operandi and demand for personal loyalty. As the Cheney episode illustrated, Trump's supporters engaged in a cleansing and purification exercise on his behalf to rid the party of those opposing Trump and what he stood for. The 2018 midterm elections had already forced out some moderate Republican members of Congress who had objected to Trump. Senators Jeff Flake and Bob Corker decided not to run for reelection. Flake, for example, said that "There was no way I could stand on a campaign stage with that man," while Trump insulted his colleagues, adding that "You have to live with yourself, sleep at night, and face your kids."[87] Moreover, Representative Mark Sanford (R-SC) and a few others were defeated by hard-core Trump supporters in the primaries. Roughly 40 percent of congressional Republicans who were in office when Trump became president were gone by the time he left the White House. What remained, according to political scientist Daniel Drezner, was a majority of steadfast Trump loyalists – the "Trump rump."[88]

For all the reasons just discussed, the Republican Party remained very much under Trump's thumb. Epitomizing its willingness to kowtow to him was the fight over convening a bipartisan January 6 Commission to investigate the causes of the Capitol insurrection. In the House every Democrat but only thirty-five Republicans – just 16 percent of the Republican caucus – supported and passed a bill in May 2021 to form the commission. However, Mitch McConnell blocked it in the Senate. In a closed-door meeting with his caucus McConnell warned that the commission could hurt the party's chances in the 2022 midterm elections and beyond because it might uncover damaging revelations about Trump's role in the uprising.[89] Trump himself had called the

---

[84] Milligan 2021.   [85] Barrett et al. 2021.   [86] Coleman 2021; Warren 2021a.
[87] Milligan 2021.   [88] Drezner 2020, pp. 199–200.   [89] Everett 2021.

commission a "Democrat trap."[90] Other Republican senators thought it was simply time to move on from the events of January 6 – that it was time to forget about the past. Although most of the Senate voted for the bill, it got only a handful of Republican votes, not enough to defeat a filibuster and get the sixty votes needed for passage. Even some Republicans, including Senators Pat Toomey (R-PA) and Richard Burr (R-NC), who had voted to convict Trump during his second impeachment trial for inciting the riot, now opposed the commission. Murkowski blasted her Republican colleagues for putting the party's short-term interests in the midterms above the national interest of finding out what caused the Capitol insurrection so that they could prevent something like it from happening again.[91] Nevertheless, much of the Republican Party remained loyal to Trump.

Of course, Democrats were outraged too. Senator Jon Tester (D-MT) put it bluntly in terms of the Republican cult of personality: "We've got to get to the bottom of this...It's a nonpartisan investigation of what happened. And if it's because they're afraid of Trump then they need to get out of office."[92] Republican opposition to the commission highlighted the power Trump still had over most of the party.[93] The fear Tester referred to stemmed from the ease and effectiveness with which Trump demanded fealty from Republicans or bullied them into submission. Eventually, the House launched its own investigation into the January 6 insurrection, but only after Speaker Pelosi rejected Minority Leader McCarthy's nomination of several Trump sycophants to the committee and ended up with only two Republican members, Adam Kinzinger and Liz Cheney. In 2022 the RNC censured both for serving on the House committee and downplayed the events of January 6 as simply an example of ordinary citizens engaging in "legitimate political discourse," a characterization to which only a handful of Republican legislators objected.[94]

Let's put Trump's grip on the Republican Party into historical perspective. When Richard Nixon ran for reelection in 1972, he established the Committee to Re-Elect the President, which operated out of the White House and was run by his former attorney general John Mitchell.[95] The Committee was involved in the infamous Watergate scandal. Congressional hearings revealed that Nixon and his team had conspired to cover up the scandal and that Nixon had lied about it. Eventually, after the House had drawn up articles of impeachment, the White House was forced to release a secret audio tape – the so-called smoking gun – which proved Nixon's culpability in the affair. Soon thereafter, Republican leaders from the House and Senate visited Nixon in the White House and told him that he needed to resign the presidency or face impeachment and likely conviction. Nixon bowed to their wishes and resigned from office. In contrast, when Trump faced impeachment, not once but twice, nobody from his party went to the White House and encouraged him to resign. Even after January 6,

---

[90] Jalonick 2021.   [91] Nobles et al. 2021; Rogers et al. 2021.   [92] Everett 2021.
[93] Nobles et al. 2021.   [94] Weisman and Epstein 2022.   [95] Skowronek et al. 2021, p. 51.

only a few scattered Republicans called for his resignation.[96] During the first impeachment, no House Republican voted to impeach and only one Senate Republican voted to convict despite considerable evidence in Special Counsel Robert Mueller's report that Trump had conspired to obstruct justice, notably by firing FBI director James Comey and trying to squelch the Mueller investigation. I'll have more to say about this in the next chapter. During the second impeachment, only ten House Republicans voted to impeach and just seven Senate Republicans voted to convict. The fact that most of the party had coalesced around Trump showed how powerful and radically transformative leaders can be in certain circumstances if they have Trump's leadership characteristics.

4.5 BIPARTISANSHIP IN RETREAT

Trump's ability to redefine the meaning of republicanism reverberated beyond the party throughout American politics causing further institutional damage. Complimenting civil political discourse is the willingness to negotiate and compromise in a bipartisan manner. Of course, Republicans, particularly those in the Senate led by Mitch McConnell, had become increasingly obstructionist since Obama was first elected. And Democrats occasionally dug in their heels too as Congress became increasingly polarized along party lines.[97] But Trump's presidency exacerbated the demise of bipartisanship in several ways.

Research in political science and communications studies has shown that Trump's scorched earth rhetoric, embracing demagoguery, cultural invective, scapegoating and lying, pitted people against each other along racial, gender, religious and politically partisan lines in ways that severely undermined bipartisanship.[98] For example, Trump promised to build a wall along the Mexican border to better control immigration. In fact, leading Democrats had voted in 2006 for the Secure Fence Act, which would have built hundreds of miles of fencing there. But Trump's racist and xenophobic rhetoric about Mexicans and the wall was so offensive that it was difficult politically for them to support his plan. His discourse ruined the possibility of serious bipartisan discussion of the issue.[99] Furthermore, when it came to confirming presidential appointments, procedural delays skyrocketed. Trump faced more filibusters of his nominees than any other president before him. Democrats said they held up Trump's picks because many of his nominees were different from previous president's choices – they were partisan, unqualified, and thus worth opposing – and because the Republicans, for the first time ever, abandoned all pretense of pursuing bipartisan consensus in the confirmation process. Even some Republicans put holds on Trump's nominees for similar reasons. It's extremely

---

[96] Woodward and Costa 2022, p. 260.   [97] Shafer and Wagner 2019.
[98] Gilmore et al. 2020, p. 559. See also Edwards (2020, pp. 309–310).
[99] Edwards 2020, p. 314.

unusual for members of the president's own party to block his nominees. So, this was also another example of Republicans at war with themselves.[100]

Recent experimental research has found that when political leaders treat each other disrespectfully, their followers are less willing to compromise with the opposition than when leaders treat each other politely.[101] The problem, according to political scientist Francis Lee, is that since the 1980s, as control of Congress became more competitive, compromise became increasingly illusive in the legislative branch. Why? In part because political messaging in the Senate, and, following Gervais and Morris, I would add the House, shifted more toward denigrating the opposition party on the grounds of incompetence, lack of integrity, and cultural differences rather than challenging its policy agenda.[102] But Lee also found that presidential leadership was important in this.[103] It follows, then, that because Trump's treatment of political leaders in the Democratic Party was often insulting he contributed to the decline of bipartisanship, cooperation, and compromise in Congress. However, Trump also undermined the possibilities for political compromise in other ways.

We've already seen that moderate Republicans in Congress have left public service on Trump's watch giving way to more combative people less inclined toward bipartisanship. That's what happened to Paul Ryan, Jeff Flake, and Bob Corker, opponents of Trump who quit politics. In addition, party activists and party leaders have more frequently recruited extremist candidates like Marjorie Taylor Greene and Matt Gaetz to run for office. As a result, more Trump-styled Republicans took over the party machinery. As one observer put it, "The Republican coalition of today lacks any significant liberal or moderate factions who might pull it back to a more centrist position."[104] Political polarization and the possibility for bipartisanship suffered accordingly.[105] Thomas Mann and Norman Ornstein found in their research that the decline of bipartisanship in today's Congress is due to the Republican Party having moved so far to the right because of its increasingly homogeneous positions on race, religious traditionalism, and other cultural issues – things that Trump pushed hard. They conclude that the party has become "one of the most extreme – even radical – conservative parties in the democratic world."[106]

Figure 4.3 presents average (median) scores for each party's ideological profile in each congress during the twenty-first century. Scores for each party are based on their combined Senate and House roll-call votes. The scale was developed by a team of political scientists at the University of California-Los Angeles. The farther below zero a score is, the more liberal the party is; the farther above zero a score is, the more conservative the party is. Not surprisingly, Democrats are generally more liberal than Republicans. More important, the ideological gap

---

[100] Everett and Levine 2020.   [101] Huddy and Yair 2021.
[102] Gervais and Morris 2018; Lee 2016.   [103] Lee 2016, 2009, p. 3.
[104] Drutman 2020. See also Howell and Moe (2020, pp. 148–153, 169).   [105] Reynolds 2018.
[106] Mann and Ornstein 2020.

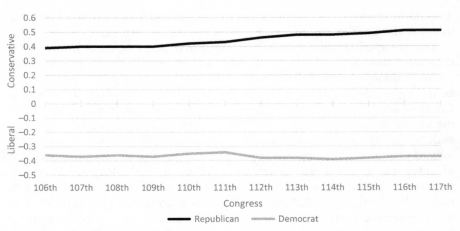

FIGURE 4.3. Median party ideology.
Source: Lewis et al. (2021).

between the two parties widened. And the change is attributable primarily to the increasing conservatism of the Republicans, which reached a high point during the 115th and 116th congresses during the Trump presidency. Figures 4.4a and 4.4b provide a more fine-grained look at the data for the House and Senate, respectively, broken down into roll-call votes for economic/redistributive and noneconomic legislation. The story is much the same. Again, the widening gap between the two parties is almost entirely attributable to House and Senate Republicans becoming significantly more conservative and, again, hitting a high point during the Trump presidency. Trump certainly didn't initiate these trends, but the data are consistent with the argument that he helped sustain, if not exacerbate, them with his inspirational rhetoric and discourse and his bullying and insistence on personal loyalty.

The more conservative and combative wing of the Republican Party, now the majority, is tightly aligned with Trump. Consider who supported impeachment after the Capitol insurrection. Heritage Action for America scores all members of Congress on how much their votes align with the organization's very conservative agenda. Its most recent scorecard showed that on a scale of 0 to 100, with 100 being a perfect conservative score, the average House Republican scored 95 and the average Senate Republican got 91. However, the House Republicans who voted to impeach Trump the second time averaged only a 77 score while the Senate Republicans who voted to convict Trump in the second trial averaged only 81.[107] Moreover, those members whose support

---

[107] Heritage Action for America (2021) and author's calculations. The exception was Liz Cheney who received a score of 98 but was pilloried by Trump and most of her House colleagues for voting to impeach Trump.

(a)

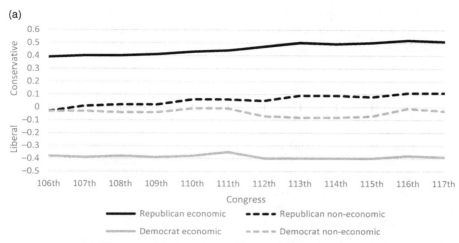

FIGURE 4.4A. Median party ideology in the House

(b)

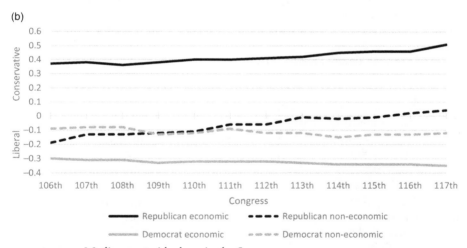

FIGURE 4.4B. Median party ideology in the Senate.
Source: Lewis et al. (2021).

for Trump during the impeachment was among the most shrill and uncompromising – including Ted Cruz, Jim Jordan, Marjorie Taylor Greene, Tom Cotton, Josh Hawley, and Matt Gaetz – all scored 98. In sum, it was the moderate Republicans who tended to oppose Trump and the more conservative ones who tended to support him. If moderates are more amendable to negotiation and compromise, then it stands to reason that those who aligned themselves with Trump in increasing numbers were among those least likely to compromise on legislation either within their own party or with their colleagues across the aisle.

4.6 CONCLUSION

Trump's rhetoric and behavior were a radical assault on the well-institutionalized norms of political discourse and civility. It helped drive the Republican Party up to and over a tipping point, which also involved an escalation of the culture wars as well as the dissemination of all sorts of conspiracy theories and falsehoods, particularly about the 2020 election. The Republican Party was torn apart and transformed into a cult of personality thanks in large part to Trump's brand of inspirational, transactional, and bullying leadership as well as his narcissistic demands for personal loyalty, which went a long way in redefining what it meant to be a Republican. Much of the party and its electoral base fell under his spell. As Patrick Buchanan noted, "The Republican establishment today bends the knee to Caesar." In other words, it's now the Party of Trump.[108] Political polarization increased and bipartisanship became as elusive as anyone could remember in a very long time. The institutional transformation was profound, and the damage was severe.

For American democracy to function well, it needs two reasonable political parties willing to negotiate and compromise. Without that the consequences can be dangerous. According to Thomas Mann, political parties have been a source of moderation in years past, trying to appeal to a wide swath of voters. But now the Republican Party is doing the opposite. In Mann's view, "We've had demagogues speaking out and sometimes winning high office. The difference this time is that they're being encouraged rather than constrained by party and election officials." By failing to check radicalism, he says, "Our whole system breaks down."[109]

For decades Republicans had alluded to Ronald Reagan as the symbol of what they and their party stood for – conservative norms including those of decency and civility. Even Trump invoked Reagan from time to time, for example, telling an audience that Reagan had tried for years to build a border wall like the one Trump wanted, even though this wasn't true.[110] More important, Reagan was much different from Trump. He too was charismatic, enjoyed a loyal following, and used conservative rhetoric, but it wasn't uncivil or overtly insulting. Moreover, according to Emily Elkins of the libertarian Cato Institute, "there were ideas associated with that [Reagan] era. With Trump, it does seem to be more about the individual person."[111] Put differently, with

---

[108] Peters 2022, p. 298.   [109] Wines 2021.   [110] Milligan 2021; Schladebeck 2018.
[111] Bunch 2009.

Trump it was all about his narcissistic self-importance and demands for loyalty. Finally, whatever success Reagan had in pushing his party toward culture wars, it fell far short of what Trump did. The truth is that Trump's sway over the party drove it farther and farther away from Reagan's legacy into a world of conspiracy theories and lies quite antithetical to Reagan's and the party's traditional norms. What it meant to be a Reagan Republican wasn't too far out of step with what it had meant to be a Republican for much of the late twentieth and early twenty-first centuries. Thanks to Trump's leadership and tipping point opportunities, the same can't be said for what it means to be a Trump Republican.

It was no coincidence, then, that in 2021 Paul Ryan spoke at the Ronald Reagan Presidential Library and chastised Republicans for following in Trump's footsteps. As he put it, "If the conservative cause depends on the populist appeal of one personality, or on second-rate imitations, then we're not going anywhere." He cautioned further that Republican voters should "not be impressed by the sight of yes-men and flatterers flocking to Mar-a-Lago." And he warned that "We win majorities by...staying faithful to the conservative principles that unite us."[112] What he was implying, of course, was that the meaning of republicanism, including the norms of civility and compromise, had been badly damaged by the cult of personality and surrounding rhetoric that Trump had fostered.

I mentioned in Chapter 1 that some believe we have already slipped into a world of Latin American presidentialism where the core tenets of democracy have been irreparably damaged; where the door is open for autocratic rulers to regain power in future elections; and where elections will forevermore be viewed by many with suspicion as corrupt and rigged. In other words, some believe that the changes Trump wrought were not just radical but truly revolutionary, fundamentally transforming our democratic institutions. This and the preceding chapter show that we have taken several big steps in that direction thanks to Trump's behavior and the recent behavior of the Republican Party. But it is still too early to know whether we have finally crossed the line from democracy to autocracy. Much will depend on the sort of resistance I have described so far and that appears in the chapters that follow. But the damage Trump caused was not limited to America's democratic institutions. It also extended into key parts of the state apparatus to which we now turn.

[112] Karni 2021.

5

Blind Justice?

To the left of the steps leading up to the US Supreme Court is a massive marble statue of a woman seated and holding a small figurine of a lady who is blindfolded and embracing a set of scales in her arms. The scales represent the Court's duty to weigh each side of an argument and the blindfold signifies the Court's responsibility to do so fairly – reminders to all who enter the Court that America's system of justice is supposed to be impartial and free from bias, political or otherwise. Not so in Trump's view. He wanted it to serve his personal and political interests and he tried hard to make that happen.

This chapter is about Trump's attempts to transform the federal justice system, specifically the courts and Department of Justice (DOJ), to do his bidding, how he reacted if it didn't, and the institutional ramifications involved. It illustrates several arguments I made earlier about institutional change. First, institutions are more than just rules and norms. They also involve mechanisms for monitoring and enforcing them. That's why the federal judiciary and DOJ have been such important parts of the American state for so long – they are responsible for much of that monitoring and enforcement.[1] That's also why Trump's attempts to change them were so significant. Second, in addition to altering institutional structures – such as rules and norms – institutional change can also entail changing institutional functions. This involves reorienting how rules and norms are interpreted and the purposes to which they are put. Trump tried to functionally reorient the justice system so that it would better serve his interests. This was as clear a sign as any of his narcissistic leadership, putting his own interests above all else. Finally, institutional change varies in degree. Trump's attacks on the justice system represented sharp breaks from the past, but some were more radical than others in terms of their longevity. Given that

---

[1] Skowronek 1982.

his appointments to the bench but not law enforcement agencies were tenured for life, the institutional changes he made to the courts were more radical and potentially more damaging than the changes he made to the DOJ. Nevertheless, the DOJ's reputation for independence and even-handedness was badly tarnished.[2]

Once again leadership and tipping points mattered. In addition to his narcissism, Trump's transactional and bullying leadership styles and demands for personal loyalty came into sharp focus. So did his habit of surrounding himself with people that he presumed he could trust to back him up when the going got tough. Insofar as the judiciary was concerned, two tipping points were important. One involved the availability of vacancies on the federal bench; the other involved the criteria used for filling them.

5.1 A JUDICIAL TIPPING POINT

The night before Barack Obama was inaugurated as president in January 2009, Senate Minority Leader Mitch McConnell and a handful of other high-ranking Republicans met in an upscale Washington DC restaurant to discuss how to deal with the new president. McConnell announced that he wanted to make Obama a one-term president by doing everything he could to obstruct and otherwise thwart Obama's agenda and undermine his popularity.[3] Everyone agreed. Their capacity for obstruction was bolstered by Republicans winning control of the Senate in 2015. McConnell had no qualms about exercising that capacity by stonewalling Obama's nominations to the federal district and appellate courts.

The epitome of McConnell's stonewalling involved Obama's nominee for the US Supreme Court, Merrick Garland, a circuit court judge whose credentials and record were impeccable by all accounts. Obama's opportunity to nominate Garland arose due to the untimely death of Justice Antonin Scalia, one of the most conservative justices on the Court. Although Garland was a centrist, Republicans worried that his appointment would shift the ideological balance on the Court too far to the left. As a result, McConnell stalled. Obama nominated Garland in March 2016, but McConnell blocked the confirmation process for ten months, refusing either to meet with Garland or schedule a hearing for him. Eventually, the nomination expired in January 2017 with the end of the 114th Congress, the last of Obama's presidency. Now it would be up to the new president, Donald Trump, to fill Scalia's seat. Later, McConnell announced that "one of my proudest moments was when I looked Barack Obama in the eye and I said, 'Mr. President, you will not fill the Supreme Court vacancy.'"[4]

---

[2] Skowronek et al. 2021, p. 77.
[3] Capehart 2012; Franken 2017, pp. 235–236, 246; Hacker and Pierson 2010, pp. 262–263.
[4] Rogers and Guillon 2019, p. 36.

But there was much more to Republican stonewalling. Consider the district courts.[5] Compared to his three two-term predecessors (Ronald Reagan, Bill Clinton, and George W. Bush), there was nothing special about how many nominations Obama either made or had confirmed to the district courts until the Republicans gained control of the Senate in the 114th Congress. In his last year in office the Senate confirmed only 30 percent of his nominees, much fewer than it had for Reagan (66 percent), Clinton (50 percent), or Bush (68 percent) at the end of their presidencies. As a result, on Obama's watch, district court vacancies nearly doubled from thirty-three to sixty-five between April 2015 and April 2016. Although all these presidents had to contend with Senate confirmation hearings controlled by the opposition party, McConnell's Republicans alone dug in their heels and refused to confirm the vast majority of Obama's nominees, or in some cases even hold hearings for them.[6]

The point is that by the time Trump won the White House, there was a backlog of empty seats on the federal bench waiting to be filled – a tipping point where he could pack the courts with judges that he believed would do his bidding.[7] Figure 5.1 illustrates the situation. At the end of Obama's second term in office, the 114th Congress, the Senate had "returned" to the president, that is, blocked or otherwise failed to confirm, 70 percent of his nominees for district courts and nearly 80 percent of those for the circuit courts of appeals. This was far more than at any time previously in his presidency or during his predecessor George W. Bush's presidency. The Senate confirmed only one appellate court appointment in each of Obama's last two years in office, the fewest since the Carter administration.[8] As a result, during his first three months in office, Trump had 116 federal court vacancies to fill – more than any president since Reagan. By contrast, during his first three months in office Joe Biden had sixty-eight vacancies to fill – *fewer* than any president since Reagan.[9]

[5] The federal court system has 94 US district courts and 13 US courts of Appeals (US courts 2020).

[6] Wheeler 2016. Republicans used a variety of tactics to create vacancies on the federal bench during Obama's tenure in the White House, including encouraging judges to retire and exercising their automatic veto privileges under the Eastland rule, which gave any senator the right to veto any nominee to a judgeship in their state – a privilege that Democrats granted to Republicans when they controlled the Senate Judiciary Committee but that Republicans refused to grant Democrats once they took control of the committee (King and Ostrander 2020, p. 595; Millhiser 2020; Ruiz and Gebeloff 2020).

[7] King and Ostrander 2020, p. 593.

[8] US Congressional Research Service 2020c. The rate of confirmations during presidential election years tends to be lower than in other years.

[9] Wheeler 2021. A "vacancy" is a judgeship with no incumbent. They occur when judges leave "active status," such as by retiring to part-time work or retiring altogether; resigning; being appointed to another judgeship; or dying. Congress can also create new judgeships.

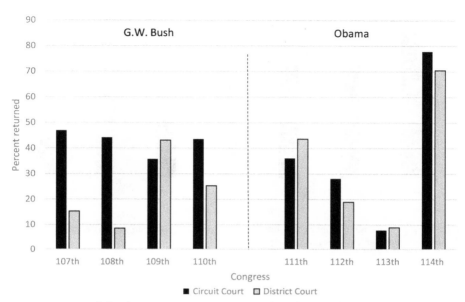

FIGURE 5.1. US federal court nominations returned to the president by the Senate. *Source:* US Congressional Research Service (2019).

5.2 STACKING THE DECK

Soon after taking office, Trump began filling federal judgeships at a record pace.[10] Figure 5.2 shows that the annual rate of judicial appointments Trump made exceeded that of every president since Jimmy Carter. Three and a half years into his presidency, Trump was responsible for having appointed almost a quarter of all the active federal judges in the country.[11] By December 1, 2020, the Senate had confirmed 229 of his nominees with another 48 pending.[12] When he took office, 40 percent of the sitting appellate court judges had been appointed by Republicans but by the time he left office 54 percent were Republican appointees.[13]

It isn't surprising that a Republican president would nominate conservative judges to the bench. However, one thing that distinguished Trump from his Republican predecessors was how *many* conservative judges he nominated. So, this was a radical quantitative transformation of the federal judiciary. But quantity is one thing; quality is something else. Here Trump distinguished himself again from former Republican presidents by implementing another radical institutional change. The American Bar Association (ABA) rates the

[10] Edmondson 2021b.   [11] Gramlich 2020.   [12] Ballotpedia 2020.   [13] Wheeler 2021.

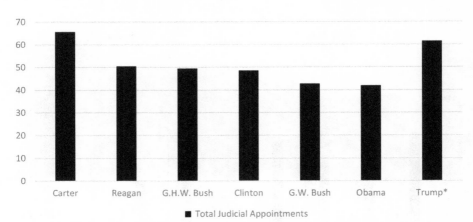

FIGURE 5.2. Average number of judicial appointments made per year by each president.
*Through December 31, 2020, for Trump.
Source: Ballotpedia (2021).

quality of all presidential judicial nominations. It's Standing Committee
on the Federal Judiciary has been doing this since 1953 for both Democratic
and Republican presidents. Only members of the highest professional status
and integrity are appointed to the Committee. They do not propose, recommend, or endorse nominees to the bench; they simply rate their qualifications
for the job.[14] The Committee's ratings are based on assessments of a wide
variety of information about a nominee, including their written responses to
questions posed by the Senate Judiciary Committee as well as their legal
writings, court decisions, briefs, legal memoranda, publications, speeches,
and transcripts of court hearings. The assessment also involves interviews
about the nominee with a broad cross-section of judges, lawyers, and others.
The process is painstaking and thorough – and, importantly, is done without
reference to the nominee's judicial philosophy, political affiliation, or
ideology.[15]

The Standing Committee rates nominees as being "well qualified," "qualified," or "not qualified" but, to reiterate, it does not recommend candidates for
nomination. If found not qualified, the Committee has decided that "the
nominee does not meet the Committee's standards with respect to one or more
of its evaluation criteria – integrity, professional competence or judicial tem-
perament." So, for example, the ABA rated all but one of the US Supreme Court
justices – both conservative and liberal – on the court at the end of Trump's
presidency as being "well qualified." Clarence Thomas was the exception with

[14] American Bar Association 2020a.   [15] American Bar Association 2020a.

TABLE 5.1. *Official ratings by the American Bar Association for nominees confirmed by the Senate, 1977–2018*

	Circuit Court Nominees			District Court Nominees		
	Percent Well Qualified	Percent Qualified	Percent Not Qualified	Percent Well Qualified	Percent Qualified	Percent Not Qualified
Carter	75.0	25.0	0.0	51.0	47.5	1.5
Reagan	56.6	43.4	0.0	53.8	46.2	0.0
G.H.W. Bush	61.9	38.1	0.0	57.4	42.6	0.0
Clinton	75.4	24.6	0.0	58.7	40.0	1.3
G.W. Bush	68.9	31.1	0.0	69.3	29.1	1.5
Obama	80.0	20.0	0.0	58.6	41.4	0.0
Trump	80.0	13.3	6.7	62.3	34.0	3.8

Source: US Congressional Research Service (2019).

a "qualified" rating by the majority of the Committee but a "not qualified" rating by the minority.[16] The Committee reports its rating to the Senate Judiciary Committee, which is responsible for reviewing all nominations and voting whether to confirm them before reporting their recommendation to the full Senate for a final vote. The ABA Committee also submits its assessments to the White House and the DOJ. The idea is to ensure that the most professionally qualified people serve on the federal bench.

It is extremely rare that nominees for the federal bench receive a "not qualified" rating. Table 5.1 summarizes the ABA's ratings for all district and appellate court nominees going back to the Carter administration. Until the Trump administration, no appellate court nominee received a "not qualified" rating. However, nearly 7 percent of Trump's nominees did. Similarly, virtually none of the district court nominees were rated "not qualified" until Trump's presidency at which point nearly 4 percent were deemed not qualified. This is especially disconcerting when it comes to the appellate courts for reasons I will explain later.

The Trump administration suddenly ended the long-standing practice of using the ABA's Standing Committee review to assess the professional qualifications of prospective nominees to the federal bench. Instead, it turned to the Federalist Society, an overtly conservative organization founded in 1980 whose members are lawyers, judges, law school professors and law students holding libertarian, judicial restraint, and originalist or other conservative views of the law and the constitution. It was designed as a counterweight to the ABA, which

---

[16] American Bar Association 2020b.

it viewed as being too liberal.[17] Its budget and membership are much smaller than the ABA's, although it still boasts a membership of 42,000 conservative lawyers, 150 law school campus chapters, and about seventy-five lawyers' groups nationally. Its top donors have included the Bradley, Olin, and Scaife Foundations, the Charles Koch Charitable Foundation, David Koch, and Koch Industries Inc., all well known for supporting libertarian and other conservative causes.[18]

Unlike the ABA, which maintains an arms-length distance from the nomination process, the Federalist Society is more intimately involved because although it does not rate nominees for federal judgeships, it does make recommendations for nominations. Its members have assumed informal yet influential positions in the judicial nomination process and Republicans have used society membership as a litmus test in making judicial appointments because it signifies an individual's commitment to conservative principles. According to political scientist Steven Teles, the society's membership network provides crucial information about the ideological preferences of potential nominees to the federal bench. Remember that the ABA does not evaluate judges based on their ideology.[19]

The Federalist Society has been advising Republican presidents and senators on judicial nominations since its founding. But its influence relative to that of the ABA's grew over the years among Republican administrations.[20] It reached a tipping point with the Trump administration when the Federalist Society no longer just supplemented the ABA ratings but completely supplanted them. Trump worked closely with McConnell to appoint hundreds of judges to the federal bench that had been identified by the Federalist Society as reliably conservative.[21] This was another sudden and radical institutional change. As political scientist Amanda Hollis-Brusky has observed, "the Trump administration has openly and publicly handed over the reins of judicial selection to the Federalist Society network."[22]

In fact, this is exactly what Trump had promised voters during the 2016 election campaign when he said, "We're going to have great judges, conservative, all picked by the Federalist Society."[23] But why make such a promise? Whether Trump really cared about the Federalist Society's advice isn't clear, but what is clear was his political motivation. Trump's conservative credentials were

---

[17] There is some evidence that ABA ratings are somewhat biased toward liberals – that is, appointments by Democrats (Smelcer et al. 2012). However, the ABA pales in comparison to the Federalist Society when it comes to willfully exerting influence over the judicial nomination process. Proof of this is the fact that the liberal wing of the legal profession created the American Constitution Society as a mirror image of the Federalist Society to counterbalance its influence not only over the judicial nomination process but also its influence throughout law schools and the legal profession (Hollis-Brusky 2019, epilogue).

[18] Mayer 2016, p. 110.   [19] Teles 2008, chap. 5.   [20] Palazzolo 2017.
[21] Gerstle 2022, p. 270.   [22] Hollis-Brusky 2019, p. x.   [23] Millhiser 2020.

somewhat suspect during the campaign. Jeb Bush accused him during the primaries of having been a Democrat longer than a Republican in the last decade – and not without reason. Trump told MSNBC on several occasions that "I identify with some things as a Democrat." Between July 1987 and April 2012, he switched his party registration six times.[24] So, his promise to rely on the Federalist Society for his judicial picks was one way to improve his conservative image and fulfill his ambition of becoming president.[25]

Of the first thirteen judicial nominees confirmed by the Senate during Trump's presidency, ten were either current or former members of the Federalist Society.[26] By late March 2019 nearly 90 percent of Trump's appellate court judges, not to mention his two Supreme Court justices, were members.[27] According to the Federalist Society executive vice president Leonard Leo,

What President Trump has done with the judicial selection and appointments is probably at the very center of his legacy and may well be his greatest accomplishment thus far. By the end of this year [2018], he probably will have transformed about 30 percent of the federal appellate courts in our country, and that's quite significant when put against other administrations in modern history.[28]

In other words, Trump was radically reorienting the federal bench. Reinforcing that effect, Trump's nominees to the bench tended to be younger than those appointed by previous presidents, which is one reason why the ABA rated some of them as being not qualified; they didn't have much experience on the bench. Youthfulness was especially evident for Trump's nominations to the appellate courts, which along with his Supreme Court nominees tended on average to be about four years younger than appointees by presidents dating back to Richard Nixon. Because federal judges have lifetime appointments, Trump's impact on the federal judiciary promised to be long-lasting. Recall that longevity is one indicator of how radical an institutional change is. Trump's appellate court nominees averaged 48 years in age. Since the average retirement age of an appellate court judge is 68 years, Trump's appointees are likely to influence appellate court rulings for a generation, if not longer. Trump's district court appointments averaged 51 years of age with an average retirement age of 66 years, again giving them at least a generation of influence on the federal bench.[29] As Hollis-Brusky notes, "it is no overstatement to say that Trump has changed the face and ideological balance of the federal judiciary, appointing young, conservative Federalist Society type judges for lifetime terms."[30]

I mentioned earlier that Trump's appointments to the appellate courts were especially important. There are several reasons for this. First, these courts rule as three-judge panels and are the last word on a case unless it goes to the

[24] Gillin 2015.   [25] Millhiser 2016; Peters 2022, pp. 214–215.   [26] Wheeler 2017.
[27] Whitehouse 2019.   [28] Quinn 2018.   [29] Syed 2020.   [30] Hollis-Brusky 2019, p. x.

Supreme Court. Of the roughly 50,000 cases filed annually with the appellate courts, only about 10 percent end up being submitted to the high court where fewer than 100 of these are heard. So, most appellate decisions are final.[31] Second, as Supreme Court Justice Sonia Sotomayor has said, "the court of appeals is where policy is made," during these intense years of polarization and gridlock in Washington politics. Third, the rate at which Trump appointed these judges was roughly twice the rate of all previous presidents since Carter.[32] Trump appointed fifty-three appellate court judges by November 2020. That was more than one-quarter of all active appellate court judges, and more than Reagan, Clinton, or George W. Bush appointed in twice the time – that is, in two terms in office, not just one.[33] As a result, and given the youthfulness of his nominees, Trump's impact on the federal judiciary – and especially the appellate courts – was unprecedented.[34]

In sum, Trump's impact on judicial institutions was both structural and functional, was radical even by mainstream Republican standards, and will have lasting effects. His abandoning the nonpartisan ABA ratings and reliance instead on Federalist Society recommendations, which take into consideration a nominee's ideological profile as well as their intellectual qualifications, was a dramatic structural change in the institutional process by which federal judges were appointed. But he also caused a remarkable functional reorientation of judicial institutions by pushing judicial decision making in a much more conservative direction.[35] For instance, research has shown that judges sitting on the appellate courts who belong to the Federalist Society are significantly more likely to vote conservatively on the bench than other judges, even after controlling statistically for their political ideology, race, gender, and seniority. In other words, membership has a substantively large impact on judicial decision making.[36] So does their youth. As Joshua Fischman, a law professor at the University of Virginia, explained, "We've seen a huge conservative shift. A lot of these judges are very young, and they'll be there for a long time." Mitch McConnell agreed. Reflecting on the possibility that the Democrats might soon win the White House thus ending Trump's presidency, McConnell explained that "a lot of what we've done over the last four years will be undone sooner or later by the next election...[But] they won't be able to do much about this for a long time."[37] So, as the Federalist Society's Leonard Leo predicted, Trump's appointments to the federal bench may be among his most lasting – and most radical – institutional legacies. The same is true of his Supreme Court appointments.

5.3 SUPREME COURT APPOINTMENTS

Part of the tipping point that McConnell helped create involved stonewalling Obama's choice for the US Supreme Court, Merrick Garland, after the death of

---

[31] US courts 2021.   [32] Ballotpedia 2020.   [33] Millhiser 2020.   [34] Millhiser 2020.
[35] Hult 2021, p. 41.   [36] Scherer and Miller 2009.
[37] Ruiz and Gebeloff 2020. See also Hollis-Brusky (2019, pp. x–xi).

Justice Scalia. McConnell's move to block the Garland appointment was technically legal but normatively unprecedented given the many months Obama still had left in his presidency. Democrats were outraged. McConnell's publicly stated rationale was that his move was appropriate because the government was divided in a presidential election year: the Congress was under Republican control while the White House was in the Democrats' hands. Democrats viewed this as ridiculous and a desecration of well-institutionalized congressional norms, especially because the election was almost a year away. Nevertheless, McConnell stuck to his guns and killed the Garland nomination.

When Trump took office, he moved quickly to appoint Neal Gorsuch to Scalia's seat. Gorsuch sat on the Tenth Circuit Court and apparently pandered to the Federalist Society for their blessing as a potential Supreme Court justice. He did this by writing a series of opinions indicating how, if given the chance, he would limit the regulatory reach of federal agencies, a legal view with which the Society was enamored. It worked. His anti-regulatory views attracted the attention of the Society, which endorsed him, and then Trump who eventually nominated him. The Republican-controlled Judiciary Committee approved his nomination in a straight 11-to-9 party-line vote, the first time in more than a decade that such a partisan vote had happened for a Supreme Court nomination. The full Senate followed suit confirming the nomination with all Republicans voting in favor and all but three Democrats voting against. Gorsuch took his seat on the high court.[38]

It is rare for a president to make three appointments to the Supreme Court, but Trump did it in a single term in office. He next nominated Brett Kavanaugh, a staunch conservative, to replace Justice Anthony Kennedy, a more moderate justice who had announced his retirement. Kennedy was a swing vote, sometimes siding with the liberals on the Court and sometimes with the conservatives. Kavanaugh had clerked for Kennedy and now sat on the powerful DC Circuit Court. His name was part of a list of over 20 judges put together by Trump's White House counsel Don McGahn with the help of the Federalist Society's Leonard Leo. The list had been publicized as part of the effort, noted earlier, to convince voters in 2016 that Trump was a true conservative and would appoint conservatives to the federal bench if he were elected.[39] The list was loaded with people touting membership and other connections to the Federalist Society. After a vicious and highly partisan Senate Judiciary Committee hearing where Kavanagh was accused of sexual assault when he was an undergraduate at Yale, his nomination was confirmed.[40] Again, the committee voted largely along partisan lines as did the full Senate.

Amy Coney Barrett, a University of Notre Dame law professor and member of the Seventh Circuit Court in Chicago, was Trump's third nomination for the Supreme Court, and another one steeped in controversy. She had clerked for

---

[38] Millhiser 2020.   [39] Hollis-Brusky 2019, p. x.   [40] Achenback 2018.

Justice Scalia, shared many of his views, and was a deeply religious social conservative.[41] She, too, was on Trump's list of judges as well as a member of the Federalist Society. Her nomination was prompted by the death of Justice Ruth Bader Ginsberg, a liberal, less than two months before the 2020 presidential election. Disregarding the fact that he had stalled the Garland hearings for ten months prior to the 2016 election, McConnell rushed with Trump's encouragement to confirm Barrett in record time. She was sworn in as the newest justice just nine days before the election. Again, Democrats cried foul, charging that McConnell's haste was the epitome of hypocrisy because it flew in the face of his own rationale for holding up the Garland appointment – that the people should have some influence over the appointment in a presidential election year. Although the time between her nomination and the election was weeks rather than several months, as it had been for Garland, McConnell and his fellow Republicans pushed back arguing that this time was different because Republicans controlled both Congress and the White House – government was not divided as it had been during the Garland case. But his logic didn't matter; he had the votes.[42] The Judiciary Committee approved her nomination with all the Republicans supporting it and all the Democrats boycotting the vote in protest. In the full Senate, only one Republican voted against the nomination as did all the Democrats.[43] She was confirmed. As we shall see in a moment, her nomination was an extraordinary example of Trump's transactional expectations of loyalty and service to his own personal interests.

Overall, then, Trump's historic opportunity to appoint three justices to the high court stemmed from the same tipping point mentioned earlier – the accumulation of Court vacancies, this time due to a combination of fate (two deaths and a retirement) and McConnell's control of the confirmation process. Like Trump's lower court appointments, Justices Gorsuch, Kavanaugh, and Barrett were relatively young when confirmed – 50, 53, and 48 years of age, respectively – which meant that they would likely serve three decades or longer. And as with Trump's lower court appointments, his Supreme Court picks – a third of all justices – marked a radical institutional change, quickly shifting the Court to a solid 6–3 conservative supermajority and giving the Court its most conservative complexion since at least 1950.[44]

5.4 A BULLY IN THE BULLY PULPIT

Trump demanded unconditional loyalty to an extent unheard of in other modern American presidencies. In his words, "I value loyalty above everything else – more than brains, more than drive and more than energy."[45] This was something he learned in the cutthroat New York City real estate market.[46] For

---

[41] Greenhouse 2021b, pp. 50, 58.   [42] Greenhouse 2021b, pp. 44–45.   [43] Chalfant 2020.
[44] Bailey 2020.   [45] Kruse 2018.   [46] Bernstein 2020; Cohen 2020.

anything he gave, he wanted something in return – or else. This became especially clear in his treatment of judicial appointments. He appointed people to the federal bench whom he believed would support his policies and protect his own political interests. So, when they ruled against him, he lashed out at them from his presidential bully pulpit.[47] In this regard, Trump combined three leadership characteristics – expectations of personal loyalty, transactional appointments, and aggressive bullying – to facilitate institutional change. This was one reason why he insisted that Amy Coney Barrett should be confirmed quickly – so that she could decide in his favor if questions about the fairness and legitimacy of the 2020 presidential election, which he suspected of being rigged against him, ended up having to be resolved by the Supreme Court.[48] As Trump put it when asked why there was such a rush to confirm her, "We need nine justices. You need that with the millions of ballots that they (Democrats) are sending. It's a scam. It's a hoax. You're going to need nine justices. . .I think this (election) will end up in the Supreme Court. It's very important. We must have nine justices."[49]

But Trump's plan backfired. After he lost the election, the Texas Republican attorney general filed a lawsuit with Trump's blessing asking the high court to overturn the election results in four battleground states. This was the legal equivalent of a sixty-yard Hail Mary pass in football, a desperate last-second attempt to win the game. If successful, the suit would have disenfranchised millions of voters, but the Court threw out the case.[50] Trump was outraged, in part because he had appointed a third of the justices and expected their loyalty in return.[51] He launched a series of scathing tweets like this one: "The Supreme Court really let us down. No Wisdom, No Courage!" Barrett as well as his two other picks for the Court agreed with the rest of the justices to reject the suit. It was the second time in a week that the high court rebuffed Republican requests to meddle in the election.[52]

In fact, Trump criticized federal judges throughout his presidency, often on Twitter, when they ruled against his wishes. For instance, he belittled four judges early in his term who struck down his travel ban on Muslims entering the United States. He railed against Judge Amy Berman Jackson who presided over a case involving Roger Stone, Trump's long-time friend, when she sentenced Stone to jail on several felony counts connected to the investigation of Russian interference in the 2016 election. Trump also called Judge Jon Tigar of the Ninth Circuit "a disgrace" and "an Obama judge" for overturning his executive order banning certain people from coming to the United States seeking asylum. In Tigar's defense, Chief Justice John Roberts responded publicly – a startling break from the Supreme Court's protocol of staying out of politics. According to Roberts:

[47] Lyons 2019.   [48] Chait 2020.   [49] Greenhouse 2021b, p. 70.   [50] Liptak 2020a.
[51] Chait 2020; Leonnig and Rucker 2021, pp. 371, 411, 513.   [52] Merchant et al. 2020.

[The United States doesn't have] Obama judges or Trump judges, Bush judges, or Clinton judges. What we have is an extraordinary group of dedicated judges doing their level best to do equal right to those appearing before them. The independent judiciary is something we should all be thankful for.[53]

Trump's dispersions indicated that he rejected the idea that the courts should be independent – in his view they should serve his interests, at least insofar as he appointed the judges and justices. Yet despite Roberts' unusual reprimand, Trump continued to attack judges that ruled against him. He also suggested breaking up the Ninth Circuit because in his view "Every case that gets filed in the Ninth Circuit we get beaten."[54] He also leveled personal attacks at Supreme Court justices Sotomayor and Ginsberg calling for them to recuse themselves in any matter before the Court that involved him, and at one point calling for Ginsberg to resign.[55] At another time he went so far as to charge that the entire federal court system was "broken and unfair," that is, unfair to him.[56]

Presidents have historically exercised great restraint, refraining from criticizing the courts and especially from attacking judges personally, out of deference to the important role the judiciary plays as an apolitical check on the power of the executive and legislative branches of government.[57] Hence, Roberts' rebuke of Trump. But Trump continued attacking these institutional norms and said publicly that he didn't care if people objected. He added that his administration was taking "decisive action" to improve its vetting procedures to avoid the problem in the first place.[58] In other words, he would do a better job of nominating judges that would do his bidding so he wouldn't have to criticize them at all. But his criticisms continued.[59] Trump wore his disregard for norms of judicial independence on his sleeve. Indeed, in a fiery speech on the Ellipse in front of millions of television viewers just moments before insurrectionists stormed the Capitol on January 6, he ripped into the Supreme Court for placing their loyalty to the law and country above their loyalty to him. His sense of transactional betrayal and narcissistic self-importance were obvious.[60]

5.5 REORIENTING THE JUDICIARY

Trump's transformation of the judiciary was quite extraordinary given the large number of conservative appointments he made quickly and the fact that they were likely to last a long time given their tenure. In fact, his appointments had a significant effect on judicial decision making. An analysis by *The New York*

[53] Brennan Center for Justice 2020b. [54] Brennan Center for Justice 2020b.
[55] Brennan Center for Justice 2020b. [56] Lyons 2019, p. 6. [57] Totenberg 2017.
[58] Brennan Center for Justice 2020b. [59] Brennan Center for Justice 2020b.
[60] Greenhouse 2021b, pp. 116, 135.

Times of over 10,000 published decisions during the first three years of the Trump administration found that the president's picks for the appellate courts were significantly more likely than past Republican appointees to disagree with their fellow judges who were selected by Democrats and significantly more likely to agree with those who were selected by Republicans. A follow-up of 1,700 more opinions during the last six months of the Trump administration indicated that this trend had intensified. What this meant was that the federal courts had become significantly more polarized politically as well as more conservative on Trump's watch.[61]

Polarization also occurred on the Supreme Court. Since Trump's three justices arrived, unusually bitter rifts among the justices have marked several of their decisions.[62] For instance, in one case the conservative Court upheld a new Arizona election law that eviscerated the Voting Rights Act. According to Justice Elena Kagan's steaming dissent, "the Court has (yet again) rewritten – in order to weaken – a statute that stands as a monument to America's greatness...the Court has damaged a statute designed to bring about the end of discrimination in voting."[63] The Court's decision was a radical departure from past precedent and an omen of things to come. Others predicted that the Court's decisions going forward would "weaken or reverse *Roe vs. Wade*, heighten the role of money in politics, favor business over consumers, favor the wealthy over the poor, expand the public role of religion, limit gun control, roll back affirmative action, limit government programs and regulations, and in general curtail what government can do to address the problems of its citizens."[64] Linda Greenhouse, who has observed and reported on the Court for decades, has shown that civility on the Court has eroded lately, its long-established legal precedents have become more precarious, and that with the addition of Justice Barrett the Court has taken a fundamentally new turn to the right. Since the late 1970s, she argues, the Court always had a swing justice, occupying middle ground facilitating moderation and a modicum of compromise among the justices. But since Barrett's arrival, a swing justice is missing, leaving the Court exposed and vulnerable to charges of being just another political branch of government.[65] Its legitimacy is at risk. Justice Steven Breyer said as much in an April 2021 speech to the Harvard Law School. He warned that "if the public sees judges as 'politicians in robes,' its confidence in the courts, and in the rule of law itself, can only diminish, diminishing the court's power, including its power to act as a 'check' on the other branches."[66] In short, federal judicial institutions have been functionally reoriented in a much more conservative, not to mention politically contentious, direction thanks to Trump.

[61] Ruiz and Gebeloff 2020.   [62] Greenhouse 2021b; Liptak 2020b.
[63] Stohr and Bloomberg 2021.   [64] Howell and Moe 2020, p. 94.
[65] Greenhouse 2021b, chap. 2, pp. 66–67, 98, 233–235.   [66] Greenhouse 2021b, pp. 233–234.

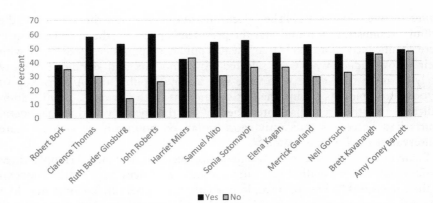

FIGURE 5.3. Would you like to see the Senate vote in favor of this nominee serving on the US Supreme Court?.
Note: Gallup did not ask this question for Antonin Scalia when he was nominated and confirmed. Bork failed to receive Senate confirmation. Miers's nomination was withdrawn.
Source: Gallup Polling (2021c).

It appears that Trump's reorientation, politicization, and public bullying of the federal judiciary did not bode well for its legitimacy. First, Figure 5.3 shows that Trump's three Supreme Court appointments were more controversial compared to most of those stretching back to Ronald Reagan's nomination of Robert Bork, which marked the beginning of a much more contentious Senate confirmation process.[67] Roughly twice as many people surveyed by Gallup supported Merrick Garland's nomination – the one that Mitch McConnell stonewalled – than opposed it. This level of support was much larger than it was for any of Trump's nominees, especially Kavanaugh and Barrett where those either supporting or opposing the nomination were divided about equally. Furthermore, according to another poll when asked whether Trump should fill Justice Ginsberg's seat shortly before the 2020 election half of the respondents said he should not and that the nomination should be left up to the winner of the election while only about a third said that he should nominate someone right away.[68] Of course, Trump proceeded to fill the seat anyway. All of this suggests that much of the public took a dim view of Trump's handling of his Supreme Court nominations.[69]

Second, although the public's confidence in the Supreme Court generally declined since the late 1990s, once all of Trump's justices had taken their seats

---

[67] Rogers and Guillon 2019, pp. 31–43; Scherer and Miller 2009, p. 376.   [68] Shepard 2020.
[69] The Trump era is not the first time the Supreme Court has been significantly politicized (Barton 2019).

on the high court and began making decisions, things took a turn for the worse.[70] Gallup found a dramatic decline in the public's approval of the Supreme Court. When respondents were asked, "Do you approve or disapprove of the way the Supreme Court is handling its job?" the Court's approval rating dropped from 49 percent of those questioned in July 2021 to 40 percent in September 2021 – the lowest it had been since Gallup began asking the question in 2000.[71] According to Irv Gornstein, executive director of Georgetown Law's Supreme Court Institute, "Not since *Bush vs. Gore* has the public perception of the Court's legitimacy seemed so seriously threatened." The Court knows it too. Several justices have recently found it necessary to publicly defend the Court's reputation. Justice Barrett, for instance, told a Kentucky audience in September 2021 that "my goal today is to convince you that this Court is not comprised of a bunch of partisan hacks." Ironically, she made these remarks at the University of Louisville's McConnell Center after being introduced by Mitch McConnell, for whom the Center was named and who helped rush her highly politicized confirmation through the Senate.[72] Liberal justices worried about the public's perceptions too and were especially concerned that if the Court overturned *Roe vs. Wade* now that Trump had tilted its composition so sharply to the right, the Court would pass a tipping point from which its legitimacy could not recover. Justice Breyer summarized their concern saying that if the high court is perceived as being made up of politicians rather than judges, "that's what kills us as an American institution."[73]

A presidential commission investigating the need for changes to the Supreme Court amplified Breyer's concerns. It was formed in part due to the bitter partisan conflict swirling around Trump's three nominations. It concluded that the confirmation process for Garland, Gorsuch, Kavanaugh, and Barrett had "come under severe strain from partisan conflict" and had "given rise to multimillion dollar lobbying campaigns seeking to mobilize public pressure for or against particular nominations," especially for or against the nominations of Justices Kavanaugh and Barrett. The icing on the cake was McConnell's pledge in 2021 that if his party won a majority in the Senate in the 2022 midterm elections, he would not commit to acting on any Supreme Court nomination Biden might bring forward, particularly if it was during the 2024 presidential election year. In short, McConnell threatened to stonewall Biden's Supreme Court nominations for two years! The commission concluded that all of this posed a significant danger to the

---

[70] Gallup Polling 2021c.
[71] Jones 2021. The recent poll was done shortly after the Court declined to block a controversial Texas law restricting abortion.
[72] Liptak 2021a.   [73] Liptak 2021b.

high court's legitimacy, its independence, and its fundamental relationship to democracy.[74]

The Court's legitimacy was undermined further in two unprecedented ways. First, it became clear that it was relying far more than ever on the so-called "shadow docket" whereby it issued decisions without hearing oral arguments and without either signing or explaining those decisions. Previously, the shadow docket was used for mundane things like denying an appeal from a lower court or giving a party more time to file a brief. But now it was being used to issue more substantive decisions that affected millions of Americans' lives. For instance, in a 5-to-4 shadow docket decision the Court revived a Trump administration regulation that limited the ability of states and tribes to restrict projects that might damage waterways or reduce water quality – a move by the Court's conservative majority that undermined the Clean Water Act and upended decades of settled law. Through the shadow docket the Court also blocked an Occupational Safety and Health Administration rule mandating COVID-19 vaccinations for employees of large firms; refused to block Texas' ban on most abortions after six weeks; and reinstated congressional district maps that two Alabama lower courts had struck down as violating the Voting Rights Act. Even Chief Justice John Roberts, a conservative in his own right, sided with the liberal dissent in six shadow docket cases, criticizing the conservative majority for abusing the shadow docket process and short-circuiting ordinary procedures to reach their desired results without sufficient explanation.[75]

Second, in June 2022, the Court's conservative majority overturned *Roe* v. *Wade* by upholding a Mississippi ban on most abortions after fifteen weeks of pregnancy. The decision ended nearly a half-century of federal constitutional protection of abortion rights, allowing each state to decide for itself whether to restrict or ban abortion. The decision was an earthshattering reversal of settled law and Supreme Court precedent that suddenly allowed laws banning or severely curbing abortion to snap into place in over twenty states and sparked demonstrations across the country. Six conservative justices, including Trump's three appointees, voted for the opinion while the Court's three liberal justices opposed it. Chief Justice Roberts tried to urge moderation in the Court's decision but was outgunned by his five conservative colleagues. The decision cast doubt on the precedents governing other non-abortion rulings, particularly because of Justice Clarence Thomas's concurring opinion urging the Court to overrule three "demonstrably erroneous decisions" regarding same-sex marriage, gay intimacy, and contraception.[76] In his 2005 Senate confirmation hearing Roberts said that the Court should be wary of overturning precedents because doing so threatens the Court's legitimacy. Justices Kavanaugh and

---

[74] Presidential Commission on the Supreme Court of the United States 2021.
[75] Bouie 2022; Vladeck 2022.   [76] Liptak 2022; Savage 2022a.

Gorsuch assured senators privately and during their confirmation hearings that they respected the precedent set by *Roe* and led the Judiciary Committee members to believe that they would not overturn it. But they did. All of this further damaged the trustworthiness of the confirmation process and the Court's legitimacy.[77] Although it's too soon to be sure, it is likely that overturning *Roe* will probably weaken the public's already record-low trust in the Court.[78] Just a day before the Supreme Court ruling overturning *Roe* was announced, Gallup reported that the public's confidence in the Court had already hit a new historic low in June 2022. Only 25 percent of those surveyed said they had either a "great deal" or "quite a lot" of confidence in the Court – an 11-point drop from a year earlier and a decline of roughly twice that of any other government institution that experienced a decline in confidence that year. The poll was taken a month after a draft of the Court's decision on *Roe* was leaked to the press, which may explain the sharp decline because Gallup also found that Americans opposed overturning *Roe* by nearly a 2-to-1 margin.[79]

Overturning *Roe* and the Court's extensive use of the shadow docket for substantive decision-making underscored how effectively Trump had functionally reoriented the judicial system at the highest level. By one standard measure used by political scientists the Court's term ending in June 2022 was the most conservative since 1931.[80] Other recent decisions confirmed this conservative shift. For example, in 2020 the Court ruled that the president could fire the director of the Consumer Financial Protection Bureau; in 2021 the Court struck down the Center for Disease Control and Prevention's moratorium on evicting tenants who lived in counties experiencing substantial or high levels of COVID-19 transmission rates and who demonstrated financial need; and, as noted, in 2022 the Court struck down the Occupational Safety and Health Administration rule mandating that businesses with 100 or more employees could require COVID-19 vaccinations. All these decisions were supported by Trump's appointees to the Court in coalition with the other conservative Republican appointees. The liberal justices appointed by Democrats were in opposition. Overall, this illustrated the successful attack on the deep state's administrative structure that Trump envisioned, particularly because Congress was too paralyzed to pass new legislation to reverse the impacts of these rulings.[81]

5.6 REORIENTING THE JUSTICE DEPARTMENT

Nowhere was Trump's transactional loyalty-based leadership style, narcissistic sense of self-importance, bullying tendencies, and efforts to reorient an institution's function clearer than in his appointments to high-level positions at the DOJ, which like the courts is supposed to be above the political fray, serving as

[77] Hulse 2022.   [78] Beauchamp 2022.   [79] Gallup Polling 2022.
[80] Liptak and Parlapiano 2022.   [81] Savage 2022b.

a key mechanism for monitoring and enforcing the law of the land. The DOJ's legitimacy and effectiveness depend on the public's perception that it is doing its business impartially and free from political interference. In other words, it should be functionally oriented toward serving the public interest in a fair and objective way. To ensure that, long-standing DOJ and White House guidelines limit communications between the White House and DOJ regarding specific law enforcement matters. The effort to insulate the Justice Department from White House meddling has been strong ever since the Nixon Watergate scandal. After Watergate the DOJ developed rules and memoranda spelling out an ethos that applied to both Democratic and Republican administrations whereby the administration could set the DOJ's overall policy direction but not interfere in its specific cases, especially if the president were implicated. Congress reinforced this norm by insisting during all attorney general and FBI director confirmation hearings that they must act independently of White House control.[82] However, in a radical departure from institutional practice, Trump ignored all that and insisted that the DOJ and FBI be functionally reoriented toward his own political interests – or suffer the consequences. Four notorious examples illustrate the point.

The first involved Trump's first attorney general, Jeff Sessions, an ultraconservative Republican US Senator from Alabama. Sessions had been the first senator to endorse Trump's bid for the presidency in 2016, long before most people gave Trump a chance of winning the Republican nomination, let alone the White House. He lent Trump some of his top staffers for the campaign and helped him with his first major foreign policy speech. True to his transactional ways, Trump saw Sessions as a loyal lieutenant, which was why he appointed him. But their relationship soon soured.[83]

Sessions had been questioned during his confirmation hearing about his involvement with Russians interfering in the Trump 2016 election campaign. He denied having had any contact with the Russians. But it turned out later that he had had two conversations with the Russian Ambassador, Sergei Kislyak, during the campaign.[84] Soon thereafter, on advice from the DOJ's ethics staff, he began to consider recusing himself from overseeing the Department's ongoing Russia investigation. The DOJ rules were clear that no department official should be involved in a criminal investigation if they had been involved with people or organizations party to that investigation. Trump was furious and felt that Sessions' recusal would be a personal betrayal – a violation of Trump's transactional expectations.[85] He believed that Sessions' job was to protect him and ordered his White House counsel to talk Sessions out of recusing. But despite this and other pressure from the White House Sessions refused to back down. He eventually recused himself and, as a result, suffered

[82] Pfiffner 2021, p. 108; US Senate Judiciary Committee 2021, pp. 7–11.
[83] Rucker and Leonnig 2020, pp. 48–49.   [84] Mueller 2019 vol. I, pp. 197–198.
[85] Hennessey and Wittes 2020, p. 168.

Trump's wrath because, according to Sessions, the president feared that the Russia investigation would spin out of control without him overseeing it as attorney general. But things soon got worse, and Trump's bullying escalated.[86]

Deputy Attorney General Rod Rosenstein took over supervising the Russia investigation. When he appointed Special Counsel Robert Mueller to run it Trump went ballistic, again telling Sessions that "you were supposed to protect me" but you "let me down."[87] This was a remarkably transparent example of Trump's transactional loyalty-based leadership style. Now Sessions considered resigning altogether as attorney general but was deterred by others. Eventually, Trump ordered one of his staff to tell Sessions to limit the scope of the Mueller investigation, but that message was never delivered. Trump also persisted in ridiculing Sessions like a schoolyard bully both publicly and behind his back.[88] In the end, however, the die had been cast. He finally forced Sessions to resign in the fall 2018. True to transactional form, rather than appointing Rosenstein as the acting attorney general, Trump picked Matthew Whitaker, Sessions' chief of staff and a Trump loyalist who had publicly criticized the Mueller investigation. This was someone Trump believed he could trust to accommodate his wishes until he could appoint a new attorney general.[89] In Trump's view Rosenstein had also been disloyal to him by appointing the special counsel in the first place. The special counsel's report eventually confirmed that Trump had tried to obstruct the Russia investigation and had leaned heavily on Sessions and others to do so on his behalf. This was an obvious attempt to functionally reorient the DOJ to serve Trump's personal interest and a blatant disregard for the institutional precedent of DOJ independence from the White House.[90]

A second example of Trump's narcissistic, loyalty-demanding, transactional, and bullying leadership traits as well as an attempt at institutional reorientation was his treatment of FBI director James Comey. The FBI operates under the DOJ's jurisdiction. In late July 2016, the FBI opened an investigation into possible Russian interference in the upcoming presidential election. A few days after Trump took office, he summoned Comey to dine with him privately at the White House.[91] According to Comey, the dinner conversation soon turned to a discussion about whether he wanted to remain as FBI director and that Trump needed to trust the people who worked for him. In Comey's telling, Trump said, "I need loyalty. I expect loyalty." Comey's evasive response was simply that he would perform "reliably" in his position as director and be "honest" with him. His concern that Trump was suggesting a transactional quid pro quo – keeping his job in exchange for personal loyalty to the president – was so disconcerting that he wrote up detailed notes on the dinner conversation as soon as he left the

---

[86] Mueller 2019 vol. II, pp. 48–52; Rucker and Leonnig 2020, pp. 42–54, 70–76, 107–108.
[87] Rucker and Leonnig 2020, p. 70. See also Woodward (2020, p. 45).
[88] Mueller 2019 vol. II, pp. 90–96.   [89] Rucker and Leonnig 2020, pp. 312–315.
[90] Mueller 2019 vol. II, pp. 97–98.   [91] Mueller 2019 vol. II, p. 33.

White House.[92] The White House denied that Trump had demanded loyalty at the meeting but Comey's memory of the details of the dinner remained consistent as he reported them on several occasions – in his own memorandum, in congressional testimony under oath, to the Mueller team, and in his own book.[93]

Days later Comey met Trump alone in the Oval Office. This time the president asked him to drop the investigation of Michael Flynn, his National Security Advisor, whom the FBI had recently interviewed in connection with the Russia probe. Flynn had lied to FBI agents when questioned. Trump told Comey, "I hope you can see your way clear to letting this go, to letting Flynn go. He is a good guy. I hope you can let this go."[94] Again, Comey wrote a memo about the meeting. In subsequent meetings Trump repeated his concern about the Russia investigation and told him that he hoped "the cloud" of the investigation might be lifted. Trump also urged Comey to let it be known publicly that the president was not under investigation in connection with the Russia probe. Comey declined to respond realizing that what Trump was asking was again far from appropriate, precisely because the FBI and Justice Department were supposed to operate independently from the White House and politics. Trump was livid that Comey had failed to say publicly or in congressional testimony that he was not under investigation.[95] And so, soon thereafter on a trip to California Comey learned on the television news that unbeknownst to him he had "resigned." Trump had sacked him and then tweeted a warning: "James Comey better hope there are no 'tapes' of our conversations before he starts leaking to the press."[96] The bullying didn't stop even after Comey was gone. Moreover, even after Comey's departure, Trump frequently considered firing his replacement, Christopher Wray, whom Trump suspected eventually of disloyalty and being "a Comey guy." He also considered sacking other FBI personnel and replacing them with loyalists.[97] Trump was especially irate and threatening toward Wray for not supporting his unfounded claims of voter fraud in the 2020 election.[98]

The third example of Trump's aggressive transactional leadership characteristics and efforts to bend the DOJ to his will involves Sessions' replacement as attorney general, William Barr – someone who did much to undermine the Justice Department's image of political independence. The Mueller report was released in 2019. As attorney general, Barr received an advance copy of the report and called a press conference to summarize its findings. He described the report's conclusions in what many, including Mueller, believed was a whitewash designed to protect the president, particularly when it came to the issue of whether Trump should be indicted for obstruction of justice having tried to

---

[92] Comey 2018, chap. 13; Woodward 2020, p. 55.   [93] Mueller 2019 vol. II, p. 35.
[94] Comey 2018, chap. 14.   [95] Mueller 2019 vol. II, p. 54.
[96] Comey 2018, chap 14; Woodward 2020, chap. 7.
[97] Leonnig and Rucker 2021, pp. 132–138.   [98] Allam et al. 2021.

interfere with the Russia investigation, notably by bullying Sessions and Comey. According to Barr, Mueller's team had found no evidence that Trump had tried to obstruct justice. But it turned out that this was an excessively generous interpretation of the report. The Mueller report was clear that according to the DOJ's Office of Legal Counsel (OLC) charging a sitting president with a crime was legally "not an option" for the Mueller team. So, as the report explained and as Mueller reiterated later in congressional testimony, he felt that the report could only go so far. As a result, it stopped short of saying that Trump should be indicted, but it didn't let him off the hook either. These were the report's keywords: "Accordingly, while this report does not conclude that the president committed a crime, it also does not exonerate him."[99] The report did, however, systematically document how Trump had tried to undermine the DOJ's independence by meddling in its investigation to protect his interests. 700 former federal prosecutors agreed that the Mueller report showed multiple acts of obstruction of justice and that the president wasn't charged simply because of the DOJ's policy of not indicting a sitting president. In a subsequent Freedom of Information Act lawsuit, a federal judge concurred that Barr had grossly distorted the report's findings.[100]

The Mueller report, although heavily redacted, was published online and received widespread media coverage as did accusations that Barr had tried to put a dishonestly positive spin on it for the president's sake. Despite the report's ambiguity, the impression left in many people's minds, including various legal scholars and even a few Republicans, was that there was enough evidence to indict Trump had Mueller wanted to disregard the OLC precedent. But Barr continued to insist on behalf of the president that Mueller had refrained from charging obstruction because he found no evidence of it.[101] The discrepant interpretations of the report spilled over into the public domain. Roughly half of those polled in a Gallup survey said that based on what they knew about the report they felt that Trump should be impeached. The partisan differences were huge – 6 percent of Republicans, 55 percent of independents, and a whopping 89 percent of Democrats favored impeachment.[102] Even more damning evidence against Trump was revealed in the impeachment inquiry and subsequent trial. Now people were aware of how he had tried repeatedly to interfere in DOJ business to protect his political interests. None of this made Barr look particularly good publicly but the president continued to favor him as one of his most loyal and steadfast allies.

In fact, Barr was viewed by Democrats and others, including other lawyers, as Trump's toady – someone who bent over backward to defend the president's position on a variety of issues, often with dubious justification.[103] For instance, in addition to his Panglossian interpretation of the Mueller report, he let the

---

[99] Mueller 2019, vol. II, p. 2. [100] Woodward and Costa 2021, p. 29. [101] Johnson 2019.
[102] Gilberstadt 2019; McCarthy 2019. [103] Kirby 2020; Lynch 2020.

DOJ file a brief with the Supreme Court in support of the citizenship question on the US Census, discussed in Chapter 3; he pressured US attorney Geoffrey Berman, whose office was investigating several Trump business associates, into resigning; and he intervened on behalf of Roger Stone to reduce his sentence.[104] Most notably, in the months prior to the 2020 election Barr echoed Trump's prediction that there would be major problems of voter fraud due to mail-in ballots. In a September interview Barr warned without confirming evidence that with mail-in ballots people could sell their vote, be coerced or intimidated into voting for a particular candidate, and engage in voter fraud.[105] He suggested as well that foreign countries could print large numbers of counterfeit absentee ballots and send them to voters, and that states were "playing with fire" to be resorting to the widespread use of mail-in ballots.[106] It was backstopping like this throughout Barr's tenure as attorney general that endeared him to Trump, who appreciated his loyalty and often praised him publicly. It appeared, then, that Trump had succeeded in undermining the DOJ's institutional independence from politics and reorienting it to his personal narcissistic interests. But all that came to a screeching halt after the 2020 presidential election.

On December 1, Barr announced that the DOJ had found no evidence of widespread voter fraud that could change the outcome of the presidential election. This, of course, directly contradicted Trump's own repeated claims about the election and the Big Lie. Moreover, despite Trump's urging, Barr refused to appoint special counsels to investigate either the 2020 election or Hunter Biden, Joe Biden's son, whose business activities were an issue in the campaign.[107] Trump was incensed about all of this and took it as a personal betrayal by someone who had previously been one of his most loyal stalwarts. He retweeted a post that Barr was "A big disappointment." He also told reporters when asked that he wasn't sure whether he would fire Barr or not. But before it came to that, Barr resigned.[108] Although Trump and Barr exchanged pleasantries during his resignation announcement at a press conference, it was clear that Barr had seen the writing on the wall and quit, fed up with Trump's excessively transactional and bullying leadership styles, and perhaps his repeated efforts to distract the DOJ from its proper institutional function.[109] However, according to a Senate Judiciary Committee investigation, Barr's resignation didn't stop Trump from "repeatedly [asking] DOJ leadership to endorse his false claims that the election was stolen and to assist his efforts to overturn the election results."[110] This brings us to the last example

---

[104] Fried and Larson 2020; Thomsen and Barber 2020; Truax 2020; Weissmann 2020. According to Leonnig and Rucker (2021, pp. 56–59), it isn't clear that Barr's intervention on Stone's behalf was prompted by Trump, but it certainly left that impression in many people's minds both inside and outside the DOJ.

[105] Christie 2020.   [106] Polantz and Kelly 2020.   [107] Balsamo 2020.   [108] Klein 2020.

[109] Karl 2021, pp. 199–200; Kirby 2020; Swan 2021a.

[110] US Senate Judiciary Committee 2021, p. 2.

of Trump's efforts to reorient the DOJ's functioning to his own interests in quid pro quo fashion and by bullying its leadership.

Jeffrey Clark was an acting assistant attorney general who ran the Justice Department's civil division. Clark quietly approached Trump with a scheme to use the DOJ to pressure Georgia election officials into overturning the results of the 2020 presidential election in their state. Trump asked Clark if he would be willing to serve as acting attorney general and pursue the plan of leaning on Georgia officials if Trump fired the current acting attorney general, Jeffrey Rosen.[111] Trump thought it was a great way to leverage his personal agenda and bully others who were not kowtowing to his wishes. Trump wanted to get rid of Rosen because he had refused Trump's request to help overturn the election in Georgia and appoint special counsels to investigate various unfounded accusations of election fraud. Trump abandoned Clark's plan to fire Rosen only after learning that all the Justice Department's senior leadership, who by now had discovered the plot, had threatened to quit if Rosen was fired, and that this would likely trigger mass resignations elsewhere in the DOJ.[112] Why? According to *The New York Times*, which broke the story, "The Clark plan, the officials concluded, would seriously harm the department, the government and the rule of law."[113] Here was yet another case of Trump's attempt to radically reorient the normative, if not the legal, institutions governing the DOJ. The Senate Judiciary Committee's subsequent investigation of the matter suggested that "in attempting to enlist DOJ for personal, political purposes to maintain his hold on the White House, Trump grossly abused the power of the presidency. He also arguably violated the criminal provisions of the Hatch Act, which prevent any person – including the president – from commanding federal government employees to engage in political activity."[114]

In sum, Trump's efforts to twist the DOJ to serve his interests revealed again his important leadership characteristics: a narcissistic sense of self-importance above all else; demands for loyalty; a transactional approach to his political appointments; and a habit of bullying anyone who refused to do his bidding.

5.7 RESISTANCE AT THE JUSTICE DEPARTMENT

Threats by senior DOJ leadership to quit if Trump carried out Clark's plan were only the tip of the iceberg. Resistance had mounted in and around the Justice Department as Trump tried to politicize its activity and reorient it toward his own interests.

---

[111] US Senate Judiciary Committee 2021, p. 28.
[112] US Senate Judiciary Committee 2021, pp. 37–39.
[113] Benner 2021a, 2021b; Benner and Savage 2021; Benner and Edmondson 2021. See also Karl (2021, pp. 250–254).
[114] US Senate Judiciary Committee 2021, pp. 2–3.

To begin with, many people recognized that Trump's appointments and other efforts to influence the DOJ were direct attacks on the well-institutionalized principle that the DOJ should operate independently from the president. In February 2020 more than 2,000 former DOJ career officials and political appointees who had served in Republican and Democratic administrations signed a statement calling for Barr to resign. This was triggered by the sudden resignation of all four federal prosecutors in the Roger Stone case after Barr, calling for a more lenient punishment, overruled their sentencing recommendation to the court. According to their statement,

Mr. Barr's actions in doing the president's personal bidding unfortunately speak louder than his words. Those actions, and the damage they have done to the Department of Justice's reputation for integrity and the rule of law, require Mr. Barr to resign. But because we have little expectation that he will do so, it falls to the Department's career officials to take appropriate action to uphold their oaths of office and defend nonpartisan, apolitical justice.[115]

Several current DOJ prosecutors were also outraged over political interference at the Justice Department. They expressed concern that both judges and juries would worry that cases were not being brought fairly and objectively and that clients were now wary of cooperating with them for fear that the DOJ would act improperly and put them in jeopardy.[116] This was another example of Trump's institutional attack being met with resistance from within the bureaucracy. They were worried about the institutional damage Trump was causing.

It didn't end there. There were numerous examples of staff at both the DOJ and FBI pushing back against Trump's efforts to exert undue political influence on their work.[117] For example, in October 2020, a former assistant US attorney of 36 years resigned. Philip Halpern served under 19 attorneys general and six presidents but called it quits because, in his words, "Donald Trump has made it crystal clear that there's simply no place in his administration for anyone who places loyal service to their country over blind obedience to him...And unfortunately, it's become all too clear that Bill Barr has chosen typically to play the lapdog and follow this president's lead." Others concurred noting that Barr "has wielded the power of the Justice Department more deeply in service of a president's political agenda than any attorney general in a half-century."[118] But Halpern further justified his decision to resign with reference to several additional political intrusions into DOJ business, including the president's call for criminal indictments of Obama and Joe Biden. Other prosecutors quit as well due to their concerns about the politization of the Justice Department.[119] Some

---

[115] Jarrett 2020.   [116] Jarrett 2020.   [117] Skowronek et al. 2021, chap. 6.
[118] Klein 2020.   [119] Shapiro 2020.

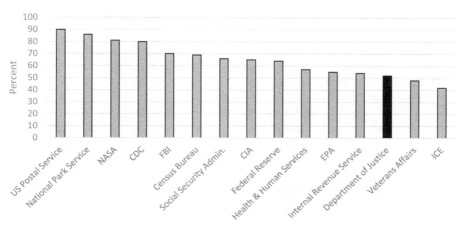

FIGURE 5.4. Percent who have a favorable opinion of each federal agency.
Source: Pew Research Center (2019a).

offered soulful public apologies for being complicit in Trump's abuse and politicization of the Department.[120]

The point is that Justice Department staff, concerned with how politics were interfering with their duties to pursue justice objectively and impartially, were going public and criticizing the Department and its operation. As a result, people outside the DOJ were sounding alarms too. This was another legitimation crisis like that described in Chapter 3 where concerns raised inside the state became public and triggered objections from outside.

Noah Bookbinder, another former federal prosecutor, lamented that Barr's service to Trump "has done tremendous damage to the Department of Justice and to the American people's very faith in our justice system."[121] He was right judging from the public's opinion of the DOJ. Figure 5.4 shows that in late 2019 barely half of those surveyed by the Pew Research Center reported that they had a favorable opinion of the Justice Department. This was worse than almost all the other federal agencies listed in the survey and a significant decline since Trump took office.[122] As Bob Bauer and Jack Goldsmith have noted, "Trump's attacks on Justice Department independence did enormous damage to the department's reputation and to the legitimacy of many of its actions."[123] This may be why the House committee investigating the January 6 insurrection at the Capitol was torn over whether it should make a criminal referral to the DOJ suggesting that Trump and his allies may have tried to obstruct a congressional proceeding and conspired to defraud the American people. The committee's concern was that a referral would taint the current DOJ investigation

---

[120] Newland 2020. [121] Lynch 2020. [122] Pew Research Center 2019a.
[123] Bauer and Goldsmith 2020, p. 153.

because some people would think the DOJ was acting on behalf of the Democrats.[124]

Moreover, according to the Pew polling, public attitudes toward the DOJ had become increasingly politicized. Republican views of the Justice Department improved after Trump's election, while the Democrats' views turned more negative. By April 2020, three-quarters of Republicans viewed the DOJ favorably, up from 61 percent the previous fall and the highest positive rating by Republicans for the Department in a decade. But only half of Democrats held favorable opinions of the Department, the lowest rating by Democrats in a decade. The gap between the Democrat and Republican favorability opinions of the DOJ increased from 18 to 26 points between 2010 and 2020. Democrats and Republicans tended to share the same opinions of most other government agencies in 2020, but not when it came to the Justice Department.[125]

Trump's Justice Department was not the first to suffer accusations of presidential interference. John Kennedy appointed his brother, Robert, as attorney general. George W. Bush fired seven US attorneys, allegedly for political reasons. But these isolated examples fall far short of Trump's systematic, self-interested, and prolonged interference in DOJ business.

It is especially important to understand two things about Trump's effort to radically reorient the DOJ's institutional functions. First, although he sought sudden and sharp breaks from past institutional practices, he didn't always succeed. Resistance and pushback limited some of the changes he wanted. Notably, Barr was far more willing to defend Trump's interests than Sessions, Comey or Rosenstein were, and the Clark plan blew up in Trump's face and was abandoned. Second, some effects of Trump's interference in DOJ business will last longer than others. On the one hand, the department's low public approval rating will take years to fix. Reputations are not repaired overnight. On the other hand, Trump's DOJ appointments will be short-lived. For instance, new presidents always appoint a new attorney general. So, when Joe Biden took over as president he appointed Merrick Garland, the Obama Supreme Court nominee that McConnell had stonewalled. In announcing his pick for attorney general Biden minced no words explaining that the DOJ would operate under different rules than it had under Trump. Speaking directly to Garland at the press conference, he said, "You won't work for me. You are not the president or the vice president's lawyer."[126] Biden also selected several heavyweight lawyers to work under Garland as US attorneys thus reversing many of the changes and some of the damage that Trump had caused at the DOJ.[127] The point is that Trump's radical attack on law enforcement institutions was serious but lacked longevity – at least insofar as his DOJ appointments were concerned.

---

[124] Schmidt and Broadwater 2022.   [125] Pew Research Center 2020a.   [126] Rigby 2021.
[127] Rigby 2021.

5.8 CONCLUSION

In countries where rulers have reoriented judicial and law enforcement institutions to serve their personal interests, democracy has suffered. Similarly, as several others have argued, Trump's efforts to change our federal judicial and law enforcement institutions posed a clear and present danger to American democracy.[128] The justice system is the core institutional mechanism for monitoring and enforcing federal law. Trump tried to radically reorient it to suit his own rather than the country's interests. He did so by installing people in transactional fashion whom he believed would be personally loyal to him above all else. He expected them to support his personal interests and when they defied his expectations, he bullied them mercilessly, and in some cases got rid of them. From a leadership perspective, his was an egregious narcissistic attempt to transform the justice system's institutional functions.

The changes he wrought to the judiciary were the most successful and the institutional damage the most serious because he replaced a record number of judges and justices, appointing them to lifetime positions. And by shifting the high court as well as the lower federal courts in a significantly more conservative direction, the institutional ramifications and damage going forward promise to be substantial insofar as the courts overturn fundamental pieces of legislation and their own legal precedents. Trump's attack on the DOJ's independence was less successful. Biden's ability to appoint a new attorney general and others in the department means that the institutional damage Trump caused will have a much shorter half-life than that which he inflicted on the judiciary, although questions about the DOJ's institutional integrity may linger in the public's mind.

The episodes described in this chapter reinforce and sometimes expand on arguments I made earlier. First, packing the courts with conservatives in lifetime appointments heralded a radical change in the functional orientation of the courts.[129] This supports the point that understanding institutional change requires paying attention to the function as well as the structure of institutions.

Second, the accumulation of judicial seats for Trump to fill and the gradual rise of the Federalist Society's influence on judicial nominations, which culminated in Trump's sudden and complete rejection of the traditional ABA rating system, were two tipping points that facilitated radical change in the judiciary. But Trump's judicial appointments may have also created a new tipping point – the possibility for the courts to radically reorient the law going forward. Tipping points can be both the cause and effect of institutional change.

Finally, this chapter suggests that the impact and longevity of radical institutional change depend on several things. Two already mentioned are the

---

[128] Kaufman and Haggard 2019; King and Ostrander 2020; Levitsky and Ziblatt 2018; Skowronek et al. 2021, p. 79.
[129] Ruiz and Gebeloff 2020.

presence of tipping points and the institutional capacity of new leaders to reverse or modify that change later. That capacity, of course, depends on the institutionalized rules determining who gets to make appointments and how long they last. By law, Biden was able to quickly replace Trump's personnel in the Justice Department but not on the federal bench or Supreme Court, although he did manage to fill new vacancies on the bench when they appeared, including appointing Ketanji Brown Jackson to the Supreme Court. A third thing that affects the impact and longevity of radical institutional change is the balance of power. Attempts at radical change often generate resistance. We've seen plenty of examples of that in this chapter. In the end, Trump's leadership skills were unable to overcome that resistance, which is one reason why he pardoned dozens of his personal allies and cronies at the end of his presidency – it was apparently payback, an effort to "lash out at the criminal justice system" for not having given him what he expected from it.[130] Transactional and bullying leadership, demands for personal loyalty, and narcissistic scheming didn't always yield the results Trump wanted, in part because professionals refused to be pushed around. As it turned out, that sort of resistance also emerged in other areas of the federal bureaucracy and civil service that Trump targeted for change.

[130] Schmidt et al. 2021.

6

You're Fired!

About a year into Trump's presidency, I sat on a flight home from Europe next to a twenty-year veteran of the US State Department. I asked him how things were going since Trump's Secretary of State, Rex Tillerson, had taken charge. He hesitated for a minute but then explained that things weren't going that well. Neither Trump nor Tillerson listened much to their career civil service professionals. Morale was as low as he'd ever seen it, several senior people had decided to take early retirement, and those remaining were often at odds with administration policies. He also said that because the State Department's reputation had been tarnished because of Trump's insulting and often isolationist foreign policies, it was having trouble recruiting young people to work there – a problem, he explained, that was creating a generational vacuum of expertise that would remain for years even after Trump was gone.

This anecdote illustrates a key part of Trump's attack on the deep state – his efforts to purge the federal bureaucracy, especially of people whose expertise he didn't respect or whom he felt were disloyal to him. Trump had no government experience but did know how to sack people and was famous for it, thanks to his television show *The Apprentice* where he confronted contestants who fell short of his expectations with two words: "You're fired!" This behavior was not limited to the Justice Department examples I described earlier – it was widespread throughout much of the federal bureaucracy.[1]

Bear in mind that institutions involve more than just rules, monitoring and enforcement mechanisms, and meaning systems. They also need people who sustain them by creating these rules, interpreting their meaning, and monitoring and enforcing their implementation. And in doing so they influence the functional orientation and efficacy of these institutions. The previous chapter

---

[1] Karl 2021, pp. xvi, chaps. 5 and 10.

showed how Trump tried to transform the deep state by functionally reorienting justice system institutions. This chapter explains how he tried to transform
the deep state by undermining the functional efficacy of the federal bureaucracy. He did this by targeting many government departments and agencies and
then changing their leadership, replacing them with his acolytes, getting rid of
senior civil service staff, and ignoring experienced and expert advice. This
attack benefited from a tipping point, rising public dissatisfaction with the
federal government. And it was rooted in key elements of Trump's leadership
style: demand for personal loyalty, intellectual arrogance, transactional and
bullying tactics, and narcissism. Bluntly put, this was a radical attempt at
bureaucratic sabotage that was broad in scope. It often triggered resistance,
which is why it didn't always succeed.[2] But when it did, the results
were damaging.

6.1 A TIPPING POINT AND THE NUMBERS

During the 2016 campaign Trump promised to slash the federal bureaucracy.
At one appearance he said he would "cut so much your head will spin." Trump
had spotted another tipping point. Political scientists William Howell and Terry
Moe have explained that public perceptions of ineffective government had been
mounting for decades, fostering anger and anxiety, and fueling support for
populist appeals. The Tea Party movement was one manifestation of that
discontent. Trump's election as president was another. According to a Gallup
poll, the public's level of dissatisfaction with the government had been growing
for at least two decades. In 2001, 30 percent of Americans said they were either
"dissatisfied" or "very dissatisfied" with how well the government worked but
by 2016 that number had more than doubled to 64 percent. Similarly, those
who reported being either dissatisfied or very dissatisfied with the size and
power of the federal government jumped from 47 percent to 62 percent.[3]
Howell and Moe show that Trump capitalized on this public discontent by
"spotlighting the failures of government, stoking the fires of populist anger, and
adopting a demagogic style of leadership that is right out of the populist playbook."[4] In short, Trump inspired voters who were fed up with the federal
government.

Once in office, Trump seemed to get off to a good start in delivering on his
promise. At the beginning of his term many people left the federal bureaucracy –
both civil servants and political appointees – and Trump imposed a hiring
freeze. During his first six months in office, more than 71,000 career employees
quit or retired, up from 50,000 who left during Obama's first half-year as
president.[5] However, the size of the federal civil service – those career civil

[2] Skowronek et al. 2021, p. 22.   [3] Gallup Polling 2021a.   [4] Howell and Moe 2020, p. 17.
[5] Rein 2017.

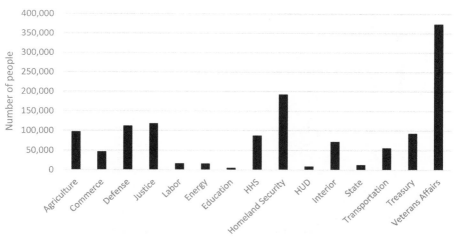

FIGURE 6.1. Cabinet department staffing, 2016.
Source: US Office of Personnel Management (2021).

servants hired based on merit and who typically keep their jobs during transitions of political leadership – eventually grew by about one hundred thousand positions.[6] The civil service is the essential core of the federal bureaucracy.

Although the civil service workforce grew by about 4 percent under Trump, this did not mean that his attack on the deep state bureaucracy failed. To begin with, there was a lot of variation across departments. Figure 6.1 compares the size of the civilian workforce in all the cabinet departments in 2016 just before he took office. Some like the Department of Veterans Affairs and Department of Homeland Security (DHS) were much larger than others. More important, Figure 6.2 shows how uneven the changes in staffing levels were under Trump. Nine of these fourteen departments suffered staff reductions. The Departments of Labor, Education, and Interior took the biggest hits. Meanwhile, growth was especially large in the DHS, Veterans Affairs, and Commerce. However, the Commerce Department was an anomaly because it conducts the US Census, which was taken in 2020 and, therefore, required a temporary increase in staffing.[7] But the point is that staff in most departments was reduced.

Furthermore, staffing reductions undermined agency performance – that is, institutional efficacy. For example, between 2016 and 2019 the Internal Revenue Service (IRS) staff declined by 6 percent, over 4,300 people. As a result, the agency's ability to audit wealthy individuals and corporations

---

[6] Light 2020; US Congressional Research Service 2020a.   [7] US Census Bureau 2018.

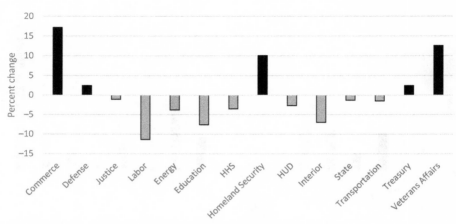

FIGURE 6.2. Change in cabinet department staffing, 2016–2020.
Note: Data are from September 2016 and 2020.
Source: US Office of Personnel Management (2021).

diminished too. Notably, the percentage of tax returns from rich people and corporations that the IRS audited dropped sharply after Trump came into office. This now costs the federal government roughly $175 billion a year in lost revenue due to tax evasion just by the super-rich.[8]

Similar stories unfolded at other agencies. Staff at the Centers for Disease Control and Prevention (CDC) dropped by 4 percent on Trump's watch.[9] At the Occupational Safety and Health Administration (OSHA) during Trump's first year in office inspection staff also declined by 4 percent. That number of employees continued to fall and by mid-2019 it had reached its lowest point in the agency's history. The effect of these reductions was not uniform. Nationwide the number of OSHA inspections remained fairly constant, but they declined significantly in several states. In Mississippi, for instance, which has one of the country's highest worker fatality and injury rates, the number of OSHA inspections fell by 26 percent during Trump's first year in office. Even after these positions are refilled, it takes months of training and experience in the field for inspectors to get up to speed. According to Jordan Barab, an OSHA inspector under Obama, "Even after OSHA hires someone, they can't just send them out to do an inspection by themselves. This will have an impact for years."[10] This is another example of the generational vacuum problem mentioned earlier.

---

[8] Ingraham 2021; US Internal Revenue Service 2019, Tables 17A, 31, and 32.
[9] Centers for Disease Control and Prevention 2021.
[10] Khimm 2018; Rainey 2019; US Occupational Safety and Health Administration 2021.

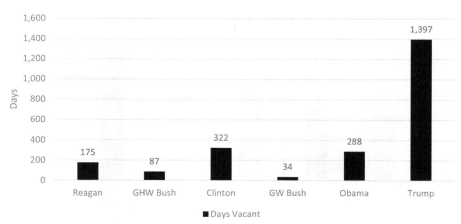

FIGURE 6.3. Cumulative days cabinet positions were vacant (as of June 6 in their third year).
Source: Witherspoon (2019).

Another illustration of how staff reductions hurt agency performance was the Environmental Protection Agency (EPA) where staffing fell to its lowest levels in at least a decade and cuts reduced expertise.[11] Annual surveys of federal employees conducted by the US Office of Personnel Management found that during Obama's last year in office 73 percent of EPA respondents reported that their agency was successfully accomplishing its mission but by 2019, two years into Trump's presidency, only 57 percent said so.[12] In short, by cutting staff the Trump administration seriously damaged the institutional efficacy of many state agencies and departments.

Perhaps more troubling was Trump's propensity for leaving top leadership positions empty. His move in this direction was unparalleled. For example, Figure 6.3 compares the cumulative number of days that positions in Trump's cabinet, such as the Secretary of State or Secretary of Defense, remained vacant compared to his five predecessors. Each day a cabinet position was vacant counts as one day. So, for instance, if the Secretary of Defense and Secretary of Commerce posts were each vacant for a week, the cumulative number of vacancy days would be fourteen. The vacancy number for each president depicted in the chart includes all vacancies through the middle of the third year of their first term in office. During this time various cabinet positions remained open for a total of almost 1,400 days during Trump's presidency.[13] All other

[11] Plumer and Davenport 2019; Sullivan et al. 2021; US Environmental Protection Agency 2021.
[12] US Office of Personnel Management 2016, 2019c.
[13] The following cabinet positions were left vacant: EPA director (237 days), Secretary of Homeland Security (191 days), chief of staff (160 days), UN representative (157 days),

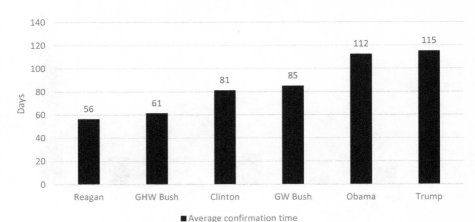

FIGURE 6.4. Average number of days for the Senate to confirm presidential nominations. *Source:* Center for Presidential Transition (2020).

presidencies paled in comparison. Bill Clinton and Barack Obama were the next closest to Trump. Yet Trump's cabinet experienced more than four times as many vacancy days as either the Clinton or Obama cabinets.[14]

It's possible that Trump's high vacancy score wasn't his fault. A new president needs to fill 3,000 to 4,000 political appointments of which about 1,200 require Senate confirmation. This includes cabinet positions. It might be, as Trump claimed, that the problem was that the Senate took a very long time to confirm his nominations. But this is unlikely judging by the average number of days the Senate took to confirm all of Trump's appointments.[15] Figure 6.4 reports the average time it took the Senate to confirm presidential appointments for presidents Reagan through Trump.[16] The average Senate confirmation time grew longer for each successive president. This was due to the increasingly common practice of senators delaying the confirmation process by placing "holds" on nominations or filibustering them. More to the point, the difference

Secretary of Defense (157 days), Secretary of Veterans Affairs (124 days), Secretary of Health and Human Services (122 days), attorney general (99 days), Secretary of the Interior (99 days), Secretary of State (26 days), and CIA director (25 days) (Witherspoon 2019).

[14] See also Lewis and Richardson (2021, p. 57).

[15] Lewis et al. 2018, p. 489; Lewis and Richardson 2021, p. 59.

[16] The data presented in Figure 6.4 only represent the time from the president's formal nomination of an individual to the time the Senate votes to confirm them. It excludes the time for vetting, background checks, security clearances, and other work that occurs prior to the president's formal nomination. This preliminary groundwork takes on average about 70 percent of the time involved in bringing someone through the full nomination and confirmation process. Nowadays the entire process can take anywhere from six months to a year (Center for Presidential Transition 2020).

between the average Senate approval time for Obama's and Trump's nominations was only three days, a miniscule difference especially when compared to the vast difference in the number of days that cabinet positions remained vacant for these two presidents – 1,109 days – as shown in Figure 6.3. Cabinet nominations were generally confirmed quicker than subcabinet nominations but, again, there was virtually no difference between Obama and Trump in the time involved for confirmation.[17] Trump's record number of days of cabinet vacancies was his own doing, not the Senate's.

6.2 QUANTITY VS. QUALITY

Changes in the federal civilian workforce were more than just a matter of numbers. They also involved a deterioration of experience and expertise. Events prior to Trump's inauguration foreshadowed this problem. The presidential nominees of both major political parties form transition teams in case they win the White House.[18] As a candidate Trump picked New Jersey governor Chris Christie to run his team. It prepared briefing books, agency landing teams, and lists of names to fill the most important of the president's many appointed positions. But soon after the election, Trump replaced Christie with vice president-elect Mike Pence and Trump's son-in-law Jared Kushner. They tossed out much of the work Christie's team had prepared and did very little to get ready for a transition. Furthermore, the Obama administration took extensive efforts to prepare seminars, presentations, briefing books and other materials for them. But Trump's team often ignored these efforts, sometimes not even showing up for briefings.[19] Finally, many highly qualified people in the bureaucracy were not invited to stay as they normally are during a transition of power. Nor were well-qualified replacements found for them.[20]

Once in office, Trump appointed people at the highest levels who often had absolutely no experience for their posts.[21] To name but a few, Secretary of State Rex Tillerson, former ExxonMobil CEO, had no foreign policy experience or diplomatic training. Secretary of Housing and Urban Development Ben Carson, a former pediatric neurosurgeon, had no experience for his post either. Betsy DeVos, who hailed from a billionaire family of big-time Republican donors, became the Secretary of Education. She had no experience as an educator or school administrator. Jared Kushner was appointed senior advisor to the president with an expansive portfolio including reforming criminal justice, managing relations with Mexico and China, orchestrating a government-wide reorganization, coping with the opioid epidemic, brokering peace between the

---

[17] Center for Presidential Transition 2020; Cook 2020.
[18] In 2015 Congress required each sitting president to provide briefings to the winner's transition team, although it had already been happening informally before that.
[19] Burke 2018; Cohen 2020, p. 310 ; Lewis 2018; Lewis et al. 2018.   [20] Lewis 2018, part II.
[21] Herbert et al. 2019, p. 80.

Israelis and Palestinians, and eventually organizing procurement of COVID-19 pandemic-related equipment – jobs for which he was extraordinarily ill prepared given that he was a high-end real estate developer. The president also brought in Ivanka Trump, his daughter and Kushner's wife, as another senior White House advisor although she, too, had no political or government experience.

Appointments like these were made for three reasons. One was that high-quality people with experience, integrity, and who took pride in their work – and in their reputations – often refused to consider taking positions in Trump's administration.[22] Another was that Trump had no political experience – a serious disadvantage for any leader – and, therefore, lacked the roster to fill many positions, especially second and third tier positions in the federal bureaucracy. Nor did he know many people who knew people who could fill them.[23] Finally, Trump privileged loyalty above all else. He was much less concerned with competence and merit than with fealty from his staff. This was also an indication of Trump's transactional leadership style. Indeed, he often fired perfectly competent people whom he believed had crossed him in one way or another. For instance, soon after Trump's first impeachment acquittal he fired several people who had testified under oath in ways that he perceived as being disloyal. This was a retribution campaign to root out deep-state foes and others he believed to have been his enemies.[24]

Underscoring Trump's obsession with loyalty was his appointment of Johnny McEntee, his long-time "body guy" who runs errands for the president and carries his bags on trips, to head the Presidential Personnel Office. His job was to vet and often hire presidential appointees throughout the federal government. McEntee had no experience for this job but was a loyal acolyte during the 2016 campaign and was charged with rooting out anybody in the government who might be disloyal to Trump, a task that he tackled with relish. As Jonathan Karl explains, McEntee was Trump's most loyal lieutenant and "would lead a witch hunt, browbeating cabinet secretaries, scouring voting records and social media accounts of officials high and low, conducting loyalty interviews, and installing inexperienced people with questionable backgrounds into some of the most sensitive and important positions in the US government."[25] The result was a massive purge from the federal bureaucracy of anyone McEntee and his team suspected of disloyalty to Trump. His targets included people at the DOJ, the EPA, the DHS, the Department of Housing and Urban Development, and the Department of Defense among others suspected of working against Trump inside the deep state.[26]

[22] Howell and Moe 2020, pp. 86–88.

[23] Herbert et al. 2019, pp. 145; Lewis et al. 2018, p. 489; Lewis and Richardson 2021, p. 59.

[24] Leonnig and Rucker 2021, pp. 49–50, 237, 361–362   [25] Karl 2021, p. 4.

[26] Karl 2021, chaps. 5 and 10. McEntee lost his White House job in 2018 for security reasons but Trump brought him back into the fold in February 2020 (Woodward and Costa 2021, p. 164).

Making matters worse, many of Trump's cabinet appointments were opposed to their department's traditional missions and were instructed to shrink the size of their departments and leave vacant jobs open, which meant that many posts – including many requiring the most experience – remained unfilled for months if not years.[27] As Stephen Bannon, one of Trump's senior White House advisors, put it, "If you look at these Cabinet appointees, they were selected for a reason and that is deconstruction of the administrative state."[28] For example, during the 2016 presidential campaign, Rick Perry, who Trump appointed later as Secretary of Energy, had vowed to shut down that agency if he ever got a chance. And Secretary of State Tillerson cut 30 percent of his department's staff, primarily through attrition and buyouts. Between December 2016 and September 2017, the size of the State Department's civilian workforce dropped by 6 percent and foreign service positions fell by 12 percent. A disproportionately large number of the departures were from the department's most senior and experienced ranks. As I was told on my flight home from Europe, few fresh faces were being hired to replace them. Ron Neumann, a 37-year foreign service veteran and former ambassador observed that, "You're throwing out the people at the top, so you're losing expertise. If you don't bring in people at the bottom...you're setting up a long-term problem."[29] That problem, of course, was a deterioration in the State Department's institutional efficacy.

Requiring Senate confirmation for many of the president's appointments is intended ostensibly as a source of quality control – another way to help ensure institutional efficacy. However, the Trump administration often side-stepped that process. One way was by appointing officials to high-level positions on an "acting" basis – that is, on a temporary basis, which did not require confirmation. For example, after Trump fired Defense Secretary Mark Esper for disagreeing with him – and in McEntee's eyes for failing the loyalty test – he appointed Christopher Miller, an apparent Trump loyalist, as Acting Secretary without Senate confirmation.[30] Trump liked this approach because he said it gave him the flexibility to install whomever he wanted for whatever reason without worrying about Senate approval. In Trump's first three years in office, he had twenty-eight acting cabinet secretaries – roughly the same number that both Obama and Clinton each had in their eight years in office.[31] The problem was that acting officials slow down the government and undermine its effectiveness. It's like running a school with a team of substitute teachers – caretakers with little interest in or effect on policymaking and long-term planning.[32] But the Federal Vacancies Reform Act limits how long a position can be filled in this way, usually about seven months.

[27] Herbert et al. 2019, chap. 4; Sanger 2021.
[28] Pfiffner 2018, p. 159. See also Lewis and Richardson (2021, p. 54). [29] Corrigan 2018.
[30] Karl 2021, chap. 10. [31] Bach 2019. Clinton had 27 cabinet secretaries and Obama had 23.
[32] Lewis et al. 2018, p. 491.

So, another way Trump avoided Senate confirmation – and circumvented the Vacancies Reform Act – was to put people into positions that didn't require confirmation at all and then delegate authority to them from vacancies higher up in the bureaucracy that did need Senate approval. For example, William Perry Pendley was appointed without the need for Senate confirmation as the deputy director of policy programs at the Bureau of Land Management. He was then delegated the authority of the director, a vacant position above his that did require confirmation.[33] In effect, he became the de facto director without Senate approval.

It's true that these strategies gave Trump flexibility in the appointment process. But critics charged that they were also used as an end-run around the Senate to install and promote people who would have had trouble passing muster in a confirmation hearing because they were either too inexperienced or represented fringe positions unacceptable to most senators – fringe positions that were consistent with Trump's personal views. Insofar as delegation was concerned, critics also worried that it was often used to hire people who knew that they could be fired arbitrarily at any time and, therefore, felt weak, vulnerable, and in a position where they had to kowtow to the president's wishes to keep their jobs. Put differently, the administration gave authority to people through acting appointments and delegation that ensured their loyalty to the president irrespective of their qualifications for the job. This was an egregious example of Trump's transactional leadership style.[34] According to Rebecca Jones at the Project on Government Oversight, a Washington watchdog organization, this sort of gamesmanship reached unprecedented levels under Trump.[35] Others agreed that "there was nothing subtle about this in the Trump administration."[36]

As a result, several agencies and departments became very politicized. This undermined employee morale, hurt prospects for recruiting a new generation of talented civil servants and, therefore, further compromised institutional efficacy. It was also one reason why quits and retirements rose on Trump's watch.[37] Again, the EPA is a case in point where more than 700 employees, including over 200 scientists, quit, retired, or took a buyout during the Trump years. Many left because they were shocked at administration policies designed either to roll back or gut long-standing environmental regulations, or stifle research and fact-based policymaking. Elsewhere in the federal bureaucracy, people were also discouraged by several government shutdowns and hiring freezes. Others were simply fed up with the lack of leadership in their departments, such as the Department of Housing and Urban Development, which seemed to drift aimlessly under the direction of its inexperienced leader, Ben Carson. Finally, morale deteriorated because many employees felt that in the

---

[33] Rose 2020; Skowronek et al. 2021, pp. 144–146.   [34] Skowronek et al. 2021, chap. 8.
[35] Rose 2020.   [36] Skowronek et al. 2021, p. 139.   [37] Rein 2017.

(a)

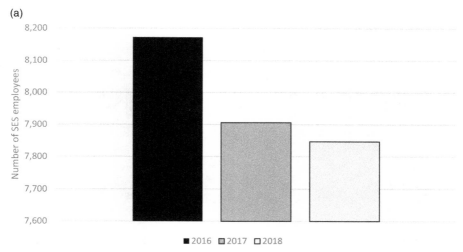

FIGURE 6.5A. Senior Executive Service employees, 2016–2018.

president's view, they were the enemy – part of the conspiratorial and corrupt deep state, not to be trusted or respected.[38]

What was particularly alarming was that although the number of departures from the rank-and-file civil service under Trump was not much greater than in past administrations, the number of departures from the Senior Executive Service (SES) – the top civil servant corps – was. Figure 6.5a shows that the total number of SES employees dropped sharply during the first two years of Trump's presidency. Figure 6.5b provides a more fine-grained view of these trends in all civilian cabinet departments. Except for the DHS, Veterans Affairs, and the Department of Transportation, all cabinet departments suffered net losses of SES personnel. These are the leaders who provide the major link – the transmission belt – between presidential appointees, such as cabinet secretaries and undersecretaries, and the rest of the career civil service. They are often responsible for policy decisions. In fact, under Trump they left at roughly twice the rate that they had during the early years of the Obama administration, often expressing concerns that Trump's political leadership was undermining career staff and, according to the US Office of Personnel Management's open-ended surveys, operating in ways that they described as "disturbing," "delusional," or "deceitful." The top factor influencing their departures, which were often voluntary, was the political environment in their department or agency – that is, conflicts with the Trump administration. Their departures wouldn't have been so troubling had they been replaced at a comparable rate. But they weren't – departures exceeded replacements. The hollowing out of the SES

---

[38] Badger et al. 2021.

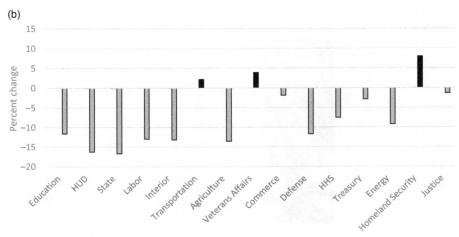

FIGURE 6.5B. Change in Senior Executive Service employees by cabinet department, 2016–2018.
Source: US Office of Personnel Management (2019a).

meant that there was less direction, oversight, and mentorship for the rest of the civil service than there would have been otherwise. This was a significant blow to the civil service bureaucracy, particularly because it exacerbated the generational leadership vacuum.[39]

The point is that Trump's prolonged vacancies, lackluster appointments, and staff cuts often reduced experience and expertise and, therefore, radically damaged institutional efficacy not just in the few agencies I've already mentioned, but across much of the federal bureaucracy. According to the Brookings Institution's John Hudak, Trump's promise to "drain the swamp" and reduce the size of government resulted in a flight of senior-level leadership and staff from the executive branch, a loss of expertise, and a deterioration in morale in many agencies and departments.[40] It happened in the Departments of Agriculture, Treasury, Homeland Security, State, and several others.[41] David Richardson and Mark Lewis surveyed thousands of high-level appointed and career federal civil servants in 2007 and again in 2020 to gauge their views of the competence of all types of government workers. By this metric they found a dramatic decline in the average competence of political appointees, senior civil servants, and low- to mid-level civil servants with the largest decline seen among Trump's political appointees. Nearly two-thirds of respondents – a sharp increase over time – also agreed that an inadequately skilled workforce

---

[39] Doherty et al. 2018; Lim 2020; US Office of Personnel Management 2019a, 2019b.
[40] The Brookings Institution 2020.   [41] Drezner 2020, pp. 194–196.

had made it more difficult for their agency to fulfill its mission.[42] Trump's transactional, bullying, and loyalty-based leadership was often to blame.

6.3 SCHEDULE F

Trump's most insidious and sweeping personnel strategy for transforming the federal bureaucracy's profile came just two weeks before the 2020 election. He issued Executive Order 13957 creating a new class of federal employees – the Schedule F classification – for positions of a "confidential, policy-determining, policy-making, or policy-advocating character" not normally subject to change because of a presidential transition.[43] These included scientists, regulators, public health experts, attorneys, and other senior civil service officials. This move did two important things that broke sharply with institutional precedent. On the one hand, it circumvented some but not all of the normal federal civil service rules that protected professional civil servants from political interference and arbitrary dismissal.[44] On the other hand, it made it easier to fill civil service positions with political appointees because Schedule F appointments required less scrutiny of their professional qualifications than would be the case for a regular civil service appointment. In other words, Schedule F would allow far more political leeway over who department and agency heads could fire and hire.

Departments and agencies throughout the government were ordered to identify positions for reclassification to Schedule F status. Tens of thousands of employees were eligible for reclassification. For instance, the Office of Management and Budget reclassified 88 percent of its positions, 425 employees, to Schedule F status – suddenly all could be sacked and replaced more easily. Republicans praised this and other moves like it. House Oversight and Reform Committee member James Comer (R-KY) saw it as another way to "drain the swamp" of "unelected, unaccountable federal government [employees] with the power to create policies that impact Americans' everyday lives."[45] But Democrats in Congress insisted that this was a ploy to purge the government of personnel who had been disloyal and critical of Trump and his policies.[46] Employee unions, federal management and advocacy organizations, and good government groups agreed. They feared that there would no longer be an independent civil service and that it was a step toward an authoritarian government.[47]

Some were also worried that the Schedule F order would accelerate the practice of "burrowing," that is, converting Trump's current political appointees to civil service status, thereby making it more difficult to fire them once a new

---

[42] Lewis and Richardson 2021.   [43] Lewis and Richardson 2021, p. 65.

[44] Even under Schedule F, however, civil service workers could not be fired for their political affiliation, whistleblower status, or for claiming discrimination or harassment.

[45] Ogrysko 2020.

[46] Alms and Mazmanian 2020; *The Los Angeles Times* 2020; Wagner 2020.

[47] Ogrysko 2020.

administration came to power. People classified as Schedule F were still part of the civil service and, therefore, harder to dismiss than someone who was just a political appointee like a cabinet secretary, undersecretary, or White House advisor. Here again Trump was playing the long game – installing loyalists that would remain for years after he was gone. It was like hiding booby traps in a field that would slow down anyone trying to move through it later.[48] This was a real concern. Ronald Sanders, who resigned as chair of the Federal Salary Council in protest over the Schedule F order, explained that although it would be easy for the next president to rescind the executive order, those political appointees who had already been converted to civil service status would be harder to remove.[49]

In sum, in a last-minute effort to undermine the deep state Trump's executive order sought to politicize much of the federal civil service, strip away some protections for nonpartisan expertise, and increase protections for his political hacks and faithful minions. Because the executive order language was so vague it could apply to any civil servant who had any discretion in giving policy advice or making decisions. It signaled a return to the patronage system where government jobs were awarded based on political loyalty rather than expertise and qualifications.[50] This was another manifestation of Trump's leadership traits – his insistence on personal loyalty and staff who told him what he wanted to hear. A group of House Democrats also feared that "the executive order…could precipitate an exodus from the federal government, leaving federal agencies without deep institutional knowledge, expertise, experience, and the ability to develop and implement long-term policy strategies."[51] Other critics agreed.[52] In other words, this was an unprecedented institutional change that would amplify the federal government's generational vacuum and further damage its institutional efficacy.

6.4 ADMINISTRATIVE CHURNING

Trump's attack on the deep state and his obsession with purging it of those suspected of disloyalty also caused a tremendous amount of turnover in his administration.[53] This was another example of radical institutional change. The turnover rate under Trump far exceeded that of the Obama, George W. Bush, and Clinton administrations.[54] For instance, Figure 6.6 compares the rate of turnover in cabinet positions in Trump's presidency with that of

---

[48] Sanger 2021.

[49] Alms and Mazmanian 2020; *The Los Angeles Times* 2020; Wagner 2020. The Federal Salary Council represents federal civil service employees and advises the administration on pay and salary issues. It is composed of presidential appointees, including three experts in labor relations and pay policy and six representatives of trade unions and other organizations representing these workers.

[50] Mitnick 2021.   [51] Wagner 2020.   [52] Ogrysko 2020.

[53] Hult 2021; Kumar 2019; Pfiffner 2018; Tenpas 2018.   [54] Yu and Yourish 2019.

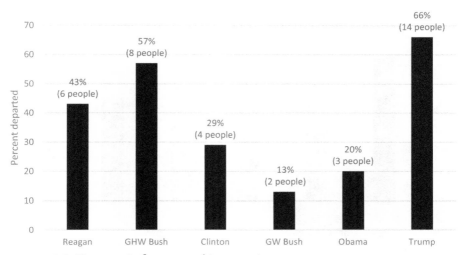

FIGURE 6.6. Turnover in first-term cabinet appointments.
Source: Tenpas (2020).

these other presidents during their first terms in office. Two-thirds of Trump's cabinet appointments left for one reason or another. This was three times the rate of departures seen during Obama's first term and five times the rate seen during George W. Bush's first term.[55]

The turnover rate was even higher when it came to the so-called "A Team," which included trusted and influential confidants, such as counselors to the president like Bannon and Kellyanne Conway; press secretaries like Sean Spicer and Sarah Huckabee Sanders; and various policy wonks, behind-the-scenes advisors, and others close to the president. These were people in the Executive Office of the President and did not include cabinet positions. Figure 6.7 compares A-team turnover during the first terms of Trump and his five predecessors. Over 92 percent of all A-team positions had at least one replacement on Trump's watch, far more than under the other presidents.[56] However, Figure 6.7 does not tell the whole story of A-team turnover because it does not reflect the fact that some positions turned over not once but several times. In other words, there was also a lot of churning *within* A-team positions. Table 6.1 shows how extensive these repeated turnovers were. Nearly half of the sixty A-team positions experienced at least two turnovers.[57] For instance, there were seven different communications directors and seven different deputy national security advisors in the Trump administration – roughly a new one every six months. Such record-breaking turnover created chaos and ineptitude

---

[55] Tenpas 2021.   [56] See also Tenpas 2018.   [57] Tenpas 2021.

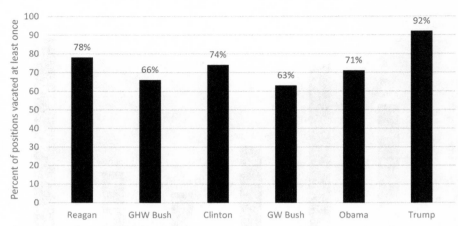

FIGURE 6.7. Percent of first-term A-team positions experiencing turnover.
Source: Tenpas (2021, 2020).

in the White House and throughout much of the Trump administration. By some accounts, it was so bad that some meetings were held in the dark because people couldn't find the lights and guests wandered around the West Wing looking for an exit after their meetings because the people in charge were so new that they didn't know their way around the place.[58] More alarming, a high turnover led to what some call a "random walk" presidency marked by indecision and constant flip-flopping on important policy issues.[59] Institutional efficacy suffered accordingly.

All in all, a revolving door marked Trump's administration at the highest levels: political loyalists entered while those he or his minions thought had either crossed him, or whose advice he didn't like left.[60] Trump's transactional and bullying leadership styles were obvious here too. But it was also apparent elsewhere. As political scientist Jeremy Mayer explains:

Trump demanded personal loyalty not just from political appointees, but from everyone throughout the federal government in a way unknown since the spoils system of the nineteenth century...No bureaucrat or cabinet officer could do or say anything even slightly out of sync with Trump's view of the day – for fear of public humiliation via Twitter.[61]

Others concur, noting that people in the administration learned that to stay in the president's good graces and keep their jobs required demonstrating fealty

---

[58] Karl 2021, pp. 151–152; Lewis et al. 2018, p. 486. See also Burke (2018), Pfiffner (2018), and Kumar (2019).
[59] Mayer 2021. For examples of such flip-flopping, see Edwards (2020, pp. 316–317).
[60] Herbert et al. 2019, chap. 6 and p. 205.   [61] Mayer 2020, p. 642.

TABLE 6.1. *Trump A-team positions that turned over twice or more*

Position	Number of Occupants	Position	Number of Occupants
Deputy Chief of Staff	4	National Security Adviser	4
Chief of Staff to the Vice President	3	Deputy National Security Adviser	7
Chief of Staff to the First Lady	3	AP for Homeland Security & Counterterrorism	4
Communications Director	7	Chief of Staff & Executive Secretary, NSC	4
Press Secretary	4	Senior Director of Intelligence, NSC	3
Director of Strategic Communications	3	Senior Director for Europe and Russia, NSC	6
Principal Deputy Press Secretary	4	Senior Director for Africa, NSC	3
Director of Public Liaison	3	Director of Domestic Policy Council	3
Director of Oval Office Operations	4	Deputy Director, National Economic Council & International Economic Affairs	5
Director of Presidential Personnel	3	Chair, White House Council of Economic Advisors	4
Staff Secretary	3	Deputy Director of the Domestic Policy Council & Director of Budget Policy	3
Director of Presidential Advance	4	White House Director of Legislative Affairs	4
Deputy White House Counsel	3	AP for Intergovernmental & Technology Initiatives	3

Source: Tenpas (2021).

to Trump rather than professional competence.[62] This created problems especially for people with experience and professional expertise.

6.5 DISDAIN FOR EXPERTISE

Trump was suspicious of and likely to turn against people who had facts, data, and expert opinions that contradicted his views. To disagree with Trump was often seen as evidence of disloyalty and an affront to his transactional leadership

---

[62] Mayer 2021, p. 85; Tenpas 2018. See also Kumar (2019, p. 232) and Pfiffner (2018).

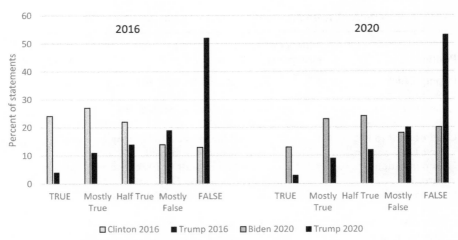

FIGURE 6.8. Truthfulness of public sentiments.
Source: PolitiFact (2021).

style. It was a clear manifestation of Trump's intellectual arrogance. After all, he often thought that he was the smartest person in the room and proclaimed himself a "stable genius" on several occasions.[63] The result was a radical depletion of expertise and experience in his administration and the federal bureaucracy, neither of which bode well for the government's institutional efficacy.

Trump's contempt for experts whose opinions differed from his own wasn't surprising insofar as he had a long track record of playing fast and loose with the truth and had expressed his distrust of experts long before he became president.[64] Figure 6.8 shows data from PolitiFact, a nonpartisan fact-checking organization, comparing the truthfulness of a sample of statements made by Hillary Clinton and Trump during the 2016 presidential campaign and Joe Biden and Trump during the 2020 campaign. What stands out in the graph is that Trump was far more likely to distort or misrepresent the facts than either Clinton or Biden. Judging especially from the very high percentage of falsehoods from Trump – more than twice that of either Clinton or Biden – it appears that Trump was far less wedded to the facts than the others – another dramatic departure from conventional political discourse.[65] By one estimate, Trump uttered over 30,000 factually incorrect statements during his tenure in office – averaging over twenty per day and as many as fifty a day in the run-up

---

[63] Rucker and Leonnig 2020, p. 6.
[64] Herbert et al. 2019, pp. 79–87; Karl 2021, pp.27, 52, 94–95.
[65] The data on "false" statements combines two PolitiFact categories – statements that are false (factually incorrect) and statements that are termed "pants on fire" (not only incorrect but ridiculous).

to the 2020 election, culminating, of course, in the Big Lie.[66] By some accounts, Trump's disdain for expertise and facts has caused institutional damage that will not be easily remedied.[67] Let me explain.

Reflecting his contempt for expertise and facts if they didn't suit his purposes, many of Trump's loyal political appointees shut down or impeded government scientific research on his behalf in areas including the environment, climate change, health, agriculture, and the economy where the research threatened Trump's beliefs or policy preferences. Professor of law, Wendy Wagner, who studies the use of science by policymakers wrote that these moves "mark a sharp departure with the past," a radical institutional change.[68] A 2018 survey of scientists at sixteen federal agencies found that half of the respondents said that their work had come under attack from Trump's political appointees and that political interests "hindered the ability of their agencies to make science-based decisions."[69] Hundreds of frustrated government scientists departed as a result. As a former top climate-policy expert in the Interior Department told reporters, "Regulations come and go, but the thinning out of scientific capacity in the government will take a long time to get back."[70] Indeed, after Trump left office, recruitment continued to suffer because government science jobs were no longer viewed as insulated from politics so people – especially young people – were reluctant to go into government service. For example, Stan Meiburg, a 38-year EPA veteran now directing graduate studies in sustainability at Wake Forest University, reported that "my students have told me, 'I believe in what EPA's trying to do, but I'm worried that the outcomes of my work will be dictated by the political leaders and not by what the science actually says.'"[71] His students were reluctant to work for the federal government. This was evidence of Trump's intellectual arrogance permeating his administration and creating a generational vacuum of experience and expertise undermining the government's institutional efficacy.

Examples of Trump's disregard for well-established expert knowledge are legion.[72] For instance, he insisted on deep cuts in individual and corporate income taxes dismissing advice from some of his own advisors and congressional experts that it would significantly increase budget deficits and the national debt.[73] He also rejected conclusions from his intelligence agencies in early 2019 that North Korea would keep developing its nuclear arsenal; that China and Russia were serious cyber threats to the United States; and that the Islamic State of Iraq and Syria (ISIS) would continue to stoke violence in the Middle East. Despite evidence to the contrary, he also refused to believe that Iran remained in compliance with a 2015 nuclear agreement. He was wrong about all of this; his advisors were right. Trump's first Defense Secretary James Mattis, a former

---

[66] Packer 2021; Spocchia 2021.   [67] Stuckey 2021, p. 135.   [68] Plumer and Davenport 2019.
[69] Badger et al. 2021.
[70] Plumer and Davenport 2019. See also Davenport and Friedman (2019).
[71] Davenport et al. 2021.   [72] Sanger and Barnes 2019.   [73] Blom 2018; Tankersley 2018.

four-star Marine Corps general, was clear in his letter of resignation that he was quitting because Trump wouldn't listen to him.[74] Similarly, after being fired by Trump, Rex Tillerson told a reporter that during his tenure as Secretary of State he had become increasingly exasperated with a president who disregarded his advice and was clueless about how to conduct foreign policy. According to Tillerson, "When the president would say, 'Here's what I want to do and here's how I want to do it.' And I'd have to say to him, 'Well Mr. President, I understand what you want to do, but you can't do it that way. It violates the law. It violates treaty.'" Tillerson added that it had been frustrating working for a man who "doesn't read briefing reports [and] doesn't like to get into the details of a lot of things" that his advisors bring to his attention.[75] To state the obvious, both Mattis and Tillerson, not to mention others, left the administration – sometimes voluntarily but sometimes not – after telling Trump things that he didn't believe and didn't want to hear.[76] In short, they couldn't stand Trump's inexperience, intellectual arrogance, and obsession with loyalty anymore.

At times Trump's willingness to ignore the most basic scientific evidence was laughable. For instance, in September 2019 he said publicly that hurricane Dorian would hit Alabama before moving up the east coast. This was a mistake and when asked about it the National Weather Service said that according to their modeling the storm would miss Alabama. Yet Trump refused to concede his error. And a few days later he tried to back up his statement at a press conference holding up a National Weather Service map projecting the hurricane's path, but with that track extended on the map into Alabama, apparently by the hand of someone with a black Sharpie marker – Trump's preferred writing instrument – which suggested to many people that Trump had doctored the map to fit his erroneous prediction.[77] Poking fun at the president, the media quickly labeled the episode "Sharpiegate."

At other times, Trump's disdain for scientific expertise wasn't funny. For instance, the Department of Agriculture relocated most staff positions at two of its key research agencies from Washington DC to Kansas City, Missouri. One was the National Institute of Food and Agriculture (NIFA), which funds and coordinates agriculturally related scientific research. The other was the Economic Research Service, which studies global food production and related issues. The administration said this was a move to improve efficiency, but critics complained that it was an attempt to undermine the quality and breadth of the work these two agencies did. In particular, they charged that the relocation was an attack on science and the agencies that produce it in the public interest, notably the science of climate change and its impact on agriculture. Trump had long been skeptical of climate change and the science around it. Critics also accused the Department of Agriculture of burying politically sensitive research reports that the Trump administration didn't like, and, assuming that many

---

[74] Mattis 2018.   [75] Straqualursi 2018.   [76] Karl 2021, chaps. 1 and 5.   [77] Shepard 2019.

people would refuse to move to Kansas City, that the relocation was simply a ruse to gut both agencies of their research staff and stifle their work. It worked. About 75 percent of the employees working in these two agencies refused relocation and quit. As a result, according to Tom Bewick, a national program leader at NIFA, "All of that expertise is gone." However, he also explained that some of the people who agreed to move, including himself, did so partly as an act of resistance "to make sure that NIFA's legacy as the preeminent science organization is not completely lost."[78] Nevertheless, the former director of NIFA told reporters that "it will take 5 to 10 years to rebuild" that staffing and expertise.[79] Similar relocation efforts were underway at the Bureau of Land Management and other agencies.[80] A former toxicologist at the EPA said that the loss of experienced scientists can erase years or decades of institutional memory.[81] These were all cases where Trump was creating generational vacuums of expertise that seriously undermined the long-term efficacy of state institutions – a key indication of radical institutional change.

A staff report for the House Committee on Science, Space and Technology concluded that the Trump administration had displayed "open hostility towards federal scientists and the federal workforce in general" and that "the four years of the Trump Administration were devastating for the federal scientific workforce. Throughout many of the federal government's civilian scientific agencies, career scientists experienced political interference, bureaucratic obstruction, and personal retaliation."[82]

Trump's disregard for expert advice bled into policymaking. For instance, as noted earlier, he pulled the United States out of the Iran nuclear agreement after rejecting evidence from his advisors and the intelligence community that Iran was complying with the terms of that agreement. He also announced a sudden troop withdrawal from Syria despite warnings from his military advisors that this might lead to the slaughter of Syrian Kurds who had worked with the United States by Turkish forces on the border. Both decisions exacerbated dangerous tensions in the Middle East and soured America's relationships with several of its allies in the region and beyond. He ignored data showing that immigrants were less inclined toward criminal activity and terrorism than American citizens and unlikely to take away Americans' jobs or reduce their wages. Instead, he moved quickly to restrict immigration from several predominantly Muslim countries and tried to bully Congress into authorizing funds to build a wall along the Mexican border to keep asylum seekers from Mexico and Central America from entering the country – a wall that just about everyone in Washington realized would not solve the problem. Furthermore, and again

---

[78] Morris 2019; US Congressional Research Service 2020b. In fact, the Senior Executive Service experienced a sharp rise in the percentage of reassignments requiring relocation after Trump took office (US Government Accountability Office 2020, Figure 2).
[79] Plumer and Davenport 2019.   [80] Beck 2020.   [81] Plumer and Davenport 2019.
[82] US House Committee on Science, Space, and Technology 2021.

contrary to expert advice, Trump encouraged the heads of his own government agencies to scale back all sorts of regulations and their enforcement, including those designed to prevent another financial crisis, protect the environment, and mitigate climate change.[83] In July 2019, in a nod to the industry, the administration also relaxed rules on infection control in nursing homes, a move that disturbed public health experts and eventually contributed to the spread of COVID-19 in these facilities.[84] It is clear from these and other examples that Trump was more than willing to turn his back on the experienced and expert advice he was receiving from his advisors and staff because he assumed that he knew best what to do.

Thanks to the Trump-inspired bureaucratic brain drain, by the time Joe Biden took over much of the government's scientific work remained unfinished. For example, intelligence agencies were far behind schedule for delivering risk assessments to the president regarding climate change because even with new people in place it took time to train them and integrate them into the day-to-day work of these agencies. The EPA faced what one former agency scientist called "a massive backlog" of work; new climate rules and clean air regulations ordered by Biden would likely be held up for years. The Department of Energy was behind on designing efficiency standards for appliances. The Defense Department was behind on evaluating the risks of climate change for national security. And the Interior Department was behind on studying the impacts of drought, heat waves and rising sea levels.[85]

Trump's contempt for scientific and policy expertise was underscored by the fact that he even ignored the advice of experts that he had appointed and who eventually pushed back against him. For instance, Trump's wish to pull the United States out of the NAFTA and the Trans-Pacific Partnership was opposed by several in the administration, including Gary Cohen, who headed the National Economic Council and who, until he left the NEC, quietly spirited away drafts of withdrawal letters from the president's desk before Trump had a chance to see and sign them.[86] Similarly, Defense Secretary Mark Esper and Joint Chiefs of Staff chairman Mark Milley often delayed actions that Trump thought were a good idea until he changed his mind, but that defense and military experts knew were dangerously misguided and under most circumstances illegal, including deploying the US Army to quell Black Lives Matter protests.[87] Furthermore, in late 2019, the EPA's Scientific Advisory Board, which evaluates the scientific integrity of EPA policies, condemned the Trump administration's plans to rewrite Obama-era regulations curbing tailpipe emissions, to roll back part of the Clean Water Act, and to limit the scientific data that could be used to draft health regulations. The scientists on the panel, over a quarter of whom were Trump appointees and often from industry, charged that

---

[83] Wolf 2019.   [84] Koronowski et al. 2020.   [85] Davenport et al. 2021.
[86] Skowronek et al. 2021, pp. 66–71.   [87] Karl 2021, pp. 42, 161.

the administration's policies were without scientific merit. They worried that the agency's institutional efficacy was being radically eroded.

These were not the only times that the government's institutional efficacy was damaged either because Trump ignored the science and counsel of his own experts whom he didn't believe, or because he pushed aside people whom he suspected of disloyalty simply because they contradicted him.[88] But one example of such intellectual arrogance stood out from all the rest. And the results were deadly.

6.6 THE COVID-19 PANDEMIC

By the time Trump left office in January 2021, nearly 400,000 Americans had died of COVID-19 and more than 24 million had been infected. The Trump administration badly fumbled how it handled the crisis. In part this was because Trump was obsessed with the upcoming election rather than the pandemic – an indication of his extraordinary narcissism.[89] But it was also due to his desire to reduce, sideline, or ignore government departments, agencies, programs, and individuals as part of his attack on the deep state because he didn't believe what they said, because they undermined his political ambitions, or because he doubted their loyalty. Scientific expertise took a back seat to political expediency in ways that grossly undermined the institutional efficacy of the government's public health apparatus and the administration's response to the pandemic.

To begin with, the Obama administration held a pandemic-response briefing for incoming Trump administration officials, which detailed specific challenges they might face in the event of a pandemic. These included coping with shortages of antiviral drugs, ventilators, personal protective equipment, and other essential medical paraphernalia. That was three years before the COVID-19 pandemic hit. By mid-March 2020 – three months into the coronavirus crisis – two-thirds of the Trump administration's representatives at that briefing were no longer in the administration and these supply shortages had not been fixed.[90]

The administration also cut staff and funding for the CDC and appointed key directors for reasons of political loyalty rather than merit, all of which demoralized doctors and other professionals, many of whom left the agency as a result.[91] The administration tossed aside the Obama administration's sixty-page pandemic playbook on how to limit America's exposure to a dangerous virus, and stopped pandemic modeling by the DHS, which it had been doing since 2005 to predict the impact a pandemic would have on hospitals, clinics, and other key infrastructure.[92] Trump also disbanded the

---

[88] Davenport and Friedman 2019. [89] Karl 2021, p. 54.
[90] Koronowski et al. 2020; US House Committee on Oversight and Reform 2020.
[91] Gerstle 2022, p. 281. [92] Koronowski et al. 2020.

Obama administration's Global Health Security and Biodefense Unit, which since its establishment in 2014 had been responsible for pandemic prepared-ness. Its head, Timothy Ziemer, the top National Security Council (NSC) official for pandemic preparedness, quit. His departure followed the removal of Tom Bossert, a DHS advisor who had called for a comprehensive biode-fense strategy against pandemics. Bossert's exit was part of the elimination of the Trump administration's NSC global health national security team. The administration claimed that this was a move to streamline and shrink NSC staff. Whether this improved NSC efficiency is debatable, but it did little to improve the Trump administration's response to the COVID-19 crisis.[93] In fact, Trump got rid of many of the national security and intelligence advisors who might have urged him to take the pandemic more seriously and replaced them with loyal yet inexperienced people, often in "acting" capacities as described earlier.[94]

Before the pandemic Trump also disregarded a September 2019 warning from his Council of Economic Advisors that a pandemic could kill a half-million people and wreck the economy. He ignored similar warnings from the intelligence community after the COVID-19 outbreak in China in late 2019 and then in the United States in early 2020. By early February, warnings like these had grown more urgent. CDC director Robert Redfield and Alex Azar, head of the Department of Health and Human Services (HHS), were raising red flags in the White House. In typical bullying fashion Trump labeled Azar an alarmist and badgered Redfield to tow the party line. During this time public health experts at the White House were at odds with the president trying to convince him that he needed to take bold steps to prevent a major public health and economic disaster. Yet for months Trump denied that there was a serious problem. It wasn't until March 13, 2020 that he declared a national emergency.[95]

There are many other examples of Trump's arrogant disdain for expert public health and medical advice that damaged the government's institutional efficacy in handling the pandemic.[96] For instance, Trump and his staff repeat-edly undercut or ignored CDC analysis and advice about the pandemic. The US House Subcommittee on the Coronavirus Crisis found that the White House blocked CDC briefings and media appearances for months; that Trump officials in the Office of Management and Budget played a central role in altering CDC public health guidance; and that CDC officials were instructed to destroy evidence proving that the administration had tried to stop the publication of truthful scientific reports believed to be damaging to Trump.[97] In one case, the

---

[93] Mayer 2020, pp. 633, 639; Reuters Fact Check 2020.   [94] Mayer 2020, p. 633.
[95] Glanz and Robertson 2020; Koronowski et al. 2020.
[96] The examples that follow are documented in Koronowski et al. (2020).
[97] US House Subcommittee on the Coronavirus Crisis 2021.

administration edited CDC guidelines removing recommendations that houses of worship consider suspending in-house services and other programs for the foreseeable future in order to help mitigate the spread of the virus. At one point four former CDC leaders condemned Trump's politicization of the agency's COVID-19 guidelines saying that for the first time in their collective memory the CDC's "sound science is being challenged with partisan potshots."[98] In another case, the administration ordered hospitals to stop reporting COVID-19 data to the CDC and instead send it to HHS for analysis. Several public health experts expressed alarm that this would politicize and taint the data analysis. Thomas File, president of the Infectious Diseases Society of America, said that "COVID-19 data collection and reporting must be done in a transparent and trustworthy manner and must not be politicized...Collecting and reporting public health data is a core function of the CDC, for which the agency has the necessary trained experts and infrastructure."[99] CDC scientists were being stripped of much of their authority and independence in responding to the pandemic.[100] All this amounted to a systematic effort to bully experts into submission for Trump's personal political interests.

Another example of how Trump used the pandemic to further his own political interests involved his treatment of certain state governments. He used the precautions that some state governments were taking to contain the virus as a wedge issue in the culture wars I mentioned in Chapter 4. In the name of individual freedom, he urged his supporters to "liberate" states like Michigan, Virginia, and Minnesota from the restrictions their governors had imposed to thwart COVID-19's spread. Here he was pandering to his political base. Furthermore, when governors criticized his handling of the pandemic, he threatened that they wouldn't receive federal help in procuring pandemic supplies – another example of his transactional and bullying leadership style as well as putting his own political interests ahead of the public health of the country.[101] At one point Trump accused the Food and Drug Administration (FDA) of sabotaging vaccine development and authorization, suggesting publicly that this was a deep-state conspiracy to slow down the process and hurt his chances for reelection – an accusation dripping in paranoid suspicions of disloyalty. In his words, "The deep state, or whoever, over at the FDA is making it very difficult for drug companies to get people to test the vaccines and therapeutics. Obviously, they are hoping to delay the answer until after November 3rd," which was election day.[102] There was no evidence to support his accusation. The FDA was following its own well-established scientific review protocol and publicly rejected Trump's charges. Eight high-level FDA

---

[98] Pfiffner 2021, pp. 102–103.   [99] Jercich 2020.   [100] Kaplan et al. 2020.
[101] Mayer 2020, p. 637.
[102] Pfiffner 2021, p. 103. See also Woodward and Costa (2021, pp. 113–115).

administrators issued a joint statement warning that real or perceived political interference could destroy the agency's credibility.[103]

Even as public health experts reported that coronavirus infections and deaths were surging exponentially in the United States, Trump continued to ignore this evidence and deny that things were out of control, downplaying the severity of the crisis and blaming the rising rates on improved and more widespread testing for the virus – another claim that did not stand up to scientific scrutiny.[104] Again, it was all about making himself look good in the eyes of the voters, not getting the pandemic under control. This was narcissism in the extreme.

In April 2020, Dr. Rick Bright, the director of the Biomedical Advanced Research and Development Authority (BARDA), and a leading expert on coronavirus vaccine development resigned, charging that he was pushed out because he resisted Trump's efforts to divert research funding toward unproven treatments, including hydroxychloroquine, a malaria drug that Trump had touted during a press conference as a possible cure for the virus. This was yet another example of an expert being fired for disloyalty. Bright called for the HHS Inspector General to investigate why Trump pressured BARDA to fund companies with political connections to pursue treatments lacking scientific promise.

By late summer 2020 Trump was tweeting criticisms against Drs. Anthony Fauci and Deborah Birx, both esteemed members of the White House Coronavirus Task Force, for sounding alarms and issuing continually pessimistic – that is, realistic, data-based – warnings about the spread of the disease. Unbeknown to Birx, he brought in Kevin Hassett, his former chairman of the Council of Economic Advisors, on a special assignment to quietly work with a small team to build a statistical model showing far fewer COVID-19 fatalities than Birx's model had shown. Trump targeted Fauci because he often publicly contradicted Trump's false claims about the pandemic – and perhaps because his public approval ratings, much to Trump's chagrin, were much higher than the president's.[105] So, Trump eventually brought in Dr. Scott Atlas to serve as his new pandemic advisor. Atlas was a radiologist who had no background in either epidemiology or infectious disease but was a senior fellow at the conservative Hoover Institute and appeared frequently on Fox News supporting Trump's views on the pandemic. Atlas' recommendations that, for instance, wearing masks and social distancing were ineffective and that the country should seek herd immunity without efforts to mitigate the spread of the virus, were roundly criticized by the expert medical and public health community. Yet

---

[103] Kaplan et al. 2020. See also Leonnig and Rucker (2021, pp. 281, 284, 368).
[104] Trump later claimed that he knew how serious the danger was but didn't want to say so publicly for fear of creating a panic (Woodward 2020, p. 286).
[105] Leonnig and Rucker 2021, pp. 98, 218–221.

it was Atlas who had the president's ear because he told Trump what he wanted to hear, pandering to the president's intellectually arrogant leadership style and demand for loyalty.[106] Atlas took over because Trump believed he was a loyal lieutenant; Trump and Birx were sidelined because they didn't demonstrate enough fealty to the president.

Given Trump's dismissal of so much public health information and advice, it was little surprise when the Harvard School of Public Health released a scathing report lambasting the administration's handling of the pandemic. The report concluded that "the evidence suggests that ineffective national policies and responses, especially as compared to those of other wealthy nations or compared to the intricate preparation and planning by previous administrations of both parties, have been driving the terrible toll of COVID-19 and its inequities in the U.S."[107] The prestigious British medical journal, *The Lancet*, drew similar conclusions charging that Trump's "Disdain for science and cuts to global health programs and public health agencies have impeded the response to the COVID-19 pandemic, causing tens of thousands of unnecessary deaths."[108] *The Lancet* found that roughly 40 percent of coronavirus deaths in the United States during the Trump administration could have been prevented if the average COVID-19 death rate matched that of other wealthy nations.[109] Other estimates were equally if not more damning.[110]

The combination of demanding transactional fealty, trying to advance his personal political interests above all else, and dismissing inconvenient facts and advice took a serious toll on the administration's institutional capacity for effectively handling the pandemic. As political scientist Kenneth Mayer put it, COVID-19 exposed the pathologies of Trump's approach to the presidency – particularly his intellectually arrogant dismissal of administrative expertise – in a catastrophic fashion.[111] By ignoring the advice of government experts at the CDC, FDA, HHS, and other agencies, Trump tried to minimize the seriousness of the pandemic, to make himself look good in an election year.[112] He bullied and tried to dispense with those who disagreed with him and failed to express their loyalty. By some accounts, Trump's crisis response was among the worst in presidential history.[113] To his credit, however, he did heed the advice of some scientific advisors and launched Operation Warp Speed, which encouraged the pharmaceutical industry to move fast to develop effective vaccines, although his administration did not develop a coherent vaccine distribution plan.[114] Nevertheless, millions of Americans got sick, and hundreds of thousands died – many needlessly – because Trump's refusal to listen to his own expert advisors seriously damaged the state's institutional efficacy. His downplaying of the crisis, his public disdain for mask-wearing and social distancing, and his refusal

---

[106] Leonnig and Rucker 2021, pp. 229–230.   [107] Hanage et al. 2020.
[108] Woolhandler et al. 2021.   [109] Woolhandler et al. 2021, p. 7.
[110] Sebenius and Sebenius 2020.   [111] Mayer 2021, p. 80. See also Stuckey (2021, p. 140).
[112] Shear et al. 2021.   [113] Mayer 2020, p. 629.   [114] Woodward and Costa 2021, p. 113.

to say whether he had been vaccinated all helped fuel an anti-vaccination, anti-mask-wearing, and antisocial distancing backlash that perpetuated the crisis with disastrous effects even after he left office. The administration's inept response to the pandemic also damaged Trump's political support among voters, notably suburban middle-class Republicans and independents, which probably cost him the 2020 election.[115]

6.7 CONCLUSION

Trump carried out his radical attack on the federal bureaucracy on several fronts. The results were mixed. Some of his efforts succeeded: positions remained vacant; civil servants were replaced with political appointees; scientists and other experts were ignored or purged; and generational vacuums of experience, knowledge, and expertise were created. Some of his efforts failed, notably the attempt to reduce the overall size of the civil service. Of those that failed, some were resisted, and some were eventually reversed. But by the end of Trump's tenure there were so few competent people left around the president that some politicians on Capitol Hill worried privately that "all of the guardrails were gone" to prevent Trump from doing dangerous things.[116] They weren't the only ones concerned. Chairman of the Joint Chiefs Mark Milley was so worried that Trump might try to do something terrible during the final weeks of his administration that he twice contacted his Chinese counterpart in the People's Liberation Army, first to reassure him that the United States would not attack China and that if an attack were imminent Milley would warn him ahead of time, and second to tell him that despite the January 6 insurrection at the Capitol the United States was not on the verge of a revolution. He also helped deter Trump from sending federal troops against Black Lives Matter protestors and dissuaded him from attacking Iran. And on several occasions Mitch McConnell and various cabinet members tried to keep Trump's demands and orders within the range of normal presidential behavior.[117]

In addition to his suspicions of and disdain for the deep state, three things drove much of Trump's attack on the bureaucracy. One was his intellectual arrogance – that is, his belief that he was at least as smart as anyone who might try to give him advice. This was one of the pillars upon which his transactional leadership style rested. Another was his insistence on personal loyalty. And the two were intimately connected. After all, why wouldn't someone who was supremely confident in their intellectual abilities – a self-proclaimed stable genius – expect loyalty from those working for them who presumably weren't as smart as the boss? The final thing underlying his attack on the bureaucracy, at least insofar as handling the pandemic was concerned,

[115] Gerstle 2022, p. 281.   [116] Leonnig and Rucker 2021, pp. 341, 493.
[117] Woodward and Costa 2021, chaps. 19–22, 25–26.

was his narcissistic conviction that his interest in reelection took precedence over the public interest in moving beyond the crisis. All of this was a matter of deeply flawed leadership.

The radical nature of Trump's attack on the deep state was clear. First, his effort to sabotage the deep state bureaucracy was not incremental – it was a sharp and decisive break from the past. He ordered his cabinet to make swift and dramatic personnel cuts in their departments. He failed to fill cabinet-level vacancies leading to the accumulation of an unprecedented number of days where departments were operating without a permanent secretary or director. He signed an extraordinary executive order – Schedule F – that would have reclassified tens of thousands of federal civil servants, making them more vulnerable to dismissal and, therefore, more likely to support his policies, or at least keep quiet if they disagreed with them. He disparaged and ignored expert advice and scientific evidence. Compared to previous modern-day presidents, this was all quite extraordinary and sudden. It all points to the fact that if you want to orchestrate radical institutional change, you can do it not only by attacking rules, norms, monitoring, and enforcement, but also by attacking the people responsible for these things and for how effectively institutions are run.

Second, the changes Trump orchestrated were sweeping in scope. Many departments and agencies suffered personnel cuts. Many cabinet positions were filled with loyalists lacking appropriate experience for their jobs. High rates of leadership turnover occurred across the administration and bureaucracy.

Third, some of Trump's moves had long-lasting effects. Notably, the reputational consequences of what Trump had been doing to the State Department, EPA, research units in the Department of Agriculture, and other targeted departments and agencies were bad enough and well-known enough that it would be difficult any time soon to refortify them with young talented recruits. Indeed, many agencies witnessed the development of generational vacuums of expertise and experience that would be difficult to rectify in the near term. Senior-level experience, talent, and expertise would be especially hard to replace. The government's institutional efficacy would suffer as a result. This suggests that the continued efficacy of institutions depends in part on perceptions of their legitimacy, both to insiders who might be so disillusioned with them that they quit or blow the whistle, and to outsiders who might otherwise be interested in joining them. As I explained in previous chapters, when the legitimacy of an institution breaks down internally and then spills over into the public realm, the institution suffers, and that damage may last for a long time.

That said, the arrival of a new president – a change in leadership – muted some of these potentially long-term effects. Biden moved quickly to fill many but certainly not all of the administrative vacancies left by Trump. He also replaced Trump's administrative appointees as best he could. According to *The New York Times*, "The Biden team arrived in Washington not only with [personnel] plans for each department and agency, but the spreadsheets detailing who would carry them out."[118] He moved quickly to nominate or install about 1,000 officials, roughly a quarter of all the political appointee jobs in the federal government, within a few weeks of his inauguration.[119] At the NSC Biden nearly doubled the number of staff ready to begin working to rebuild state capacities in climate, cyber, global health security, biodefense, and other policy areas that Trump had depleted. Similar stories about rebuilding state capacities played out at the DOJ, the HHS, the DHS, the EPA, and other departments and agencies.[120]

Furthermore, Biden rescinded the Schedule F order. He also moved to dismiss many holdovers from the Trump administration regardless of the legal consequences of doing so, including those that Trump had burrowed into the bureaucracy. Biden was fully aware that people like this had been installed in the first place as part of Trump's plan to neuter the deep state and prevent his policies from being overturned by a new administration. Biden sacked people like this, put others on administrative leave, or found other ways to sideline them.[121] According to the House Majority Leader Steny Hoyer (D-MD), "This begins the process of reversing the Trump Administration's all-out assault on federal employees."[122] But as Hoyer implied, this was only a start. It would take years to repair all the administrative damage Trump had done.

Biden also tried to replace inexperience with experience and expertise. For instance, he vowed to fill State Department vacancies with well-trained professional career officials or retired foreign service officers rather than partisan political loyalists as Trump had done. He replaced inexperienced people at the Department of Housing and Urban Development with others well-versed in tackling housing and urban problems.[123] But again, this was just a start.

For these reasons Trump's radical attack on the federal bureaucracy was not entirely successful – at least not in the long run. The point is that leadership mattered, which is why it behooves institutional theorists to take it more seriously than they have in the past. Of course, Biden was able to do all this because he had decades of experience in government, knew people to appoint, or at least knew people who knew who to appoint, and was willing to listen to advisors whose views might differ from his own. Quite the opposite from Trump, for Biden loyalty was nice but competence was what counted.

But beyond that, two other factors limited Trump's long-term impact on the bureaucracy. One was institutional. Although Schedule F made it easier to hire and fire, it didn't eliminate all protections for civil servants. In other words, there were still rules in place that prevented Trump and his minions from doing even more damage to the civil service. Another factor was political. There was plenty of pushback and resistance from people inside and occasionally outside

---

[118] Sanger 2021. [119] Sanger 2021. [120] Sanger 2021. [121] Sanger 2021.
[122] Mitnick 2021; Alms 2021. [123] Sanger 2021.

the federal bureaucracy: some NIFA employees agreed to move in order to defend and protect the agency's scientific work, senior staff spirited away documents from the president's desk before he could sign ill-advised policies into law, the EPA's Scientific Advisory Board condemned Trump's environmental policies, and members of the coronavirus task force insisted on publicly correcting the president's false claims and statements. To reiterate what I've said in previous chapters, the point is that efforts to radically change institutions are contingent and depend partly on power struggles and pushback by those affected and on other rules and norms that limit what can be changed. This is why sometimes radical change succeeds and sometimes it doesn't; why its impact is sometimes long-lived and sometimes not.

7

Economic Rocket Fuel

Institutions cannot be sustained unless people have enough resources to make them work. That includes political institutions, which is why taxes have been called the "lifeblood" of the state – without them states simply cannot function; their institutional efficacy dwindles.[1] Trump understood this. If he wanted to attack the deep state, then cutting its revenue supply and spending was an excellent way to do it. That's what he tried to do.

Republicans have long favored lower taxes and government spending and Trump's policies were no exception. In this sense, his promises to slash taxes and budgets didn't seem out of the ordinary. But his approach was far more radical than what most Republicans had imagined. His tax cuts, passed as the Tax Cuts and Jobs Act (TCJA) of 2017, were among the deepest in modern American history.[2] They were facilitated by a tipping point stemming from years of pent-up demand for tax cuts. But they were also enabled by Trump's leadership – his inspirational yet ill-informed and false claims about the economic benefits they would yield and his willingness to cut deals with and bully politicians who might otherwise have stood in the way of passing them.

It was a different story when it came to spending. Trump spotted another tipping point – growing public dissatisfaction with government inefficiency and waste. Given the breadth and depth of the budget cuts he proposed, this was another attempt at radical institutional change. But it was far beyond what Republicans would accept. So, Congress balked, refusing to cut spending as much as he wanted. In this case, Trump's leadership characteristics failed him.

---

[1] Braun 1975, p. 243. Karl Marx (1969, p. 482) agreed writing that taxes are the state's "source of life."

[2] Marnin 2021; Petulla and Yellin 2018.

As a result, rather than setting the government on a new institutional path toward reducing deficits and national debt, as he had promised, cutting taxes but not spending reinforced the same path the government had been on for decades – running deficits and accumulating debt to cover them. In fact, it got worse. Insofar as rising budget deficits and debt generate political opposition that reduces the government spending that society needs, they can damage the state's institutional efficacy.

This chapter explains all this and in doing so illustrates three important points made in Chapter 1. First, institutions come in sets and these sets often entail complementarities, whereby each one needs to fit the others to perform up to par. Put differently, institutional efficacy often depends on institutional complementarity. When one institution changes, but the others don't, the outcome will be counterproductive, particularly if the institutional change involved is radical and, therefore, dramatically undermines the complementarities within the set. This happened on Trump's watch as revenues declined but expenditures continued to rise generating more budget deficits and driving debt to new heights. This signified a deterioration in the complementary relationship between the fiscal institutions of taxing and spending. Second, attempts at radical change can be foiled by political resistance. In this case, the institutional separation of powers and Congress's reluctance to cut budgets stopped Trump's draconian budget-cutting plans dead in their tracks. Finally, unintended consequences are often associated with radical institutional change. Although Trump succeeded in slashing taxes, the results were not what he promised or anticipated. This was because he failed to heed warnings and evidence that the benefits from lower taxes that he predicted were unlikely to materialize. Here, then, was another striking example of Trump's intellectual arrogance – an unwillingness to consider the facts before him.

The distinction between deficits and debt is important. A budget deficit is the shortfall that occurs when the government spends more than it collects in revenues each year. The government often borrows to cover a deficit. Government debt, also called national or public debt, is the accumulated value of all that borrowing less whatever portion of it the government pays back to its creditors. It's the same as if you spend more in a year than you earn. If you borrow from your bank to cover that deficit, you incur debt, which grows if you do this year after year without paying it back. However, there is one big difference between you and the government – Uncle Sam can print money to pay off its debt; you can't, at least not legally. But as we shall see, printing money isn't necessarily a panacea.

7.1 TAX CUTS

The TCJA slashed the corporate income tax rate from 35 percent to 21 percent. Tax rates for individual income were also cut sharply. But unlike the rate cut for corporations, which was permanent, many of those for individuals were temporary and set to expire in 2025.[3] Trump touted the legislation's historic nature: "And just as I promised the American people... we enacted the biggest tax cuts and reforms in American history. Our massive tax cuts provide tremendous relief for the middle class and small business."[4] This was more than just a minor adjustment to the tax code; it was a major overhaul that touched most individuals and businesses in the United States. According to William Howell and Terry Moe, "By any definition this was a hugely consequential shift in policy."[5] According to the Committee for a Responsible Budget's analysis of US Treasury data, in terms of revenue lost in inflation-adjusted dollars, the corporate tax cut was projected to be the largest in US history and the entire TCJA tax cut package would be the fourth largest in nearly a century.[6]

Passage of the TCJA benefited from what Byron Shafer and Regina Wagner explained was "a collective buildup of policy wishes so intense as to precipitate...a giant log-roll pulling all these pent-up demands into one legislative spasm."[7] In other words, it reflected a tipping point, which in this case consisted of three interlinked trends. First, in exchange for supporting the bill members of Congress saw legislative opportunities to finally get things they had long yearned for, such as permission to drill for gas and oil in the Arctic National Wildlife Refuge – political pork that Trump and congressional leaders were more than willing to give to secure the bill's passage.[8] It was an opportunity for transactional horse-trading.

Second, public concern that middle-income Americans were paying too much in taxes had been growing steadily for many years. It accelerated in the late 1970s when inflation was pushing people into higher tax brackets and anti-tax movements emerged around the country. The Tea Party movement protests of 2009 amplified demands for tax cuts.[9] By the early 2000s a Gallup poll found that about 40 percent of those surveyed felt that taxes on middle-income people were too high but by April 2017 that number had risen to 51 percent. Trump capitalized on that trend during the 2016 campaign stressing that he would cut taxes on the middle class. But he promised to cut taxes for corporations and wealthy individuals too even though roughly two-thirds of those surveyed in the same poll complained that upper-income individuals and corporations were paying too little in taxes.[10] I'll explain in a moment how Trump finessed that contradiction.

Third, congressional Republicans, who controlled both the House and Senate during Trump's first two years in office, had long wanted tax cuts.

---

[3] For details on changes in tax rates and other reforms in the legislation, see Gale et al. (2018) and Floyd (2020).
[4] Floyd 2020.   [5] Howell and Moe 2020, p. 128.
[6] Committee for a Responsible Federal Budget 2017; Gittleson 2018.
[7] Shafer and Wagner 2019, p. 351.   [8] Shafer and Wagner 2019, p. 351.   [9] Martin 2008.
[10] Newport 2017.

Both Speaker of the House Paul Ryan and Senate majority leader Mitch McConnell had favored tax cuts for years and, having been unable to pursue them during the Obama administration, were eager to back Trump's effort to pass the TCJA.[11] They knew that the public's desire for tax cuts had been building. And they realized that Trump and the Republicans needed a big legislative win to help them in the 2018 midterm elections. So, when Trump took office, they all realized that they were suddenly able to do something about it. A window of opportunity for radical tax reform had opened. The time was ripe for a big institutional change. A tipping point had arrived.

The Democrats objected that the legislation would boost deficits and debt and favor the wealthy. So did others, including the nonpartisan Center on Budget and Policy Priorities, which warned at the time that the TCJA was "a costly tax cut that's heavily tilted to the nation's wealthiest households and corporations."[12] A number of prominent economists including four winners of the Nobel Prize in Economics agreed and lambasted the legislation.[13] But Trump didn't listen. Opposition forces were outgunned and their efforts to block the legislation were stymied.

Trump's leadership qualities, notably his inspirational promises of the economic benefits that tax cuts would yield, helped garner public support for the TCJA. He claimed that the new law would restore competitiveness to the American economy by stimulating investment and, as a result, boosting economic growth, creating thousands of jobs, and increasing wages for more than 3.5 million workers.[14] That's why, in Trump's view, people shouldn't object to tax cuts for corporations and the rich; they would be the ones using their tax savings to make most of the job-creating and growth-creating investments. Furthermore, in contrast to the naysayers he promised that these tax cuts along with other reforms in the bill would not increase federal budget deficits or the nation's public debt. On the contrary, the legislation would reduce them. How? According to Trump's Treasury Secretary Steven Mnuchin, "The tax plan will pay for itself with economic growth." Trump was more effusive assuring Americans that the TCJA "will be rocket fuel for our economy."[15] So, while the Treasury forecast that the new law would increase revenues by about $1.8 trillion dollars over ten years the White House doubled down putting that figure at $5.5 trillion.[16] Trump's flair for motivating his supporters with inspirational claims like these helped gin up enthusiasm among Republican voters for the tax cuts. On average, 72 percent of Republicans polled supported the bill while only 10 percent of Democrats did.[17]

Trump's inspirational pitch also helped garner support for the legislation among Republicans in Congress. But for those not on board initially, Trump

[11] Herbert et al. 2019, p. 78.   [12] Parrott et al. 2018.   [13] Stein 2017.
[14] The White House 2018.   [15] Horsley 2019.
[16] US Department of the Treasury 2017; The White House 2018.
[17] Enton 2017; Williamson 2018.

deployed other leadership talents. Some Republicans from high-tax states were only swayed to support the bill after the House with Trump's blessing added a provision for property tax deductions – important in places like California, New York, and New Jersey where people paid very high property taxes. In one case, Trump dispatched Mnuchin and his daughter, Ivanka, to a reluctant congressman's district in New Jersey to build public support for the tax bill and put pressure on him to get with the program. All this exemplified Trump's transactional, if not bullying, leadership style: I'll give you political support if you vote for my tax reform, or else.[18] It didn't always work. A handful of Republicans, notably those spooked about deficits and debt, voted against the legislation. But most supported it and Trump signed the bill into law on December 22, 2017.

7.2 FAILED PROMISES AND UNINTENDED CONSEQUENCES

Trump's inspirational pitch for the TCJA was based on supply-side economics – the idea that tax cuts would increase, not decrease, the federal government's revenues and, therefore, help reduce federal budget deficits and pay down the government's debt. Reducing taxes to increase revenue may seem counterintuitive. But Trump and his minions insisted that tax cuts would increase investment and, therefore, economic growth so much that the tax revenues generated in the long term would more than compensate for those lost in the short term from the initial rate reductions. The argument was based on the theory of Arthur Laffer, an economist who had popularized the controversial idea during the Reagan administration and who had been influential in Republican circles ever since. Laffer also had a hand in crafting the TCJA. Trump eventually awarded him the Medal of Freedom, the nation's highest civilian honor, because, in the president's words, "Few people in history have revolutionized economic thought and policy like Dr. Art Laffer."[19] Perhaps. But according to a University of Chicago survey of dozens of top economists around the country the theory was wrong. A whopping 95 percent of those polled said so.[20] Not surprisingly a variety of respectable nonpartisan budget analysts, including the Congressional Joint Committee on Taxation and the Committee for a Responsible Federal Budget, dismissed Trump's supply-side claim that the legislation would reduce deficits and debt as utter nonsense.[21]

They were right. Consider the data in Figure 7.1. During the Obama administration (2009–2016) the federal budget deficit initially grew rapidly due to a sudden burst of federal borrowing and spending to counteract the 2008 financial crisis and subsequent Great Recession but later got smaller as the economy

---

[18] Marcos and Jagoda 2017.   [19] Trump 2019.   [20] Booth School of Business 2012.
[21] Floyd 2020.

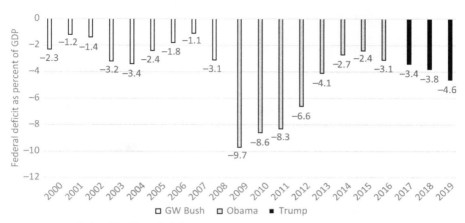

FIGURE 7.1. Federal budget deficit, 2009–2019.
Source: US Federal Reserve Bank (2020b).

began to improve. This was classic Keynesian deficit financing – run-up deficits by borrowing and spending in times of economic crisis to revitalize the economy but then once the recovery starts reverse course and begin reducing deficits. In contrast, although the economy continued to grow every year Trump was in office until the COVID-19 pandemic hit, the deficit increased, including 2018 and 2019, the first two years after the TCJA went into effect. This was the opposite of what he had promised that the legislation would do.

Consequently, the new law neither reduced the debt nor slowed its growth as Trump had also promised. The national debt had increased sharply as the Obama administration tried to contain the Great Recession but then stabilized at the end of his presidency as the economy recovered. However, debt began to increase again after Trump took office in 2017 even though the economy continued to grow.[22] This too was the opposite of what he had promised. Public debt jumped more than $2 trillion in the first two years after the TCJA was passed, reinforcing America's position as one of the most indebted countries in the world.[23] In 2019 the United States had the fifth largest public debt as a percentage of GDP of all the advanced countries and ranked first in the world in terms of the sheer amount of dollars it owed its creditors.[24] This level of debt was not just the Trump administration's fault, but the TCJA helped exacerbate it. Thanks partly to Trump's tax cuts the national debt was projected to grow between $7 trillion and $10 trillion over the next decade.[25]

---

[22] US Federal Reserve Bank 2021d.   [23] Duffin 2021.   [24] Desjardins 2019; OECD 2021b.
[25] Committee for a Responsible Federal Budget 2019.

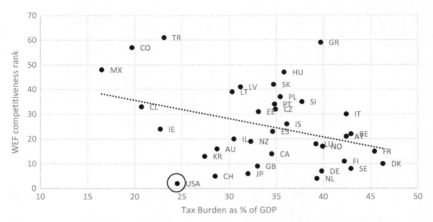

FIGURE 7.2. Tax burden and economic competitiveness in thirty-seven OECD countries, 2019.

Note: Austria (AT); Australia (AU); Belgium (BE); Canada (CA); Chile (CL); Columbia (CO); Czech Republic (CZ); Denmark (DK); Estonia (EE); Finland (FI); France (FR); Germany (DE); Great Britain (GB); Greece (GR); Hungary (HU); Iceland (IS); Ireland (IE); Israel (IL); Italy (IT); Japan (JP); Latvia (LV); Lithuania (LT); Luxembourg (LU); Mexico (MX); Netherlands (NL); New Zealand (NZ); Norway (NO); Poland (PL); Portugal (PT); Slovakia (SK); Slovenia (SI); South Korea (KR); Spain (ES); Sweden (SE); Switzerland (CH); Turkey (TR); United States (USA).

Sources: OECD (2020c); World Economic Forum (2019).

Trump's claim that lower taxes were the key to improved economic growth and international economic competitiveness was also off the mark. For one thing, the United States had been among the most competitive economies in the world for years long before the TCJA. Since at least 2008 the World Economic Forum (WEF) had ranked the United States among the top ten most competitive economies in the world every year, and since 2013 it was in the top five every year.[26] It was hard to see, therefore, how the TCJA could have improved US economic competitiveness much at all because there wasn't much room left for improvement to begin with. For another thing, Trump was wrong about the relationship between taxes and competitiveness. Figure 7.2 compares the WEF economic competitiveness rankings of the Organization for Economic Cooperation and Development (OECD) countries in 2019 with the size of their tax burdens – the percentage of GDP each government collected in taxes. The lower the WEF number, the more competitive the economy. That year the United States was ranked the most competitive economy in the OECD and the second most competitive economy in the world. It also had a much lighter tax burden than many other countries,

---

[26] These rankings are available online in the annual WEF *Global Competitiveness Reports*.

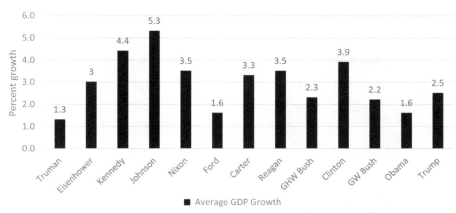

FIGURE 7.3. Average annual GDP growth during presidential administrations, 1945–2019. *Note:* Data for Trump does not include 2020, the pandemic year. If you include 2020, the average annual GDP growth rate under Trump was 0.4 percent. *Source:* Amadeo (2020).

collecting just under 25 percent of GDP in taxes from all levels of government. This would seem to corroborate Trump's claim that low taxes were associated with strong international economic competitiveness. However, the trend line in the data shows the opposite. As the tax burden for these countries rises, their economic competitiveness rankings don't deteriorate; they improve, which is contrary to Trump's supply-side mantra.[27]

The point is that Trump either ignored or didn't care about the facts regarding his tax-cutting plan – an indication of his intellectual arrogance. Nor did the economic advisors he had appointed. They told him what he already believed, which was further evidence of his tendency to surround himself with ideological cheerleaders rather than objective advisors.

The TCJA fell short of Trump's promises in other ways too. First, economic growth during Trump's first three years in office was less than spectacular. Despite his claims that the economy was doing far better than it had in a very long time, it only grew at a modest pace. Figure 7.3 compares average annual economic growth rates across all presidencies since the Second World War. During Trump's first three years in office – that is, until the pandemic wrecked the economy – economic growth averaged 2.5 percent annually, which was worse than it was in seven of the dozen administrations preceding his and not much better than two others. More important, this was a lower growth rate than the administration had forecast that the TCJA tax reforms would generate, which meant that it was not enough growth for the tax cuts to pay for

---

[27] The correlation coefficient is –0.343, which is significant at the p < .05 level.

TABLE 7.1. *Federal government revenue as a percent of GDP*

	Individual Income Tax	Payroll Taxes	Corporate Income Tax	Other Revenues	Total Revenue	Total Outlays
FY2017	8.2	6.0	1.5	1.4	17.2	20.7
FY2018	8.3	5.8	1.0	1.3	16.4	20.3
FY2019	8.1	5.9	1.1	1.3	16.3	21.0
FY2020	7.7	6.2	1.0	1.4	16.3	31.2

Source: US Congressional Budget Office (2018, 2019, 2020).

themselves.[28] The TCJA had not provided the rocket fuel that Trump had guaranteed.

Another thing that went wrong with the TCJA involved the labor market. Unemployment during Trump's first three years in office averaged 4 percent annually, which was lower than any administration's since the Second World War. This was consistent with Trump's promises and especially impressive when compared to the Obama presidency's Great Recession-induced average of 7.4 percent.[29] Given supply-side logic, one might think that with such a low unemployment rate personal income tax revenues would have surged despite tax cuts because there were simply a lot more people earning taxable income. But this didn't happen either – at least judging from the evidence on federal taxation and expenditures presented in Table 7.1. Both individual income tax revenues and payroll tax revenues, which tend to rise and fall in tandem with the unemployment rate, declined slightly as a percentage of GDP from 2017 through 2019. Why? To begin with, if we include underemployed and part-time workers seeking full-time jobs, the corrected unemployment rate was much higher – 7 percent in 2019.[30] Furthermore, although average wages and household incomes were beginning to climb, they had been stagnant for decades and didn't rise much. As a result, many Americans still struggled to make ends meet and were not suddenly flush with taxable income. That's one reason why people continued to borrow, and why household debt reached an all-time high of nearly $14 trillion in 2019.[31] So, even though more people were

---

[28] Based on estimates from the Treasury Department, Office of Management and Budget, and Council of Economic Advisors, the administration assumed growth in real GDP of 2.5 percent in 2018; 2.8 percent in 2019; and 3.0 percent for the following eight years (US Department of the Treasury 2017).

[29] Coleman 2021.   [30] US Bureau of Labor Statistics 2020a.

[31] Richter 2019. Three caveats are necessary. First, rising wages were largely due to states raising the minimum wage, which had nothing to do with Trump's economic policies. Second, borrowing was likely helped by low interest rates. Third, since the financial crisis, household debt as a percentage of net disposable personal income dropped from a high of 143 percent in 2007 to a low of 105 percent in 2018, and debt service payments as a percentage of disposable household income declined from 13 percent in 2007 to 9.6 percent in early 2020 (OECD 2020a; US Federal Reserve Bank 2020a). However, these data lump together borrowing by households

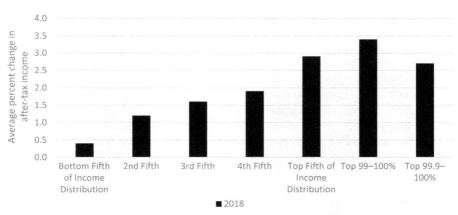

FIGURE 7.4. Change in after-tax personal income due to the TCJA, 2018.
Source: Investopedia (2020).

working, and wages were beginning to increase, those changes were not nearly enough to compensate for the individual income tax revenues lost through the TCJA.

Third, the benefits of Trump's personal income tax cuts were tilted heavily in favor of the rich. These were the people who had benefited the most from what economic growth there was on Trump's watch, particularly because they were the ones most likely to have reaped the benefits of the booming stock market. After all, they owned most of the stock.[32] Figure 7.4 reports the average change in after-tax income for different income groups due to the TCJA. In 2018 the higher the income group, the more they benefited from the TCJA's tax cuts and other reforms. Growth in after-tax income for people in the bottom fifth of the income distribution was less than half a percent on average. But it rose steadily across the higher income groups reaching nearly 3.5 percent for the top one percent of the income distribution – the richest people in the country. Higher income groups provide a larger portion of federal income tax revenue than lower income groups. For example, in 2017 the top half of the income distribution paid roughly 97 percent of all the personal income tax while the bottom half paid only about 3 percent. The top 10 percent alone shouldered 70 percent of all the income taxes paid.[33] By giving the most generous tax breaks to those

---

spanning the income range. It is impossible to tell from these data how much better or worse different income groups fared in terms of their relative debt and debt service burdens.

[32] Heeb 2019; Jacobson 2018.

[33] National Taxpayers Union Foundation 2019. This doesn't mean that the bottom half of the income distribution is off the hook. They still pay payroll taxes, property taxes, sales taxes, and all sorts of fees to the government at federal, state, and local levels.

who provided most of the individual income tax revenue the TCJA made it just that much harder for tax cuts to pay for themselves.[34]

But what about corporate income taxes? Might not reducing the corporate tax rate make up for the revenue lost from the individual income tax cuts and related reforms? Apparently not. Take another look at Table 7.1. It shows that individual income taxes provide half of all federal revenue – more than any other source. By contrast, corporate income taxes yield only about 7 percent of all federal revenue.[35] It's hard to see how the corporate tax cuts could make up for all the revenue lost elsewhere. Nevertheless, there was still much ado about the corporate tax cuts preceding the enactment of the TCJA. Trump claimed that corporate taxes were a terrible drag on the economy because they deprived firms of capital that they would otherwise invest in research and development, new plant and equipment, upskilling the labor force and other things that would provide the rocket fuel for economic growth. He also said that what he viewed as exorbitant corporate taxes had to be lowered to make American business competitive internationally and particularly to keep firms and jobs from moving to other countries with lower taxes – a problem Trump harped on throughout the 2016 presidential campaign and beyond. All of this was part of his inspirational pitch to garner public support for his plan. In fact, he said that corporate tax breaks were "probably the biggest factor in this plan."[36]

There were several problems with this argument. As Figure 7.5 shows, one was that although the statutory corporate tax rate in the United States had been the highest among the G20 countries before the TJCA was passed, the effective rate – that is, the rate corporations actually paid after taking advantage of tax credits and deductions – was less than half that size and more in line with many of these other countries. In other words, the corporate tax rate allegedly undermining competitiveness was much less problematic and the tax incentive for American-based firms to move to other countries was much less compelling than Trump suggested. Another problem, as studies have shown, was that taxes play a much less important role in determining where firms decide to invest and locate jobs than a host of other factors, including, for instance, the quality of the labor force and infrastructure, wage rates, political stability, the quality of institutions, and access to key markets.[37] A third problem was that a plethora of factors including those just noted – not just taxes – affect a country's economic competitiveness.[38] So, a country might have high corporate tax rates but still be very competitive, particularly if its government spends the revenue from those high tax rates on things that boost economic competitiveness. It's no wonder, then, that according to the WEF the ten most competitive economies in the world in 2019 had corporate income tax rates ranging from 8.5 percent

---

[34] Heeb 2019.

[35] Social insurance payroll taxes (36 percent), excise taxes (3 percent) and other taxes (5 percent) produce the rest of the federal revenue (Tax Policy Center 2021).

[36] Pramuk 2017.   [37] Jensen 2006.   [38] Hall and Soskice 2001.

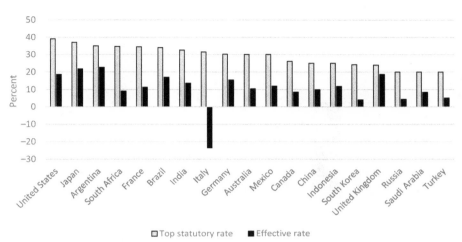

FIGURE 7.5. G20 corporate tax rates, 2012.
Source: Investopedia (2020).

(Switzerland) to 25 percent (Netherlands) in no systematic order.[39] Nor is it perplexing, as Figure 7.2 shows, that the greater the overall tax burden, the more economically competitive a country tends to be.

Finally, corporate tax cuts didn't trigger more investment as Trump predicted they would. Figure 7.6 compares the annual rate of change in business investment for the two years before and the two years after the legislation was passed. The rate of investment declined by about 25 percent after the TCJA corporate tax reforms were enacted even though the rate of economic growth, also shown in the figure, remained the same. Why didn't the TCJA reforms lead to more investment? One reason was that on average many of the country's large corporations invested only 20 percent of their tax savings in growth-producing ways. They spent the remaining 80 percent on things like stock buybacks and paying dividends to their stockholders.[40]

Overall, then, the TCJA was both a success and a failure. Trump's inspirational rhetoric and transactional and bullying skills helped ensure the bill's passage. And, as advertised, it was a radical change in the tax code that successfully reduced the government's reach into people's wallets, particularly the wealthy and corporations. But beyond that it fell short in ways that Trump neither intended nor anticipated. It didn't provide much in the way of economic rocket fuel; it didn't improve US economic competitiveness much; and it didn't help balance the state's books by reining in deficits and debt. In other words, the institutional structure of the tax code changed dramatically but its

---

[39] World Economic Forum 2019. Tax rates are from the OECD (2021a).
[40] Hendricks and Hanlon 2019.

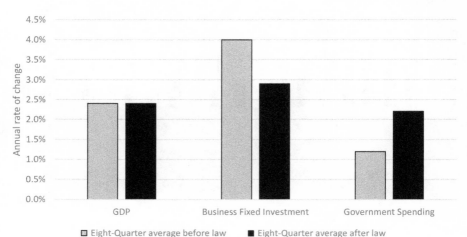

FIGURE 7.6. Effects of the Tax Cuts and Jobs Act.
Note: The pretax law period reflects 2015 Q4 to 2017 Q4. The posttax law period reflects 2017 Q4 to 2019 Q4.
Source: US House Committee on the Budget (2020).

institutional efficacy, at least as promised, did not. This shouldn't be surprising. It all reflected another important characteristic of Trump's leadership style – his unwillingness to face facts and consider arguments contrary to his beliefs.

7.3 THE BUDGET

The efficacy of political institutions depends not only on access to resources but on how those resources are used. Similarly, the size of government deficits and debt depend on spending as much as they depend on revenue, which means that there is a complementary relationship between the institutions governing taxation and government spending. That complementarity, already on shaky ground, broke down badly on Trump's watch.

Trump's first preliminary budget proposed radical cuts to nearly all major nondefense budget categories – reductions much deeper than those of either Barack Obama or George W. Bush.[41] Then, less than two months after signing the TCJA, Trump released his 2019 annual budget proposal, which, as Table 7.2 shows, called for draconian cuts in all cabinet departments and major agencies except those related to national security and commerce. On average, these cuts amounted to about a 15 percent reduction per department and agency targeted. If passed in full by Congress, this too would have been a radical institutional change – a sharp and sweeping reduction in spending.

---

[41] Fahey and Wells 2017.

TABLE 7.2. *President's budget request for FY 2019*

	2019 Budget Request ($ Billions)	Change from 2017 Budget Enacted (Percent)
Cabinet Departments		
Agriculture	19.0	−16.0
Commerce	9.8	6.0
Defense	686.0	13.0
Education	59.9	−10.5
Energy	29.0	−3.0
Health and Human Services	68.4	−21.0
Homeland Security	46.0	8.0
Housing and Urban Development	39.2	−18.3
Interior	11.3	−16.0
Justice	28.0	−1.2
Labor	9.4	−21.0
State and Other International Programs	25.8	−26.0
Transportation	15.6	−19.0
Treasury	12.3	−3.0
Veterans Affairs	83.1	11.7
Major Agencies		
Corps of Engineers	4.8	−20.0
Environmental Protection Agency	5.4	−34.0
National Aeronautics and Space Administration	19.6	2.6
Small Business Administration	0.8	−5.9

Source: US Office of Management and Budget (2018).

But why seek such deep budget cuts? After all, wouldn't supply-side tax cuts generate enough revenue to sustain current spending? In Trump's mind, that was probably beside the point. Although tax cuts would allegedly spur economic growth and generate additional revenue, he still wanted to slash the budget to reduce the size and impact of the deep state. Whatever money was left over could then be used to reduce deficits and pay down the debt. However, there are complexities here that require explanation.

First, recall from Chapter 6 that public dissatisfaction with and distrust of the federal government had been growing for decades. This spilled over into people's preferences for government spending but with strong partisan differences. By 2017, Republicans were far less supportive of spending on just about everything except veterans' benefits than Democrats, including notably assistance to the needy and unemployed. Overall, 74 percent of Republicans and Republican-leaning independents favored smaller government with fewer services whereas 67 percent of Democrats and Democrat-leaning independents favored bigger government with more services.[42] That gap had been widening since the mid-1990s. So was the partisan difference in views on government waste. Since 2001 Republicans had become increasingly more concerned about this than Democrats.[43] This presented another tipping point opportunity for Trump to exploit.

Second, fiscal conservatives – deficit hawks – in Washington worry about debt because it must be paid off eventually and in their view it's not fair to reap the benefits of borrowing today and put the burden of debt payment on future generations. Prior to the pandemic Trump's Federal Reserve Board Chairman Jerome Powell, among many others, warned that the United States had not been on a "sustainable" fiscal path for a while because the nation's debt was growing faster than the economy.[44] Trump's message to Congress in his 2019 budget echoed that concern:

The United States is laboring under the highest level of debt held by the public since shortly after the Second World War. The current fiscal path is unsustainable and future generations deserve better. The Budget makes the hard choices needed to stop wasteful spending, lower the national debt, and focus Government on what matters most – protecting the Nation.[45]

Trump's focus on wasteful spending and unsustainable deficits and debt hinted at a looming fiscal crisis. But he blamed it on out-of-control spending, not insufficient taxes. His 2019 budget proposal was explicit about this. And it explained that Trump's mission had always been to implement cost-cutting reforms to fix that. For example, the proposal noted that he had mandated by executive order that all regulatory agencies eliminate two existing regulations for each new one created – a target the administration claimed had saved the government over $8 billion. The administration had also either withdrawn or delayed over 1,500 regulations already in the pipeline and planned to go even further at an additional estimated cost saving of nearly $10 billion. Furthermore, the White House proposed $65 billion in reductions for nondefense discretionary spending. It also proposed changes to the welfare system by requiring state governments to strengthen welfare-to-work requirements and devise other cost-saving measures.[46]

But Congress, not the president, held the government's purse strings, which meant that even though Trump had to sign off on the appropriations bills, he didn't get everything he wanted. Far from it. Here was an especially clear example of how resistance can blunt a leader's drive for radical institutional change. The Republican-controlled Congress rejected most of the cuts he asked for in his 2019 budget. So he renewed his requests in his 2020 budget proposal,

---

[42] Pew Research Center 2019b.   [43] Pew Research Center 2015c.   [44] Sergent et al. 2020.
[45] US Office of Management and Budget 2018, p. 1.
[46] US Office of Management and Budget 2018, pp. 11–14.

which they again rejected. As a result, while total revenue fell as a percent of GDP after the TCJA was passed, government spending increased. Take a second look at Figure 7.6. It shows that government spending rose much faster after the TCJA was passed than before it went into effect. But that's not surprising for two reasons.

First, government spending had been increasing for decades and was bound to continue, as everyone knew, including those who claimed that the TCJA would reduce deficits and debt. Why? Because the costs of nondiscretionary entitlement programs, especially Medicare and debt service, were rising. But increased military spending – something Trump pushed for – was also significant.[47]

Second, although conventional Republican rhetoric insists on reducing the size of government, since the late 1960s the reality was that the party had become less interested in shrinking government spending than in reorienting it for the Republicans' own conservative purposes, such as enhancing national security, border protection, local policing, and establishing more market-oriented policies in business, education, energy, and the environment. Some call this conservative statism.[48] Whether Trump knew this isn't clear. He was, after all, inexperienced in the ways of fiscal policy and Republican politics in Washington. Yet to appeal to his base, Trump accommodated the more conventional Republican rhetorical profile promising deep budget cuts. So, although his budget-cutting plan may have been in step with Republican Party rhetoric and his base, it broke sharply with the Republican reality in Congress.

Whatever leadership qualities Trump may have employed to garner support for his proposed budget cuts, they weren't enough to overcome the forces supporting increased spending. Why? Because unlike his assaults on electoral institutions, the Republican Party, the justice system, and the federal bureaucracy, his capacity for shaping the budget, not to mention the tax code, involved crafting and passing legislation. And that meant that he couldn't just dictate orders and bully people into submission; he had to negotiate with Congress or face resistance. As institutional theorists know, once in place government programs tend to breed constituents who benefit from them and, therefore, are ready to fight for them if they come under attack.[49] As I explained in Chapter 1, that's one reason why institutions are sticky. This is the essence of the path-dependent theory of incremental change.

This gets back to the issue of real and apparent Republican preferences. When it comes to the budget, cutting spending is an idea that most Republicans tend to favor in theory, but not in practice when it means cutting spending for *their* pet programs or for things that benefit *their* constituents. So, even when the Republicans controlled both the House and Senate, Trump faced an uphill

[47] US Congressional Budget Office 2018, p. 4.   [48] Jacobs et al. 2019.
[49] Pierson 1994; Kenworthy 2014.

battle to win support for his budget-cutting proposals. The challenge grew even steeper after the 2018 midterm elections when the Democrats won control of the House.

The point is that when it came to the budget, inspiration, deal-making, and strong-arming often failed him. Trump ran into an institutional barrier that he couldn't overcome – the need to share power with another branch of government and eventually another party rather than act unilaterally as he did in the four other cases of institutional change discussed in previous chapters. He couldn't overcome the resistance that sprang from this institutional environment. And he didn't have the political experience to anticipate that this would likely happen, or know how to handle it when it did.

In sum, both the tax and budget-cutting initiatives were attempts at radical institutional change. However, only the tax cuts were passed. As a result, spending continued to rise and outpace revenues from 2017 through 2019.[50] Not only did Trump's institutional attack on the deep state fail to reduce spending, but it also failed to reverse the government's existing fiscal trajectory of racking up deficits and more debt – instead it accelerated that trajectory. Such were the unintended consequences of a further breakdown in institutional complementarity – change in one fiscal institution without a corresponding change in the other.

One caveat is important. Supply-side economics can be a game of smoke and mirrors obscuring ulterior motives. Republicans in the past used supply-side rhetoric as a ploy to help them attack state programs that they disparaged.[51] For example, Ronald Reagan's supply-side rhetoric concealed the fact that his aggressive tax cuts in 1981 were intended at least in part to reduce revenues and, as a result, put pressure on deficit hawks in Congress to cut spending for government programs that conservatives found to be abhorrent, notably welfare.[52] The same may have been true of Trump who didn't have any love for the welfare state either, or for that matter, many other government programs. As Table 7.2 shows, many of his budget cuts were targeted at departments that provided health, housing, and other forms of assistance to low- and moderate-income families. And in a Fox News town hall meeting in 2020 he admitted that he planned to propose cuts to Medicare, Social Security, and other benefit programs in his second term.[53] But regardless of Trump's real views on supply-side economics, two things are clear. One is that he used rosy supply-side rhetoric as an inspirational tool to win support for his election and then to elicit support for his tax reforms. The other is that Trump's success in cutting taxes and his failure to reduce budgets further eroded the state's fiscal footing

---

[50] In dollar terms, spending increased 11.6 percent and revenues increased 4 percent from 2017 through 2019 (US Congressional Budget Office 2020).

[51] Bernhard and O'Neill 2019, p. 322,   [52] Greider 1981; Roberts 1984.

[53] Rupar 2020. His staff claimed that he didn't really mean this, although he reiterated it later during the campaign.

by continuing to drive up deficits and debt. In other words, it damaged the state's institutional efficacy by making it harder politically to provide for the needs of its citizens. Then COVID-19 struck.

7.4 THE PANDEMIC

When the pandemic hit, not only was it devastating in terms of lives lost but also for the damage it did to the economy. The Trump administration's fumbling of the response to the pandemic, discussed in Chapter 6, certainly made things worse than they would have been otherwise. By the beginning of September 2020 an estimated 164,000 small businesses had closed permanently due to the crisis and tens of thousands were in jeopardy.[54] GDP shrank by 9 percent in the second quarter of 2020 – the steepest single-quarter decline on record – and finished down by 3.5 percent by the end of the year, the economy's worst performance since the Second World War.[55] The official unemployment rate (excluding underemployed and part-time workers seeking full-time jobs) skyrocketed from 4 percent to about 13 percent, a height not seen since the Great Depression, then declined but was still nearly 7 percent by the end of the year.[56]

All of this triggered a massive increase in deficits and public debt as the government scrambled to minimize the economic damage. The Fed cut interest rates nearly to zero, but they were already so low that even before the crisis hit Fed Chairman Powell admitted that this would do little to stimulate the economy if it were necessary.[57] So, the Fed began buying up Treasury bonds and other securities to pump more money into the economy to save it from collapsing.[58] It did this by crediting the accounts of big banks and others at the Fed – in effect "printing money" out of thin air with a few computer keystrokes.[59] However, according to the Brookings Institution at that time, "The Fed's powers and tools, as impressive as they are, aren't sufficient to cope with the economic harm of the COVID-19 crisis." Powell himself acknowledged that the Fed didn't have the capacity to handle the crisis alone.[60]

This is why Congress passed four economic relief bills in early 2020 totaling $2.4 trillion, a staggering sum that was projected to push the federal debt up to 122 percent of GDP by the end of the year – higher than it was even during the Second World War. Initially, Trump opposed this direct stimulus, favoring

[54] Sardana 2020.   [55] OECD 2020b; Statista 2021c; US Federal Reserve Bank 2021c.
[56] US Bureau of Labor Statistics 2020b.   [57] Smialek et al. 2020.
[58] US Federal Reserve Bank 2019.
[59] This is called quantitative easing and involves putting newly created money into the Federal Reserve accounts of several thousand domestic and foreign banks, sovereign wealth funds, and other entities who then pump that money into the economy in various ways (Cochrane 2020; Schrotenboer 2020).
[60] Cheng et al. 2020.

instead an indirect payroll tax reduction, which, of course, wouldn't help the millions of unemployed. But it was an election year and Trump decided that putting stimulus checks directly into people's pockets would help him win the election because it would remind voters of his concern for their welfare. So, he capitulated to the congressional plan, but not before insisting that his name be put on those checks – a narcissistic demand that officials warned would delay those checks from reaching the people who needed them immediately and another sign that Trump was willing to put his own political interests above those of the country. This was the first time in history that a president's name appeared on an IRS disbursement.[61] But he wanted to make sure that voters would give him credit at election time.

Much of this money was borrowed.[62] But it wasn't enough to stop the economic hemorrhaging. So, Democrats in the House passed the HEROES Act in May 2020 to pump another $3 trillion into the economy, with Republican opponents screaming that the deficits and debt that would result would be catastrophic. Congressman Gary Palmer (R-AL), for example, posted this explanation for his opposition to the bill on his website: "I opposed the misnamed HEROES Act today because it constitutes a real threat to our national security...Debt levels of this magnitude are not sustainable and threaten Social Security, Medicare, household income, and most critically threaten our national security."[63] Senate Republicans echoed this sentiment and refused to pass it. Majority leader McConnell told reporters, "Given the extraordinary numbers that we're racking up to the national debt...we need to be as cautious as we can be. We can't borrow enough money to solve the problem indefinitely."[64]

Just a few days before Christmas, and after months of negotiations with Democrats, McConnell and his caucus finally agreed to pass a scaled-down $900 billion version of the House bill. Given the gravity of the economic situation – and Republican concerns that they might lose control of the Senate in two upcoming runoff elections in Georgia unless they approved additional aid – the deficit hawks backed off.

The amount of money appropriated on Trump's watch to combat the coronavirus and rescue the economy was huge. As Table 7.1 shows, government spending jumped as a percentage of GDP by nearly 50 percent in 2020, the first year of the pandemic, and exceeded revenues by almost 100 percent.[65] As a result, national debt soared. Historian Adam Tooze warned that the enormous amount of debt

---

[61] Burns 2020.

[62] Schrotenboer 2020; Sergent et al. 2020. The first relief bill was for $8 billion; the second was for $192 billion; the third (the CARES Act) was for $1.7 trillion; and the fourth was for $483 billion. That said, the cost of government borrowing was low. The discount rate for the United States was only 0.25 percent in November 2020 while the yield on a 10-year government bond was 0.87 percent (US Federal Reserve Bank 2021a, 2021b).

[63] Palmer 2020.   [64] Matthews 2020.   [65] Smith 2020.

incurred during the coronavirus crisis "will be the battering ram for a new campaign of austerity," which means further attacks on budgets and the state's capacity to fulfill its institutional obligations because "debt service will be taken out of other spending, whether that be schools, pensions, or national defense."[66] Put differently, deficit hawks would be even more emboldened to resist budget increases and cut spending in ways that could damage the state's institutional efficacy.

Tooze was right. With Democrats controlling the House and Senate, once Joe Biden took over the presidency and proposed a $1.9 trillion COVID-19 economic relief bill, Republicans dug in their heels refusing to vote for it because, they argued, it would raise the national debt to horrendous heights. It passed anyway – with no supporting Republican votes. The irony, if not the hypocrisy, of all their handwringing over deficits and debt was that concerns like these were never part of their conversation when they passed the TCJA or refused to cut spending as Trump had requested.

The point is that although debt would have surged due to the pandemic anyway, it would never have reached the extreme level that it did – 128 percent of GDP or roughly $28.1 trillion by 2021 – were it not for Trump's massive tax cuts, his failure to cut spending and his botched response to the coronavirus crisis with its devastating effect on the economy. The institutional complementarity between fiscal institutions – that is, the balance between revenue collection and expenditures – was in tatters and deficits and debt surged. As a result, the state's institutional efficacy had been damaged. Politicians in Congress had become increasingly reluctant to spend what was necessary to stop the pandemic's economic hemorrhaging.

To be sure, governments in the advanced countries have long run deficits and incurred debt, but the American situation had become extreme. Figure 7.7 compares the level of national government debt as a percentage of GDP in the United States and Europe. During the financial crisis in 2008 debt levels on both sides of the Atlantic were roughly comparable. They increased after that, but the increase was greater in the United States, and it skyrocketed on Trump's watch during the pandemic. As a result, Trump unintentionally amplified the conditions for what may become another tipping point that causes further institutional damage to the United States – a deterioration in the dollar's strength. Understanding the danger involved requires reviewing what others have seen as they gazed into the future through their crystal balls.

7.5 INFLATION AND THE DOLLAR

Debt can be an insidious disease for the long-term institutional efficacy of a government. It wrought havoc, for instance, throughout Latin America in the 1980s leading to hyperinflation, a deterioration in the value of local currencies,

---

[66] Tooze 2020. See also Kelton and Chancellor (2020).

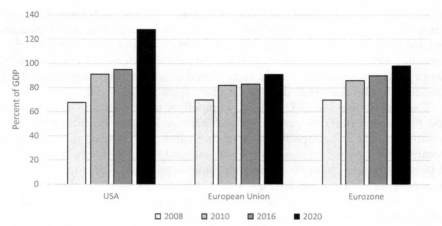

FIGURE 7.7. Government debt as a percentage of GDP.
Source: Trading Economics (2021b).

and eventually austerity programs to solve these problems that took a heavy toll on government budgets and programs throughout the region – often generating political instability. Debt also contributed to fiscal austerity and political problems in Europe after the 2008 financial crisis.[67] Concerns are growing in some quarters that a version of this story, likely not as extreme, awaits the United States if its already sizable debt gets much larger. One fear is that continued borrowing in combination with structural changes in the economy will trigger inflation and erode the value of the dollar. In turn, this would damage the US government's institutional efficacy by undermining its worldwide economic power. How?

First, borrowing often fuels increased government spending, which creates more economic demand that puts upward pressure on prices – inflation. Second, demands for higher wages were often blamed for inflation during the 1970s and 1980s. Some worry that wage-push inflation is poised to return if it hasn't already. For a while it dissipated due to globalization, which enabled employers to move jobs to low-wage countries like Mexico and China, thus neutralizing the ability of workers in high-wage countries like the United States to demand inflationary pay increases. But some say that this globalization effect has just about run its course. Wages are rising in many of the developing countries, so wage-push inflation may be on the rebound in America, exacerbated at least temporarily by the fact that many people who were laid off during the pandemic have not yet returned to work thus creating labor shortages throughout much of the economy. Third, in the absence of tax increases, as

[67] Campbell and Hall 2021, chaps. 3 and 5.

the Baby Boom generation gets older, it will require more inflationary government borrowing and spending for health care and social security.[68] What all this adds up to is the development of another tipping point where more and more borrowing and spending suddenly push the economy over the edge into a period of significant inflation. Whether he intended it or not, by jacking up government debt to record heights, Trump's institutional attack on the deep state, combined with enormous borrowing and spending on COVID-19 relief, will have contributed to this potential tipping point.

Others disagree. Those subscribing to a new brand of economics called modern monetary theory (MMT) don't fret about debt because the United States controls its own currency and so can pay that debt down whenever it wants simply by printing money.[69] Nor do they agonize about inflation. First, they point out that, although the government has chalked up so much debt, inflation hovered below 2 percent for most of the last decade, which was below the Fed's target rate. Second, unemployment was very low in America during the first three years of Trump's presidency yet there was no sign of wage-push inflation.[70] Third, at least until recently, surveys have shown that the public didn't expect inflation to erupt anytime soon, a belief that undermined the effect of the inflationary self-fulfilling prophecy whereby people buy things today because they expect them to be more expensive tomorrow thus causing near-term demand to rise faster than supply and drive-up prices. But despite all this, MMT economists still admit that if the government prints and pumps too much money into the economy, all that spending can eventually trigger inflation.[71] Indeed, that's what happened in the 1960s and early 1970s.[72] In other words, they too realize that there is a tipping point. The question is where is that threshold? As I explained in Chapter 1, predicting tipping points is next to impossible. However, inflation was projected to be 5 percent in 2021 and by February 2022 was nearing 8 percent so it may be approaching.[73]

But how would all this affect America's worldwide economic power – its international institutional efficacy? Here a little historical background is necessary. In 1944 the allies forged the Bretton Woods agreement, a set of rules governing the postar international monetary system that was based on the dollar being the world's strongest and safest currency. As a result, the dollar has long been a central institutional pillar of the world economy and, therefore, US economic hegemony. This gives the United States certain powerful

[68] Cochrane 2020; *The Economist* 2021, pp. 15, 25–27; Irwin 2021; Kelton and Chancellor 2020; Tooze 2020.
[69] Kelton 2020.
[70] However, even before the pandemic crashed the economy, there was slack in the labor market. The Brookings Institution reported that "there [was] still a considerable amount of underutilized labor and many people for whom the labor market [was] not providing adequate opportunities" (Nunn et al. 2019). This helps explain why there was no wage-push inflation.
[71] Kelton 2020, chaps. 2 and 3.   [72] Garten 2021.
[73] Trading Economics 2022; US Federal Reserve Bank 2021e.

advantages – what the French call exorbitant privilege. For example, the US government can borrow at favorable interest rates. The dollar is the preferred currency of central banks and capital markets, and it is the favored form of foreign exchange reserves, all of which make the dollar highly desirable. Most international transactions are cleared in dollars through the SWIFT international payments transfer system over which the United States has considerable influence, which means that the United States can weaponize this system if it wants to by cutting off foreign actors' access to it.[74] However, concern is growing that America's mounting debt will weaken the dollar with serious institutional consequences. Again, there is considerable debate about this.

On one side are the pessimists who believe that the dollar will get weaker as government spending continues to grow and its debt expands, particularly if the government prints dollars to finance this and inflation kicks in as a result. All else being equal, by creating more and more dollars the value of the dollar is watered down and its value relative to other currencies deteriorates.[75] On the other side are the optimists who say that because the dollar is the world's preeminent reserve currency and because there are not many alternatives, it will likely remain strong. After all, they say, roughly a fifth of world trade outside the United States is denominated in dollars and 88 percent of all deals in the $6.6 trillion daily currency market are traded against the dollar.[76] Cornell University economist Eswar Prasad adds in his excellent book *The Dollar Trap* that the dollar's supremacy also rests on a strong set of American institutions that instill great confidence in it among sovereign wealth funds, foreign governments, and other investors around the world. These institutions include strong, open, and transparent democratic processes, a solid legal framework, an effective set of government checks and balances, and an executive branch subject to the rule of law.[77]

I am less optimistic and worry that the dollar may be approaching a tipping point beyond which its foundational status as the world's premiere currency and the monetary backbone of US economic hegemony will begin to wobble – at least given Prasad's institutional argument. His analysis was convincing during the pre-Trump era, when his book was published, but things have changed since then thanks to Trump's institutional attack on the deep state. Confidence in the strength of America's democratic institutions was badly damaged by Trump. Notably, even before the January 6 Capitol insurrection Pew Research found that international confidence in America's president plummeted during Trump's term in office. Furthermore, on average only 17 percent of respondents in sixteen advanced countries said that the United States was a good example of democracy that other countries should follow. 57 percent said that it used to be a good example but hasn't been in recent years.[78] And, of

---

[74] *The Economist* 2020, 2019; Rappeport 2019.   [75] *The Economist* 2020.
[76] Smith et al. 2020.   [77] Prasad 2014, pp. 301–307. See also Garten (2021, p. 322).
[78] Wike et al. 2021.

course, people around the world were aghast as they watched the Capitol riot on television and heard about so many Americans' undying belief in the Big Lie. None of this bolstered confidence in the stability of American political institutions that Prasad argued is important for the dollar's strength. Nor has the persistent and widespread belief in the Big Lie, the civil war in the Republican Party, politicization of the legal system, or the attack on the federal bureaucracy's experience and expertise that I discussed in previous chapters. Add to that America's current bout with inflation and its record-breaking level of government debt and we may have a recipe for the dollar's fall from grace as the world's leading currency.

In fact, even before Trump came into the picture there was evidence that confidence in the dollar was beginning to erode. China started to reduce its dependence on the dollar and elevate its own currency on the world stage by promoting bilateral currency swap agreements and allowing trade deals with Japan and other countries to be settled without using dollars. The Bank of Japan opened swap lines with India and the European Central Bank. Emerging economies have done similar things. The United States' financial clout diminishes as countries expand local currency agreements like these.[79] Trump's aggressive rhetoric and punitive and unpredictable trade policies toward many of these countries – an international version of his bullying leadership style – exacerbated these trends. Furthermore, before Trump took office the International Monetary Fund added the Australian and Canadian dollars to its list of the world's safest currencies – a list that already included four others – the euro, the British pound sterling, and the Japanese yen as well as the dollar.[80] As such, the dollar was facing increasing competition as a safe haven for investors in times of trouble. Some countries are also talking about establishing an alternative to the SWIFT system. Mauro Guillén, Dean of Cambridge University's business school, has worried that "The dollar and the country whose government issues it, and stands by it, is showing clear signs of fatigue." Not only is the dollar becoming less important as an anchor for other currencies, said Guillén, but its share of world currency reserves dropped from close to 100 percent in the 1950s to roughly 60 percent by 2015.[81]

More recently, the value of the dollar dropped precipitously after Congress passed its four massive $2.4 trillion coronavirus rescue packages in 2020. The so-called "Dixie Index" (DXY), which measures the value of the dollar against a basket of other currencies, fell more than ten percent from mid-March 2020 to the end of the year, making up only about half of that loss by December 2021.[82] As one currency-tracking website noted:

---

[79] Khanna 2019, p. 144; Prasad 2014, pp. 209–214, 239–247.
[80] International Monetary Fund 2013; Kirshner 2014, chap. 6.   [81] Guillén 2015, p. 111.
[82] Trading Economics 2021a. The US Dollar Index (DXY) measures the performance of the dollar against a weighted basket of other currencies including the euro, Japanese yen, British pound sterling, Canadian dollar, Swedish krona, and Swiss franc.

The US dollar continues to face heavy selling pressure. . .as prospects of a swift economic recovery eroded safe-haven demand for the dollar. Adding to diminished interest for safety were concerns about rising levels of debt in the US. Unprecedented spending led to large budget and current account deficits and has made the greenback an increasingly unattractive investment. The dollar's weakness is likely to continue well into 2021 as investors shift to risky assets.[83]

Historically, dollars and US debt have been extremely safe investments because they are backed by the "full faith and credit" of the US government, which means that investors rest assured that they will get their money back when they want it. After all, the government can always print money if it must as a last resort. The question is when do investors begin to worry that they can't count on the government's "full faith and credit" anymore? That's when they will become more reticent to lend the federal government money and rely on the dollar for all sorts of transactions. And that's when it will get harder and more expensive for the government to finance its institutional obligations.[84] Its institutional efficacy will suffer accordingly. Although Trump's institutional attack on the deep state didn't cause all these problems single-handedly, it certainly amplified them. And in doing so he may have inadvertently helped create a future tipping beyond which the sanctity of the dollar is permanently damaged, and the institutional foundation of US economic hegemony – its exorbitant privilege – is undermined.

Of course, that hasn't happened yet. Inflation hit a forty-year high in early 2022. As a result, the Fed began to aggressively raise interest rates, which made some dollar-denominated assets like Treasury bonds more attractive to investors. Moreover, growth in emerging markets is expected to be weak in the near term; China's crackdown on democracy is unlikely to abate soon; worries that the pandemic will continue to wreak havoc on national economies persist; pandemic-related supply-chain disruptions continue; and Russia's bloody invasion of Ukraine promises to be long lasting. So, for the time being all this has created enough uncertainty such that the dollar still looks like a relatively safe investment having regained by March 2022 the value it lost since early 2020. How long these extraordinary conditions persist is anyone's guess.[85] As one Wall Street economist told *The New York Times* in May 2022, "It's unusual for the dollar to strengthen at the same time as commodity prices are rising."[86]

Regardless of who's right or wrong in these debates, the fact that people are discussing these issues at all is significant.[87] Nobody was having this conversation ten years ago, which further underscores that one of the institutional mainstays of US economic hegemony may be weakening, thanks in part to Trump's radical attack on the deep state.[88]

---

[83] Trading Economics 2021a.   [84] Kelton and Chancellor 2020.
[85] Ahmed 2021; Ashworth 2021.   [86] Sommer 2022.   [87] Kirshner 2014, p. 137.
[88] Kirshner 2014, pp. 122–130.

7.6 CONCLUSION

Trump's proposed tax and spending cuts were intended to be sharp breaks with past institutional precedent. They were also designed to be broad in scope – the tax cuts would affect most Americans and businesses; the spending cuts would affect most government departments and agencies. In this sense, these were attempts at radical institutional change. But longevity was another matter. The spending cuts never happened. Some of the tax cuts will expire automatically in a few years. And Biden and congressional Democrats have already threatened to rescind some of them before that. Meanwhile, deficits persist, and debt continues to grow, possibly threatening to undermine the sanctity of the dollar – an institutional pillar of US economic hegemony.

The famous Austrian economist Joseph Schumpeter once wrote that the study of public finances is one of the best starting points for an investigation of society, its politics, and the fate of the nation.[89] That is certainly true in this case. We see now that it can also shed light on how political institutions change. First, Trump's capacity for causing radical change was qualitatively different when it came to fiscal institutions like taxing and spending than it was for the other institutional features of the American political system that I have discussed in this book. For fiscal institutions, he had to reckon with Congress whereas in the other areas he could act with a much freer hand. This was especially problematic when it came to his attempt to reform the budget because Congress refused to abide by his wishes. Put differently, reforming fiscal institutions involved a formidable institutional hurdle – the constitutionally mandated separation of powers and the need for Congress to embrace the changes that Trump wanted. The political resistance that hurdle presented was much harder to overcome than most of the obstacles he encountered in the other areas discussed in this book. It was easily overcome when Trump's interests aligned with Congress but was insurmountable when they did not, which is why his leadership qualities failed him in pushing his budget proposals through Congress.

Second, the fates of the TCJA and Trump's budget proposals lend support to the argument that institutionalists have made about the complementary nature of institutions.[90] As noted earlier, institutions don't exist in isolation; they come in sets. As a result, the effects of one often affect those of the others. So, when someone tries to radically overhaul one institution it may be disastrous if the complementary institutions aren't also adjusted. That's what happened here where the tax code was changed but the budget wasn't. The result, of course, was a further deterioration of the state's balance sheet – deficits and debt increased with potential knock-on effects for America's economic hegemony and the state's institutional efficacy at home.

This chapter also underscores the observation of previous chapters that tipping points can be both the cause and effect of radical institutional change. In this case, Trump's tax reform stemmed from a political tipping point but may

---

[89] Schumpeter 1954, pp. 6–7.   [90] Campbell 2010; Crouch 2005; Hall and Soskice 2001.

also help create new ones – mounting political resistance to new or expanded government programs. In fact, Biden's "Build Back Better" social infrastructure initiative was killed by Republicans and a few Democrats, notably West Virginia's Democrat Senator Joe Manchin, who worried that it would push deficits, debt, and inflation too high. This was another indication of how Trump's attack on the deep state may have unintended consequences that further damage the state's institutional efficacy.

Finally, it's worth noting, perhaps ironically, that a radical policy change, such as the TCJA, does not necessarily set things off in an entirely new direction as punctuated equilibrium theory might suggest. That assumption doesn't hold in this case for two reasons. One is that the TCJA merely amplified the long-standing incremental march toward ever-larger debt. In that sense rather than causing a sharp break with the past it reinforced a trajectory already in motion that was inherited from the past. The other reason is that only part of the TCJA – the corporate tax cut – was designed to be permanent. The individual cuts were scheduled to expire within a few years. Even radical institutional changes may be temporary and reversible – sometimes by design.[91]

---

[91] I have discussed this at greater length elsewhere in connection with the sudden seemingly revolutionary changes to the political economies of post-communist Europe (Campbell 2003).

8

Damage Assessment

The day after Donald Trump was elected president in 2016, I attended a panel discussion at the Brookings Institution in Washington DC. The panel included liberals, moderates, and conservatives. The moderator asked them why the election turned out as it did and what the Trump administration was likely to do during the next four years. The panelists offered a lot of different answers, and the debate was lively. But in the end, they all agreed on one thing. Given Trump's promises to lay siege to the deep state, the next four years might be one of the toughest tests ever for America's political institutions. They wondered how well the institutional guardrails of American politics and democracy would hold.

We are now able to address that question and others. Did the guardrails hold? How bad was the damage? And what lessons can we draw from what happened about institutional change in general? This chapter begins with a quick review of the evidence I have presented and how radical Trump's attack on the deep state was. Next it assesses the damage Trump caused and why it could have been worse. Finally, it puts my general argument about institutional change into a broader perspective and discusses what we can learn about radical institutional change from the Trump presidency. Without understanding how change like this occurs, it is impossible to fully understand how Trump caused the damage he did. And without that understanding, we risk falling prey again to another leader just as dangerous, if not more so, to America's political institutions.

8.1 A QUICK REVIEW

Trump won office in the first place by spotting and capitalizing on long-developing trends in the economy, race relations, ideology, politics, and political institutions. Together they created a tipping point that afforded him a

TABLE 8.1. *Trump's attack on the deep state*

Target	Success	Failure
Electoral Institutions: Attack formal rules and informal norms of democracy.	• Undermined legitimacy of the electoral system. • Challenged peaceful transfer of power.	• Failed to overturn election results. • Failed to insert citizenship question and speed up data analysis on US Census.
Republican Party Institutions: Reinterpret institutional meaning of republicanism.	• Upset norms of political civility. • Fomented civil war within the Republican Party. • Upset norms of bipartisanship and compromise within the party and across the aisle.	• Some Republicans resisted Trump's rhetoric trying to save the party.
Justice Institutions: Functionally reorient the justice system's monitoring and enforcement institutions.	• Partisan Federalist Society dominated judicial appointments. • Stacked federal courts thus reorienting the judiciary in a conservative direction. • Upset norms of judicial and DOJ independence from politics.	• Courts, Attorneys General and FBI director sometimes failed to do Trump's bidding.
Bureaucratic Institutions: Attack personnel and functional efficacy of deep state.	• Reduced and ignored civil service experience and expertise. • Created generational vacuums of experience and expertise, especially in Senior Executive Service. • Undermined civil service morale and efficacy.	• Failed to reduce the overall size of civil service bureaucracy.
Fiscal Institutions: Attack resources and functional efficacy of deep state.	• Historic tax cuts for corporations and individuals. • Possibly threatened the long-term supremacy of the dollar.	• Failed to cut budgets. • Failed to cut deficits and public debt.

chance to inspire enough voters so that he could snatch victory from Hillary Clinton in the Electoral College. Once in office he mounted a multipronged attack on a variety of political institutions hoping to make radical changes in all of them. Table 8.1 summarizes the results.

Trump's attack on the nation's electoral institutions built on already escalating doubts about the fairness of national elections – another tipping point – that began to develop with Al Gore's loss to George W. Bush in 2000, grew thanks to the Birther Movement and then Trump's persistent false claims of voting fraud in the 2016 election, and culminated in his insistence on the Big Lie that he had won the 2020 election. In the end, he undermined the legitimacy of the electoral system. As a result, hundreds of his supporters stormed the Capitol and challenged the peaceful transition of power by trying violently to stop Congress from certifying the Electoral College vote. They failed just as Trump had failed to alter the decennial census to give Republicans an advantage in future elections. Throughout all this the full range of Trump's leadership qualities was on display. He inspired his supporters and political allies to believe the Big Lie. In true transactional style, he demanded allegiance and support in his challenges to the 2020 election results from people that he felt were beholden to him, including judges, Supreme Court justices, his attorney general, and his vice president. Much of this was driven by his intellectual arrogance and narcissism – his belief that he could not have lost the election unless it was rigged; his belief that those he had appointed to be loyal allies would not resist him; and his belief that respect for the preservation of long-held institutions, notably the peaceful transition of power, was not more important than his own interest in retaining the presidency. He bullied state election officials and others mercilessly in the process. In the end, Trump challenged long-standing institutional norms governing electoral protocol, political discourse, and American democracy itself.

Much of this spilled over into the Republican Party, which fell under Trump's spell thanks to his ability to exploit another tipping point, rooted in increasingly inflammatory Tea Party rhetoric and the culture wars, which were coming to a political boil. He energized Republicans with inspirational talk about the Big Lie and the need to "stop the steal." Politicians who proclaimed their loyalty and supported him received his support; those who didn't and resisted suffered his wrath. As such, Trump's transactional and bullying leadership styles, rooted in his narcissism and demand for personal loyalty, were joined at the hip. Consequently, the party became increasingly split between Trump's supporters and opponents. The possibilities for compromise within it and for bipartisanship across the aisle virtually disappeared. So did the traditional norms of political civility and reason that had governed the Republican Party for many decades. Although most Republicans fell in line with Trump and didn't resist, some refused to capitulate and called him out for putting his own political interests and demands for loyalty above the interests of the party and the country. By reinterpreting the long-institutionalized meaning of republicanism Trump transformed the party itself.

Trump's attack on America's electoral institutions and his vice-like grip on the Republican Party were direct assaults on the core of American democracy – our system of selecting political representatives and our system of two-party governance. If the legitimacy of the electoral system is drawn into question and if one of the two major political parties in America's two-party system falls into disarray, American democracy is in serious trouble. But Trump's attack went much farther. It also aimed at key elements of the state apparatus, which if weakened enough can compromise the government's ability to operate effectively. This is where Trump's efforts to transform the justice system, the federal bureaucracy and the state's finances came into play.

When it came to changing the justice system – the state's core monitoring and enforcement institutions – Trump benefited from two tipping points. One was created by Mitch McConnell and his Republican colleagues' preservation of an unprecedented number of judicial vacancies. The other stemmed from the Federalist Society's growing influence in the judicial nomination process. As a result of Trump's decision to rely on Federalist Society advice to fill these vacancies, the courts shifted sharply to the right, which is what he had promised to inspire voters. Assuming that his judicial appointments would do his bidding, Trump maligned them when they ruled against him. The same was true of his attorneys general and his first FBI director. When they failed to uphold their end of what Trump presumed to be a transactional deal – pledge loyalty to Trump in exchange for their jobs – he bullied them and if possible, got rid of them. Again, his inflated sense of self-importance was clear. The idea was to functionally reorient the justice system in a more conservative direction and often to defend Trump's own personal interests. It didn't always work but in trying to do so Trump trampled all over the rules and norms of political independence whereby the courts and Justice Department were supposed to be insulated from White House meddling.

Trump's move to drain the swamp of bureaucratic ineptitude, inefficiency, and disloyalty – another promise intended to inspire his supporters – also benefited from a tipping point: growing public dissatisfaction with the size and performance of the federal government. His efforts to deliver on that promise revolved primarily around changing personnel and staff rather than altering rules and norms. The exception was his Schedule F executive order, which was designed to undermine the meritocratic civil service appointment process. Behind all of this was Trump's transactional plan to create a bureaucracy that would cater to his interests. This was a plan he tried to implement by appointing loyalists, often without appropriate expertise or experience, to his cabinet and other positions; by leaving some posts vacant; and by ignoring advice from experienced civil servants and others with whom he disagreed, often bullying them in the process either because he thought he knew better than they did or because he didn't trust them. This was an institutional attack on the people responsible for the functional efficacy of various government departments and agencies whose morale and performance often suffered as a result. Trump failed to reduce the overall size of the federal civil service but did reduce its most experienced ranks, the Senior Executive Service, and created generational vacuums of expertise that will take years to fill.

Finally, Trump delivered on his inspirational promise, based on the flawed logic of supply-side economics, to cut taxes. He did this by taking advantage of a tipping point insofar as a growing proportion of Americans and congressional Republicans, who gained control of the House and Senate, were clamoring for a middle-class tax cut. The Tax Cut and Jobs Act was a historic tax reform, but disproportionately benefited corporations and the rich. Trump also wanted to cut government spending but failed to do so. Cutting taxes and spending was a strategy to help radically reduce the size and scope of the deep state by choking off its resources. In pursuing that strategy Trump gave political pork to some lawmakers and bullied others to try to get what he wanted. Institutional changes in taxation and spending were supposed to complement each other but they didn't. Resistance to his proposed budget cuts was significant, even from within the Republican Party. As a result, budget deficits and debt continued to grow and then suddenly surged during the pandemic, partly because of Trump's mishandling of the crisis, which helped crash the economy and led to trillions of dollars in additional spending, possibly undermining the dollar's supremacy in the future.

8.2 RADICAL OR INCREMENTAL CHANGE?

Remember that in the first chapter I identified three criteria by which we can distinguish radical from incremental institutional change. The sharper the break from past institutional practice, the more rapid and long-lasting the change, and the more parts of an institution that change, the more radical that change is. Much of Trump's assault on the deep state fits this definition of radical change.

First, many of Trump's efforts to change political institutions were unprecedented and represented sharp departures from past practice. Nobody had obliterated norms of civility and cooperation to the extent that he did. Nor had anybody undermined the legitimacy of presidential elections like he did. And nobody had redefined the Republican Party's raison d'être or divided it so deeply as he did. Nor had anybody packed the courts, particularly the Supreme Court, like he did. His attack on the federal bureaucracy's civil service was also unprecedented. Finally, his tax cuts were of historic proportion and his proposed budget cuts would have been too if Congress had adopted them.

Second, nearly all of Trump's maneuvers were carried out quickly – in less than one term in office. And many are likely to have institutional effects lasting far beyond his presidency. His ravaging of the norms of civility of political discourse within the Republican Party has not abated since he left office. Repeated heckling by two Republican congresswomen during Joe Biden's first State of the Union address suggests that things may have gotten worse. Nor has the Big Lie and the pall it throws over national elections diminished, particularly as states adopt new more restrictive election laws based on the false presumption that election fraud is rampant. Trump's judicial and Supreme Court appointments will likely remain in place for decades. The generational vacuum he created in the civil service will linger too. On the other hand, however, some of Trump's radical institutional changes were short-lived, such as his political appointments and executive orders like Schedule F, which Biden quickly rescinded. And a few of the changes that Trump wrought were both incremental and unintended. Notably, he hoped to slash budget deficits and public debt but instead exacerbated them, partly because some of his plans for fiscal reform backfired.

Third, the scope of Trump's efforts to transform the deep state's institutions was extraordinary. He attacked institutions governing elections, the Republican Party, the justice system, the federal bureaucracy, and the state's public finances. These constitute some of the most important institutional parts of the US government and the American political system. Furthermore, Trump's attack zeroed in on both the structural and functional sides of America's political institutions. On the structural side, it aimed to overturn long-standing formal rules, such as the tax code, civil service appointment regulations, and rules governing the Electoral College and state-level elections. It shattered informal norms, most notably the president's willingness to accept electoral defeat and submit to a peaceful transfer of power but also the norms of presidential decorum and political civility. Other examples include abandoning the routine use of the ABA rating system as part of the judicial nomination process and ignoring assumptions of Justice Department independence. Trump's attack also involved reinterpreting the meaning of norms such as those governing the rhetoric, civility, and cooperative ethic among Republicans. On the functional side, Trump tried to reorient the law in a more conservative direction, shift Justice Department activities, and in some cases judicial decision making to benefit him personally and relegate much professional and scientific expertise to the policymaking sidelines. He also jeopardized the state's institutional efficacy by appointing inexperienced people to top-level positions, getting rid of veteran civil service employees, creating generational vacuums of expertise, and trying to curb the government's supply of critical fiscal resources.

Such a broad-based effort at radical institutional reform was rare among modern American presidents whose attempts at change have tended to be more incremental and limited in scope. Even Reagan's presidency, which is often touted as a transformative moment in American politics, was more moderate and incremental in practice than it was in rhetoric. While still president his big tax cut, for example, was pared back within a few years with his blessing after it drove up budget deficits.[1] Nor was there much special in the Carter or George H.W. Bush presidencies insofar as institutional change was concerned. Of course, Clinton was responsible for transforming the welfare system by passing the Temporary Assistance for Needy Families Act. And George W. Bush launched two wars in response to the September 11, 2001 terrorist attacks and in doing so violated international rules against torture and deceived America's allies in justifying the invasion of Iraq. But it's hard to argue that these serious departures from past institutional practice were as sweeping as

---

[1] Bunch 2009.

those that Trump launched. In recent memory the president who probably comes closest to Trump in terms of causing the most radical institutional change is Barack Obama. Due to the 2008 financial crisis Obama oversaw a massive increase in government spending and a major overhaul of regulations governing the financial services industry. He also orchestrated Obamacare. These were major institutional transformations. But they still fell short of the exceptionally broad scope of the changes that occurred on Trump's watch. Trump may go down in history as having attempted the most radical set of institutional changes of any administration since Lyndon Johnson's Great Society program in the 1960s, if not Franklin Roosevelt's New Deal thirty years earlier.

The following counterfactual scenario helps further highlight how radical Trump's institutional impact really was. What if Marco Rubio or Jeb Bush, for instance, had won the Republican nomination in 2016 instead of Trump and then been elected president? Would things have been different? Yes, almost certainly. First, it is hard to imagine that they would have engaged in the same sort of vitriolic rhetoric that Trump displayed as president. They showed little taste for it during the Republican Party's televised primary debates even when Trump baited them with name-calling and insults. It would have been easy for them to retaliate in kind. But they didn't, which suggests that they didn't suffer from narcissism like Trump did.

Second, it's doubtful that they would have inflamed the culture wars as Trump did, particularly when it came to issues of race, minorities, and immigrants. After all, Rubio was a second-generation Cuban American and Bush's wife was a first-generation Mexican American. In office both had represented large minority and immigrant constituencies. Hence, for both personal and professional reasons they were far more sensitive and sympathetic to the interests of these groups than Trump was.

Third, there is little evidence to suggest that they would have appointed so many political neophytes, pushed away experts and professional civil servants, or tried to drain the swamp as Trump did. Unlike Trump, Rubio and Bush were experienced politicians who had a wealth of connections and talent from which to choose skilled and experienced people for executive branch positions. Neither one was intellectually arrogant as Trump was. Neither one claimed to be a "stable genius" or the only person who could fix all that ailed America as Trump did. So, it's likely that they would have heeded the advice of the people they appointed. They would have likely listened to and tolerated varied points of view too.

Fourth, like Trump they would probably have filled the courts with conservative judges and justices but there is no reason to believe that they would have thrown out the nonpartisan American Bar Association ratings. Indeed, unlike Trump during the 2016 campaign, nobody doubted Rubio or Bush's conservative credentials. So, there would have been no reason for them to promise to rely exclusively – and very publicly – on the Federalist Society's recommendations to convince people that they really were conservatives. Nor is there any evidence that they would have put personal loyalty above all else in appointing advisors, judges, or justices, or that they would have launched a fusillade of insults at them when they ruled against them.

Finally, we have no reason to expect that if Rubio or Bush had lost the presidential election to Joe Biden that they would have been so intellectually arrogant and narcissistic that they would have concocted and perpetuated a Big Lie. After all, unlike Trump, neither one trafficked in lies, falsehoods, or conspiracy theories during their political careers any more than most other professional politicians. Neither one complained of election fraud – even when they lost the Republican nomination to Trump. Nor did they have histories of filing countless lawsuits to harass their opponents as Trump did in business. So, there is no reason to think that they would have used that tactic to challenge the election results as Trump did.

The point is that Trump's attack on America's political institutions was unusually radical not only in terms of past institutional precedent or what other presidents have done but also in terms of what would probably have happened if one of his Republican opponents in 2016 had won the presidency instead of him. But how damaging was his attack?

8.3 HOW BAD IS THE DAMAGE?

I realize that not everyone agrees that Trump's actions damaged America's political institutions. Congressional Republicans, for instance, claimed that cutting taxes on Trump's watch fueled an economic expansion and that raising them again would hobble a post-pandemic economic recovery.[2] The fact is, as I have shown, that the promised benefits of Trump's tax cuts for economic growth and investment never materialized as promised. Some people continue to believe despite any proof that the 2020 election was riddled with fraud and that Trump should have won a second term in office. For them there was no Big Lie, and the damage was done by those *not* believing that the election was stolen. Furthermore, despite all sorts of scientific evidence showing that wearing masks, maintaining social distance, and being vaccinated were necessary to wrestle the coronavirus into submission when it first emerged, many of Trump's supporters still believe his claims that there was little need for any of this and that science and the experts advocating these things were – and still are – wrong.[3] Many also believe that stacking the courts with conservative judges and justices is good because it will lead to tougher restrictions on abortion, get

---

[2] Pramuk and Breuninger 2021.
[3] A state-by-state analysis of data from July 2020 found an extraordinarily high correlation (.83) between the percentage of people vaccinated against COVID-19 and the percentage of votes cast for Biden in the 2020 election. Those who voted for Biden were far more likely to have been vaccinated than those who didn't vote for him. I thank Michael Allen for these data.

rid of the Affordable Care Act, loosen controls on gun ownership, and prevent the legalization of marijuana, among other things that conservatives tend to cherish even though their views run against the grain of public opinion.[4]

Others have suggested that Trump's presidency wasn't particularly unusual and so by implication couldn't have been very damaging. I noted in Chapter 1 that political scientist Jon Herbert and his colleagues recognized that Trump was an unusual *president* in terms of his bombastic and unpredictable personality and leadership style.[5] But judging from his policy achievements they said that his *presidency* was rather ordinary. In their view, even his two major accomplishments – passing the big tax reform bill and appointing conservative judges and justices – were in line with mainstream Republican policy preferences.[6] However, as noted, the depth of the tax cuts and the quantity and quality of these judicial appointments were more extreme than most Republicans could imagine. In this case, the problem is that their arguments are based on evidence only from the first half of Trump's presidency, so they missed a lot that came later. For instance, they didn't see the effect that his tax cuts had on driving up federal deficits and pushing the national debt to unprecedented heights with possible knock-on effects for inflation, the dollar, and US economic hegemony. They didn't anticipate the full effect that his judicial appointments had in tilting the federal bench, and especially the Supreme Court, sharply to the right. They also missed that Trump threw the Republican Party into a tizzy; undermined the legitimacy of the electoral system; meddled in the Justice Department; and eviscerated important parts of the senior civil service. These are dramatic outcomes – far from ordinary – that can't be ignored. Besides, my argument is less about policy outcomes per se than it is about the impact Trump had on a much broader set of political institutions, which, as I've indicated, was substantial.

Much the same can be said for Dino Christenson and Douglas Kriner's otherwise excellent analysis of the Trump regime, which shows that in many ways he was an outlier among recent presidents but that his potentially extraordinary executive actions and legislative achievements were rather limited due to a variety of constraints stemming from public, congressional, and judicial antipathy.[7] For instance, they argued that several of his initiatives were blocked by Republicans as well as Democrats in Congress responding to public opinion. But like Herbert and his colleagues, their research examined only the first half of the Trump administration. As a result, it missed several of Trump's most serious and damaging attacks on our political institutions, most notably his assault on electoral norms and the legitimacy of the 2020 presidential election,

---

[4] Recent polls show that the nearly two-thirds of Americans do not want *Roe vs. Wade* overturned (Brenan 2018); half are satisfied with the Affordable Care Act (Saad 2019); only 8 percent want less strict gun laws (Brenan 2021); and 68 percent favor the legalization of marijuana (Brenan 2020).

[5] Herbert et al. 2019.   [6] Herbert et al. 2019, p. 180.   [7] Christenson and Kriner 2020.

which, as I've shown, received tremendous support – not opposition – from members of his own party who gradually fell under his spell and were increasingly prone to defending the Big Lie as well as his other initiatives.

However, the damage Trump caused was uneven; some aspects of it ran deeper than others. Much like a car that grazes the guardrail on a highway and suffers a minor scratch or dent, many bureaucratic appointments could be fixed easily. Just as a body shop can easily buff out the scratch or pop out the dent, Biden moved immediately and deftly to replace many of Trump's top-level appointees to political and civil service positions with more qualified people. Unlike Trump he had decades of government experience and so had a long roster of experienced people from which to choose. This included those he put in charge of managing the response to the COVID-19 pandemic, notably Dr. Anthony Fauci, the world-renowned expert on infectious disease whom Trump had sidelined during the pandemic, but that Biden immediately appointed as his chief medical advisor. Furthermore, in contrast to Trump's first cabinet, which had lots of people with little experience or qualifications for their posts, Biden's cabinet was loaded with relevant experience and expertise. For instance, his Secretary of State, Antony Blinken, wasn't a corporate CEO as Rex Tillerson had been but a former diplomat, a deputy security advisor, and deputy Secretary of State. His attorney general, Merrick Garland, wasn't a politician as Jeff Sessions had been but a circuit court judge and one-time Supreme Court nominee. His Treasury Secretary, Janet Yellen, wasn't a Wall Street titan as Steve Mnuchin had been but held a PhD in economics and had chaired the Federal Reserve. Biden's Secretary of Education, Miguel Cardona, wasn't a billionaire Republican donor as Betsy DeVos had been but a former schoolteacher with a master's degree in bilingual and bicultural education as well as a PhD in education. And his Secretary of Housing and Urban Development, Marcia Fudge, wasn't a pediatric neurosurgeon as Ben Carsen had been but a congresswoman and former city mayor with vast experience working on issues of affordable housing and urban economic development.

Like trying to repair a badly smashed fender or door instead of just a scratch or dent, other sorts of institutional damage will be harder to mend. Budget deficits caused by steep tax cuts can be fixed in one budget cycle if politicians muster the political courage to raise taxes and limit spending but paying down the national debt is much more difficult because it would be extraordinarily expensive and require either tremendous sacrifice among Americans or printing trillions of new dollars. Biden has signaled his willingness to raise taxes on corporations and the wealthy but must get Congress to cooperate to do that. He would also require their help to reduce deficits or resolve the debt problem. None of this would be easy or guaranteed.

Unfortunately, some things are virtually impossible to fix. A car that crashes through the guardrails into a deep ravine and suffers not only bad scratches, dents, and a crushed door but also a bent frame may be beyond repair. At best, it will never run as well as it did before the accident. Rebalancing the Supreme

Court is out of Biden's reach unless one or two of the more conservative justices retire or die soon.[8] Appointing Ketanji Brown Jackson to the Court was not enough. Damage to the Court is serious because it creates the appearance, if not the reality, that it has been politicized to the point where impartial, objective, and fair rulings are no longer assured. Recognizing that problem, Biden formed the bipartisan commission of legal and constitutional experts, mentioned in Chapter 5, to explore the possibility of reforming the Supreme Court, such as by limiting justices' length of service, increasing the size of the Court, and modifying its case selection rules and practices.[9] Whether any of these things come to fruition is a long shot given the congressional resistance that would likely materialize if Biden tried to significantly alter the Court. Meanwhile, the three justices appointed by Trump helped overturn *Roe vs. Wade*, ease restrictions on firearms, and permit states to fund students attending parochial schools that offer religious instruction. All of this appears to be part of a breathtaking attempt to weaponize the high court and eviscerate long-established Supreme Court precedents.[10]

Another thing that may be beyond repair is the general tenor of politics. By decimating the norms of civility, moderation, and compromise in American politics, not to mention collegiality within the Republican Party, Trump sharply amplified the rising vulgarity of political discourse, the increasingly contentious nature of politics, and the political polarization in Congress and the electorate – all of which undermine the social cohesion necessary for well-functioning politics and society. Damage to the Republican Party is especially serious because a two-party system requires two well-functioning and reasonably sensible parties. Now, the Republican Party does not fit that bill. As long as Trump holds sway over the party unifying it will be a very heavy lift and the possibility for bipartisanship between the Republican and Democratic Parties will remain elusive.

However, the most serious damage that Trump caused involves the Big Lie itself. Undermining electoral legitimacy threatens the very core of American democracy. And even if the Big Lie is finally laid to rest, its destructive effects will reverberate for a long time, particularly if Republican-led states pass some of the many dozens of proposed bills that make it harder to vote and that inject political partisanship into how elections are run and supervised, all ostensibly to stop voter fraud and election rigging for which there is no proof. Passing such legislation would represent a trickling down of Trump's attack on the deep state to state and local governments and institutionalize the remnants of the Big Lie for years to come. Biden has called out these efforts, warning that they constitute a twenty-first century version of Jim Crow and the most dangerous threat to American democracy since the Civil War. His Justice Department has sued the state of Georgia for passing such reforms. And he has encouraged

---

[8] Durkee 2021.   [9] The White House 2021.   [10] Greenhouse 2021a.

Congress to pass the John Lewis Voting Rights Advancement Act of 2021 and the For the People Act of 2021 to override what these state legislatures are trying to do. So far, Republicans with Trump's blessing have blocked these efforts.

8.4 IT COULD HAVE BEEN WORSE

Although Trump pushed well beyond the limits of a normal presidency, he did not operate with carte blanche. There were three reasons for this, which begin to bring us back to theories of institutional change. To begin with, Trump operated within an institutional milieu that limited how much leeway he had to work with.[11] Of course, institutions sometimes enabled him to do what he wanted. He enjoyed the power of appointment and sometimes found ways to increase it by taking advantage of rules to circumvent the Senate confirmation process. He also took advantage of his institutional authority to issue executive orders, which he did frequently. But sometimes institutions stymied what he could do. The courts refused to uphold his challenges to the 2020 election results either because there was insufficient evidence to support his claims, or because the arguments to overturn the election results didn't make legal sense. Some of his executive orders, notably various bans on immigration, were also struck down because they failed to stack up legally. Congress and Vice President Mike Pence refused to overturn the 2020 Electoral College vote choosing instead to perform their duty as prescribed by the constitution. In fact, Trump was frustrated by several laws and regulations that he either didn't understand or that didn't allow him to do what he wanted. Recall, for example, that this was one of the things his former Secretary of State Rex Tillerson found to be so frustrating in working for Trump.

The system of checks and balances among the three branches of government – the horizontal separation of power – also made institutional change more difficult than it might have been otherwise. For instance, Trump could have had his way more easily in a system like Britain's where power is far more concentrated in the executive and legislative branches with fewer veto points, or in a country like Denmark where the judiciary's willingness to curtail political initiatives has been so eroded over the decades that, according to some legal scholars, it is governed by an unwritten set of unenforceable constitutional customs and conventions.[12]

Another institutional constraint that Trump faced was American federalism – the vertical decentralization of power.[13] This meant that sometimes he had to face a plethora of possible veto points – that is, he and his allies had to fight

---

[11] Christenson and Kriner 2020; Herbert et al. 2019.

[12] For Denmark, see (Rasmussen 2006, pp. 199–200); for Britain, see Fukuyama (2014, pp. 494–497) and Steinmo (1993).

[13] Fukuyama chap. 34, especially pp. 492–496.

their battles across a wide and uneven political terrain. Challenging election returns, for example, meant filing suits in many different states, each with its own peculiar election laws, regulations, procedures, and officials. Had the election been organized nationally as it is in many European countries, things might have turned out differently. Furthermore, Trump's executive orders and regulatory policies were open to challenge in several state, district, and appellate courts. Had it not been for these most basic elements of America's political institutions, the damage Trump caused might have been much worse.

Second, beyond these institutional constraints there was outright political resistance. Some members of his cabinet pushed back against his wishes but eventually left in frustration either voluntarily or by being fired or forced to resign. Civil servants pushed back against his efforts to curtail research and expert-based policymaking at various agencies and departments, such as the Environmental Protection Agency, the Department of Agriculture, and the Census Bureau. The state's public health experts and scientists challenged his handling of the pandemic. Sometimes his attorneys general and FBI director refused to kowtow to his wishes, enraging him in the process. Experienced Justice Department officials objected publicly to his meddling in the department's internal affairs, perhaps most notably when he tried to replace his acting attorney general with someone who had agreed with him to press Georgia's election officials and governor to change the state's 2020 election results. In that case a phalanx of senior US attorneys threatened to quit if he carried out his plot. And Congress rejected his budget cuts.

The point is that the success of Trump's attack on the deep state depended partly on how much resistance he encountered in pursuing his goals and the institutional barriers and opportunities he ran into along the way – resistance, barriers, and opportunities that varied a lot across the state's terrain and over time. This should not surprise us. Political sociologists and political scientists have long recognized that the state is not a monolithic whole but rather a complex ensemble of agencies, departments, and branches of government all operating amidst a plethora of rules, regulations, laws, customs, and traditions whose interpretation, monitoring, and enforcement depend on thousands of people and vast amounts of resources.[14] This is why Trump's promise to get rid of the "deep state" may finally turn out to have been a fool's errand.

The third reason that Trump didn't operate with carte blanche was sheer luck, which also affected what Trump was able to do. As political scientist Judith Goldstein has shown, "For even the best-laid plans, it may be Fortuna that decides" how things turn out.[15] Again counterfactuals reinforce the point. For example, had it not been for the deaths of Justices Scalia and Ginsberg and Justice Kennedy's retirement Trump would not have filled any Supreme Court

---

[14] Classic statements on the issue include Evans et al. (1985) and Skowronek (1982).
[15] Goldstein 1993, p. 16.

vacancies. Without McConnell's shrewd stonewalling of Obama's judicial nominations Trump would have appointed far fewer federal judges. Had the Democrats not regained control of the House in the 2018 midterm elections, the political constraints on Trump would have been weaker when it came to dealing with Congress. Had Biden's margin of victory in the 2020 election been significantly smaller, the political ramifications of the Big Lie would have been magnified. And had there not been a pandemic, Trump might have won a second term in which case the possibility for him to have inflicted even more change on America's political institutions would have been greater. Social scientists don't like to talk much about contingencies like these because they don't always fit neatly into their theories and models. But they are important anyway. They certainly were in this case.

8.5 GENERALIZING THE ARGUMENT

To put my argument about radical institutional change, tipping points, and presidential leadership into perspective, consider another president's effort to radically overhaul long-standing institutions. In 1971, Richard Nixon decided suddenly and quite unexpectedly to close the gold window – that is, to stop exchanging gold for US dollars at the price of $35 an ounce. This cut the legs out from under the international monetary system established by the allies at Bretton Woods in 1944. America's willingness to exchange dollars for gold stabilized international exchange rates for a quarter-century and helped facilitate the rebuilding of the West European and Japanese economies after the Second World War. As Jeffrey Garten explained in his fascinating book *Three Days at Camp David*, the so-called "Nixon shock" was nothing less than a "fundamental transition" between the immediate post-war era to one where power and responsibility for developing the world economy would now be shared more equitably with America's major allies through multilateral cooperation rather than Washington's unilateral dictates.[16] In short, it was a radical institutional change. Further, in Garten's view we have witnessed another transition recently of equal magnitude, which he calls the Trump shock – the Trump administration's subversion of international agreements and organizations and, I would add, the domestic institutions I have discussed in this book. So, it's worth noting the similarities between the characteristics and dynamics of these two shocks, which suggest that my argument about the nature of tipping points, leadership, and radical institutional change may indeed have broad explanatory reach.

To begin with, the Nixon shock fit the definition of radical institutional change. Just as Trump's institutional assault was broad in scope, covering several aspects of the American political system, Nixon's assault on the

[16] Garten 2021, pp. 325–326.

Bretton Woods institutions involved several aspects of the international and American political economies. Among other things, as Garten explains, in addition to abandoning the convertibility of dollars into gold, which would lead to the dollar's devaluation, Nixon imposed wage and price controls on American business and labor as well as tariffs on imports. He also offered a variety of tax cuts and investment incentives, promised to cut budgets to reduce fiscal deficits, and relentlessly pressured the Federal Reserve to keep interest rates low. All of this was intended to stabilize the international and domestic political-economic systems after Nixon shut the gold window. Second, as a result, the Nixon shock was a sharp break with several past institutional precedents. Finally, many of Nixon's policies were implemented quickly – within a year or less – and some had long-lasting effects. In particular, the days of fixed exchange rates were suddenly gone forever, and although some countries continued to peg the value of their currencies to the dollar, they were no longer obliged to do so by international agreement. Interest rates remained low for several years. But not all of Nixon's packages enjoyed such longevity. Wage and price controls lasted only about two years before being abandoned; fiscal restraints were largely ignored; and import tariffs have come and gone through various administrations. In other words, just like Trump's institutional changes, some of Nixon's enjoyed longevity while others did not.

Both the Nixon and Trump shocks were driven by tipping points, each of which constituted a combination of trends that had been developing for years. In Nixon's case several stand out. Most important, foreigners had been accumulating more and more dollars, largely because of the Marshall Plan, American military expenditures overseas, and US investment abroad. The result was that the United States' supply of gold was no longer sufficient to buy back all the dollars held overseas should foreigners demand to exchange them. Additionally, the United States was facing growing balance of payments deficits; accelerating inflation thanks to exorbitant spending for the Vietnam War, the Great Society program, and other initiatives; and rising unemployment. The Nixon shock was intended to resolve these problems now that they had come to a head, which brings us to the question of leadership.

As I've explained, Trump had a particular set of leadership characteristics that affected how he pursued radical institutional change. Nixon didn't have all of them. However, he assembled a team that did possess some that were especially important, which meant that at least by proxy they were at his disposal. For example, Nixon and his economic advisors all recognized that the country had reached a dangerous tipping point where something dramatic needed to be done to resolve its problems. His team also realized that to sell their package on the home front they needed to mollify all the relevant interest groups to garner their support. Transactional deal-making was the order of the day. So, labor got import tariffs; business got investment tax credits; the automobile industry got the elimination of an auto excise tax; conservatives got budget cuts; liberals got wage and price controls; and consumers got a freeze on price increases. Moreover, the devaluation of the dollar would boost exports thus creating more jobs and economic growth for everyone. On the international front, Secretary of State Henry Kissinger proved to be an excellent representative of the team whose transactional capabilities went a long way in convincing the Europeans and Japanese to agree to Nixon's program when it came time to implement it. The team also had members who were not averse to bullying anyone standing in Nixon's way. Treasury Secretary John Connolly relished the chance to strong-arm troublemakers, both in Congress and abroad, and was good at it. And when it came to providing an inspirational boost to Nixon's plan Paul Volker, Connolly's Under Secretary for Monetary Affairs, was instrumental in persuading reticent members of the team and Congress to buy into it. Nixon himself demonstrated inspirational skill when he announced his plan on national television, explained that it had something for everyone and portrayed it as necessary to make the international economy fairer to the United States.

The reason why Nixon surrounded himself with people who possessed these capacities is important because it points to some important differences between his and Trump's leadership qualities. First, Nixon recognized that he was not an expert in these matters and so brought people to Camp David to discuss them. In this regard, he lacked Trump's intellectual arrogance. Second, he was an experienced politician, so he knew the experts to put on his team in the first place. Third, in this case Nixon was not obsessed with personal loyalty. He had advisors who disagreed with his views and were willing to tell him so. There was much debate and discussion during that long weekend at Camp David among those assembled about how to best handle the problems that Nixon worried about. Sometimes the disagreements were intense. Nixon read the various briefs and proposals that were presented to him and was fully engaged in hours-long discussions. This was a far cry from Trump's short attention span, unwillingness to read briefs and proposals, and reluctance to spend hours engaged in arcane debates about policy details. In the end, instead of dismissing people's opinions that contradicted his own views, Nixon listened carefully and sometimes changed his mind after weighing each side of the argument. Finally, even though a presidential election was approaching, and he knew that some of his plans might not sit well with various constituents, Nixon kept his narcissistic tendencies under control and in this case put the country's best interests above his own.

There is much debate over how well the Nixon shock accomplished its goals. But given Garten's rendition of events, there is no doubt that the radical nature of its institutional changes stemmed from both a tipping point and Nixon's leadership qualities.[17]

---

[17] Garten 2021, pp. 324–325.

8.6 FURTHER LESSONS FOR INSTITUTIONAL THEORY

Overall, then, the degree to which Trump succeeded in radically changing institutions was a function of several things. First were the unique opportunities afforded him by several tipping points. Second was his unique leadership style. Third were the resistance and institutional constraints he faced. Radical institutional change is a complex process.

One of the most glaring omissions in theories of institutional change has been the significance of tipping points. Without them the chances that Trump could have mounted so many efforts at radical change would have been very slim. Recall Judith Goldstein's insight that luck matters. She didn't specify what constituted luck, but I would argue that the presence of tipping points is an important ingredient. In this sense, Trump was extremely lucky to have enjoyed several tipping points. One reason why radical change is rare is that tipping points don't come along every day. Without them change is more incremental.

It's important not to conflate tipping points with the sudden exogenous shocks that some theorists argue are the key sources of institutional change. For one thing, as Malcolm Gladwell recognized, tipping points emerge gradually rather than suddenly. Growing public dissatisfaction with the size and efficiency of the federal government, the accumulation of judicial vacancies, and the pent-up demand for tax cuts are just a few of the examples that I have mentioned. For another thing, the development of tipping points isn't necessarily distinct from the actions of the leaders who eventually benefit from them. Someone with the right set of leadership characteristics can spot trends and help exacerbate the development of tipping points upon which they then capitalize. Notably, the development of the Big Lie – a tipping point that culminated from the gradual accumulation of doubts about election integrity – was something to which Trump contributed through his repeated claims of voter fraud throughout and after the 2016 and 2020 election campaigns and that he then weaponized for his own purposes. Similarly, the Republican Party's ultimate transformation into what some now call the Party of Trump or "Trump rump" stemmed partly from the culture wars and a rising tide of political incivility to which Trump had been contributing for years. The point is that leaders don't just inherit tipping points; sometimes they help create them in the first place.

I explained in Chapter 1 that scholars who have sought to explain institutional change have often left people out of the equation – that is, they have relied on structural arguments about things like exogenous shocks, critical junctures, path-dependence, and punctuated equilibrium and have neglected how important living and breathing actors are in facilitating or inhibiting institutional change. Moreover, those who take people and agency seriously often do so without carefully specifying what leadership traits might be involved. Following Richard Samuels, I have argued that these consist of several things: the ability to inspire people to support change; the ability to engage in transactional deal-making with people to garner their cooperation;

the ability to bully people into backing the leader's policies; and, as Gladwell showed, the ability to spot and capitalize on tipping-point opportunities for change in the first place. Trump utilized all these characteristics to varying degrees as he lay siege to America's political institutions. The importance of leadership qualities is another omission in many theories of institutional change.

However, leaders also possess other traits that matter too. In Trump's case, obsessive demands for personal loyalty, inexperience and a tendency to appoint people who were also inexperienced, intellectual arrogance, and a narcissistic sense of self-importance all played a role in his efforts to orchestrate radical institutional change. Insofar as scholars recognize the importance of entrepreneurial and leadership skills, they dwell on the strengths that leaders need to be successful but ignore the weaknesses that either stymie their attempts to change things or cause serious damage even if they succeed in changing things a lot. Put differently, there are two sides to leadership that need to be taken into consideration to understand episodes of dramatic institutional change – leadership strengths and leadership weaknesses.

Three additional points about people, agency, and institutional change are important. First, I have only scratched the surface when it comes to specifying the importance of leadership characteristics and hope that others will continue to explore the issue. More work is needed to specify what it takes to be inspirational, what the most effective ways are to gin up support for policies through transactional deal-making, and the conditions under which bullying either works or backfires. Similarly, more work is required to identify how narcissism, demands for personal loyalty, inexperience, and intellectual arrogance affect what leaders can and cannot do. In other words, we need to pay closer attention to how and when different leadership qualities matter – and which ones tend to be the most important.

Second, institutional change is not just a matter of revising rules, norms, monitoring and enforcement mechanisms, and meaning systems – that is, institutional structure. It can also involve altering institutional functions. That means changing either the efficacy or orientation of institutions – how well they work and the purposes toward which they are put. Even when formal institutional structures remain intact, their functions may shift.[18] People matter a great deal here. By replacing personnel Trump influenced how effectively certain agencies were able to pursue their institutional mandates. For example, the Internal Revenue Service suffered staffing cuts that reduced its efficacy in auditing and pursuing wealthy tax evaders. By stacking the courts Trump reoriented the functional purposes toward which the law was put. Indeed, recent Supreme Court decisions indicate that his conservative supermajority is willing to ignore and roll back some of the Court's own long-standing legal

---

[18] Ashbee 2020, p. 1038.

precedents and point the law in new and much more conservative directions. Justice Sotomayor has argued more than once that "now, it seems, the Court is willing to overrule precedent without even acknowledging it is doing so, much less providing any special justification."[19]

Third, institutional change is contingent on the relationship between leaders and their staff. Where that relationship is strong and supportive change is more likely than where it is weak and conflictual thus breeding legitimacy crises that can block change. Trump recognized this, which is why he tried to purge the government of people he suspected of disloyalty. Max Weber recognized this too when he argued that serious legitimation problems emerge when leaders lose the support of their staff.[20] Attempts to overhaul political institutions can flounder if there is resistance to them from staffers within the state.

In this regard, it is also worth noting that much of the resistance Trump ran into within the state came from professionals, scientists, and other experts. These are highly educated and well-trained people whose knowledge base and experience are their sources of political power and influence. Modern bureaucracies, including states, are staffed increasingly with people like this. As a result, the tensions and possibilities for conflict between political and bureaucratic leadership and their professionally trained staff increases.[21] It behooves those studying institutional change to pay close attention to the role that professionally trained, knowledgeable people play in fomenting or resisting institutional change. This is another way in which systematically bringing people back into the analysis of change is important.

We also need to remember that many scholars studying institutional change focus on formal rules, laws, and regulations at the expense of informal norms. But we have seen that changing norms can be just as consequential if not more so. Stephen Skowronek and his colleagues noticed the same thing in their analysis of past presidencies remarking that the quality of government "ultimately depends on common understandings of what good government entails. It really is all just a matter of norms."[22] This was particularly evident in the effect Trump had on the norms of political civility and the Republican Party. As William Howell and Terry Moe point out:

The normative universality that has long unified and democratically constrained the presidents of both parties is giving way (for now) to a new normative arrangement that is bifurcated by party...The normal presidency will continue to live on when Democrats hold office, but probably not when Republicans do, at least for the foreseeable future.[23]

---

[19] Liptak 2021.
[20] Weber 1978, pp. 212–213, 264, 278–280. See also Parsons (1964, pp. 58–60), Gouldner (1979) and Wilson (1980, pp. 372–382).
[21] Friedson 1994; Gouldner 1979. See Fukuyama (2014, chap. 35, especially pp. 509–511) for a discussion of how this affects states and policymaking.
[22] Skowronek et al. 2021, p. 198.   [23] Howell and Moe 2020, p. 173.

There is also a lesson about unintended consequences to be gleaned from Trump's attack on the state. Trump intended to achieve certain goals, such as cutting taxes, balancing the budget, reducing public debt, and driving out scientific expertise from certain areas of the executive branch of government. Sometimes what resulted turned out to be quite different from what he either intended or imagined. For instance, Trump's corporate tax cuts were associated with a reduction rather than an increase in corporate investment. When his administration tried to sideline scientific expertise in the Department of Agriculture by moving its research arm from Washington DC to the Midwest, he emboldened some of its scientific staff, whom he had intended to quit. Instead, they dug in their heels and accepted the transfer to push back and preserve some of the expertise and research that Trump was trying to get rid of. Much the same thing happened when he tried to shelve scientists and public health advisors during the pandemic. There was a backlash. Most notably, rather than letting himself be muzzled, Anthony Fauci frequently granted interviews to the media in which he contradicted Trump's claims about the virus being under control, about various crackpot treatments, and about the futility of wearing masks, social distancing and observing other scientifically proven public health precautions. Fauci became a pariah in the Trump administration but a media darling appearing almost nightly on TV news programs. And rather than calming the public as Trump apparently intended, pushing out Fauci raised all sorts of public doubts and concerns about the government's capacity for handling the pandemic. Indeed, Trump's mishandling of the pandemic may have cost him the election in 2020.[24]

Wolfgang Streeck, Kathleen Thelen, and others discussed in Chapter 1, who have studied incremental change have suggested that the outcomes of change are often unintended. Institutions may drift slowly in new directions, displace other institutions, and even become exhausted and disappear, all almost as if by accident. It turns out that the consequences of more radical institutional changes may also be unintended and may even come back to haunt those who instigated those changes in the first place. But we shouldn't be surprised by this. As Timur Kuran explained about the frequency and importance of unintended consequences, "The root reason for unintended consequences is that the choices we make on one issue impinge on issues we have been treating as unrelated, and possibly also on matters not yet recognized as issues."[25] Put differently, failing to recognize or accommodate the complementary relationships among institutions can lead to surprises when change is afoot. The mismatch between Trump's tax reforms and Congress' refusal to cut spending is the best example.

One unintended consequence of radical institutional change may be to create new tipping points in the future. For example, while Trump managed to capture the hearts and minds of the Republican Party, he may have also unintentionally changed the Democratic Party. Although the Democrats managed to retain control of the House and gain control of the Senate in the 2020 election, their majorities were razor-thin; only a handful of seats in the House and exactly half the seats in the Senate with a Democratic vice president providing the tie-breaking vote when necessary. This is a grave liability insofar as Democrat incumbents in red and deeply purple states may now feel compelled by electoral insecurity to embrace more conservative, if not reactionary, positions on the issues than they would have otherwise. In short, the Democratic Party may have reached a tipping point in the sorts of policies they are willing to advocate. One indication is the opposition of Senators Joe Manchin (D-W.VA) and Kristin Sinema (D-AZ), both Democrats, to Biden's "Build Back Better" social infrastructure proposal. Their refusal to support the bill killed it and enraged the left wing of the party as well as many moderates.[26] It may also have put the brakes on the Democrats' more progressive policy agenda.

This is not the only example of Trump's assault on the deep state unintentionally creating the possibility of new tipping points in the future. Trump's handling of the country's fiscal affairs may have inadvertently helped spark inflation and may yet weaken the dollar, which, as I explained in Chapter 7, may push the country further toward a tipping point for American international hegemony. Making matters worse, Trump's extraordinary behavior on the international stage – his lack of civility and respect for diplomatic protocol, not to mention his disregard for international treaties and agreements – undermined America's reputation and standing among other countries, which was one reason why the level of confidence and trust foreigners had in the United States plummeted while he was in office. A Pew Research Center survey found that America's reputation among many key allies and partners reached an all-time low by 2020. According to Pew researchers, "In several countries, the share of the public with a favorable view of the US is as low as it has been at any point since the center began polling on this topic nearly two decades ago."[27] Several European leaders expressed doubts that they could count on US leadership anymore. Of course, they welcomed Biden's election as a sign that the United States would resume some of its former leadership roles. His leadership in mobilizing an international response against Russia's ruthless invasion of Ukraine in 2022 mollified some of their concerns. But Trump's behavior left a bad taste in their mouths. Our allies can never be quite sure whether Biden's successor might not turn his or her back on them again.[28] The same is true for America's adversaries. The Biden administration has tried to revitalize an agreement with Iran whereby it would not develop nuclear weapons if the United States lifted sanctions imposed by Trump. But the

---

[26] Many thanks to Alex Hicks for this insight.   [27] Wilke et al. 2020.   [28] Erlanger 2020.

Iranians have said that they will refuse to strike a new bargain without guarantees that the next president won't reimpose similar sanctions. Once trust is lost it is very hard to restore. In other words, Trump may have helped generate and then push America past a tipping point where its international reputation and influence are permanently tarnished. Insofar as US leadership on the world stage would help tackle problems like the pandemic, cyberthreats, nuclear proliferation, rogue states, and climate change, the unintended consequences of Trump's behavior and policies may be especially damaging in the long run.

Trump's attack on the deep state's institutions was unprecedented, abrupt, and sweeping. Many of the results will be long-lasting. But even though Trump is no longer president the danger has not passed. The institutional siege is not over yet. Republicans have learned a lot by watching him, which is why they moved quickly in so many states to revamp election rules and get rid of nonpartisan election officials. They have also learned that playing fast and loose with the truth can be a winning political strategy. As a result, we now live in a brave new world where people must choose between facts and falsely contrived "alternative facts." Trump has learned a lot too, which is why he has tried to remove people who were obstacles to his reelection in 2020 and why he has supported candidates for local, state, and national offices who have pledged allegiance to him.[29] We are still waiting to see if he will run again for president. All of this is dangerous for American democracy. From now on there will always be the risk that another president with Trump's leadership qualities will follow in his footsteps, pursuing new and perhaps even more radically damaging institutional changes to democracy and the state than those discussed in this book.[30]

In Hollywood, it's often true that the sequel to a movie is worse than the original. Americans need to remain vigilant that the same thing doesn't happen in presidential politics now that Trump has left the White House.

----

[29] Goldmacher 2022.
[30] Bauer and Goldsmith 2020, pp. 3, 354–355; Hennessey and Wittes 2020; Howell and Moe 2020; Skowronek et al. 2021.

References

Abrajano, Marisa, and Zoltan Hajnal. 2015. *White Backlash: Immigration, Race and American Politics.* Princeton, NJ: Princeton University Press.

Abramowitz, Alan. 2019. "Did Russian Interference Affect the 2016 Election Results?" Rasmussen Reports, August 8. www.rasmussenreports.com/public_content/polit ical_commentary/commentary_by_alan_i_abramowitz/did_russian_interference_ affect_the_2016_election_results.

2013. *The Polarized Public?* New York: Pearson.

Abramson, Alana. 2017. "President Trump's Allies Keep; Talking about the 'Deep State'. What's That?" *Time*, March 8. https://time.com/4692178/donald-trump-deep-state-breitbart-barack-obama/.

Achenbach, Joel. 2018. "A Look at the List Helping Trump Reshape the Supreme Court." *Chicago Tribune*, July 8. www.chicagotribune.com/nation-world/ct-trump-supreme-court-list-20180708-story.html.

Adams, Scott. 2017. *Win Bigly: Persuasion in a World Where Facts Don't Matter.* New York: Penguin.

Agiesta, Jennifer, and Sonya Ross. 2012. "AP Poll: Majority Harbor Prejudice against Blacks." *Ebony*, October 12. https://www.ebony.com/news/ap-poll-us-majority-harbor-prejudice-against-blacks/

Ahlquist, John, and Margaret Levi. 2011. "Leadership: What It Means, What It Does, and What We Want to Know about It." *Annual Review of Political Science* 14:1–24.

Ahmed, Saqib Iqbal. 2021. "Dollar Dominates as Inflation Heats Up." *Reuters*, November 15. www.reuters.com/business/finance/dollar-dominates-inflation-heats-up-2021-11-15/

Aichholzer, Julian, and Johanna Willmann. 2020. "Desired Personality Traits in Politicians: Similar to Me But More of a Leader." *Journal of Research in Personality* 88:1–11.

Aistrup, Joseph. 1996. *The Southern Strategy Revisited.* Lexington: University of Kentucky Press.

Alba, Richard. 2015. "The Myth of a White Minority." *New York Times*, June 11. www.nytimes.com/2015/06/11/opinion/the-myth-of-a-white-minority.html.

Alberta, Tim. 2022. "The Freshman." *The Atlantic*, January/February, 46–55.

Alemany, Jacqueline, Hannah Allam, Devlin Barrett et al. 2021. "Red Flags: During." *Washington Post*, October 31. www.washingtonpost.com/politics/interactive/2021/jan-6-insurrection-capitol/.

Allam, Hannah, Devlin Barrett, Aaron C. Davis et al. 2021. "Red Flags: Before." *Washington Post*, October 31. www.washingtonpost.com/politics/interactive/2021/jan-6-insurrection-capitol/.

Allen, Jonathan, and Amie Parnes. 2017. *Shattered: Inside Hillary Clinton's Doomed Campaign*. New York: Crown.

Alms, Natalie. 2021. "Biden Repeals Schedule F, Rolls Back Trump-Era Workforce Policy." *FCW: The Business of Federal Technology*, January 22. https://fcw.com/articles/2021/01/22/schedule-f-official-time-orders-repealed.aspx.

Alms, Natalie, and Adam Mazmanian. 2020. "Schedule F Workforce Plan Survives Funding Bill." *FCW: The Business of Federal Technology*, December 21. https://fcw.com/articles/2020/12/21/funding-bill-civil-service-order-stays.aspx.

Amadeo, Kimberly. 2020. "How Every President since Hoover Has Affected the Economy." *The Balance*, March 27. www.thebalance.com/gdp-growth-by-president-highs-lows-averages-4801102.

American Bar Association. 2020a. "Standing Committee on the Federal Judiciary: What It Is and How It Works." www.americanbar.org/content/dam/aba/administrative/government_affairs_office/backgrounder-9-21-2020.pdf.

  2020b. "Supreme Court Nominations." www.americanbar.org/groups/committees/federal_judiciary/resources/supreme-court-nominations/.

American Psychological Association. 2016. "Speaking of Psychology: How Politics Became So Uncivilized." October. www.apa.org/research/action/speaking-of-psychology/incivility-politics.

Angelucci, Charles, Julia Cage, and Michael Sinkinson. 2020. "Media Competition and News Diets." National Bureau of Economic Research, working paper 26782. www.nber.org/papers/w26782.

Arnsdorf, Isaac. 2021. "Trump Spawned a New Group of Mega-Donors Who Now Hold Sway Over the GOP's Future." *ProPublica*, May 6. www.propublica.org/article/trump-spawned-a-new-group-of-mega-donors-who-now-hold-sway-over-gops-future.

Ashbee, Eddie. 2020. "Roundtable." *Journal of American Studies* 54(5):1032–1048.

Ashworth, Marcus. 2021. "Still the King, the U.S. Dollar Throws Shade at Currency Weaklings." Bloomberg, November 17. www.bloomberg.com/opinion/articles/2021-11-17/despite-a-strengthening-yuan-the-u-s-dollar-has-no-real-rival-in-the-world.

Bach, Natasha. 2019. "All the Acting Heads of Trump's Presidency." *Fortune*, November 27. https://fortune.com/2019/11/27/trump-acting-heads-cabinet-presidency/.

Badger, Emily. 2020. "Most Republicans Say They Doubt the Election. How Many Really Mean It?" *New York Times*, November 30. www.nytimes.com/2020/11/30/upshot/republican-voters-election-doubts.html.

Badger, Emily, Quoctrung Bui, and Alicia Parlapiano. 2021. "The Government Agencies That Became Smaller, and Unhappier, under Trump." *New York Times*, February 1. www.nytimes.com/2021/02/01/upshot/trump-effect-government-agencies.html.

Bailey, Michaell. 2020. "If Trump Appoints a Third Justice, the Supreme Court Would Be the Most Conservative It's Been since 1950." *Washington Post*, September 22. www.washingtonpost.com/politics/2020/09/22/if-trump-appoints-third-justice-supreme-court-would-be-most-conservative-its-been-since-1950/.

Baker, Peter, Maggie Haberman, and Annie Karni. 2021. "Pence Reached His Limit with Trump. It Wasn't Pretty." *New York Times*, January 13. www.nytimes.com/2021/01/12/us/politics/mike-pence-trump.html.

Ballotpedia. 2021. "Federal Courts." June 9. https://ballotpedia.org/Federal_judicial_appointments_by_president

     2020. "Federal Courts." December 14. https://ballotpedia.org/Federal_judicial_appointments_by_president

Balsamo, Michael. 2020. "Disputing Trump, Barr Says No Widespread Election Fraud." *Associated Press*, December 1. https://apnews.com/article/barr-no-widespread-election-fraud-b1f1488796c9a98c4b1a9061a6c7f49d

Barber, James. 1972. *The Presidential Character*. Englewood Cliffs, NJ: Prentice-Hall.

Barrett, Devlin, Aaron C. Davis, Josh Dawsey et al. 2021. "Red Flags: After." *Washington Post*, October 31. www.washingtonpost.com/politics/interactive/2021/jan-6-insurrection-capitol/.

Barry, Dan. 2020. "'Loser': How a Lifelong Fear Bookended Trump's Presidency." *New York Times*, November 26. www.nytimes.com/2020/11/26/us/politics/trump-election-loss.html.

Bartels, Larry. 2016. *Unequal Democracy*: Princeton, NJ: Princeton University Press.

Barton, Benjamin. 2019. "American (Dis)Trust of the Judiciary." *Institute for the Advancement of the American Legal System*. September. Denver, CO: University of Denver.

Barzel, Yoram. 1989. *Economic Analysis of Property Rights*. New York: Cambridge University Press.

Bauer, Bob and Jack Goldsmith. 2020. *After Trump: Reconstructing the Presidency*. Washington, DC: Lawfare Press.

Baumgartner, Frank and Bryan Jones. 1993. *Agendas and Instability in American Politics*. Chicago, IL: University of Chicago Press.

Beauchamp, Zack. 2022. "What Happens When the Public Loses Faith in the Supreme Court?" *Vox*, June 24. www.vox.com/23055620/supreme-court-legitimacy-crisis-abortion-roe.

Beck, Madelyn. 2020. "BLM Move Prompt about Half of D.C. Staff to Quit." *Boise State Public Radio News*, KRCC, March 10. www.cpr.org/2020/03/06/blm-move-prompts-about-half-of-d-c-staff-to-quit/.

Béland, Daniel and Robert Cox, editors. 2011. *Ideas and Politics in Social Science Research*. New York: Oxford University Press.

Benner, Katie. 2021a. "Trump and Justice Dept. Lawyer Said to Have Plotted to Oust Acting Attorney General." *New York Times*, January 22. www.nytimes.com/2021/01/22/us/politics/jeffrey-clark-trump-justice-department-election.html.

     2021b. "Watchdog to Examine Whether Justice Dept. Helped Trump Effort to Overturn Election." *New York Times*, January 25. www.nytimes.com/2021/01/25/us/politics/justice-department-inspector-general-trump-voter-fraud.html

Benner, Katie, and Catie Edmondson. 2021. "Pennsylvania Lawmaker Played Key Role in Trump's Plot to Oust Acting Attorney General." *New York Times*, January 23.

www.nytimes.com/2021/01/23/us/politics/scott-perry-trump-justice-department-election.html.

Benner, Katie, and Charlie Savage. 2021. "Jeffrey Clark was Considered Unassuming. Then He Plotted with Trump." *New York Times*, January 24. www.nytimes.com/2021/01/24/us/politics/jeffrey-clark-trump-election.html.

Bergman, Elizabeth, Dari Sylvester Tran, and Philip Yates. 2019. "Voter Identification." Pp. 102–113 in *Electoral Integrity in America*, edited by Pippa Norris, Sarah Cameron and Thomas Wynter. New York: Oxford University Press.

Berhnard, Michael, and Daniel O'Neill. 2019. "Trump: Causes and Consequences." *Perspectives on Politics* 17(2):317–324.

Berman, Ari. 2015. "A Voter-Fraud Witch Hunt in Kansas." *The Nation*, June 11. www.thenation.com/article/archive/voter-fraud-witch-hunt-kansas/

Bernstein, Andrea. 2020. "Where Trump Learned the Art of the Quid Pro Quo." *The Atlantic*, January 20. www.theatlantic.com/ideas/archive/2020/01/trumps-brand-of-transactional-politics/604978/

Bevor, Anthony. 2009. *D-Day: The Battle for Normandy*. New York: Penguin.
	1998. *Stalingrad: The Fateful Siege: 1942–1943*. New York: Penguin.

Binder, Sarah. 2014. "Polarized We Govern?" Center for Effective Public Management, The Brookings Institution. Washington, DC: Brookings Institution. www.brookings.edu/research/polarized-we-govern/

Blake, Aaron. 2017. "Donald Trump Claims None of Those 3 to 5 Million Illegal Votes Were Cast for Him. Zero." *Washington Post*, January 26. www.washingtonpost.com/news/the-fix/wp/2017/01/25/donald-trump-claims-none-of-those-3-to-5-million-illegal-votes-were-cast-for-him-zero/

Blanchard, Oliver, Rudiger Dornbusch, Paul Krugman, Richard Layard, and Lawrence Summers. 1992. *Reform in Eastern Europe*. Cambridge: Massachusetts Institute of Technology Press.

Blom, Terry. 2018. "CBO's Projections of Deficits and Debt for the 2018–2028 Period." April 19. Washington, DC: Congressional Budget Office. www.cbo.gov/publication/53781.

Bluestone, Barry and Bennett Harrison. 1988. *The Great U-Turn: Corporate Restructuring and the Polarizing of America*. New York: Basic Books.

Blumenthal, Paul. 2021. "Capitol Insurrectionists Said They Were Following Trump's Orders." *Huffington Post*, January 16. www.huffpost.com/entry/capitol-insurrection-trump-orders_n_6002040ac5b6efae62f88f31.

Blyth, Mark. 2013. *Austerity*. New York: Oxford University Press.

Booth School of Business. 2012. "Laffer Curve." *The Initiative on Global Markets*, June 26. www.igmchicago.org/surveys/laffer-curve/.

Borowitz, Andy. 2022. *Profiles in Ignorance: How America's Politicians got Dumb and Dumber*. New York: Avid Reader Press.

Bouie, Jamelle. 2022. "You May Not Find Many Friends on This Power-Hungry Supreme Court." *New York Times*, April 8. www.nytimes.com/2022/04/08/ketanji-brown-jackson-supreme-court.html.

Bowles, Nigel. 1999. "Studying the Presidency." *Annual Review of Political Science* 1:1–23.

Braun, Rudolf. 1975. "Taxation, Sociopolitical Structure, and State-Building: Great Britain and Brandenburg-Prussia." Pp. 243–327 in *The Formation of National*

States in Western Europe, edited by Charles Tilly. Princeton, NJ: Princeton University Press.

Brazile, Donna. 2017. *Hacks: The Inside Story of the Break-ins and Breakdowns That Put Donald Trump in the White House*. New York: Hechette Books.

Brenan, Megan. 2021. "Americans Remain Largely Dissatisfied with U.S. Gun Laws." Gallup Polling, February 19. https://news.gallup.com/poll/329723/americans-remain-largely-dissatisfied-gun-laws.aspx.

2020. "Support for Legal Marijuana Inches Up to a New High of 68%." Gallup Polling, November 9. https://news.gallup.com/poll/323582/support-legal-marijuana-inches-new-high.aspx.

2018. "Nearly Two-Thirds of Americans Want Roe v. Wade to Stand." Gallup Polling, July 12. https://news.gallup.com/poll/237071/nearly-two-thirds-americans-roe-wade-stand.aspx.

Brennan Center for Justice. 2022. "FOIA Documents from Trump Administration on 2020 Census." January 13. www.brennancenter.org/our-work/research-reports/foia-documents-trump-administration-2020-census.

2020a. "Debunking the Voter Fraud Myth." New York University School of Law. www.brennancenter.org/sites/default/files/analysis/Briefing_Memo_Debunking_Voter_Fraud_Myth.pdf.

2020b. "In His Own Words: The President's Attacks on the Courts." February 14. www.brennancenter.org/our-work/research-reports/his-own-words-presidents-attacks-courts.

British Broadcasting Company. 2020a. "Trump Says Universal Mail-In Voting Would be 'Catastrophic'." *BBC News*, August 16. www.bbc.com/news/world-us-canada-53795876.

2020b. "Trump Blocks Postal Funds to Prevent Expanded Mail-In Voting." *BBC News*, August 13. www.bbc.com/news/election-us-2020-53772526

2016. "Trump Claims Millions Voted Illegally in Presidential Poll." *BBC News*, November 28. www.bbc.com/news/world-us-canada-38126438.

Brock, David, Ari Rabin-Havt and Media Matters. 2012. *The Fox Effect*. New York: Anchor.

Bump, Philip. 2021. "How the Culture-War Divide in the U.S. Compares to Other Democracies." *Washington Post*, May 7. www.washingtonpost.com/politics/2021/05/07/how-culture-war-divide-us-compares-other-democracies/.

Bunch, Will. 2009. *Tear Down This Myth: How the Reagan Legacy Has Distorted Our Politics and Haunts Our Future*. New York: Free Press.

Burke, John. 2018. "'It Went Off the Rails: Trump's Presidential Transition and the National Security System." *Presidential Studies Quarterly* 48(4):832–844.

Burns, Alexander, and Jonathan Martin. 2022. "'I've Had It with This Guy': G.O.P. Leaders Privately Blasted Trump After Jan. 6." *New York Times*, April 21. www.nytimes.com/2022/04/21/us/politics/trump-mitch-mcconnell-kevin-mccarthy.html.

Burns, Katelyn. 2020. "Trump Wants His Name on Millions of Stimulus Checks, Even If It Delays Them." *Vox*, April 15. www.vox.com/policy-and-politics/2020/4/15/21222046/trump-name-stimulus-checks-delays.

Bycoffe, Aaron, Ella Koeze, and Nathaniel Rakich. 2020. "Did Americans Support Removing Trump From Office?" *FiveThirtyEight*, February 12. https://projects.fivethirtyeight.com/impeachment-polls/.

Campbell, James E. 2016. *Polarized*. Princeton: Princeton University Press.

Campbell, John L. 2018. *American Discontent: The Rise of Donald Trump and Decline of the Golden Age*. New York: Oxford University Press.

2010. "Institutional Reproduction and Change." Pp. 87–116 in *The Oxford Handbook of Comparative Institutional Change*, edited by Glenn Morgan, John L. Campbell, Colin Crouch, Ove Kaj Pedersen and Richard Whitley. New York: Oxford University Press.

2004. *Institutional Change and Globalization*. Princeton, NJ: Princeton University Press.

2003. "States, Politics and Globalization: Why Institutions Still Matter." Pp. 234–259 in *The Nation State in Question*, edited by T. V. Paul, G. John Ikenberry and John A. Hall. Princeton, NJ: Princeton University Press.

2002. "Ideas, Politics and Public Policy." *Annual Review of Sociology* 28:21–38.

1998. "Institutional Analysis and the Role of Ideas in Political Economy." *Theory and Society* 27:377–409.

1987. "Legitimation Meltdown: Weberian and Neo-Marxist Interpretations of Legitimation Crisis in Advanced Capitalist Society." *Political Power and Social Theory* 6:133–158.

Campbell, John L., and John A. Hall. 2021. *What Capitalism Needs: Forgotten Lessons of Great Economists*. New York: Cambridge University Press.

Campbell, John L., and Ove K. Pedersen. 2014. *The National Origins of Policy Ideas: Knowledge Regimes in the United States, France, Germany and Denmark*. Princeton, NJ: Princeton University Press.

2007. "The Varieties of Capitalism and Hybrid Success: Denmark in the Global Economy." *Comparative Political Studies* 40(3):307–332.

2001a. "The Rise of Neoliberalism and Institutional Analysis." Pp. 1–23 in *The Rise of Neoliberalism and Institutional Analysis*, edited by John L. Campbell and Ove K. Pedersen. Princeton, NJ: Princeton University Press.

2001b. "Conclusion: The Second Movement in Institutional Analysis." Pp. 249–283 in *The Rise of Neoliberalism and Institutional Analysis*, edited by John L. Campbell and Ove K. Pedersen. Princeton, NJ: Princeton University Press.

Campbell, John L., and Ove K. Pedersen, editors. 1996. *Legacies of Change*. New York: Aldine de Gruyter.

Capehart, Jonathan. 2012. "Republicans Had It in for Obama Before Day 1." *Washington Post*, August 10. www.washingtonpost.com/blogs/post-partisan/post/republicans-had-it-in-for-obama-before-day-1/2012/08/10/0c96c7c8-e31f-11e1-ae7f-d2a13e249eb2_blog.html?utm_term=.6fd86a311738

Capoccia, Giovanni. 2016a. "Critical Junctures." Pp. 89–106 in *The Oxford Handbook of Historical Institutionalism*, edited by Orfeo Fioretos, Tulia Falleti and Adam Sheingate. New York: Oxford University Press.

2016b. "When Do Institutions 'Bite'? Historical Institutionalism and the Politics of Institutional Change." *Comparative Political Studies* 49(8):1095–1127.

Capoccia, Giovanni, and Daniel Kelemen. 2007. "The Study of Critical Junctures: Theory, Narrative, and Counterfactuals in Historical Institutionalism." *World Politics* 59:341–369.

Centers for Disease Control and Prevention. 2021. "Justification of Estimates for Appropriations Committees." (FY 2021–2015). Washington, DC.: U.S.

Department of Health and Human Services. www.cdc.gov/budget/fy2015/congres sional-justification.html.

Center for Presidential Transition. 2020. "Senate Confirmation Process Slows to a Crawl." Partnership for Public Service, January 20. https://presidentialtransition .org/publications/senate-confirmation-process-slows-to-a-crawl/.

Center for Responsive Politics. 2021. OpenSecrets.Org. www.opensecrets.org/.

Chait, Jonathan. 2020. "Trump Tells the Supreme Court It's on His Election Team." *New York Magazine*, October 30. https://nymag.com/intelligencer/2020/10/trump-supreme-court-republican-vote-biden-pack.html.

Chalfant, Morgan. 2020. "Barrett Sworn in as Supreme Court Justice by Thomas." *The Hill*, October 26. https://thehill.com/homenews/administration/522889-barrett-sworn-in-as-supreme-court-justice-by-thomas.

Cheng, Jeffrey, Dave Skidmore, and David Wessel. 2020. "What's the Fed Doing in Response to the COVID-19 Crisis? What More Could it Do?" The Brookings Institution, June 12. www.brookings.edu/research/fed-response-to-covid19/.

Chinni, Dante. 2020. "New Electoral Map Comes into Focus Ahead of 2020 Census." *NBC News*, January 5. www.nbcnews.com/politics/meet-the-press/new-electoral-map-comes-focus-ahead-2020-census-n1110546

Choi, Matthew. 2021. "Ignoring Calls to Pull Back, Gaetz Slams Cheney in Her Home State." *Politico*, January 28. www.politico.com/news/2021/01/28/matt-gaetz-liz-cheney-rally-463582

Christenson, Dino, and Douglas Kriner. 2020. *The Myth of the Imperial Presidency*. Chicago, IL: University of Chicago Press.

Christie, Bob. 2020. "US Attorney General Levels Broadside on Voting by Mail." *Associated Press*, September 10. https://apnews.com/article/arizona-voting-arch ive-phoenix-william-barr-68d48ba67b8f2da58853f8bdde9bde94

Cillizza, Chris. 2014. "How Citizens United Changed Politics, in 7 Charts." *Washington Post*, January 22. www.washingtonpost.com/news/the-fix/wp/2014/01/21/how-citi zens-united-changed-politics-in-6-charts/?utm_term=.5ee609bb9463

Clark, Dartunorro. 2020. "As Census Deadline Looms, Experts Warn Rushing Count Will Come At Great Cost." *NBC News*, December 21. www.nbcnews.com/politics/ politics-news/we-need-more-time-experts-sound-warnings-about-flawed-census-n1 251774

Clawson, Dan, Alan Neustadtl, and Mark Weller. 1998. *Dollars and Votes*. Philadelphia, PA: Temple University Press.

Clayton, Katherine, Nicholas Davis, Brendan Nyhan et al. N.D. "Does Elite Rhetoric Undermine Democratic Norms?" Unpublished paper, Department of Government, Dartmouth College, Hanover, New Hampshire. www.dartmouth.edu/~nyhan/ democratic-norms.pdf.

CNN. 2021. "Embargoed for Release: Wednesday, September 15 at Noon." September 15. http://cdn.cnn.com/cnn/2021/images/09/15/rel5e.-.elections.pdf.

2016. CNN Politics: Exit Polls. www.cnn.com/election/results/exit-polls.

Cobb, Jelani. 2021. "What is Happening to the Republicans?" *New Yorker*, March 8. www.newyorker.com/magazine/2021/03/15/what-is-happening-to-the-republicans.

Cochrane, John. 2020. "How the Fed Plans to Pay the Country's Bills." *Chicago Booth Review*, May 12. https://review.chicagobooth.edu/public-policy/2020/article/how-fed-plans-pay-country-s-bills.

Coe, Kevin, and Dakota Park-Ozee. 2020. "Uncivil Name-Calling in the U.S. Presidency, 1933–2018." *Presidential Studies Quarterly* 50(2):264–285.

Cohen, Marshall, Jason Morris, and Christopher Hickey. 2021. "Timeline: What Georgia Prosecutors Are Looking At as They Investigate Trump's Efforts to Overturn the Election." CNN, August 5. https://edition.cnn.com/interactive/2021/08/politics/trump-georgia-2020-election/.

Cohen, Michael. 2020. *Disloyal: A Memoir: The True Story of the Former Attorney to President Donald J. Trump.* New York: Skyhorse.

Cohen, Patricia. 2008. "Conservatives Try New Tack on Campuses." *New York Times*, September 22.

Coleman, David. 2021. "Unemployment Rates by President, 1948–2016." *Research: History in Pieces*, January 5, 2021. https://historyinpieces.com/research/us-unemployment-rates-president.

Coleman, Justine. 2021. "Trump Vows 'No More Money for RINOS,' Instead Encouraging Donations to his PAC." *The Hill*, March 8. https://thehill.com/home news/campaign/542244-trump-vows-no-more-money-for-rinos-while-encouraging-donations-to-his-pac.

Collins, Michael. 2020. "Trump Jokes He Might Leave the Country if He Loses to Joe Biden in Nov. 3 Election." *USA Today*, October 16. www.usatoday.com/story/news/politics/elections/2020/10/16/trump-jokes-he-might-leave-country-if-he-loses-joe-biden/3688173001/.

Comey, James. 2018. *A Higher Loyalty: Truth, Lies, and Leadership.* New York: Flatiron.

Committee for a Responsible Federal Budget. 2019. "CBO's Analysis of the President's FY 2020 Budget." May 9. www.crfb.org/papers/cbos-analysis-presidents-fy-2020-budget.

2017. "Is President Trump's Tax Cut the Largest in History Yet?" October 25. www.crfb.org/blogs/president-trumps-tax-cut-largest-history-yet.

Conran, James, and Kathleen Thelen. 2016. "Institutional Change." Pp. 51–70 in *The Oxford Handbook of Historical Institutionalism*, edited by Orfeo Fioretos, Tulia Falleti and Adam Sheingate. New York: Oxford University Press.

Cook, Nancy. 2020. "Trump's Staffing Struggle: After 3 Years, Unfilled Jobs across the Administration." *Politico*, January 20. www.politico.com/news/2020/01/20/trumps-staffing-struggle-unfilled-jobs-100991.

Corasaniti, Nick. 2021. "G.O.P. Seeks to Empower Poll Watchers, Raising Intimidation Worries." *New York Times*, May 2. www.nytimes.com/2021/05/01/us/politics/republican-pollwatchers.html.

Corasaniti, Nick, Jim Rutengerg, and Kathleen Gray. 2020. "As Trump Rails Against Loss, His Supporters Become More Threatening." *New York Times*, December 9. www.nytimes.com/2020/12/08/us/politics/trump-election-challenges.html.

Corrigan, Jack. 2018. "The Hollowing-Out of the State Department Continues." *The Atlantic*, February 11. www.theatlantic.com/international/archive/2018/02/tiller son-trump-state-foreign-service/553034/.

Crouch, Colin. 2005. *Capitalist Diversity and Change.* New York: Oxford University Press.

Daly, Natasha. 2021. "19 Unforgettable Quotes From Political Leaders on a Day That Will Live in Infamy." *National Geographic*, January 6. www.nationalgeographic.com/history/2021/01/unforgettable-quotes-from-political-leaders-on-a-day-that-wi ll-live-in-infamy/

Danziger, Sheldon, and Peter Gottschalk. 1995. *America Unequal*. Cambridge: Harvard University Press.

Darcy, Oliver. 2020. "News Anchors Forcefully Call Out Trump for Prematurely Declaring Victory." *CNN Business*, November 4. www.cnn.com/2020/11/04/media/tv-networks-trump-speech-election-night/index.html.

Davenport, Coral, and Lisa Friedman. 2019. "Science Panel Staffed with Trump Appointees Says E.P.A. Rollbacks Lack Scientific Rigor." *New York Times*, December 31. www.nytimes.com/2019/12/31/climate/epa-science-panel-trump.html

Davenport, Coral, Lisa Friedman, and Christopher Flavelle. 2021. "Biden's Climate Plans Are Stunted After Dejected Experts Fled Trump." *New York Times*, August 1. www.nytimes.com/2021/08/01/climate/biden-scientists-shortage-climate.html.

Davis, Gerald, Doug McAdam, W. Richard Scott and Mayer Zald, editors. 2005. *Social Movements and Organization Theory*. New York: Cambridge University Press.

Deeg, Richard and Gregory Jackson. 2007. "Towards a More Dynamic Theory of Capitalist Variety." *Socio-Economic Review* 5(1):149–179.

Deliso, Meredith, Catherine Thorbecke, and Marc Nathanson. 2020. "Election 2020: A Look at Trump Campaign Election Lawsuits and Where They Stand." *ABC News*, November 28. https://abcnews.go.com/Politics/election-2020-trump-campaign-election-lawsuits-stand/story?id=74041748.

Desjardins, Jeff. 2019. "$69 Trillion of World Debt in One Infographic." *Visual Capitalist*, November 14. www.visualcapitalist.com/69-trillion-of-world-debt-in-one-infographic/.

Diamond, Jeremy. 2015. "Trump: 'I Will Be a Great Unifier'." *CNN Politics*, October 26. www.cnn.com/2015/10/25/politics/donald-trump-democrats-republicans-bipartisanship-great-unifier/.

DiMaggio, Paul. 1988. "Interest and Agency in Institutional Theory." Pp. 3–21 in *Institutional Patterns and Organizations*, edited by Lynne Zucker. Cambridge: Ballinger.

DiMaggio, Paul, and Walter Powell. 1983. "The Iron Cage Revisited: Institutional Isomorphism and Collective Rationality in Organizational Fields." *American Sociological Review* 48:147–160.

Dimock, Michael, and John Gramlich. 2020. "How America Changed during Donald Trump's Presidency." Pew Research Center, September 23. www.pewresearch.org/2021/01/29/how-america-changed-during-donald-trumps-presidency/.

Dionne, E.J. 2016. *Why the Right Went Wrong: Conservatism from Goldwater to the Tea Party and Beyond*. New York: Simon & Schuster.

Dionne, E.J., Norman Ornstein, and Michael Mann. 2017. *One Nation After Trump*. New York: St. Martin's Press.

Dobbin, Frank. 1994. *Forging Industrial Policy*. New York: Cambridge University Press.

Doherty, Carroll. 2016. "Five Facts about Trump Supporters' Views on Immigration." Pew Research Center, August 25. www.pewresearch.org/fact-tank/2016/08/25/5-facts-about-trump-supporters-views-of-immigration/.

Doherty, Kathleen, David Lewis, and Scott Limbocker. 2018. "Executive Control and Turnover in the Senior Executive Service." *Journal of Public Administration Research and Theory* 29(2):159–174.

Domhoff, G. William. 2014. "Is the Corporate Elite Fractured, or Is There Continuing Corporate Dominance? Two Contrasting Views." *Class, Race and Corporate Power* 3(1):1–42.

Douglas, Mary. 1986. *How Institutions Think*. Syracuse: Syracuse University Press.

Drake, Bruce, and Jocelyn Kiley. 2019. "Americans Say the Nation's Political Debate Has Grown More Toxic and 'Heated' Rhetoric Could Lead to Violence." Pew Research Center, July 18. www.pewresearch.org/fact-tank/2019/07/18/americans-say-the-nations-political-debate-has-grown-more-toxic-and-heated-rhetoric-could-lead-to-violence/.

Draper, Robert. 2022. "'This was Trump Pulling a Putin'." *New York Times*, April 17. www.nytimes.com/2022/04/11/magazine/trump-putin-ukraine-fiona-hill.html.

Drezner, Daniel. 2020. *The Toddler in Chief*. Chicago, IL: University of Chicago Press.

Drutman, Lee. 2020. "Why There Are So Few Moderate Republicans Left." *FiveThirtyEight*, August 24. https://fivethirtyeight.com/features/why-there-are-so-few-moderate-republicans-left/.

Duffin, Erin. 2021. "Public Debt of the United States from 1990 to 2020." *Statista*, October 21. www.statista.com/statistics/187867/public-debt-of-the-united-states-since-1990/

Duina, Francesco. 2018. *Broke and Patriotic: Why Poor Americans Love Their Country*. Stanford, CA: Stanford University Press.

Durkee, Alison. 2021. "Progressives Demand 'Breyer Retire' So Biden Can Appoint Supreme Court Justice." *Forbes*, April 9. www.forbes.com/sites/alisondurkee/2021/04/09/progressives-demand-stephen-breyer-retire-so-biden-can-appoint-supreme-court-justice/?sh=7588637aad96.

   2020. "Trump Campaign Lawyers Quite Pennsylvania Lawsuit – Again." *Forbes*, November 16. www.forbes.com/sites/alisondurkee/2020/11/16/trump-campaign-lawyers-quit-pennsylvania-lawsuit-again/?sh=36313f2d443b.

Edelman, Murray. 1967. *The Symbolic Uses of Politics*. Urbana: University of Illinois Press.

Edmondson, Catie. 2021a. "Greene's Holocaust Comparisons Cause New Headaches for G.O.P." *New York Times*, May 25. www.nytimes.com/2021/05/25/us/politics/greene-holocaust.html.

   2021b. "Senate Confirms Biden's 40th Judge, Tying a Reagan-Era Record." *New York Times*, December 19. www.nytimes.com/2021/12/18/us/politics/biden-judges-reagan-record.html.

Edsall, Mary, and Thomas Byrne Edsall. 1992. *Chain Reaction: The Impact of Race, Rights, and Taxes on American Politics*. New York: Norton.

Edsall, Thomas Byrne. 2012. *The Age of Austerity: How Scarcity Will Remake American Politics*. New York: Doubleday.

   1984. *The New Politics of Inequality*. New York: Norton.

Edwards III, George. 2020. "The Bully in the Pulpit." *Presidential Studies Quarterly* 50 (2):286–324.

Enton, Harry. 2017. "The GOP Tax Cuts Are Even More Unpopular Than Past Tax Hikes." *FiveThirtyEight*, November 29. https://fivethirtyeight.com/features/the-gop-tax-cuts-are-even-more-unpopular-than-past-tax-hikes/.

Epstein, Reid. 2022. "Fringe Scheme to Reverse 2020 Election Splits Wisconsin G.O.P." *New York Times*, February 20. www.nytimes.com/2022/02/19/us/politics/wisconsin-election-decertification.html.

Erlanger, Steven. 2020. "Europe Wonders if It Can Rely on U.S. Again, Whoever Wins." *New York Times*, October 22. www.nytimes.com/2020/10/22/world/europe/europe-biden-trump-diplomacy.html

Evans, Peter, Dietrich Rueschemeyer, and Theda Skocpol, editors. 1985. *Bringing the State Back In*. New York: Cambridge University Press.

Everett, Burgess. 2021. "Senate GOP Moderates Fume as McConnell Prepares to Block Jan. 6 Commission." *Politico*, May 27. www.politico.com/news/2021/05/27/republicans-to-block-january-6-commission-491162.

Everett, Burgess, and Marianne Levine. 2020. "The Senate's Record-Breaking Gridlock Under Trump." *Politico*, June 8. www.politico.com/news/2020/06/08/senate-record-breaking-gridlocktrump-303811.

Fahey, Mark, and Nick Wells. 2017. "Comparing Trump's Budget Changes to Previous Presidents'." *CNBC*, March 17. www.cnbc.com/2017/03/17/comparing-trumps-budget-changes-to-previous-presidents.html.

Ferguson, Thomas, and Joel Rogers. 1986. *Right Turn*. New York: Hill and Wang.

Feur, Alan, Maggie Haberman, Michael Schmidt, and Luke Broadwater. 2022. "Trump Had Role in Weighing Proposals to Seize Voting Machines." *New York Times*, January 31. www.nytimes.com/2022/01/31/us/politics/donald-trump-election-results-fraud-voting-machines.html.

Firozi, Paulina. 2021. "Romney Booed at Utah GOP Convention Before Failed Vote to Censure Him." *Washington Post*, May 2. www.washingtonpost.com/politics/2021/05/02/romney-booed-utah-gop-censure/.

Fligstein, Neil, and Doug McAdam. 2012. *A Theory of Fields*. New York: Oxford University Press.

Floyd, David. 2020. "Explaining the Trump Tax Reform Plan." *Investopedia*, January 20. www.investopedia.com/taxes/trumps-tax-reform-plan-explained/#citation-28.

Fontaine, Sam, and Daniel Gomez. 2020. "Going Social: A Comparative Analysis of Presidents' Official and Social Media Messages." *Presidential Studies Quarterly* 59 (3):507–538.

Fortune Magazine. 2016. "Donald Trump Says He Would Dismantle Dodd-Frank Wall Street Regulation." May 18. http://fortune.com/2016/05/18/trump-dodd-frank-wall-street/.

Frank, Thomas. 2016. *Listen, Liberals*. New York: Picador.

Franken, Al. 2017. *Al Franken, Giant of the Senate*. New York: Twelve.

Fried, Charles, and Edward Larson. 2020. "How Far Bill Barr Has Fallen." *The Atlantic*, June 27. www.theatlantic.com/ideas/archive/2020/06/how-far-bill-barr-has-fallen/613582/

Friedson, Eliot. 1994. *Professionalism Reborn*. Chicago, IL: University of Chicago.

Frum, David. 2018. *Trumpocracy: The Corruption of the American Republic*. New York: Harper.

Fukuyama, Francis. 2014. *Political Order and Political Decay*. New York: Farrar, Straus and Giroux.

Gabriel, Trip, and Dana Goldstein. 2021. "Disputing Racism's Reach, Republicans Rattle American Schools." *New York Times*, June 1. www.nytimes.com/2021/06/01/us/politics/critical-race-theory.html.

Gale, William, Hilary Gelfond, Aaron Krupkin, and Mark Mazur. 2018. *Effects of the Tax Cuts and Jobs Act: A Preliminary Analysis*. Washington, DC: Urban Institute and Brookings Institution.

Gallup Polling. 2022. "Confidence in U.S. Supreme Court Sinks to Historic Low." https://news.gallup.com/poll/394103/confidence-supreme-court-sinks-historic-low .aspx

2021a. "Government." https://news.gallup.com/poll/27286/government.aspx.

2021b. "Race Relations." https://news.gallup.com/poll/1687/Race-Relations.aspx.

2021c. "Supreme Court." https://news.gallup.com/poll/4732/supreme-court.aspx.

2017a. "Taxes." www.gallup.com/poll/1714/taxes.aspx.

2017b. "Presidential Approval Ratings – Gallup Historical Statistics and Trends." www.gallup.com/poll/116677/presidential-approval-ratings-gallup-historical-statis tics-trends.aspx.

2016a. "U.S. Congress Approval Remains Low." www.gallup.com/poll/190598/con gress-approval-remains-low.aspx.

2016b. "Economy Continues to Rank as Top U.S. Problem." www.gallup.com/poll/ 191513/economy-continues-rank-top-problem.aspx.

2015. "Big Government Still Named as Biggest Threat to U.S." December 22. www .gallup.com/poll/187919/big-government-named-biggest-threat.aspx.

Ganz, Marshall. 2000. "Resources and Resourcefulness: Strategic Capacity in the Unionization of California Agriculture, 1959–1966." *American Journal of Sociology* 105:1003–1062.

Gardner, Amy, and Paulina Firozi. 2021. "Here's the Full Transcript and Audio of the Call Between Trump and Raffensperger." *Washington Post*, January 5. www .washingtonpost.com/politics/trump-raffensperger-call-transcript-georgia-vote/2021/ 01/03/2768eocc-4ddd-11eb-83e3-322644d82356_story.html.

Gardner, Amy, Kate Rabinowitz, and Harry Stevens. 2021. "How GOP-Backed Voting Measures Could Create Hurdles for Tens of Millions of Voters." *Washington Post*, March 11. www.washingtonpost.com/politics/interactive/2021/voting-restrictions- republicans-states/.

Garten, Jeffrey. 2021. *Three Days at Camp David*. New York: HarperColllins.

Gaventa, John. 1980. *Power and Powerlessness: Quiescence and Rebellion in an Appalachian Valley*. Champaign: University of Illinois Press.

Gerstle, Gary. 2022. *The Rise and Fall of the Neoliberal Order*. New York: Oxford University Press.

Gervais, Bryan, and Irwin Morris. 2018. *Reactionary Republicanism: How the Tea Party in the House Paved the Way for Trump's Victory*. New York: Oxford University Press.

Ghandnoosh, Nazgol. 2014. *Race and Punishment: Racial Perceptions of Crime and Support for Punitive Policies*. Washington, DC: The Sentencing Project. www .sentencingproject.org/wp-content/uploads/2015/11/Race-and-Punishment.pdf.

Ghandnoosh, Nazgol, and Josh Rovner. 2017. *Immigration and Public Safety*. Washington, DC: The Sentencing Project. www.sentencingproject.org/wp-content/ uploads/2017/03/Immigration-and-Public-Safety.pdf.

Ghazal Aswad, Noor. 2019. "Exploring Charismatic Leadership: A Comparative Analysis of the Rhetoric of Hillary Clinton and Donald Trump in the 2016 Presidential Election." *Presidential Studies Quarterly* 49(1):56–74.

Gilberstadt, Hannah. 2019. "For the First Time, Majority of Republicans Express Confidence in the Fairness of Mueller's Investigation." Pew Research Center, July 23. www.pewresearch.org/fact-tank/2019/07/23/majority-republicans-express-con fidence-fairness-mueller-investigation/.

Gillin, Joshua. 2015. "Bush Says Trump Was a Democrat Longer than a Republican 'In the Last Decade'." *Politifact*, August 24. www.politifact.com/factchecks/2015/aug/24/jeb-bush/bush-says-trump-was-democrat-longer-republican-las/.

Gilmore, Jason, Charles Rowling, Jason Edwards, and Nicole Allen. 2020. "Exceptional 'We' or Exceptional 'Me'? Donald Trump, American Exceptionalism, and the Remaking of the Modern Jeremiad." *Presidential Studies Quarterly* 50(3):539–567.

Gittleson, Kim. 2018. "US Tax Cuts: Are They the Biggest in American History?" *BBC News*, April 17. www.bbc.com/news/world-43790895.

Gladwell, Malcolm. 2000. *The Tipping Point*. New York: Little Brown and Company.

Glanz, James, and Campbell Robertson. 2020. "Lockdown Delays Cost at Least 36,000 Lives, Data Show." *New York Times*, May 22. www.nytimes.com/2020/05/20/us/coronavirus-distancing-deaths.html?auth=linked-google.

Godes, David, Elie Ofek, and Miklos Sarvary. 2009. "Content vs. Advertising: The Impact of Competition on Media Firm Strategy." *Marketing Science* 28(1):20–35.

Goldmacher, Shane. 2022. "Trump's Words, and Deeds, Reveal Depths of His Drive to Retain Power." *New York Times*, February 1. www.nytimes.com/2022/02/01/us/politics/trump-election-jan-6-voting-machines.html.

2021. "Hooked on Trump: How the G.O.P. Still Banks on His Brand for Cash." *New York Times*, July 27. www.nytimes.com/2021/07/27/us/politics/trump-republicans-fundraising-brand.html.

Goldmacher, Shane, and Maggie Haberman. 2022. "Tucker, Thiel and Trump: How J.D. Vance Won in Ohio." *New York Times*, May 4. www.nytimes.com/2022/05/04/us/politics/jd-vance-trump-ohio-fox-news.html.

Goldstein, Judith. 1993. *Ideas, Interests, and American Trade Policy*. Ithaca, NY: Cornell University Press.

Doris Kearns Goodwin. 2018. *Leadership in Turbulent Times*. New York: Simon & Schuster.

Gouldner, Alvin. 1979. *The Future of Intellectuals and Rise of the New Class*. New York: Oxford University Press.

Gramlich, John. 2020. "How Trump Compares with Other Recent Presidents in Appointing Federal Judges." Pew Research Center, July 15. www.pewresearch.org/fact-tank/2020/07/15/how-trump-compares-with-other-recent-presidents-in-appointing-federal-judges/.

Granovetter, Mark. 1978. "Threshold Models of Collective Behavior." *American Journal of Sociology* 83:1420–1443.

Green, Jon and Sean McElwee. 2019. "The Differential Effects of Economic Conditions and Racial Attitudes in the Election of Donald Trump." *Perspectives on Politics* 17 (2):358–379.

Green, Joshua. 2017. *The Devil's Bargain: Steve Bannon, Donald Trump and the Storming of the Presidency*. New York: Penguin.

Greenfield, Jeff. 2021. "A GOP Civil War? Don't Bet On It." *Politico*, May 12. www.politico.com/news/magazine/2021/05/12/gop-civil-war-dont-bet-on-it-487192.

Greenhouse, Linda. 2021a. "The Supreme Court, Weaponized." *New York Times*, December 19. www.nytimes.com/2021/12/16/opinion/supreme-court-trump.html.

2021b. *Justice on the Brink*. New York: Random House.

Greenstein, Fred. 2005. "The Person of the President, Leadership, and Greatness." Pp. 218–240 in *The Executive Branch*, edited by Joel Aberbach and Mark Peterson. New York: Oxford University Press.

Gregorian, Dareh. 2020. "'This is Getting Insane': Republicans Push Back Against Trump's False Election Claims." *NBC News*, November 5. www.nbcnews.com/politics/2020-election/getting-insane-republicans-push-back-against-trump-s-false-election-n1246700.

Greider, William. 1981. "The Education of David Stockman." *The Atlantic*, December. www.theatlantic.com/magazine/archive/1981/12/the-education-of-david-stockman/305760/.

Greif, Avner. 2006. *Institutions and the Path to the Modern Economy*. New York: Cambridge University Press.

Guillén, Mauro. 2015. *The Architecture of Collapse: The Global System in the Twenty-first Century*. York: Oxford University Press.

Gulati, Ranjay. 2022. *Deep Purpose: The Heart and Soul of High-Performance Companies*. New York: Harper Business.

Gumbel, Andrew. 2016. "The History of 'Rigged' U.S. Elections: From Bush vs. Gore to Trump vs. Clinton." *The Guardian*, October 25. www.theguardian.com/us-news/2016/oct/25/donald-trump-rigged-election-bush-gore-florida-voter-fraud.

Haberman, Maggie, Alexandra Berzon, and Michael Schmidt. 2022. "Trump Allies Continue Legal Drive to Erase His Loss, Stoking Election Doubts." *New York Times*, April 19. www.nytimes.com/2022/04/18/us/politics/trump-allies-election-decertify.html.

Hacker, Jacob, and Paul Pierson. 2010. *Winner-Take-All Politics*. New York: Simon & Schuster.

Hall, John A., and Charles Lindholm. 1999. *Is America Breaking Apart?* Princeton, NJ: Princeton University Press.

Hall, Peter, and David Soskice. 2001. "An Introduction to Varieties of Capitalism." Pp. 1–70 in *Varieties of Capitalism*, edited by Peter Hall and David Soskice. New York: Oxford University Press.

Hall, Peter, and Kathleen Thelen. 2009. "Institutional Change in Varieties of Capitalism." *Socio-Economic Review* 7(1):7–34.

Hanage, William, Christian Testa, Jarvis Chen et al. 2020. "COVID-19: US Federal Accountability for Entry, Spread, and Inequities – Lessons for the Future. *European Journal of Epidemiology* 35:995–1006. https://link.springer.com/article/10.1007/s10654-020-00689-2.

Harrell, Erika, Lynn Langton, Lance Couzens, and Hope Smiley-McDonald. 2014. "Household Poverty and Nonfatal Violent Victimization, 2008–2012." Washington, DC: U.S. Department of Justice. www.bjs.gov/content/pub/pdf/hpnvvo812.pdf.

Hart, John. 1998. "Neglected Aspects of the Study of the Presidency." *Annual Review of Political Science* 1:379–399.

Hart, Roderick. 2020. "Donald Trump and the Return of the Paranoid Style." *Presidential Studies Quarterly* 50(2):348–365.

Hasen, Richard. 2019. "Electoral Laws." Pp. 30–43 in *Electoral Integrity in America*, edited by Pippa Norris, Sarah Cameron, and Thomas Wynter. New York: Oxford University Press.

Hay, Colin. 2001. "The 'Crisis' of Keynesianism and the Rise of Neoliberalism in Britain: An Ideational Institutionalist Approach." Pp. 193–218 in *The Rise of Neoliberalism and Institutional Analysis*, edited by John L. Campbell and Ove K. Pedersen. Princeton, NJ: Princeton University Press.

Heclo, Hugh. 1977. *Studying the Presidency: A Report to the Ford Foundation*. New York: Ford Foundation.

Heeb, Gina. 2019. "U.S. Income Inequality Jumps to Highest Level Ever Recorded." *Markets Insider*, September 27. https://markets.businessinsider.com/news/stocks/income-inequality-reached-highest-level-ever-recorded-in-2018-2019-9-1028559996.

Heilbroner, Robert, and William Milberg. 1995. *The Crisis of Vision in Modern Economic Thought*. New York: Cambridge University Press.

Hendricks, Galen, and Seth Hanlon. 2019. "The TCJA 2 Years later: Corporations, Not Workers, Are the Big Winners." Center for American Progress, December 19. www.americanprogress.org/issues/economy/news/2019/12/19/478924/tcja-2-years-later-corporations-not-workers-big-winners/.

Hennessey, Susan, and Benjamin Wittes. 2020. *Unmaking the Presidency*. New York: Farrar, Straus and Giroux.

Herbert, Jon, Trevor McCrisken, and Andrew Wroe. 2020. "Roundtable." *Journal of American Studies* 54(5):1032–1048.

2019. *The Ordinary Presidency of Donald J. Trump*. New York: Palgrave Macmillan.

Heritage Action for America. 2021. "Scorecard for the 117th Congressional Session." https://heritageaction.com/scorecard/members?

Heyboer, Kelly. 2021. "Former Gov. Whitman Among 150 Republicans Ready to Ditch GOP for New Political Party Over the 'Big Lie'." NJ.com, May 13. www.nj.com/politics/2021/05/former-gov-whitman-among-150-republicans-ready-to-ditch-gop-for-new-political-party-over-the-big-lie.html.

Hirsch, Paul. 1997. "Sociology Without Social Structure: Neoinstitutional Theory Meets Brave New World." *American Journal of Sociology* 102:1702–1723.

Hirsch, Paul, and Michael Lounsbury. 1997. "Ending the Family Quarrel: Toward a Reconciliation of 'Old' and 'New' Institutionalisms." *American Behavioral Scientist* 40(4):406–418.

Hochschild, Arlie. 2016. *Strangers in Their Own Land*. New York: The New Press.

Hollis-Brusky, Amanda. 2019. *Ideas with Consequences: The Federalist Society and the Conservative Counterrevolution*. New York: Oxford University Press.

Horsley, Scott. 2019. "After Two Years, Trump Tax Cuts Have Failed to Deliver on GOP's Promises." *NPR News*, December 30. www.npr.org/2019/12/20/789540931/2-years-later-trump-tax-cuts-have-failed-to-deliver-on-gops-promises.

Howell, William, and Terry Moe. 2020. *Presidents, Populism, and the Crisis of Democracy*. Chicago, IL: University of Chicago Press.

Hudak, Zachary, Rebecca Kaplan, Caroline Linton et al. 2021. "Live Updates: Liz Cheney Removed from House GOP Leadership." *CBS News*, May 12.

Huddy, Leonie, and Omer Yair. 2021. "To Reduce Political Hostility, Civility Goes Further Than Compromise." *Behavioral Scientist*, April 5. https://behavioralscientist.org/to-reduce-political-hostility-civility-goes-further-than-compromise/.

Hulse, Carl. 2022. "Kavanaugh Gave Private Assurances. Collins Says He 'Misled' Her." *New York Times*, June 24. www.nytimes.com/2022/06/24/us/roe-kavanaugh-collins-notes.html

Hult, Karen. 2021. "Assessing the Trump White House." *Presidential Studies Quarterly* 51(1):35–50.

Ingraham, Christopher. 2021. "The Richest One Percent Dodge Taxes on More Than One-Fifth of Their Income, Study Shows." *Washington Post*, March 26. www.washingtonpost.com/business/2021/03/26/wealthy-tax-evasion/.

International Monetary Fund. 2013. "IMF Releases Data on the Currency Composition of Foreign Exchange Reserves with Additional Data on Australian and Canadian Dollar Reserves." IMF Press Releases, June 28. www.imf.org/external/np/sec/pr/2013/pr13236.htm.

Investopedia. 2020. "Explaining the Trump Tax Reform Plan." Microsimulation Model (version 2017-1). Urban-Brookings Tax Policy Center. January 20. www.investopedia.com/taxes/trumps-tax-reform-plan-explained/.

Ipsos/Reuters. 2021. "Ipsos/Reuters Poll: The Big Lie." Ipsos Press Release, May 21. www.ipsos.com/sites/default/files/ct/news/documents/2021-05/Ipsos%20Reuters%20Topline%20Write%20up-%20The%20Big%20Lie%20-%2017%20May%20thru%2019%20May%202021.pdf.

Irwin, Neil. 2021. "The Most Important Thing Biden Can Learn from the Trump Economy." *New York Times*, January 11. www.nytimes.com/2021/01/11/upshot/trump-economy-lessons-biden.html.

Jacobs, Ben. 2021. "No One Likes Marjorie Taylor Greene, But Can Anyone Stop Her?" *New York Magazine*, March 7. https://nymag.com/intelligencer/2021/03/no-one-likes-marjorie-taylor-greene-but-can-they-stop-her.html.

Jacobs, Nicholas, Desmond King, and Sidney Milkis. 2019. "Building a Conservative State: Partisan Polarization and the Redeployment of Administrative Power." *Perspectives on Politics* 17(2):453–469.

Jacobson, Louis. 2018. "What Percentage of Americans Own Stock?" *Politifact*, September 18. www.politifact.com/factchecks/2018/sep/18/ro-khanna/what-percentage-americans-own-stocks/.

Jalonick, Mary Clare. 2021. "Explainer: How Congress' Jan. 6 Commission Would Work." *Associated Press*, May 21. https://apnews.com/article/mitch-mcconnell-riots-terrorist-attacks-donald-trump-capitol-siege-ac4cf46ad3e0617a045eb926d21945eb.

Jarrett, Laura. 2020. "More Than 2,000 Former Prosecutors and Other DOJ Officials Call on Attorney General Bill Barr to Resign." *CNN Politics*, February 17. www.cnn.com/2020/02/16/politics/prosecutors-doj-officials-barr-resign/index.html.

Jensen, Nathan. 2006. *Nation-States and the Multinational Corporation: A Political Economy of Foreign Direct Investment*. Princeton, NJ: Princeton University Press.

Jercich, Kat. 2020. "White House to Hospitals: Bypass CDC, Report COVID-19 Data Directly to HHS." *Healthcare ITNews*, July 15. www.healthcareitnews.com/news/white-house-hospitals-bypass-cdc-report-covid-19-data-directly-hhs.

Johnson, Eliana. 2019. "Mueller Remarks Put Barr Back into Harsh Spotlight." *Politico*, May 29. www.politico.com/story/2019/05/29/robert-mueller-william-barr-1346881.

Johnson, Richard. 2017. "Racially Polarized Partisanship and the Obama Presidency." Pp. 161–180 in *The Obama Presidency and the Politics of Change*, edited by Edward Ashbee and John Dumbrell. New York: Palgrave Macmillan.

Jones, Jeffrey. 2021. "Approval of U.S. Supreme Court Down to 40%, a New Low." Gallup Polling, September 23. https://news.gallup.com/poll/354908/approval-supreme-court-down-new-low.aspx.

Jones, Van. 2017. *Beyond the Messy Truth*. New York: Ballantine Books.

Journal of American Studies. 2020. "Roundtable: The Ordinary Presidency of Donald J. Trump." *Journal of American Studies* 54(5):1032–1048.

Judis, John. 2016. *The Populist Explosion*. New York: Columbia Global Reports.

Jupille, Joseph, and James Caporaso. 2021. *Theories of Institutions*. New York: Cambridge University Press.

Karl, Jonathan. 2021. *Betrayal: The Final Act of the Trump Show*. New York: Dutton.

Kamarck, Elaine, and Christine Stenglein. 2020. "Low Rates of Fraud in Vote-By-Mail States Show the Benefits Outweigh the Risks." The Brookings Institution, June 2. www.brookings.edu/blog/fixgov/2020/06/02/low-rates-of-fraud-in-vote-by-mail-states-show-the-benefits-outweigh-the-risks/.

Kaplan, Sheila, Sharon LaFraniere, Noah Weiland, and Maggie Haberman. 2020. "How the F.D.A. Stood Up to the President." *New York Times*, October 20. www.nytimes.com/2020/10/20/health/covid-vaccines-fda-trump.html.

Karni, Annie. 2021. "Paul Ryan Critiques Trump's Grip on the Republican Party." *New York Times*, May 27. www.nytimes.com/2021/05/27/us/politics/paul-ryan-trump-reagan-dinner.html.

Katzenstein, Peter, and Lucia Seybert. 2018a. "Uncertainty, Risk, Power and the Limits of International Relations Theory." Pp. 27–56 in *Protean Power: Exploring the Uncertain and Unexpected in World Politics*, edited by Peter Katzenstein and Lucia Seybert. New York: Cambridge University Press.

2018b. "Power Complexities and Political Theory." Pp. 267–301 in *Protean Power: Exploring the Uncertain and Unexpected in World Politics*, edited by Peter Katzenstein and Lucia Seybert. New York: Cambridge University Press.

Katzenstein, Peter, editor. 1996. *The Culture of National Security*. New York: Columbia University Press.

Katznelson, Ira. 2003. "Periodization and Preferences: Reflections on Purposive Action in Comparative Historical Social Science." Pp. 270–301 in *Comparative Historical Analysis in the Social Sciences*, edited by James Mahoney and Dietrich Rueschemeyer. New York: Cambridge University Press.

Katznelson, Ira, and Barry Weingast. 2005. "Intersections between Historical and Rational Choice Institutionalism." Pp. 1–26 in *Preferences and Situations*, edited by Ira Katznelson and Barry Weingast. New York: Russell Sage Foundation.

Kaufman, Robert, and Stephan Haggard. 2019. "Democratic Decline in the United States: What Can We Learn from Middle-Income Backsliding?" *Perspectives on Politics* 17(2):417–432.

Kelton, Stephanie. 2020. *The Deficit Myth: Modern Monetary Theory and the Birth of the People's Economy*. New York: Public Affairs.

Kelton, Stephanie, and Edward Chancellor. 2020. "Can Governments Afford the Debts They Are Piling Up to Stabilise Economies?" *Financial Times*, May 3. file:///C:/Users/d35640y/MyFiles/America%20&%20Trump's%20Damage/4.%20Fiscal/Readings/Can%20governments%20afford%20the%20debts%20they%20are%20piling%20up%20to%20stabilise%20economies_%20_%20Financial%20Times.html.

Kenworthy, Lane. 2014. *Social Democratic America*. New York: Oxford University Press.

Khanna, Parag. 2019. *The Future is Asian*. New York: Simon & Schuster.

Khimm, Suzy. 2018. "Number of OSHA Workplace Safety Inspectors Declines Under Trump." *NBC News*, January 8. www.nbcnews.com/politics/white-house/exclusive-number-osha-workplace-safety-inspectors-declines-under-trump-n834806.

Kim, Catherine. 2020. "Poll: 70 Percent of Republicans Don't Think the Election Was Free and Fair." *Politico*, November 9. www.politico.com/news/2020/11/09/republicans-free-fair-elections-435488.

King, Jonathan, and Ian Ostrander. 2020. "Prioritizing Judicial Nominations after Presidential Transitions." *Presidential Studies Quarterly* 50(3):592–610.

Kingdon, John. 1995. *Agendas, Alternatives, and Public Policies*, 2nd edition. New York: Harper Collins.

Kirby, Jen. 2020. "Attorney General Bill Barr Contradicted Trump on Voter Fraud. Now He's Resigning." *Vox*, December 14. www.vox.com/2020/12/14/22175221/bill-barr-resigns-trump-attorney-general.

Kirshner, Jonathan. 2014. *American Power after the Financial Crisis*. Ithaca, NY: Cornell University Press.

Kjaer, Peter, and Ove K. Pedersen. 2001. "Translating Liberalization: Neoliberalism in the Danish Negotiated Economy." Pp. 219–247 in *The Rise of Neoliberalism and Institutional Analysis*, edited by John L. Campbell and Ove K. Pedersen. Princeton, NJ: Princeton University Press.

Klein, Charlotte. 2020. "Barr to Trump: You Can't Fire Me Because I Quit." *Vanity Fair*, December 7. www.vanityfair.com/news/2020/12/barr-attorney-general-con sidering-resigning-doj.

Knight, Jack. 2001. "Explaining the Rise of Neoliberalism: The Mechanisms of Institutional Change." Pp. 27–50 in *The Rise of Neoliberalism and Institutional Analysis*, edited by John L. Campbell and Ove K. Pedersen. Princeton, NJ: Princeton University Press.

  1992. *Institutions and Social Conflict*. New York: Cambridge University Press.

Kornai, Janos. 1992. "The Postsocialist Transition and the State: Reflections in the Light of the Hungarian Fiscal Problems." *American Economic Review* 82(2):1–21.

Koronowski, Ryan, Jeremy Venook, and Will Ragland. 2020. "'Blinking Red': A Running Timeline of How the Trump Administration Ignored Warnings, Misled the Public and Made the Coronavirus Crisis Worse." Center for American Progress, April 27. www.americanprogress.org/issues/democracy/news/2020/04/27/483986/blinking-red-trump-administration-ignored-warnings-misled-public-ma de-coronavirus-crisis-worse/.

Krasner, Stephen. 1988. "Sovereignty: An Institutional Perspective." *Comparative Political Studies* 21(1):66–94.

Krcmaric, Daniel, Stephen Nelson, and Andrew Roberts. 2020. "Studying Leaders and Elites: The Personal Biography Approach." *Annual Review of Political Science* 23:133–151.

Kruse, Michael. 2018. "I Need Loyalty." *Politico Magazine*, March/April. www.politico .com/magazine/story/2018/03/06/donald-trump-loyalty-staff-217227.

Kumar, Martha Joynt. 2019. "Energy or Chaos? Turnover at the Top of President Trump's White House." *Presidential Studies Quarterly* 49(1):219–236.

Kuran, Timur. 1995. *Private Truths, Public Lies: The Social Consequences of Preference Falsification*. Cambridge: Harvard University Press.

Kurzman, Charles. 2017. "Muslim-American Involvement with Violent Extremism, 2016." Triangle Center on Terrorism and Homeland Security, Department of Sociology, University of North Carolina-Chapel Hill. https://sites.duke.edu/tcths/files/2017/01/Kurzman_Muslim-American_Involvement_in_Violent_Extremism_2016.pdf.

Laughlin, Nick, and Peyton Shelburne. 2021. "How Voters' Trust in Elections Shifted in Response to Biden's Victory." *Morning Consult*, January 27. https://morningconsult.com/form/tracking-voter-trust-in-elections/.

2020. "Election Trust Tracker: Most Republicans Want Trump to Concede – If He Can't Produce Evidence of Widespread Fraud." *Morning Consult*, December 8. https://morningconsult.com/form/tracking-voter-trust-in-elections/.

Lee, Francis. 2016. *Insecure Majorities*. Chicago, IL: University of Chicago Press.

2009. *Beyond Ideology*. Chicago, IL: University of Chicago Press.

Leicht, Kevin, and Scott Fitzgerald. 2014. *Middle Class Meltdown in America*. New York: Routledge.

2006. *Postindustrial Peasants*. New York: Worth.

Leonnig, Carol, and Philip Rucker. 2021. *I Alone Can Fix It*. New York: Penguin.

Lester, Richard, and Michael Piore. 2004. *Innovation: The Missing Dimension*. Cambridge: Harvard University Press.

Levitsky, Steven, and Daniel Ziblatt. 2018. *How Democracies Die*. New York: Crown.

Lewindowski, Corey, and David Bossie. 2017. *Let Trump Be Trump*. New York: Center Street.

Lewis, David, Patrick Bernhard, and Emily You. 2018. "President Trump as Manager: Reflections on the First Year." *Presidential Studies Quarterly* 48(3):480–501.

Lewis, Jeffrey, Keith Poole, Howard Rosenthal et al. 2021. *Voteview: Congressional Roll-Call Votes Database*. https://voteview.com/parties/all.

Lewis, David, and Mark Richardson. 2021. "The Very Best People: President Trump and the Management of Executive Personnel." *Presidential Studies Quarterly* 51 (1):51–70.

Lewis, Michael. 2018. *The Fifth Risk*. New York: W. W. Norton.

Liasson, Mara. 2020. "As the Culture Wars Shift, President Trump Struggles to Adapt." National Public Radio, June 20. www.npr.org/2020/06/20/881096897/as-the-cul ture-wars-shift-president-trump-struggles-to-adapt.

Lieberman, Robert, Suzanne Mettler, Thomas Pepinsky, Kenneth Roberts, and Richard Valelly. 2019. "The Trump Presidency and American Democracy: A Historical and Comparative Analysis." *Perspectives on Politics* 17(2):470–479.

Light, Paul. 2020. "The True Size of Government is Nearing a Record High." The Brookings Institution, October 7. www.brookings.edu/blog/fixgov/2020/10/07/the-true-size-of-government-is-nearing-a-record-high/.

Lim, Daniel. 2020. "Federal Workforce Attrition under the Trump Administration." *Government Executive*, December 28. www.govexec.com/management/2020/12/federal-workforce-attrition-under-trump-administration/171045/.

Lim, Elvin. 2008. *The Anti-Intellectual Presidency*. New York: Oxford University Press.

Limon, Alexandra. 2021. "Documents: Rioters Wanted to Kill VP Pence, Speaker Pelosi." KOIN Television, February 10. www.koin.com/news/washington-dc/docu ments-rioters-wanted-to-kill-vp-pence-speaker-pelosi/.

Liptak, Adam. 2022. "June 24, 2022: The Day Chief Justice Roberts Lost His Court." *New York Times*, June 24. www.nytimes.com/2022/06/24/us/abortion-supreme-court-roberts.html

2021a. "Back on the Bench, the Supreme Court Faces a Blockbuster Term." *New York Times*, October 3. www.nytimes.com/2021/10/03/us/politics/supreme-court-new-term.html.

2021b. "Critical Moment for Roe, and the Supreme Court's Legitimacy." *New York Times*, December 5. www.nytimes.com/2021/12/04/us/mississippi-supreme-court-abortion-roe-v-wade.html.

2020a. "Supreme Court Rejects Texas Suit Seeking to Subvert Election." *New York Times*, December 12. www.nytimes.com/2020/12/11/us/politics/supreme-court-elec tion-texas.html.

2020b. "Midnight Ruling Exposes Rifts at a Supreme Court Transformed by Trump." *New York Times*, November 26. www.nytimes.com/2020/11/26/us/rifts-supreme-court-trump.html.

Liptak, Adam and Alicia Parlapiano. 2022. "A Transformative Term at the Most Conservative Court in Nearly a Century." *New York Times*, July 1. www .nytimes.com/2022/07/01/us/supreme-court-term-roe-guns-epa-decisions.html

Lopéz, Ian Haney. 2014. *Dog Whistle Politics*. New York: Oxford University Press.

Lukes, Steven. 1974. *Power: A Radical View*. New York: Palgrave.

Lynch, Sarah. 2020. "U.S. Attorney General Barr Steps Down as Trump Election Defeat Confirmed." *Reuters*, December 14. www.reuters.com/article/us-usa-trump-barr/u-s-attorney-general-barr-steps-down-as-trump-election-defeat-confirmed-idUSKBN2 8O329.

Lyons, James. 2019. "Trump and the Attack on the Rule of Law." *Institute for the Advancement of the American Legal System*. September. Denver, CO: University of Denver.

MacLean, Nancy. 2017. *Democracy in Chains*. New York: Viking.

Madsbjerg, Christian, and Mikkel Rasmussen. 2014. *The Moment of Clarity*. Cambridge: Harvard Business Review Press.

Magleby, Daniel, Michael McDonald, Jonathan Krasno, Shawn Donahue, and Robin Best. 2019. "Gerrymandering." Pp. 83–101 in *Electoral Integrity in America*, edited by Pippa Norris, Sarah Cameron and Thomas Wynter. New York: Oxford University Press.

Mahoney, James. 2000. "Path Dependence in Historical Sociology." *Theory and Society* 29:507–548.

Mahoney, James, Khairunnis Mohamedali, and Christoph Nguyen. 2016. "Causality and Time in Historical Institutionalism." Pp. 71–88 in *The Oxford Handbook of Historical Institutionalism*, edited by Orfeo Fioretos, Tulia Falleti and Adam Sheingate. New York: Oxford University Press.

Mahoney, James, and Kathleen Thelen. 2010. "A Theory of Gradual Institutional Change." Pp. 1–37 in *Explaining Institutional Change: Ambiguity, Agency, and Power*, edited by James Mahoney and Kathleen Thelen. New York: Cambridge University Press.

Mann, Thomas, and Norman Ornstein. 2020. "Five Myths about Bipartisanship." *Washington Post*, January 17. www.washingtonpost.com/outlook/five-myths/five-myths-about-bipartisanship/2020/01/17/35853dca-3873-11ea-bb7b-265f4554af6d_story.html.

2012. *It's Even Worse Than It Looks*. New York: Basic Books.

Marcos, Cristina, and Naomi Jagoda. 2017. "The 13 House Republicans Who Voted Against the GOP Tax Plan." *The Hill*, November 16. https://thehill.com/homenews/house/360780-the-13-house-republicans-who-voted-against-the-gop-tax-plan.

Marnin, Julia. 2021. "Fact Check: Did Trump Pass the Largest Tax Cut in History as He Says?" *Newsweek*, January 20. www.newsweek.com/fact-check-did-trump-pass-largest-tax-cut-history-he-says-1563210.

Martin, Isaac. 2008. *The Permanent Tax Revolt*. Stanford, CA: Stanford University Press.

Martin, Jonathan, and Alexander Burns. 2022. *This Will Not Pass: Trump, Biden, and the Battle for America's Future*. New York: Simon & Schuster.

Martin, Jonathan, and Astead Herndon. 2020. "At Rally for Georgia Senators, Trump Focuses on His Own Grievances." *New York Times*, December 6. www.nytimes.com/2020/12/05/us/trump-georgia-runoff.html.

Marwell, Gerald, and Pamela Oliver. 1993. *The Critical Mass in Collective Action*. Cambridge: Cambridge University Press.

Marx, Karl. 1969 [1889]. "The Eighteenth Brumaire of Louis Bonaparte." Pp. 394–487 in *Karl Marx and Frederick Engels, Selected Works*, vol. 1. Moscow, Russia: Progress.

Mason, Melanie. 2020. "As Trump Attacks Election Outcome, Americans Are Less Confident in the Vote Count, USC Poll Finds." *Los Angeles Times*, November 19. www.latimes.com/politics/story/2020-11-19/usc-dornsife-post-election-poll.

Massey, Doug. 2015. "The Real Hispanic Challenge." Pp. 3–7 in *Pathways* (Spring). Stanford, CA: Stanford Center on Poverty and Inequality.

Massey, Doug, and Kerstin Gentsch. 2014. "Undocumented Migration and the Wages of Mexican Immigrants." *International Migration Review* 48(2):482–499.

Matthews, Dylan. 2020. "Mitch McConnell's Rediscovery of the Deficit is a Recipe for a Depression." *Vox*, April 27. www.vox.com/policy-and-politics/2020/4/27/21232672/federal-budget-deficit-4-trillion-stimulus-coronavirus.

Mattis, James. 2018. "Letter of Resignation." December 20. Washington, DC: U.S. Department of Defense. https://media.defense.gov/2018/Dec/20/2002075156/-1/-1/1/LETTER-FROM-SECRETARY-JAMES-N-MATTIS.PDF.

Mayer, Jane. 2021. "The Big Money Behind the Big Lie." *New Yorker*, August 9, pp. 30–41.

2016. *Dark Money: The Hidden History of the Billionaires Behind the Rise of the Radical Right*. New York: Doubleday.

Mayer, Jeremy. 2020. "Two Presidents, Two Crises: Bush Wrestles with 9/11, Trump Fumbles COVID-19." *Presidential Studies Quarterly* 50(3):629–649.

Mayer, Kenneth. 2021. "The Random Walk Presidency." *Presidential Studies Quarterly* 51(1):71–95.

McAdam, Doug, and Karina Kloos. 2014. *Deeply Divided*. New York: Oxford University Press.

McCarthy, Justin. 2020. "Confidence in Accuracy of U.S. Election Matches Record Low." Gallup Polling, October 8. https://news.gallup.com/poll/321665/confidence-accuracy-election-matches-record-low.aspx.

2019. "Congress Approval, Support for Impeaching Trump Both Up." Gallup Polling, October 16. https://news.gallup.com/poll/267491/congress-approval-support-impeaching-trump.aspx?utm_source=alert&utm_medium=email&utm_content=morelink&utm_campaign=syndication.

McCarthy, Niall. 2020. "How Trust in the 2020 Election Compares to Recent Contests." *Statista*, November 11. www.statista.com/chart/23459/share-of-americans-who-consider-elections-free-and-fair/.

Merchant, Noman, Alanna Durkin Richer, and Mark Sherman. 2020. "Trump Criticizes Supreme Court after Election Lawsuit is Rejected." *Time*, December 12. https://time.com/5920883/trump-criticizes-supreme-court-lawsuit/.

Meyer, John, John Boli, and George Thomas. 1987. "Ontology and Rationalization in the Western Cultural Account." Pp. 12–37 in *Institutional Structure: Constituting*

State, Society and the Individual, edited by George Thomas, John Meyer, Francisco Ramirez and John Boli. Beverly Hills, CA: Sage.

Millhiser, Ian. 2020. "What Trump Has Done to the Courts, Explained." *Vox*, September 29. file:///C:/Users/d35640y/Desktop/Trump%E2%80%99s%20Supreme%20Court%20and%20other%20federal%20judges%20could%20spell%20doom%20for%20Democrats%20-%20Vox.html.

2016. "Trump Says He Will Delegate Judicial Selection to the Conservative Federalist Society." *Think Progress*, June 15. https://archive.thinkprogress.org/trump-says-he-will-delegate-judicial-selection-to-the-conservative-federalist-society-26f622b10c49/.

Milligan, Susan. 2021. "Trump's GOP Drives Out Reagan Republicans." *U.S. News & World Report*, May 14. www.usnews.com/news/the-report/articles/2021-05-14/trumps-gop-drives-out-reagan-republicans.

Mishel, Lawrence, Josh Bivens, Elise Gould, and Heidi Shierholz. 2012. *The State of Working America*, 12th edition. Ithaca, NY: Cornell University Press.

Mitnick, Barry. 2021. "Behind the Executive Order that Could Politicize Civil Service." University of Pittsburgh Pittwire, January 21. www.pittwire.pitt.edu/news/behind-executive-order-could-politicize-civil-service.

Mizruchi, Mark. 2013. *The Fracturing of the American Corporate Elite*. Cambridge: Harvard University Press.

Montague, Zach. 2021. "Over 100 Republicans, Including Former Officials, Threaten to Split from G.O.P." *New York Times*, May 12. www.nytimes.com/2021/05/11/us/politics/republicans-third-party-trump.html.

Morin, Rich. 2016. "Behind Trump's Win in Rural White America: Women Joined Men in Backing Him." Pew Research Center, November 17. www.pewresearch.org/fact-tank/2016/11/17/behind-trumps-win-in-rural-white-america-women-joined-men-in-backing-him/.

Morris, Frank. 2019. "Critics of Relocating USDA Research Agencies Point to Brain Drain." National Public Radio, September 10. www.npr.org/2019/09/10/759053717/critics-of-relocating-usda-research-agencies-point-to-brain-drain.

Mudge, Stephanie. 2011. "What's Left of Leftism? Neoliberal Politics in Western Party Systems, 1945–2008." *Social Science History* 35:337–380.

Mueller III, Robert S. 2019. *Report on The Investigation Into Russian Interference In the 2016 Presidential Election*. Washington, DC: U.S. Department of Justice.

Nance, Malcolm. 2016. *The Plot to Hack America*. New York: Skyhorse.

National Taxpayers Union Foundation. 2019. "Who Pays Income Taxes?" October 25. www.ntu.org/library/doclib/2019/10/2017-who-pays-income-taxes-2.pdf.

NBC News Survey. 2021. "Hart Research Associates/Public Opinion Strategies." Study #210098, April 17–20. https://assets.documentcloud.org/documents/20690434/210098-nbc-news-april-poll-4-25-21-release.pdf.

New Hampshire House. 2021. "House Bill 544: An Act Relative to the Propagation of Divisive Concepts." April 8. https://legiscan.com/NH/text/HB544/id/2238380.

Newland, Erica. "I'm Haunted by What I Did As a Lawyer in the Trump Justice Department." *New York Times*, December 20. www.nytimes.com/2020/12/20/opinion/trump-justice-department-lawyer.html.

Newport, Frank. 2017. "Majority Say Wealthy Americans, Corporations Taxed Too Little." Gallup Polling, April 18. https://news.gallup.com/poll/208685/majority-say-wealthy-americans-corporations-taxed-little.aspx.

Niedzwiadek, Nick. 2021. "McCarthy Says Trump 'Bears Responsibility' for Capitol Riot." *Politico*, January 13. www.politico.com/news/2021/01/13/mccarthy-trump-responsibility-capitol-riot-458975.

Nobles, Ryan, Ted Barrett, and Manu Ragu. 2021. "Senate Vote Delayed for January 6 Commission after Republicans Bog Down the Floor." CNN, May 28. www.cnn .com/2021/05/28/politics/january-6-commission-vote-senate/index.html.

Norris, Pippa, Sarah Cameron, and Thomas Wynter. 2019. "Challenges in American Elections." Pp. 3–42 in *Electoral Integrity in America*, edited by Pippa Norris, Sarah Cameron and Thomas Wynter. New York: Oxford University Press.

North, Douglass. 2005. *Understanding the Process of Economic Change*. New York: Oxford University Press.

1990. *Institutions, Institutional Change and Economic Performance*. New York: Cambridge University Press.

Nunn, Ryan, Jana Parsons, and Jay Shambaugh. 2019. "Race and Underemployment in the U.S. Labor Market." The Brookings Institution's "Up Front" blog, August 1. www.brookings.edu/blog/up-front/2019/08/01/race-and-underemployment-in-the-u-s-labor-market/.

Ogrysko, Nicole. 2020. "What They're Saying about the New Schedule F." *Federal News Network*, October 26. https://federalnewsnetwork.com/mike-causey-federal-report/2020/10/what-theyre-saying-about-the-new-schedule-f/.

Oladipo, Gloria. 2022. "More Than 100 Republican Primary Winners Support Trump's Baseless Election Claim." *The Guardian*, June 14. www.theguardian.com/us-news/2022/jun/14/trump-big-lie-support-republican-primary-winners-gop

Organization for Economic Cooperation and Development. 2021a. "Table II.1. Statutory Corporate Income Tax Rate." OECD.Stat. Paris: OECD. https://stats .oecd.org/Index.aspx?DataSetCode=TABLE_II1#.

2021b. "General Government Debt." OECD Data. Paris: OECD. https://data.oecd .org/gga/general-government-debt.htm.

2020a. "OECD Data, Household Debt." Paris: OECD. https://data.oecd.org/hha/household-debt.htm.

2020b. "Real GDP Forecast." Paris: OECD. https://data.oecd.org/gdp/real-gdp-forecast.htm.

2020c. "Revenue Statistics 2020-Denmark: Tax-to-GDP Ratio." Paris: OECD.

2011. *Divided We Stand: Why Inequality Keeps Rising*. Paris: OECD.

Ostrom, Elinor. 1990. *Governing the Commons: The Evolution of Institutions for Collective Action*. New York: Cambridge University Press.

Packer, George. 2021. "The Legacy of Donald Trump." *The Atlantic* (January/February): 9–12.

Palazzolo, Joe. 2017. "GOP and Bar Association Tangle over Judicial Nominees." *The Wall Street Journal*, November 14. www.wsj.com/articles/gop-and-bar-association-tangle-over-judicial-nominees-1510706943.

Palmer, Gary. 2020. "Palmer: Pelosi's $3 Trillion Bill is a Threat to National Security." Press release, Congressman Gary Palmer, Alabama 6th District. May 15. https://palmer.house.gov/media-center/press-releases/palmer-pelosi-s-3-trillion-bill-threat-national-security.

Parrott, Sharon, Aviva Aron-Dine, Dottie Rosenbaum et al. 2018. "Trump Budget Deeply Cuts Health, Housing, Other Assistance for Low- and Moderate-Income

Families." Center on Budget and Policy Priorities. February 14. www.cbpp.org/research/federal-budget/trump-budget-deeply-cuts-health-housing-other-assistance-for-low-and.

Parsons, Talcott. 1964. *Max Weber: The Theory of Social and Economic Organization.* New York: The Free Press.

Pempel, T.J. 1998. *Regime Shift: Comparative Dynamics of the Japanese Political Economy.* Ithaca, NY: Cornell University Press.

Pengelly, Martin. 2022. "Trump Pardon Promise for Capitol Rioters 'Stuff of Dictators' – Nixon Aide." *The Guardian*, January 30. www.theguardian.com/us-news/2022/jan/30/trump-pardon-promise-capitol-rioters-dictators-john-dean-nixon.

Peoples, Steve, and Jill Colvin. 2021. "Bowing to Trump? GOP Brings Leaders, Donors to His Backyard." *Associated Press*, April 9. https://apnews.com/article/donald-trump-capitol-siege-politics-florida-abcfc4015aad9629568272cccdca3982.

Perspectives on Politics. 2019. "Special Issue on the Trump Presidency." June, vol. 17, no. 2.

Peters, Jeremy. 2022. *Insurgency: How Republicans Lost Their Party and Got Everything They Ever Wanted.* New York: Crown.

Pettula, Sam, and Tal Yellin. "The Biggest Tax Cut in History? Not Quite." *CNN Politics*, January 30. www.cnn.com/2017/12/15/politics/is-trumps-bill-largest-tax-cut-in-history-no.

Pew Research Center. 2021a. "Biden Begins Presidency with Positive Ratings; Trump Departs with Lowest-Ever Job Mark." U.S. Politics and Policy, January 15. www.pewresearch.org/politics/2021/01/15/biden-begins-presidency-with-positive-ratings-trump-departs-with-lowest-ever-job-mark/.

2021b. "Broad Public Support for Coronavirus Aid Package; Just a Third Say It Spends Too Much." U.S. Politics and Policy, March 9. www.pewresearch.org/politics/2021/03/09/broad-public-support-for-coronavirus-aid-package-just-a-third-say-it-spends-too-much/.

2020a. "Growing Shares of Republicans Express Favorable Views of CDC, HHS and Justice Department." U.S. Politics and Policy, April 9. www.pewresearch.org/politics/2020/04/09/public-holds-broadly-favorable-views-of-many-federal-agencies-including-cdc-and-hhs/pp_2020-04-09_agencies_0-01/.

2020b. "Voters' Attitudes about Race and Gender Are Even More Divided Than in 2016." U.S. Politics and Policy, October 9. www.pewresearch.org/politics/2020/09/10/voters-attitudes-about-race-and-gender-are-even-more-divided-than-in-2016/.

2019a. "Public Expresses Favorable Views of a Number of Federal Agencies." U.S. Politics and Policy, October 1. www.pewresearch.org/politics/2019/10/01/public-expresses-favorable-views-of-a-number-of-federal-agencies/.

2019b. "Little Public Support for Reductions in Federal Spending." April 11. www.pewresearch.org/politics/2019/04/11/little-public-support-for-reductions-in-federal-spending/.

2018. "Public Confidence in Mueller's Investigation Remains Steady." U.S. Politics and Policy, March 15. www.pewresearch.org/politics/2018/03/15/public-confidence-in-muellers-investigation-remains-steady/.

2017. "The Partisan Divide on Political Values Grows Even Wider." U.S. Politics and Policy, October 5. www.pewresearch.org/politics/2017/10/05/the-partisan-divide-on-political-values-grows-even-wider/.

2016. "On Views of Race and Inequality, Blacks and Whites are Worlds Apart." Social and Demographic Trends, June 2016. www.pewsocialtrends.org/2016/06/27/3-discrimination-and-racial-inequality/.

2015a. "General Opinions about the Federal Government." U.S. Politics and Policy, November 23. www.people-press.org/2015/11/23/2-general-opinions-about-the-federal-government/.

2015b. "Across Racial Lines, More Say Nation Needs to Make Changes to Achieve Racial Equality." August 5. www.people-press.org/2015/08/05/across-racial-lines-more-say-nation-needs-to-make-changes-to-achieve-racial-equality/.

2015c. "General Opinions about the Federal Government." November 23. www.pewresearch.org/politics/2015/11/23/2-general-opinions-about-the-federal-government/.

2014. "Political Polarization in the American Public." U.S. Politics and Policy, June 12. www.people-press.org/2014/06/12/political-polarization-in-the-american-public/.

Pfiffner, James. 2021. "Donald Trump and the Norms of the Presidency." *Political Studies Quarterly* 51(1):96–124.

2018. "Organizing the Trump Presidency." *Presidential Studies Quarterly* 48 (1):153–167.

Pierson, Paul. 2004. *Politics in Time: History, Institutions and Social Analysis.* Princeton, NJ: Princeton University Press.

1994. *Dismantling the Welfare State.* New York: Cambridge University Press.

Pierson, Paul, and Theda Skocpol. 2002. "Historical Institutionalism in Contemporary Political Science," Pp. 693–721 in *Political Science: State of the Discipline*, edited by Ira Katznelson and Helen Milner. New York: W. W. Norton.

Plumer, Brad, and Coral Davenport. 2019. "Science under Attack: How Trump is Sidelining Research and Their Work." *New York Times*, December 28. www.nytimes.com/2019/12/28/climate/trump-administration-war-on-science.html.

Polantz, Katelyn, and Caroline Kelly. 2020. "Barr Says Voting by Mail is 'Playing with Fire'." *CNN Politics*, September 2. www.cnn.com/2020/09/02/politics/barr-mail-in-voting-playing-with-fire-situation-room/index.html.

PolitiFact. 2021. "Latest Fact-Checks." The Poynter Institute, October 7, 2016; February 12, 2021. www.politifact.com/.

Potok, Mark. 2017. "The Trump Effect." Intelligence Report, Southern Poverty Law Center, February 15. www.splcenter.org/fighting-hate/intelligence-report/2017/trump-effect.

Pramuk, Jacob. 2017. "Trump: Slashing Taxes on Corporations is 'Probably the Biggest Factor' in GOP Tax Plan." *CNBC*, December 20. www.cnbc.com/2017/12/20/trump-says-corporate-tax-cut-is-biggest-factor-in-gop-tax-plan.html.

Pramuk, Jacob, and Kevin Breuninger. 2021. "McConnell Says GOP Won't Support Biden's Infrastructure Plan, Vows to Fight Democratic Agenda." *CNBC*, April 1. www.cnbc.com/2021/04/01/mcconnell-says-gop-will-oppose-biden-infrastructure-plan.html.

Prasad, Eswar. 2014. *The Dollar Trap: How the U.S. Dollar Tightened Its Grip on Global Finance.* Princeton, NJ: Princeton University Press.

Presidential Commission on the Supreme Court of the United States. 2021. Draft Final Report, December. Washington DC: The White House. www.whitehouse.gov/wp-content/uploads/2021/12/SCOTUS-Report-Final.pdf.

Prokop, Andrew. 2019. "Trump's Census Citizenship Question Fiasco, Explained." *Vox*, July 11. www.vox.com/2019/7/11/20689015/census-citizenship-question-trump-executive-order.

Qiu, Linda. 2020. "No, Georgia's Governor Cannot 'Overrule' Its Secretary of State on Voting." *New York Times*, November 30. www.nytimes.com/2020/11/30/technol ogy/no-georgias-governor-cannot-overrule-its-secretary-of-state-on-voting.html.

Quinn, Melissa. 2018. "Trump's Stealth Victory: Reshaping the Courts." *Washington Examiner*, May 21. www.washingtonexaminer.com/policy/courts/trumps-stealth-victory-reshaping-the-courts.

Rainey, Rebecca. 2019. "Number of Workplace Safety Inspectors Fall under Trump." *Politico*, June 17. www.politico.com/story/2019/06/17/number-of-workplace-safety-inspectors-fall-under-trump-1531659.

Rappeport, Alan. 2019. "At G-20 Meeting, U.S.-China Trade Dispute Sours Global Economic Outlook." *New York Times*, June 10, p. A9.

Rasmussen, Hjalte. 2006. "Constitutional Laxity and International High Economic Performance: Is There a Nexus?" Pp. 197–244 in *National Identity and the Varieties of Capitalism: The Danish Experience*, edited by John L. Campbell, John A. Hall and Ove K. Pedersen. Montreal: McGill-Queens University Press.

Rein, Lisa. 2017. "How Trump's First Year Has Decimated Federal Bureaucracy." *The Independent*, December 31. www.independent.co.uk/news/world/americas/presi dent-donald-trump-white-house-first-year-inauguration-federal-bureaucracy-bar ack-obama-a8135921.html.

Reinhart, R. J. 2020. "Faith in Elections in Relatively Short Supply in U.S." Gallup Polling, February 13. https://news.gallup.com/poll/285608/faith-elections-rela tively-short-supply.aspx.

Republican National Committee. 2020. "Resolution Regarding the Republican Party Platform." https://prod-cdn-static.gop.com/docs/Resolution_Platform_2020.pdf.

Reuning, Kevin, and Nick Dietrich. 2019. "Media Coverage, Public Interest, and Support in the 2016 Republican Invisible Primary." *Perspectives on Politics* 17 (2):326–339.

Reuters Fact Check. 2020. "Partly False Claim: Trump Fired Entire Pandemic Response Team in 2018." *Reuters*, March 25. www.reuters.com/article/uk-factcheck-trump-fired-pandemic-team/partly-false-claim-trump-fired-pandemic-response-team-in-2018-idUSKBN21C32M.

Reynolds, Molly. 2018. "Why is the Senate Broken?" FIXGOV, The Brookings Institution, February 21. www.brookings.edu/blog/fixgov/2018/02/21/why-is-the-senate-broken/.

Rhee, Nari. 2013. "The Retirement Savings Crisis: Is it Worse than We Think?" Washington, DC: National Institute on Retirement Security. www.nirsonline.org/storage/nirs/documents/Retirement%20Savings%20Crisis/retirementsavingscrisis_final.pdf.

Richter, Felix. 2019. "This is What Nearly $14 Trillion of Household Debt Looks Like." World Economic Forum, November 25. www.weforum.org/agenda/2019/11/u-s-household-debt-climbs-to-13-95-trillion/.

Rigby, Ben. 2021. "'You Won't Work For Me' – Joe Biden Assembles Heavyweight DOJ Team." *The Global Legal Post*, January 22. www.globallegalpost.com/big-stories/you-wont-work-for-me—joe-biden-assembles-heavyweight-doj-team-95525039/.

Roberts, Paul Craig. 1984. *The Supply-Side Revolution: An Insider's Account of Policy-Making in Washington.* Cambridge: Harvard University Press.

Rogers, Alex, Manu Raju, and Ted Berrett. 2021. "What the Top Democratic and Republican Senate Leaders Are Saying about the Commission." *CNN*, May 27. www.cnn.com/politics/live-news/capitol-riot-senate-vote-congress-news/h_02f906f043addd050483ad4bc4a78a92.

Rogers, Hon. Chase, and Stacy Guillon. 2019. "Giving Up on Impartiality: The Threat of Public Capitulation to Contemporary Attacks on the Rule of Law." *Institute for the Advancement of the American Legal System.* September. Denver, CO: University of Denver.

Rose, Joel. 2020. "How Trump Has Filled High-Level Jobs without Senate Confirmation Votes." National Public Radio, March 9. www.npr.org/2020/03/09/813577462/how-trump-has-filled-high-level-jobs-without-senate-confirmation.

Rucker, Philip, and Carol Leonnig. 2020. *A Very Stable Genius: Donald J. Trump's Testing of America.* New York: Penguin.

Ruiz, Rebecca, and Robert Gebeloff. 2020. "As Trump Leaves the White House, His Imprint on the Judiciary Deepens." *New York Times*, December 17. www.nytimes.com/2020/12/17/us/politics/trump-judges-appeals-courts.html.

Rupar, Aaron. 2021. "Sidney Powell Gives Up the Game, Admits Trump Election Conspiracies Weren't Factual." *Vox*, March 23. www.vox.com/2021/3/23/22346333/sidney-powell-dominion-defamation-lawsuit-trump.

2020. "Trump: 'We'll Be Cutting' Entitlement Programs. White House: He Didn't Really Mean That." *Vox*, March 6. www.vox.com/2020/3/6/21168038/trump-on-entitlements-fox-news-town-hall.

Rutenberg, Jim, Jo Becker, Eric Lipton et al. 2021. "77 Days: Trump's Campaign to Subvert the Election." *New York Times*, February 1. www.nytimes.com/2021/01/31/us/trump-election-lie.html.

Rutenberg, Jim, Nick Corasaniti, and Alan Feuer. 2020. "Trump's Fraud Claims Died in Court, But the Myth of Stolen Elections Lives On." *New York Times*, December 27. www.nytimes.com/2020/12/26/us/politics/republicans-voter-fraud.html?action=click&module=News&pgtype=Homepage.

Saad, Lydia. 2019. "'Obamacare' Still Earns a Split Decision from Americans." Gallup Polling, April 29. https://news.gallup.com/poll/249146/obamacare-earns-split-decision-americans.aspx.

Saldin, Robert, and Steven Teles. 2020. *Never Trump: The Revolt of the Conservative Elites.* New York: Oxford University Press.

Samuels, Richard. 2003. *Machiavelli's Children: Leaders & Their Legacies in Italy and Japan.* Ithaca, NY: Cornell University Press.

Samuelsohn, Darren. 2016. "A Guide to Donald Trump's 'Rigged' Election." *Politico*, October 25. www.politico.com/story/2016/10/donald-trump-rigged-election-guide-230302.

Sanger, David. 2021. "Biden Team Rushes to Take over Government, and Oust Trump Loyalists." *New York Times*, January 28. www.nytimes.com/2021/01/27/us/politics/biden-government.html.

Sanger, David, and Julian Barnes. 2019. "On North Korea and Iran, Intelligence Chiefs Contradict Trump." *New York Times*, January 29. www.nytimes.com/2019/01/29/us/politics/kim-jong-trump.html.

Sardana, Saloni. 2020. "Yelp Says 60% of U.S. Businesses that Closed Due to Covid-19 Won't Re-Open." *Markets Insider*, September 17. https://markets.businessinsider .com/news/stocks/yelp-business-closures-permanent-covid-report-2020-9-1029598 577.

Savage, Charlie. 2022a. "Abortion Ruling Poses New Questions About How Far Supreme Court Will Go." *New York Times*, June 24. www.nytimes.com/2022/06/ 24/us/supreme-court-abortion-contraception-same-sex-marriage.html

   2022b. "E.P.A. Ruling is Milestone in Long Pushback to Regulation of Business." *New York Times*, June 30. www.nytimes.com/2022/06/30/us/supreme-court-epa-administrative-state.html

Scharpf, Fritz. 1997. *Games Real Actors Play*. New York: Westview Press.

Schelling, Thomas. 1971. "Dynamic Models of Segregation." *Journal of Mathematical Sociology* 1:143–186.

Scherer, Nancy, and Banks Miller. 2009. "The Federalist Society's Influence on the Federal Judiciary." *Political Research Quarterly* 62(2):366–378.

Schladebeck, Jessica. 2018. "Trump Invokes Ronald Reagan in Call for Border Wall Funding but Reagan Actually Supported an Open Border." *New York Daily News*, December 21. www.nydailynews.com/news/politics/ny-news-trump-reagan-border-wall-government-shutdown-20181221-story.html.

Schmidt, Michael, and Luke Broadwater. 2022. "Jan. 6 Panel Has Evidence for Criminal Referral of Trump, But Splits on Sending." *New York Times*, April 10. www .nytimes.com/2022/04/10/us/politics/jan-6-trump-criminal-referral.html.

Schmidt, Michael, Maggie Haberman, and Nicholas Fandos. 2021. "Matt Gaetz, Loyal for Years to Trump, Is Said to Have Sought a Blanket Pardon." *New York Times*, April 7. www.nytimes.com/2021/04/06/us/politics/matt-gaetz-trump-pardon.html.

Schmidt, Vivien. 2008. "Discursive Institutionalism: The Explanatory Power of Ideas and Discourse." *Annual Review of Political Science* 11:303–326.

   2002. *The Futures of European Capitalism*. New York: Oxford University Press.

Schrotenboer, Brent. 2020. "US is 'Printing' Money to Help Save the Economy from the COVID-19 Crisis, but Some Wonder How Far It Can Go." *USA Today*, May 13. www.usatoday.com/in-depth/money/2020/05/12/coronavirushow-u-s-printing-dollars-save-economy-during-crisis-fed/3038117001/.

Schumpeter, Joseph. 1954 [1918]. "The Crisis of the Tax State." *International Economic Papers*, edited by A. T. Peacock, W. Stolper, R. Turvey and E. Henderson 4:5–38.

Scott, W. Richard. 2001. *Institutions and Organizations*, 2nd edition. Thousand Oaks, CA: Sage.

Sebenius, Isaac, and James Sebenius. 2020. "How Many Needless Covid-19 Deaths Were Caused by Delays in Responding? Most of Them." *Stat News*, June 19. www .statnews.com/2020/06/19/faster-response-prevented-most-us-covid-19-deaths/.

Segers, Grace, and Cassidy McDonald. 2021. "McConnell Says Trump was 'Practically and Morally Responsible' for Riot after Voting Not Guilty." *CBS News*, February 14. www.cbsnews.com/news/mitch-mcconnell-trump-impeachment-vote-senate-speech/.

Sergent, Jim, Ledyard King, and Michael Collins. 2020. "4 Coronavirus Stimulus Packages. $2.4 Trillion in Funding. See What That Means to the National Debt." *USA Today*, May 8. www.usatoday.com/in-depth/news/2020/05/08/national-debt-how-much-could-coronavirus-cost-america/3051559001/.

Seybert, Lucia, and Peter Katzenstein. 2018. "Protean Power and Control Power: Conceptual Analysis." Pp. 3–26 in *Protean Power: Exploring the Uncertain and Unexpected in World Politics*, edited by Peter Katzenstein and Lucia Seybert. New York: Cambridge University Press.

Shafer, Byron, and Regina Wagner. 2019. "The Trump Presidency and the Structure of Modern American Politics." *Perspectives on Politics* 17(2):340–357.

Shah, Sono. 2020. "Rising Share of Lawmakers – But Few Republicans – Are Using the Term Latinx on Social Media." Pew Research Center, August 24. www.pewresearch.org/fact-tank/2020/08/24/rising-share-of-lawmakers-but-few-republicans-are-using-the-term-latinx-on-social-media/.

Shapiro, Ari. 2020. "Assistant U.S. Attorney on Why He's Leaving DOJ after More Than 30 Years." National Public Radio, October 16. www.npr.org/2020/10/16/924648161/assistant-u-s-attorney-on-why-hes-leaving-doj-after-more-than-30-years.

Shear, Michael. 2013. "Politics and Vetting Leave Key U.S. Posts Long Unfulfilled." *New York Times*, May 2. www.nytimes.com/2013/05/03/us/politics/top-posts-remain-vacant-throughout-obama-administration.html.

Shear, Michael, Maggie Haberman, Noah Weiland, Sharon LaFraniere and Mark Mazzetti. 2021. "Trump's Focus as the Pandemic Rages: What Would It Mean for Him?" *New York Times*, January 13. www.nytimes.com/2020/12/31/us/politics/trump-coronavirus.html.

Shephard, Alex. 2021. "Trump's Republicans Want a Coup." *The New Republic*, June 1. https://newrepublic.com/article/162586/michael-flynn-trump-myanmar-coup.

Shepard, Steven. 2020. "Poll: Half Say Election Winner Should Appoint Next Justice." *Politico*, September 21. www.politico.com/news/2020/09/21/poll-winner-appoint-supreme-court-justice-419523.

2019. "Was Trump Really Wrong about Hurricane Dorian's Threat to Alabama?" *Politico*, September 5. www.politico.com/story/2019/09/05/donald-trump-hurricane-dorian-alabama-1482815.

Simonton, Dean. 1987. *Why Presidents Succeed*. New Haven, CT: Yale University Press.

Skelley, Geoffey. 2021. "Most Republicans Still Won't Accept That Biden Won." *FiveThirtyEight*, May 7. https://fivethirtyeight.com/features/most-republicans-still-wont-accept-that-biden-won/.

Skocpol, Theda. 1996. *Boomerang: Clinton's Health Security Effort and the Turn Against Government in U.S. Politics*. New York: Norton.

Skocpol, Theda, and Vanessa Williamson. 2012. *The Tea Party and the Remaking of Republican Conservatism*. New York: Norton.

Skowronek, Stephen. 1982. *Building a New American State*. New York: Cambridge University Press.

Skowronek, Stephen, John Dearborn, and Desmond King. 2021. *Phantoms of a Beleaguered Republic*. New York: Oxford University Press.

Smelcer, Sudan Navarro, Amy Steigerwalt, and Richard Vining, Jr. 2012. "Bias and the Bar: Evaluating the ABA Ratings of Federal Judicial Nominees." *Political Research Quarterly* 65(4):827–840.

Smialek, Jeanna, Jim Tankersley, and Ben Casselman. 2020. "Low Interest Rates Worry the Fed: Ben Bernanke Has Some Ideas." *New York Times*, January 5. www.nytimes.com/2020/01/04/business/economy/low-interest-rates-ben-bernanke.html.

Smith, Allan. 2021. "Trump Takes Victory Lap after Cheney's Ouster from House Republican Leadership." *NBC News*, May 12. www.nbcnews.com/politics/

donald-trump/trump-takes-victory-lap-after-cheney-s-ouster-house-republican-n12
67081.

Smith, Colby, Eva Szalay, and Katie Martin. 2020. "Dollar Blues: Why the Pandemic is
Testing Confidence in the US Currency." *Financial Times*, July 31. www.ft.com/
content/7c963379-10df-4314-9bd0-351ddcdc699e.

Smith, Kelly Anne. 2020. "Should You Worry about the Record $3 Trillion Federal
Deficit?" *Forbes*, September 14. www.forbes.com/advisor/personal-finance/should-
you-worry-about-the-record-3-trillion-federal-deficit/.

Smith, Matthew, Jamie Ballard, and Linley Sanders. 2021. "Most Voters Say the Events
at the U.S. Capitol Are a Threat to Democracy." YouGov, January 6. https://today
.yougov.com/topics/politics/articles-reports/2021/01/06/US-capitol-trump-poll.

Solingen, Etel, and Wilfred Wan. 2016. "Critical Junctures, Developmental Pathways,
and Incremental Change in Security Institutions." Pp. 553–571 in *The Oxford
Handbook of Historical Institutionalism*, edited by Orfeo Fioretos, Tulia Falleti
and Adam Sheingate. New York: Oxford University Press.

Sommer, Jeff. 2022. "The Dollar is Stronger. Who Wins? Who Loses?" *New York
Times*, May 6. www.nytimes.com/2022/05/06/business/dollar-stock-bond-
currency.html.

Spocchia, Gino. 2021. "Final Tally of Lies: Analysts Say Trump Told 30,000
Mistruths – That's 21 a Day – During Presidency." *The Independent*, January
2021. www.independent.co.uk/news/world/americas/us-election-2020/trump-lies-
false-presidency-b1790285.html.

Sprunt, Barbara. 2021. "Kevin McCarthy Leads House GOP in Blasting Marjorie
Taylor Greene's Holocaust Remarks." National Public Radio, May 25. www.npr
.org/2021/05/25/1000129271/marjorie-taylor-greenes-holocaust-remarks-blasted-
by-republicans-leaders.

Statista. 2021a. "Number of Monthly Active Twitter Users in the United States from 1st
Quarter 2010 to 1st Quarter 2019." www.statista.com/statistics/274564/monthly-
active-twitter-users-in-the-united-states/.

2021b. "End of the Road for Trump's Twitter Account." www.statista.com/chart/
19561/total-number-of-tweets-from-donald-trump/.

2021c. "Annual Growth of Real GDP in the United States of America from 1930 to
2020." Historical Data, January 5. www.statista.com/statistics/996758/rea-gdp-
growth-united-states-1930-2019/.

Stein, Jeff. 2017. "37 of 38 Economists Said the GOP Tax Plans Would Grow the Debt.
The 38th Misread the Question." *Washington Post*, November 22.

Steinmo, Sven. 2010. *The Evolution of Modern States*. New York: Cambridge
University Press.

1993. *Taxation and Democracy*. New Haven, CT: Yale University Press.

Steinmo, Sven, Kathleen Thelen, and Frank Longstreth, editors. 1992. *Structuring
Politics: Historical Institutionalism in Comparative Perspective*. New York:
Cambridge University Press.

Stinchcombe, Arthur. 1997. "On the Virtues of the Old Institutionalism." *Annual
Review of Sociology* 23:1–18.

Stohr, Greg, and Bloomberg. 2021. "Supreme Court Conservative Majority Chips Away
at Voting Rights Act with a 6-3 Ruling." *Fortune*, July 1. https://fortune.com/2021/
07/01/supreme-court-conservative-majority-voting-rights-act-arizona/.

Stone, Roger. 2017. *The Making of the President 2016*. New York: Skyhorse.

Straqualursi, Veronica. 2018. "Rex Tillerson Said Trump Got 'Frustrated' When Told He Couldn't Do Something That 'Violates the Law'." *CNN*, December 7. www.cnn .com/2018/12/07/politics/rex-tillerson-donald-trump/index.html.

Streeck, Wolfgang, and Kathleen Thelen, editors. 2005a. *Beyond Continuity*. New York: Oxford University Press.

Streeck, Wolfgang, and Kathleen Thelen. 2005b. "Introduction: Institutional Change in Advanced Political Economies." Pp. 1–39 in *Beyond Continuity*, edited by Wolfgang Streeck and Kathleen Thelen. New York: Oxford University Press.

Stuckey, Mary. 2021. "The Rhetoric of the Trump Administration." *Presidential Studies Quarterly* 51(1):125–150.

Sullivan, Marianne, Chris Sellers, Leif Fredrickson et al. 2021. "Re-Envisioning EPA and Its Work in the Post-Trump Era: Perspectives from EPA Employees." *Journal of Public Health Policy* (in press). https://link.springer.com/article/10.1057/ s41271-021-00276-z.

Swan, Jonathan. 2021a. "Trump's Last Stand Part III: The Break with Barr." *Axios podcast*, February 1. https://podcasts.apple.com/us/podcast/how-it-happened/ id1549225698.

2021b. "Trump's Last Stand Part IV: The Point of No Return." *Axios podcast*, February 8. https://podcasts.apple.com/us/podcast/how-it-happened/id1549225698.

Swidler, Ann. 1986. "Culture in Action: Symbols and Strategies." *American Sociological Review* 51:273–286.

Syed, Moiz. 2020. "Charting the Long-Term Impact of Trump's Judicial Appointments." *ProPublica*, October 30. https://projects.propublica.org/trump-young-judges/.

Talkers. 2017. "2016 Talkers Heavy Hundred." www.talkers.com/heavy-hundred/.

Tankersley, Jim. 2018. "How the Trump Tax Cut is Helping Push the Federal Deficit to $1 Trillion." *New York Times*, September 25. www.nytimes.com/2018/07/25/busi ness/trump-corporate-tax-cut-deficit.html.

Tax Policy Center. 2021. "Briefing Book: A Citizen's Guide to the Fascinating (Though Often Complex) Elements of the U.S. Tax System." Urban Institute and Brookings Institution, p. 4. www.taxpolicycenter.org/briefing-book/what-are-sources-revenue-federal-government#:~:text=About%2050%20percent%20of%20federal,insurance %20programs%20(figure%201).

Teles, Steven. 2008. *The Rise of the Conservative Legal Movement*. Princeton, NJ: Princeton University Press.

Temin, Peter. 2017. *The Vanishing Middle Class*. Cambridge, MA: Massachusetts Institute of Technology Press.

Tenpas, Kathryn Dunn. 2021. "Tracking Turnover in the Trump Administration." The Brookings Institution, January 2021. www.brookings.edu/research/tracking-turn over-in-the-trump-administration/.

2020. "And Then There Were Ten: With 85% Turnover Across President Trump's A Team, Who Remains?" The Brookings Institution', April 13. www.brookings.edu/ blog/fixgov/2020/04/13/and-then-there-were-ten-with-85-turnover-across-president-trumps-a-team-who-remains/.

2018. "White House Staff Turnover in Year One of the Trump Administration: Context, Consequences, and Implications for Governing." *Presidential Studies Quarterly* 48(3):502–516.

Tesler, Michael, and David Sears. 2010. *Obama's Race*. Chicago, IL: University of Chicago Press.

The Brookings Institution. 2020. "Election 2020: State of Play and Implications." November 10. www.youtube.com/watch?v=qMqrV34ItHg.

The Economist. 2021. "Will Inflation Return" and "Briefing Inflation: Prognostication and Prophecy." December 12, pp. 15, 25–27.

2020. "Dethroning the Dollar." January 18, pp. 62–64.

2019. "Global Technology: Pinch Points." June 8, pp. 58–59.

The Los Angeles Times. 2020. "Editorial: Trump Wants to Turn Federal Bureaucracy into a Presidential Fiefdom." December 4. www.latimes.com/opinion/story/2020-12-04/trump-federal-employees-political-appointees.

The White House. 2021. "President Biden to Sign Executive Order Creating the Presidential Commission on the Supreme Court of the United States." April 9. www.whitehouse.gov/briefing-room/statements-releases/2021/04/09/president-biden-to-sign-executive-order-creating-the-presidential-commission-on-the-supreme-court-of-the-united-states/.

2018. "President Donald J. Trump Achieved the Biggest Tax Cuts and Reforms in American History." Fact Sheets, Budget & Spending, February 5. www.whitehouse.gov/briefings-statements/president-donald-j-trump-achieved-biggest-tax-cuts-reforms-american-history/.

Thelen, Kathleen. 2004. *How Institutions Evolve*. New York: Cambridge University Press.

Thelen, Kathleen, and Sven Steinmo. 1992. "Historical Institutionalism in Comparative Politics." Pp. 1–32 in *Structuring Politics*, edited by Sven Steinmo, Kathleen Thelen and Frank Longstreth. New York: Cambridge University Press.

Thomsen, Jacqueline, and C. Ryan Barber. 2020. "With Questions of What's 'Fair,' Barr Defends His Handling of Roger Stone's Sentencing." *The National Law Journal*, July 28. www.law.com/nationallawjournal/2020/07/28/with-questions-of-whats-fair-barr-defends-his-handling-of-roger-stones-sentencing/.

Thornton, Patricia, William Ocasio, and Michael Lounsbury. 2012. *The Institutional Logics Perspective*. New York: Oxford University Press.

Tooze, Adam. 2020. "Should We Be Scared of the Coronavirus Debt Mountain?" *The Guardian*, April 27. www.theguardian.com/commentisfree/2020/apr/27/economy-recover-coronavirus-debt-austerity.

Totenberg, Nina. 2017. "Trump's Criticism of Judges Out of Line with Past Presidents." National Public Radio, February 11. www.npr.org/2017/02/11/514587731/trumps-criticism-of-judges-out-of-line-with-past-presidents.

Trading Economics. 2022. "United States Consumer Price Index (CPI)." United States Consumer Price Index (CPI) – February 2022 Data – 1950–2021 Historical (tradingeconomics.com).

2021a. "United States Dollar: 1971–2021." https://tradingeconomics.com/united-states/currency.

2021b. "Government Debt to GDP." https://tradingeconomics.com/united-states/government-debt-to-gdp.

Troyer, Madison. 2020. "Top Trump Tweets Since Election Day 2020." *Stacker*, December 30. https://stacker.com/stories/6057/top-trump-tweets-election-day-2020.

Truax, Chris. 2020. "Attorney General William Barr Was Once Widely Respected. Thanks to Trump, Not Anymore." *USA Today*, July 13. www.usatoday.com/

story/opinion/2020/07/13/roger-stone-commuted-sentence-william-barr-donald-tru
mp-column/5424112002/.

Trump, Donald, and Tony Schwartz. 2005. *The Art of the Deal*. New York: Ballantine.

Trump, Donald J. 2019. "Remarks by President Trump at Presentation of the Medal of Freedom to Dr. Arthur Laffer." The White House, June 19. www.whitehouse.gov/ briefings-statements/remarks-president-trump-presentation-medal-freedom-dr-arth ur-laffer/.

U.S. Bureau of Labor Statistics. 2020a. "Graphics for Economic News Releases: Employment-Population Ratio." Washington, DC: U.S. Government Printing Office. www.bls.gov/charts/employment-situation/employment-population-ratio.htm.

2020b. "Economy at a Glance." Washington, DC: U.S. Government Printing Office. www.bls.gov/eag/eag.us.htm.

U.S. Census Bureau. 2018. "U.S. Census Bureau Needs Hundreds of Thousands of Workers." July 17. www.census.gov/library/stories/2018/07/recruiting-for-2020-census.html.

U.S. Congressional Budget Office. 2020. "Monthly Budget Review: Summary for Fiscal Year 2020." Washington, DC: U.S. Printing Office. www.cbo.gov/system/files/ 2020-11/56746-MBR.pdf

2019. "Monthly Budget Review: Summary for Fiscal Year 2019." Washington, DC: U.S. Printing Office. www.cbo.gov/system/files/2019-11/55824-CBO-MBR-FY19 .pdf

2018. "Monthly Budget Review: Summary for Fiscal Year 2018." Washington, DC: U.S. Printing Office. www.cbo.gov/system/files/2018-11/54647-MBR.pdf

U.S. Congressional Research Service. 2020a. "Federal Workforce Statistics Sources: OPM and OMB." Washington, DC: U.S. Congressional Research Service. https:// fas.org/sgp/crs/misc/R43590.pdf.

2020b. "Relocation of the USDA Research Agencies: NIFA and ERS." Washington, DC: U.S. Congressional Research Service. https://crsreports.congress.gov/product/ pdf/IF/IF11527.

2020c. "Confirmation of U.S. Circuit and District Court Nominations during Presidential Election Years: Frequently Asked Questions." CRS report R46533. Washington, DC: U.S. Congressional Research Service.

2019. "Judicial Nomination Statistics and Analysis: U.S. District and Circuit Courts, 1977–2018." www.everycrsreport.com/reports/R45622.html#_Toc4079577.

U.S. Courts. 2021. "Appellate Courts and Cases – Journalist's Guide." About Federal Courts, March 3. www.uscourts.gov/statistics-reports/appellate-courts-and-cases-journalists-guide#:~:text=Federal%20courts%20of%20appeals%20routinely,fewer %20than%20100%20cases%20annually.

2020. "About the U.S. Courts of Appeals." About Federal Courts, December 20. www.uscourts.gov/about-federal-courts/court-role-and-structure/about-us-courts-appeals.

U.S. Department of the Treasury. 2017. "Analysis of Growth and Revenue Estimates Based on the U.S. Senate Committee on Finance Tax Reform Plan." Washington, DC. December 11. www.treasury.gov/press-center/press-releases/Documents/ TreasuryGrowthMemo12-11-17.pdf.

U.S. Environmental Protection Agency. 2021. "EPA's Budget and Spending." Washington, DC. www.epa.gov/planandbudget/budget.

U.S. Federal Bureau of Investigation. 2017. "Uniform Crime Reports: Hate Crime Statistics." https://ucr.fbi.gov/ucr-publications#Hate.

U.S. Federal Register. 2020. "Combating Race and Sex Stereotyping: A Presidential Document by the Executive Office of the President on 9/28/2020." www.federalregister.gov/documents/2020/09/28/2020-21534/combating-race-and-sex-stereotyping.

U.S. Federal Reserve Bank. 2021a. "Interest Rates, Discount Rate for the United States." St. Louis: U.S. Federal Reserve Bank. https://fred.stlouisfed.org/series/INTDSRUSM193N.

2021b. "Long-Term Government Bond Yields: 10-Year: Main (Including Benchmark) for the United States." St. Louis: U.S. Federal Reserve Bank. https://fred.stlouisfed.org/series/IRLTLT01USM156N.

2021c. "Real Gross Domestic Product." St. Louis: U.S. Federal Reserve Bank. https://fred.stlouisfed.org/series/GDPC1.

2021d. "Federal Debt: Total Public Debt as Percent of Gross Domestic Product." St. Louis: U.S. Federal Reserve Bank. https://fred.stlouisfed.org/series/GFDEGDQ188S.

2021e. "Consumer Price Index, 1913–2021." Minneapolis: U.S. Federal Reserve Bank. www.minneapolisfed.org/about-us/monetary-policy/inflation-calculator/consumer-price-index-1913-.

2020a. "Household Debt Service Payments as a Percentage of Disposable Personal Income." St. Louis: U.S. Federal Reserve Bank. https://fred.stlouisfed.org/series/TDSP.

2020b. "Federal Surplus or Deficit as Percent of Gross Domestic Product. St. Louis: U.S. Federal Reserve Bank. https://fred.stlouisfed.org/series/FYFSGDA188S.

2019. "Recent Balance Sheet Trends." Washington, DC: U.S. Federal Reserve Bank. www.federalreserve.gov/monetarypolicy/bst_recenttrends.htm.

2012. "Government Debt and Macroeconomic Activity: A Predictive Analysis for Advanced Economies." Finance and Economics Discussion Series: 2013-05. Washington, DC: U.S. Federal Reserve Bank. www.federalreserve.gov/pubs/feds/2013/201305/.

U.S. Government Accountability Office. 2020. "Senior Executive Service: Opportunities for Selected Agencies to Improve Their Career Reassignment Processes." GAO-20-559, September. www.gao.gov/assets/gao-20-559.pdf.

U.S. House Committee on the Budget. 2020. "Charts & Graphs." February 11. https://budget.house.gov/charts-and-graphs.

U.S. House Committee on Oversight and Reform. 2020. "New Document Shows Inadequate Distribution of Personal Protective Equipment and Critical Medical Supplies to States." April 8. Washington, DC. https://oversight.house.gov/news/press-releases/new-document-shows-inadequate-distribution-of-personal-protective-equipment-and.

U.S. House Committee on Science, Space, and Technology. 2021. "Brain Drain: Quantifying the Decline of the Federal Scientific Workforce." March. Washington, DC. https://science.house.gov/imo/media/doc/2021-3%20EMBARGOED%20Scientific%20Brain%20Drain%20Majority%20STAFF%20REPORT%20w%20cover%20page.pdf.

U.S. House Subcommittee on the Coronavirus Crisis. 2021. "Clyburn Demands Answers From Redfield on Trump Administration Officials' Interference with CDC's Pandemic Response." Press release, November 12. https://coronavirus

.house.gov/news/press-releases/clyburn-demands-answers-redfield-trump-adminis tration-officials-interference-cdc.

U.S. Internal Revenue Service. 2019. *Internal Revenue Service Data Book, 2019*. Washington, DC: U.S. Treasury Department. www.irs.gov/pub/irs-pdf/p55b.pdf.

U.S. Occupational Safety and Health Administration. 2021. *Occupational Safety and Health Administration (OSHA) Enforcement*. Washington, DC: U.S. Department of Labor. www.osha.gov/enforcement/2020-enforcement-summary.

U.S. Office of Management and Budget. 2018. *Efficient, Effective, Accountable: An American Budget. Budget of the U.S. Government, Fiscal Year 2019*. Washington, DC: U.S. Government Publishing Office. www.govinfo.gov/content/pkg/BUDGET-2019-BUD/pdf/BUDGET-2019-BUD.pdf.

U.S. Office of Personnel Management. 2021. "Employment Trend (Year-to-Year)." www.fedscope.opm.gov/.

2019a. "Senior Executive Service: Fiscal Year 2014–2018." Office of Strategy and Innovation Data Analysis Group. www.opm.gov/policy-data-oversight/data-analy sis-documentation/federal-employment-reports/reports-publications/ses-summary-2014-2018.pdf.

2019b. "Memorandum for Human Resources Directors: Federal Senior Executive Service Exit Survey Results." June 11. www.chcoc.gov/content/federal-senior-execu tive-service-exit-survey-results.

2019c. "Federal Employee Viewpoint Survey." www.opm.gov/fevs/reports/data-reports/data-reports/report-by-agency/2019/2019-agency-report/.

2016. "Federal Employee Viewpoint Survey." www.opm.gov/fevs/reports/data-reports/data-reports/report-by-agency/2016/2016-agency-report-part-1.pdf.

U.S. Senate Judiciary Committee. 2021. "Subverting Justice: How the Former President and His Allies Pressured DOJ to Overturn the 2020 Election." Majority Staff Report. www.judiciary.senate.gov/imo/media/doc/Interim%20Staff%20Report% 20FINAL.pdf.

Vance, J.D. 2016. *Hillbilly Elegy*. New York: Harper Collins.

Vickery, Chad and Heather Szilagyi. 2019. "America in Comparative Perspective." Pp. 175–195 in *Electoral Integrity in America*, edited by Pippa Norris, Sarah Cameron and Thomas Wynter. New York: Oxford University Press.

Villeneuve, Marina. 2018. "Report: Trump Commission Did Not Find Widespread Voter Fraud." *Associated Press*, August 3. https://apnews.com/article/ f5f6a73b2af546ee97816bb35e82c18d.

Vladeck, Stephen. 2022. "Roberts Has Lost Control of the Supreme Court." *New York Times*, April 17. www.nytimes.com/2022/04/13/opinion/john-roberts-supreme-court.html.

Vogel, Kenneth, and Shane Goldmacher. 2022. "As Midterms and 2024 Loom, Trump Political Operation Revs Up." *New York Times*, January 4. www.nytimes.com/ 2022/01/04/us/politics/donald-trump-midterm-elections.html.

Wagner, Erich. 2020. "House Leadership Demands Accounting of Political Burrowing, Schedule F Activities." *Government Executive*, November 30. www.govexec.com/ management/2020/11/house-leadership-demands-accounting-political-burrowing-schedule-f-activities/170366/.

Waldman, Michael. 2016. *The Right to Vote*. New York: Simon & Schuster.

Wang, Hansi Lo. 2020. "Census Missed Year-End Deadline for Delivering Numbers for House Seats." National Public Radio, December 30. www.npr.org/2020/12/30/ 951566925/census-to-miss-year-end-deadline-for-delivering-numbers-for-house-seats.

Warren, Mark. 2001. *Dry Bones Rattling: Community Building to Revitalize American Democracy*. Princeton, NJ: Princeton University Press.

Warren, Michael. 2021a. "RNC Donors Gather in Palm Beach, the GOP's 'New Political Power Center'." *The Mercury News/CNN*, April 10. www.mercurynews .com/2021/04/10/rnc-donors-gather-in-palm-beach-the-gops-new-political-power-center/.

2021b. "The Republican Party is at War with Itself as It Charts Its Post-Trump Future." *CNN*, January 26. www.cnn.com/2021/01/26/politics/republican-party-future/index.html.

Weber, Max. 1978. *Economy and Society*, vol. 1, edited by Guenther Roth and Claus Wittich. Berkeley: University of California Press.

Weiser, Wendy, and Douglas Keith. 2017. "The Actually True and Provable Facts About Non-Citizen Voting." *Time*, February 13. https://time.com/4669899/illegal-citizens-voting-trump/.

Weisman, Jonathan, and Reid Epstein. 2022. "G.O.P. Declares Jan. 6 Attack 'Legitimate Political Discourse'." *New York Times*, February 4. www.nytimes.com/2022/02/04/us/politics/republicans-jan-6-cheney-censure.html.

Weissmann, Andrew. 2020. "America's Prosecutors Know What Bill Barr Did was Wrong." *The Atlantic*, August 5. www.theatlantic.com/ideas/archive/2020/08/bill-barr-stone-prosecutors/614929/.

Wheeler, Lydia. 2017. "Meet the Powerful Group Behind Trump's Judicial Nominations." *The Hill*, November 16. https://thehill.com/regulation/court-battles/360598-meet-the-powerful-group-behind-trumps-judicial-nominations.

Wheeler, Russell. 2021. "Can Biden 'Rebalance' the Judiciary?" The Brookings Institution, March 18. file:///C:/Users/d35640y/Desktop/Justice%20articles/Can%20Biden%20%E2%80%98rebalance%E2%80%99%20the%20judiciary_.html.

2016. "The Growing Specter of Vacant Judgeships." The Brookings Institution, April 12. www.brookings.edu/blog/fixgov/2016/04/12/the-growing-specter-of-vacant-federal-judgeships/.

Whitehouse, Sheldon. 2019. "The Third Federalist Society." March 27, Speech of U.S. Senator Sheldon Whitehouse. www.whitehouse.senate.gov/news/speeches/the-third-federalist-society.

Wike, Richard, Janell Fetterolf, and Mara Mordecai. 2020. "U.S. Image Plummets Internationally as Most Say Country Has Handled Coronavirus Badly." Pew Research Center, September 15. www.pewresearch.org/global/2020/09/15/us-image-plummets-internationally-as-most-say-country-has-handled-coronavirus-badly/.

Wike, Richard, Jacob Poushter, Laura Silver, Janell Fetterolf, and Mara Mordecai. 2021. "America's Image Abroad Rebounds with Transition from Trump to Biden." Pew Research Center, June 10. www.pewresearch.org/global/2021/06/10/americas-image-abroad-rebounds-with-transition-from-trump-to-biden/.

Williams, Joan C. 2016. "What So Many People Don't Get about the U.S. Working Class." *Harvard Business Review*, November 10. https://hbr.org/2016/11/what-so-many-people-dont-get-about-the-u-s-working-class.

Williamson, Vanessa. 2018. "The 'Tax Cuts and Jobs Act' and the 2018 Midterms: Examining the Potential Electoral Impact." The Brookings Institution, August 27. www.brookings.edu/research/the-tax-cuts-and-jobs-act-and-the-2018-midterms-examining-the-potential-electoral-impact/.

Wilson, James Q. 1980. *The Politics of Regulation*. New York: Basic Books.

Wines, Michael. 2022. "Census Memo Cites 'Unprecedented' Meddling by Trump Administration." *New York Times*, January 15. www.nytimes.com/2022/01/15/us/2020-census-trump.html.

2021. "In Arizona 2020 Election Review, Risks for Republicans, and Democracy." *New York Times*, June 7. www.nytimes.com/2021/06/07/us/arizona-recount-audit-republicans.html.

Wines, Michael, and Emily Bazelon. 2020. "Flaws in Census Count Imperil Trump Plan to Exclude Undocumented Immigrants." *New York Times*, December 4. www.nytimes.com/2020/12/04/us/census-trump.html.

Wines, Michael, and Richard Fausset. 2020. "With Census Count Finishing Early, Fears of a Skewed Tally Rise." *New York Times*, August 4. www.nytimes.com/2020/08/04/us/2020-census-ending-early.html.

Witherspoon, Andrew. 2019. "Trump's Incredibly Empty Cabinet." *Axios*, June 6. www.axios.com/trump-cabinet-vacancies-65a66f00-a140-4b49-887f-3c1bcf6469a7.html.

Wolf, Zachary. 2019. "Trump Wants Radically Less Government. Here's What That Looks Like." *CNN Politics*, April 12. www.cnn.com/2019/04/12/politics/trump-deregulation/index.html.

Wolfe, Jan. 2021. "'He Invited Us': Accused Capitol Rioters Blame Trump in Novel Legal Defense." *Reuters*, February 2. www.reuters.com/article/us-usa-trump-capitol-defense/he-invited-us-accused-capitol-rioters-blame-trump-in-novel-legal-defense-idUSKBN2A219E.

Wolff, Michael. 2018. *Fire and Fury: Inside the Trump White House*. New York: Henry Holt and Co.

Woodward, Bob. 2020. *Rage*. New York: Simon & Schuster.

Woodward, Bob, and Robert Costa. 2021. *Peril*. New York: Simon & Schuster.

Woolhandler, Steffie, David Himmelstein, Sameer Ahmed et al. 2021. "Public Policy and Health in the Trump Era." *The Lancet*, February 11. www.thelancet.com/journals/lancet/article/PIIS0140-6736(20)32545-9/fulltext.

World Economic Forum. 2019. *The Global Competitiveness Report, 2019*. Davos: World Economic Forum. www3.weforum.org/docs/WEF_TheGlobalCompetitivenessReport2019.pdf.

Wuthnow, Robert. 2018. *The Left Behind: Decline and Rage in Rural America*. Princeton, NJ: Princeton University Press.

Yourish, Karen, Larry Buchannan, and Denise Lu. 2021. "The 147 Republicans Who Voted to Overturn Election Results." *New York Times*, January 7. www.nytimes.com/interactive/2021/01/07/us/elections/electoral-college-biden-objectors.html.

Yu, Denise, and Karen Yourish. 2019. "The Turnover at the Top of the Trump Administration is Unprecedented." *New York Times*, January 14. www.nytimes.com/interactive/2018/03/16/us/politics/all-the-major-firings-and-resignations-in-trump-administration.html.

Zanona, Melanie, Olivia Beavers, and Quint Forgey. 2021. "As McCarthy Moves to Boot Cheney, a Favorite Successor Emerges." *Politico*, May 4. www.politico.com/news/2021/05/04/mccarthy-gop-cheney-485316.

Index

CPSIA information can be obtained
at www.ICGtesting.com
Printed in the USA
LVHW040042221222
735706LV00003B/241

9 781009 170192